MAURICE BOWRA

Leslie Mitchell was educated at Wadham College, Oxford, and was for many years a fellow of University College. He is a specialist on the history of England and France in the eighteenth century and has written a number of acclaimed biographies, including lives of Charles James Fox, Lord Melbourne, and Bulwer Lytton.

Praise for *Maurice Bowra: A Life*

'absorbing'
Hugh Cecil, *The Spectator*

'Leslie Mitchell's book is richly embroidered and captures, warts and all, the man who impressed so many of his peers.'
Melvyn Bragg, *Daily Telegraph*

'We are in Leslie Mitchell's debt for bringing Bowra so convincingly to life, recapturing so vividly both the attractive and the repellent features of an extraordinary academic icon'
Anthony Kenny, *Times Literary Supplement*

'... stylish biography ... Mitchell makes a spirited effort to bring Bowra back to life: he draws a perceptive and sympathetic portrait, one which allows us to hear distant echoes of the voice and to persuade ourselves that we have some inkling of his power and charm.'
Stefan Collini, *London Review of Books*

'... richly detailed biography'
Noel Malcolm, *Standpoint Magazine*

'... meticulous and elegant ... '
Peter Wilby, *New Statesman*

'Leslie Mitchell is a sure guide to the world Bowra inhabited. If anyone can resurrect Bowra for the twenty-first century, it is he.'
Adam Sisman, *Literary Review*

'... deeply illuminating and carefully researched ... Leslie Mitchell's vivid and accomplished study reminds us above all of an old-fashioned faith in the value of a university education as an end in itself.'
Mark Bostridge, *Independent*

MAURICE BOWRA: A LIFE

LESLIE MITCHELL

OXFORD
UNIVERSITY PRESS

OXFORD

UNIVERSITY PRESS

Great Clarendon Street, Oxford OX2 6DP

Oxford University Press is a department of the University of Oxford.
It furthers the University's objective of excellence in research, scholarship,
and education by publishing worldwide in

Oxford New York

Auckland Cape Town Dar es Salaam Hong Kong Karachi
Kuala Lumpur Madrid Melbourne Mexico City Nairobi
New Delhi Shanghai Taipei Toronto

With offices in

Argentina Austria Brazil Chile Czech Republic France Greece
Guatemala Hungary Italy Japan Poland Portugal Singapore
South Korea Switzerland Thailand Turkey Ukraine Vietnam

Oxford is a registered trade mark of Oxford University Press
in the UK and in certain other countries

Published in the United States
by Oxford University Press Inc., New York

British Library Cataloguing in Publication Data

Data available

Library of Congress Cataloging in Publication Data

Data available

Typeset by Laserwords Private Limited, Chennai, India
Printed in Great Britain
on acid-free paper by
CPI Antony Rowe, Chippenham, Wiltshire

ISBN 978–0–19–929584–5(Hbk.)
ISBN 978–0–19–958933–3(Pbk.)

1 3 5 7 9 10 8 6 4 2

2 4 6 8 10 9 7 5 3 1

To J.M.M.A.

Maurice Bowra (on the left) takes tea with Charlie Chaplin, 1962.

Contents

List of Plates

Plates 1–6 and 10–12 are reproduced by kind permission of Wadham College, Oxford.

List of Short Titles

In giving references, the following short titles have been employed:

Berlin MSS	Correspondence and Papers of Sir Isaiah Berlin, Bodleian Library, Oxford
Betjeman MSS	Correspondence and Papers of Sir John Betjeman, McPherson Library, University of Victoria, British Columbia
Bowra MSS	Correspondence and Papers of Sir Maurice Bowra, Wadham College, Oxford
Connolly MSS	Correspondence and Papers of Cyril Connolly, Department of Special Collections, McFarlin Library, University of Tulsa, Oklahoma
Frankfurter MSS	Correspondence and Papers of Felix and Marian Frankfurter, National Library of Congress, Washington DC
HRC	Harry Ransom Humanities Research Center, University of Texas at Austin
Murray MSS	Correspondence and Papers of Sir Gilbert Murray, Bodleian Library, Oxford
Rylands MSS	Correspondence and Papers of G W Rylands, King's College, Cambridge
Sparrow MSS	Correspondence and Papers of John Sparrow, All Souls, Oxford
Davie Mitchell Morwood	Interviews conducted by Michael Davie, Leslie Mitchell, and James Morwood
Memories	C M Bowra, *Memories 1898–1939* (London, 1966)

Preface

To write a life of Maurice Bowra is, in one sense, to describe a career in miniature. Nearly everything about him was defined by the usages and values of Oxford. He sometimes jokingly wondered how life could be sustained anywhere else. He performed on a narrow stage. His beliefs and concerns were largely Oxford in character and provenance. The tribe which inhabited that city had its own rituals and codes, which were not always those of the world outside. To understand them the biographer must accept a sense of separateness. To an extent, of course, all lives are lived in miniature. Everyone moves within certain social and geographical circles, accepting or reacting against the voices of those around them. But in Bowra's case this was particularly true. He was never a London figure and had no wish to be one. He went abroad with the first intention of meeting people like himself. He believed completely in what he took Oxford to stand for, and confidently trumpeted its claims. Had other factors not been in operation, he would have been indistinguishable from many of the city's other inhabitants.

But other factors were in operation. The miniature world of Oxford exercised a magnetism which drew in a wider world, and for many of these visitors Bowra was Oxford. His reputation quickly became formidable to many, notorious to some. Distinguished men and women came to the University, and Bowra, more often than not, was their host; Adenauer and Valéry, Charlie Chaplin and Jean Cocteau. Oxford also attracted the attention of London figures, who were happy to hear Bowra talk in the salons of Ottoline Morrell and Margot Asquith or at dinner in Wadham. Bowra's voice emanated from a small world, but it was heard appreciatively by a much wider audience. As someone with multilingual talents, he eagerly embraced a captive audience wherever one could be found. His values were for export to London and beyond, but such a diaspora of views came from a confidence in Oxford's purpose. No concessions to a wider world were either called for or necessary.

Even before Bowra died, in 1971, the capacity of Oxford to pronounce from confidence was already being eaten away. Criticisms brought against the University from those outside its walls made Bowra unintelligible no matter what language he spoke, and he was painfully aware of this development. Today, vice chancellors are rarely national figures. The British Academy rarely thunders. Academics themselves are nervous of pronouncing on what guarantees a culture or defines a civilization. The rules have changed. But Bowra had no such inhibitions. To thunder was his speciality. Yet, scarcely forty years after his death, his biography must be firmly accounted a work of history, and on that development he would doubtless have had much to say.

In writing a book of this kind, I have inevitably incurred large debts to many people and institutions. The late Michael Davie worked on this project for some time, conducting interviews and gathering information all of which he generously put at my disposal. He and I talked with many people who had known Maurice Bowra, and their kindness and encouragement must be gratefully recorded: Lord and Lady Annan, Mr and Mrs J. B. Bamborough, David Bell, Mary Bennett, Sir Isaiah and Lady Berlin, Sally Chilver, Colette Clark, Jill Day-Lewis, the Dowager Duchess of Devonshire, Lady Antonia Fraser, Peter Fraser, Sir Stuart Hampshire, Lady Harrod, Walter Hooper, George Huxley, Patrick Leigh Fermor, Lady Longford, Julian Mitchell, the Hon. Fionn Morgan, Lord and Lady Quinton, George Richardson, Leslie Rowse, Caroline Scott, Pat Thompson, Sir Robert Wade-Gery, John Walsh, Mary Wesley, Bob Williams, Lady Wilson, Noel Worswick. Some of these also allowed access to original materials in their possession. To their number must be added in this respect the names of Juliet Annan, W. M. Calder III, Professor Nancy Cartwright, Oliver Gates, Dominick Harrod, Alexander Murray, John Salmon, Nicholas Scheetz, and David Synnott. In addition, many Wadham men contributed stories and anecdotes. Few authors can have met more willing assistance.

Many institutions have also kindly given permission for quotations to be used from material in their possession: the Society of Authors (Rosamond Lehmann), the Lilly Library in the University of Indiana (Desmond and

Mollie McCarthy), the Isaiah Berlin Literary Trust, Washington State University (Edith Sitwell), the Literary Estate of Lord Dacre of Glanton, the Estate of Nancy Mitford, the Warden and Librarian of All Souls (John Sparrow), and the Pennsylvania State University Library.

In the preparation of this biography, much help was required in the smooth collecting of materials from libraries all over the world, in translating, in the discovery of out-of-the-way references, and in the technological transformation of a manuscript into a book. In these respects, I have been blessed with the assistance of Jonathan Brewer, Andrew Duncan, Robert Gerwath, Mark Hewitson, Mark Hope, Margaret Matthews, James Morwood, Michael Nicholson, James Rogers, James Ross, Lady Spender, Blair Worden, and Hugh Young. I thank them for their patience and expertise.

Inevitably, much of Maurice Bowra's correspondence remains in and around Oxford, and the archivists of the following institutions deserve heartfelt thanks: All Souls, Balliol, Christ Church, New College, Nuffield College, the Bodleian Library; Eton College Library; and the Library of King's College, Cambridge. Archivists and Librarians in North America have also responded to requests and enquiries with a professionalism that has greatly facilitated the writing of this book. I am most grateful to them, and to the institutional and private owners of manuscript collections for allowing me access to materials in their possession.

Above all, my thanks go to the Warden and Fellows of Wadham College, Oxford, who commissioned this project, and to Cliff Davies in particular for stage-managing the whole operation with discretion and diplomacy. I can only hope that they will not be disappointed with the outcome of their liberality.

Leslie Mitchell

PART
I

Formation

I

From China to Cheltenham

Kiukiang stands on the Yangste in south central China, approximately one thousand miles from the river's mouth. A centre of regional administration, the city had little else to distinguish it. Even more modest was the town of Newchwang in Manchuria, nominally under Chinese authority but increasingly subject to Russian and Japanese infiltration, as the nineteenth century came to an end. In both locations the Bowra family journal records the daily routines of small European communities battling disease, boredom, and the temptation 'to go yellow', with a perspiring integrity. From this unlikely, if exotic, world came one of the dominant Oxford figures of the twentieth century. Cecil Maurice Bowra was born in Kiukiang on Good Friday, 8 April 1898. Shortly after, his father, a senior official in the Chinese Customs Service, was transferred to Manchuria, where his new son would spend the first five years of his life. In geographical terms at least, Bowra emerged from a decent obscurity.

China was a long way from the family's roots in Kent. Bowra's father was a keen amateur genealogist, and the family journal traced the surname to beohr or bur, the Anglo-Saxon words for hill and cottage. He also noted its variants. It became Borer or Borrer in Sussex, Boorer in Surrey, and Bowra in Kent. In the seventeenth and eighteenth centuries, the family prospered under the patronage of the Sackvilles of Knole. One Bowra excelled as the opening batsman in the Duke of Dorset's private cricket team. In the 1920s, when Maurice Bowra visited Knole as the guest of Edward Sackville-West, he was therefore treading in the footsteps of ancestors. Providentially, on these visits, he was not asked to play cricket. Among the English Bowras, the most remarkable was Edward, Maurice Bowra's great-grandfather, who was credited with the invention of both the mackintosh and the gym shoe.

Considerable wealth might have accrued to the family had the inventor not been swindled out of his patents. Reviewing his ancestry, Bowra's father concluded that he came from 'a typical southern English family of the yeoman class, of no particular distinction, some members of which have gone up and some have gone down'[1]: this was generally fair comment.

The Englishness of the Bowras was, however, easy to question. Too many of them were inclined 'to seek surprising experiences in strange places'.[2] In particular, they, like so many Victorian families, grasped the opportunities offered by an expanding British Empire. In the 1840s, there were Bowras in Hong Kong, Jamaica, and New South Wales. In the latter location, a Bowraville still proclaims their prominence. There were even some in Brazil, who visited England when Maurice was a boy, and whom he thought wildly exotic. As an adult, he continued to relish his more colourful ancestors. On his mother's side, there was an illegitimate son of Lord Cornwallis, a circumstance which allowed Bowra to delight American audiences with the news that his family had been largely responsible for the United States winning its independence. Equally, when visiting Ireland, he could make much of the fact that another ancestor had fought with Wolfe Tone. Jokingly, he speculated that this glamorous association might allow him to stand for the Irish Parliament. If Bowra family roots were in Kent, they transplanted easily.[3]

Most romantic of all was Maurice's grandfather, Edward Charles Bowra. As a young man, he had been one of Garibaldi's Redshirts, fighting for the unification of Italy. His swashbuckling account of his adventures still exists among the Bowra manuscripts. At the age of twenty-two, he tried his luck in China, serving under General Gordon in the Taiping Wars before establishing himself in the Chinese Customs Service, then something of a British fief. To confirm the family's expatriate status, he married Thirza Woodward from Calcutta. In his *Memories*, Maurice Bowra wrote of his grandparents with affection. Both had courage and a determination to make their way in the world. Unfortunately, Edward Bowra died at the early age of thirty-three. He was killed by bravado. According to family tradition, he loved outdoor activities, and it was these that killed him. In swinging himself round an upright pole in a horizontal position he did irreparable damage to his heart, and on 15 October 1874, he suddenly died at East Grinstead. His children were told summarily by the Chinese amah, 'Papa he makee die'.[4] Thirza Woodward was left to bring up her family alone, but at least her husband had established a foothold in the Chinese Customs Service that would be the family's salvation.

Her eldest son, Cecil Arthur Verner Bowra, was born in Ningpo in 1869 and would spend forty years in the Service, thereby guaranteeing Maurice the family heritage of a Chinese childhood. The two men were never close. Maurice complained in letters that his father was opinionated, unclever, and out of sympathy with his own academic pretensions. Arguments were frequent. In 1926 for example, a family supper was disrupted by 'my father laying down the law on Baldwin ("I like him, he may not be clever, but he's honest") and on Ireland ("a hopeless people—not our stock"). I lost my temper twice and he always kept his.'⁵ Another such encounter three years later almost decided Maurice 'to forego the domestic life forever'.⁶ According to Maurice, his father was a true representative of a family, which, despite involvement in action and adventure, had been completely unintellectual. In this vein, it could only boast of Agnes Strickland, a distant cousin, whose lives of the queens of England had misled generations of English school children.

It is true that Cecil Bowra never understood the academic life. When entering his son for Cheltenham College, he wrote down 'barrister' as the boy's likely future profession. When Maurice approached the end of his undergraduate years, his father was counselling a life in the Civil Service, a view which his son denounced as 'intolerable' and which led him to 'doubt if my good parent has any sense at all'.⁷ Even the winning of an Oxford Fellowship was not entirely comprehensible. Cecil Bowra wrote to congratulate his son, but doubted that he would have enough to live on, and enquired if entry fees were payable.⁸ Later, he would talk proudly of his son's success in Oxford and the wider world, calling him 'The Warden' in family letters, but he had little interest in or understanding of what went to make a reputation in a university.

It was also true that Bowra's father could not be called an intellectual. His commonplace book is heavily military and patriotic in emphasis. Literary extracts are made, but Pope and Swift are mixed up with spoonerisms. Equally, his diaries suggest upright, Pooterish qualities. A keen Freemason, Cecil Bowra much enjoyed the privilege of dining with the prestigious Jerusalem Lodge while home on leave in 1903. In his words, it had been 'a very select affair'.⁹ None of this was congenial to a son, who, early in life, came to detest social snobbery and the small-minded. It cannot be a coincidence that, although Bowra was christened Cecil Maurice, he was always known by his second name. His rejection of his father's Christian name merely reflected the distance between the two men.

Yet there was more to Cecil Bowra than his son would allow. His letters and journals record forty years as a faithful employee of the Chinese government, defending its interests against Russian and Japanese depredations. When he retired in 1923, he had collected the Order of the Rising Sun from Japan, the Order of St Olaf from Norway, and the Chinese decorations of the Red Button and the Striped Tiger (second class).[10] Although a firm believer in the civilizing presence of the Anglo-Saxon in Asia, he wrote sensitively about the Chinese and claimed to understand why Boxer nationalists detested the European presence in their country. In some ways he could even be described as a freethinker. As a follower of Thomas Huxley, he enjoyed encouraging religious doubt in his children.[11] The revelations of an extramarital affair were never going to 'upset' anyone in the Bowra family.[12] Maurice faithfully noted these facts, but went on to insist that his father was endowed with 'the full code of Victorian morality'.[13] On one occasion, his father allegedly sent a young man, who had shown an unsuitable interest in one of his daughters, 'to the most plague-stricken spot in China'.[14] Maurice's construction of his father's character has a wilful quality about it in fact. The emotional distance which he describes was not necessarily felt by the other party. His father reported visits to Wadham during which 'the Warden was in fine form and everyone was in high spirits'.[15]

Misconstruction and misunderstanding issued from one simple fact. Maurice never had the opportunity to know his father. Between 1905 and 1924, they met only at rare intervals when the Bowra parents took home leave. In his *Memories*, he admitted that it was only in 1916, while taking an evening stroll around the walls of Peking with his father, that he 'came for the first time to know him'. Before that he had simply been 'frightened of him'.[16] Only now, at the age of eighteen, did he glimpse a man who could be 'tickled by odd moments of absurdity in people and events'.[17] Such moments were redeeming but rare. They had to be extracted from a man, who lived by a 'stern determination not to betray his feelings', and certainly not to his sons.[18] He prided himself in being at all times in control of himself. Maurice reacted strongly against such a code. Throughout his life he preferred upper lips to be stiff, but not if this inhibited spontaneity and laughter.

Then there was the problem of the closeness of his parents' marriage. The affection between husband and wife was so strong that it seemed there was none left over for the children. Maurice felt excluded by his parents' devotion to each other. In private correspondence, he sometimes made joking references to labouring under an Oedipus complex. He certainly resented the way his mother deferred to his father in all things, and his attempts to stir up rebellion in her came to nothing. There was never any doubt in his mind that 'if she had to chose between her husband and her children, she would have chosen her husband'.[19] Growing up without parents was a common experience for children in Victorian and Edwardian England, but it was a real and damaging aspect of Maurice Bowra's relationship with his father.

Nor could his mother fill the gap. Ethel May Lovibond came from a brewing family which by 1900 had fallen on hard times. She and Cecil Bowra had four children: Edward born in 1896, Maurice in 1898, Norah in 1904, and Ethel Francesca in 1911. All but one of the children were born in China. For all of them she was more often a mother longed for rather than present. One of the earliest letters of Maurice's brother, Edward, carries all the directness and misery of a seven year old; 'Dear Mother, when are you coming back Maurice and I want you to come back.'[20] Maurice's own account of his mother is chill, and slightly disdainful. He told a college friend that she was a woman who 'showed possibilities of intelligence and independence'.[21] She even claimed, mistakenly in Bowra's view, to understand her son:

> My mother now firmly believes that she knows all about me; this is good, but her fear of my father prevents her from telling me about herself. She simply can't do it because the Spectre of Family Respectability as raised by him forbids it. Of course really she knows nothing about me; so much the better for her. I am the harmless and touchy doctrinaire with the usual doctrinaire brutality.[22]

In fact, according to Maurice, his mother and sisters never had any chance of developing independent views or personalities. Any move in those directions would be immediately smothered by his father. As a result, the women simply spent their time 'developing their repressions in his company'.[23] In 1921, for example, Cecil Bowra decided, much against his wife's inclinations, on one more tour of duty in China. Despairingly, Maurice recorded yet another paternal victory. His father became 'more

intolerably autocratic than ever. Result; fearful nervous searchings of heart
by Ma and strong conviction that she must do what her husband says. Net
result, Pa dislikes me for interfering.'[24] When his mother died, in 1960,
Maurice's valedictory comments were regretful and formal: 'there is always
a wound ... I am glad she went off in her sleep, and she was an old lady. So
for her sake I must not complain. But we had a very good relation [sic], and I
keep on thinking of things which I can't tell her and she would have loved.'[25]

As a child of the British Empire therefore, Maurice Bowra grew up
with all the advantages and disadvantages of that situation. The privileges
were considerable. His was a world of servants. Ayahs and nannies devoted
themselves to his welfare. There was also a certain amount of wealth. The
Bowras complained from time to time about 'periodical poverty',[26] and the
outbreak of civil war in China badly hurt the family's finances, but there
was never any real distress. At his death in 1947, Cecil Bowra left each of
his children over twenty thousand pounds, making his a very considerable
estate. From his childhood onwards, Maurice had no need of skills that
most people found essential. Helpers of all kinds supplied the deficit. He
never learnt to drive, and his family found it hard to imagine him shopping.

The price of this warmth and security was, however, enormous. No
long-term, emotional relationships were formed with either his parents or
his siblings. Bowra was filial in the sense that his mother and father were
regularly invited to Oxford. He attended family weddings and funerals.
He could be totally supportive of a niece who married against her parents'
wishes.[27] In all things the forms were kept up. But his interaction with
his family was kept strictly apart from his other activities. There was a
determined segregation of these different worlds. Close friends like Isaiah
Berlin were surprised to discover after his death that Maurice had a
brother.[28] No Fellow of Wadham was ever introduced to his parents.
When he entertained his family, Bowra always described himself as 'going
into purdah'.[29] Parents and siblings created obligations which he fulfilled,
but it was a joyless business.

Sometimes Bowra fantasized about what would happen if his sharply
defined worlds collided. If his family took a holiday in Scotland, for
example, could he introduce them to the Earl and Countess of Kinross,
whose son he had come to know at Oxford:

> It is a fatal mistake to allow parents to meet any but the very best of one's
> friends. They are ... going to Edinburgh soon in a final effort to get away

from themselves. Shall I send them to see the Kinrosses? Mrs B and Caroline would get on, but the Mandarin [Cecil Bowra] is so unpresentable that I hesitate to bring them together ... Besides the Mandarin will want to lie with Pamela. He has got to the stage when he likes pink chubby girls.[30]

His doubts were based on more than mere snobbery, although the stratified society of England in the 1920s made the crossing of class lines a perilous undertaking. He worried that, if his family met friends like Basil Murray, who saw indiscretion as an art form, he would 'expose my secret life', with the result that he would never 'be able to return to this home of ancient boredom'.[31] More seriously, he accepted that the robust, intellectual world of Oxford had little in common with imperial China or suburban Kent. He told Paddy Leigh Fermor that he would always be grateful that his parents had raised no objection to his learning Latin and Greek, 'though they themselves had seen nothing in it'.[32] It was less stressful to keep worlds with different values rotating around different suns.

China, at the end of the nineteenth century, offered a European child an extraordinary mixture of privilege and threat. Bowra later recalled that, as a child, he had proudly called himself 'the son of a mandarin', who had consequently claimed to be 'a king pin' in the small world of Newchwang.[33] Candidly, he admitted that he had been 'spoilt', but, with Wildean phraseology, concluded that 'it was well worth it, and I have nothing but gratitude to those who did it'.[34] Little boys could ride, sail, and watch with fascination the endless procession of British, American, Japanese, and Russian ships passing up and down the river. The babble of languages was unforgettable. Here, in particular, Bowra had his first contact with that Russian world which would later occupy so much of his time and energies. It was all colour and exoticism. Cecil Bowra's journal records a typical family outing in 1902: 'On 8th February, we took the children, Edward and Maurice, up to the gunboats, riding on p'aitzu, or sledges, on the frozen river, and they were carried home to their great joy by a couple of English blue jackets.'[35] It was a boy's-own childhood as long as the child survived it.

In fact the same family journals calmly report the frequent deaths of Europeans through accident and disease, and Maurice experienced both in full measure. When he was two weeks old, he contracted chicken pox, and was so ill that his parents hurriedly arranged a christening by the Revd J. A. Ingle of the American Episcopal Mission. At fifteen months, he was visited by croup and was 'very ill', but at least he was not touched by the outbreak of bubonic plague in Newchwang in 1899. His father phlegmatically recorded that 'there was no panic among the European community. Everyone stuck to his post as normal and carried on.' In December 1900, both Bowra boys went down with influenza, which Cecil Bowra thought 'a troublesome complication, as on Christmas Day we had 30 people to dinner and a dance afterwards'. On Maurice's fourth birthday, the Bowra family home was consumed by fire.[36]

In the summer of 1900, danger appeared from a new quarter. The Boxer Rebellion closed in on Newchwang. Cecil Bowra could understand why Chinese nationalists should want to threaten Europeans with violence: 'It can't be said that the protest was unjustified. For years the European Powers (especially Russia and Germany) had pursued a cynical course of aggression against China, with annexation of Chinese territory, which was bound in the long run to induce savage attempts at reprisals.' Even so, he had to act to protect his own family. On 23 June, he organized patrols of European men in the town and brought all the women and children, sixty-five in all, to the Commissioner's House, which was then fortified. The Bowra home became a refugee centre:

> We had this large party of refugees occupying every corner of our dwelling, women, children and amahs lying asleep on floors, tables, and sofas, and, with one or two exceptions, accepting this strange upheaval with a courage and coolness beyond all praise...Ethel had a busy night, looking after her houseful of guests, her two children...and calming down the one or two excited ones whose nerves were unequal to the strain.[37]

Next day, all the women and children were placed onto a Japanese steamer, the *Sendai Maru*, and evacuated down river. The party included Ethel, Edward, and Maurice Bowra. As the boat made its progress towards the sea, it had to pass under the guns of Chinese forts. No one knew whether their garrisons were sympathetic to the Boxers. In the event, the journey was nerve-racking but uneventful. On 17 July, Cecil Bowra received a letter from his wife reporting that she and the boys had safely settled at Arima in Japan.[38]

The evacuation proved to be a prudent precaution. The Commissioner's House came under repeated attacks from the Boxers, and the Bowra family journals are illustrated with photographs of dead bodies lying in their garden. The European community in Newchwang was ultimately saved by the arrival of Russian soldiers, who then, much to Cecil Bowra's disgust, proceeded to butcher the Chinese indiscriminately. It was a consolation that his wife and sons returned on 23 September, safe but 'worn out ... with fatigue, anxiety, bad food, and travel in dirty Japanese ships'.[39] But it was disheartening to witness the Russian annexation of the town in all but name. When Cecil Bowra left Newchwang in 1903, his position went to a Russian. He had not been able to protect the rights of his Chinese employers, but at least his family had survived life-threatening experiences.

Maurice Bowra himself claimed that his own memories of China were merely a blur of colour and sound. All the events narrated above occurred before his fourth birthday. Yet he carried away from China a rewarding legacy. As a young don, he lived in rooms full of Chinese artefacts, which, according to his first pupils, helped to validate his exotic reputation.[40] His will spoke of Tang and Ming figures, famille verte jars, and eighteenth-century paintings on silk.[41] China, too, became a conversational resource for the rest of his life. Cyril Connolly remembered Maurice calling up 'the scenery, the culture, and the witty embittered mandarins'.[42] As a topic of discussion it was a valuable point of contact with his father.[43] To China he also owed his first contact with the sounds and rhythms of a foreign language. He proudly told pupils that he had talked Mandarin fluently 'at the age of six'.[44] Although he lost all memory of the language on returning home, he was left with the knowledge that language alone made thought and feeling possible. A competence in many tongues gave a man more options than could be enjoyed by someone trapped in mere English.

Above all, a childhood spent in Asia allowed Maurice early to appreciate societies with few of the social rules and regulations that constrained the English. Solecisms in Oxford could be excused by appealing to a Chinese past. Gleefully, he described one such occasion to an American friend:

> Our big show at the end of term was ruined by rain. Poor Lord Halifax collected reservoirs as he marched in his gold gown, and I study the papers every day to see who had died of pneumonia ... A learned lady, Miss Plumer, said that, as the daughter of a field-marshal, she could not carry an umbrella on parade, and I told here [sic] that, as the son of a Chinese mandarin, I never went on parade without one. So there we were, and she profited by my oriental habits.[45]

Maurice always enjoyed breaking the rules, and anything that justified him in doing so was to be welcomed. Asiatic civilizations were more relaxed and more knowing than western equivalents. Visiting them was always agreeable and nostalgic. After touring Iran, he reported that, 'I feel at home in Asia...because there are no rules, no discipline, no fixed laws for anything, infinite emptiness relieved by magnificent things to see, a most agreeable hugger–mugger in the bazaars...the smell of the East which reminds me of my childhood.'[46] The rebel in Bowra was properly grateful to China for giving insights and perspectives that could not possibly have resulted from a more orthodox upbringing.

On 27 April 1903, the Bowras left Newchwang for the last time. Their destination was England, for it was time to try to turn Edward and Maurice into Englishmen. The family travelled via Nagasaki, Honolulu, San Francisco, Chicago, Washington, and New York. It was an adventure for small boys. Maurice remembered San Francisco just before the great earthquake, and met Civil War veterans in Washington, one of whom presented him with a rose.[47] They crossed the Atlantic in the steamer *St Paul*. The other passengers were young ladies from a finishing school, 'who took a great fancy to the boys and spent most of the day on board amusing them'.[48] There was a danger that England would prove an anticlimax.

On reaching home, the family leased a house called Highmanswick in the village of Knockholt in Kent, from June 1903 to February 1905. It was an idyllic few months, as the Bowras settled down to a year of country life.[49] For the boys there was a governess–cart and pony, cycling, country walks, and, best of all, the undivided attention of their parents for the only time in their lives. It was in his father's company that Maurice first saw London:

> I took Edward and Maurice for a day's sight-seeing in London. We went to the Tower and St Paul's and had lunch at a chop-house. Maurice was only six years old and our sight-seeing involved some long and weary trudging, but so great was their interest and keenness that they went through it all without a murmur and returned home in the highest spirits. The only anxiety I had was when they would insist on leaning as far as possible over the parapet to the dome of St Paul's to gaze at the City beneath, a proceeding which filled me with terror, but caused them no perturbation whatever.[50]

These same months also saw both boys overcoming whooping cough, bronchitis, and enteric fever picked up on a family holiday near St Malo. Maurice would later attribute his robust good health to having exhausted all the dangers in the average, medical dictionary by the age of seven. But nothing could really undermine the joy of, for once, being close to parents.

It was all the more emotionally draining, therefore, when, in February 1905, Ethel and Cecil Bowra returned to China without their children. Cecil recorded the separation in the family journal as follows:

> We now had to face the ordeal which confronts all Anglo-Oriental parents—that of parting from our children. Our Boys were still quite young, Edward eight, and Maurice six, so that it would not have been impossible to take them back to China with a governess for a year or two. But ... I felt that it would be unfair to them ... to give them a fair chance in the world it was necessary that they should begin their English education as early as possible. We were fortunate in having my mother, step-father, and sister Mabel to leave them with. We knew that they would be well cared for as if they were with us, and, the parting once over, would be quite happy in their new home. And so indeed it turned out.[51]

On 16 January, the boys were taken to their grandmother's house, 80 Erpington Road, Putney, and farewells were said. The boys would not see their parents again for four years.

The Putney household consisted of the widow of the Garibaldino, her second husband, the Revd George Mackie, and his unmarried daughter, Mabel. As surrogate parents, they all three became figures of importance in the boys' lives. There were also visits to grandmother Lovibond, also a widow, in Blackheath, who lived with her daughters Florence and Beatrice. However, as the Lovibonds were Liberal in politics and inclined to suffragette opinions, such visits were kept to a minimum.[52] Maurice later counted himself fortunate in being brought up by one man and five women of independent opinions, which they were happy to share with the boys. These adults took trouble to amuse their charges. George Mackie did conjuring tricks and Aunt Mabel regularly took them to the theatre. They never, however, attempted to direct the boys unduly. Often they were left to themselves and their own imaginations. As for formal instruction, that was left to Ella Dell, the sister of Ethel M. Dell, the highly popular, if notorious, contemporary novelist. This was fortunate, in that both boys came to 'love' her dearly, and kept up a correspondence with her long after nursery days were over.[53]

Years later, Maurice 'greatly enjoyed' reading *The Kindly Ones* by Anthony Powell, particularly for its evocation of 'childhood before 1914, with servants and uncles and luncheons'.[54] This comment is understandable. Parting from parents had been grim, but, in every other way, he had been favoured with an Edwardian childhood of warmth and security. His elder brother, Edward, kept a schoolboy diary for much of this time. It records trips to Folkestone, church services, shopping trips to Harrods with tea at the Army & Navy, football matches, and endless hours playing with his brother. These games prophetically often involved toy soldiers. For his seventh birthday Maurice was given a 'party. 18 children fine games, lovely magic lantern. Wild cheers for every battle picture and three cheers for Uncle Ned.'[55] When he was ten, he received '3 books… 3 boxes of soldiers a fortress and a switchback to build (from me) a game (Happy Golliwog) 49 stamps a satchel a tent a gun and £2-10-0 from Mum and Dad.'[56] Christmas brought the boys yet more treasure. In 1907, they had 'heaps of presents 28 or more each', followed by Aunt Mabel's 'grand dinner lots of crackers games and concert after in the playroom'.[57] There was every reason for Maurice to be grateful that he had known a world of doting aunts and grandmothers, which invited the expression of real affection.

Unfortunately, no such bond developed between the two brothers. From 1905 to 1909, they were constantly in each other's company. Edward's diary records a daily ration of highly competitive but good-natured games playing. The names of victors and vanquished are dutifully noted. As fellow, colonial 'orphans', they may well have been drawn close to each other. If so, the affinity was of short duration. By 1918, there was distance between the two men that was unbridgeable. For Maurice, his home life, 'dismal at best', was made 'intolerable owing to the presence of my brother'.[58] Separation came as a consequence of the First World War. Maurice emerged from that conflict with a detestation of all things military. To his dismay, his brother chose to remain in the army after the War and to make it his career. This sad decision could only be explained, according to Maurice, by the fact that the Army suited men of mean intelligence, who needed its camaraderie to supply deficiencies in their own character. In 1925, he described his brother as 'a poor thing'.

> His intelligence is not so bad, but he is unfathomably envious and has an enormous inferiority complex. As he is too cowardly to admit this, one can do nothing for him. Also he expects me to spend my days playing games with him. He is no good at them but plays them out of hatred and because he is terrified of being left to himself.[59]

Maurice had no opportunity of really knowing his sisters, who grew up in China. The chance of having a brother for life was lost. None of his siblings were therefore to play a significant role in his life. They became as remote to him as his parents had been.

In February 1905, both boys were entered as pupils at Willington Preparatory School in Upper Richmond Road, Putney. The establishment was owned and managed by two sisters. Miss Annie Hale taught Scripture and English, while her sister, Ada, introduced boys to Latin and Greek. Maurice remembered both as 'excellent teachers'.[60] For recreation, the boys were offered the waltz, the two-step, and a variety of country dances. School reports suggested an academic in the making. That for April 1905 was sprinkled with 'fairs' and 'goods', and identified Maurice as a 'very promising little pupil'.[61] By November 1906, he was top of the class in every subject except arithmetic. In that he had 'good methods but inaccurate working'.[62] Teaching him as a young boy was obviously a rewarding experience. When she heard that her former pupil had become Warden of Wadham, Miss Ada wrote to congratulate him, and was happy 'to find that your early promise has been so wonderfully fulfilled'.[63] Similarly, Ella Dell, on seeing Maurice's photograph in *Vogue*, was moved to write in acknowledgment of what he, as a pupil, had given her:

> To think I once guided those hands, then like little bits of India rubber, to write some of the first words they were capable of forming, and that, for relaxation, you stood on your head in an old armchair and told me little bits of history of which I knew nothing.... Now seeing your portrait, I can trace at least some little resemblance to the boy who was my friend, and who introduced me to much that was beautiful, and certainly gave me a finer outlook on life.[64]

These are extraordinary words for a teacher to use about a small boy, but they would be rehearsed many times among Maurice's friends.

As the Bowra boys acquired the ways of England in Putney, Maurice noted that 'the memory of my father and mother inevitably grew fainter'. In 1909, therefore, before facing the rigours of boarding school, it was decided that the brothers should visit their parents, now stationed in Mukden in Manchuria. They travelled by train across Europe and continental Russia. The journey was uneventful, but sufficiently exciting for boys of thirteen and eleven. Maurice remembered train stations in which Kalmucks tried to 'sell sour milk', and 'lines of camels resting while their owners tried to sell toys or food'.[65] Although the winter of 1909-10 was unusually cold, the boys mounted ponies to visit the tombs of the Manchu emperors and the battlefield of Mukden, where the recent carnage allowed them to collect cartridges and rusty bayonets. The highlight of the holiday was a meeting with Lord Kitchener, but Maurice found him 'a huge, gross, purple-faced man with blotchy eyes, who seemed to be bursting at every point from his field-marshal's uniform'.[66] Returning home with their father they travelled by way of Hong Kong, Colombo, Suez, and Naples. Maurice celebrated his twelfth birthday in Algiers.[67] The whole experience confirmed the fact, if more evidence were wanting, that the Bowra brothers had seen more of the world than most of their contemporaries. This may or may not have compromised their Englishness, but, to someone with Maurice's sensitivity, it must have been obvious that the distance between Putney and Manchuria was more than geographical.

If this was an unsettling thought, its impact would be compounded by being thrust into the English gothic of Cheltenham College in April 1910. The choice of school had nothing to do with Maurice or his future career. As his father candidly recorded in the family journal, his eldest son had decided already on an army career. Cheltenham and Wellington had a reputation for preparing boys for Sandhurst and Woolwich. Cheltenham in fact explicitly divided boys into a military division and a classical-modern division. It was the ideal training for Edward, and Maurice simply followed his brother for reasons of convenience.[68] Cecil Bowra took the boys to their new school on 26 April 1910 and returned to China two weeks later, after being assured that they 'were settling down all right'.[69]

Such a diagnosis may have been over-optimistic. Never before had Maurice experienced such structure, such regulation, so many rules. From compulsory chapel at 8.45 every morning until bedtime there was no free space and little free time. A wish for privacy was largely out of the question, and even suspect. Baths could only be taken in the City Baths, using a ticket 'obtainable from the Bursar'.[70] Equally challenging was the exchange of the comforts of Putney and the excitements of China for something altogether colder and greyer. Maurice now found himself surrounded by the sons of respectable, middle-class England, who were, for the most part, untravelled and unbookish. Many, like his brother, were looking forward to a career in the army. In later life, Bowra's comments on men of this type were sometimes pitying and sometimes contemptuous, but he never sought their company.

Two aspects of the new regime were particularly difficult to come to terms with: team games and the OTC. After six months at Cheltenham, the headmaster reported that Maurice was 'a nice, quiet boy' who was 'making good progress', showing 'a most wonderful general knowledge', and knowing 'decidedly quaint and interesting things'. But he also reported that, 'we are trying to interest him in football. He certainly takes to it more kindly than to cricket but I should like to see him a little more interested in outdoor things.'[71] His hopes would never be fulfilled. Bowra simply found the playing of team games 'a little odd'.[72] This view was not based on any physical weaknesses. His compact and muscular physique made him a useful rugger player under the soubriquet 'Mossy'. A. J. Ayer, in remembering this fact, could easily imagine him 'scrummaging to good effect'.[73] In the same vein, Lady Longford retailed the story of Maurice repelling an attack on his New College rooms by drunken hearties, calling on his rugger training to inflict 'heavy losses on the enemy'.[74] Rather, he objected to spending two or three afternoons a week in team games as, at best, a waste of time, or, at worst, an attempt to destroy individual character in favour of corporate identities. This might be a suitable training for future soldiers, but for no one else.

Worse still was the Officers Training Corps itself. On Monday, Wednesday, and Friday afternoons, Cheltenham boys played soldiers. With the possibility of a European war coming ever closer, these afternoons took on a special significance. When Cecil Bowra visited his sons, in June 1912, he was aware that the burden of war was already being lowered onto the shoulders of his sons:

> We found the boys at a review of the OTC being held by General Glubb. After the review the General addressed the boys in the College's gymnasium and I well remember the purport of his remarks, which was to the effect that war was looming up and that we must be prepared.[75]

With these cheerful thoughts in mind he, next day, took his sons out for lunch in Stratford-on-Avon. Parades at school were supplemented by camps under canvas in the more desolate parts of Hampshire and Devon. To these Maurice and his contemporaries were expected to take two pairs of strong, well-worn boots, for 'it is better for a boy to give up Camp than to come with untried boots'.[76] There was no escaping military discipline or the anxieties of the coming war. Four of the thirteen members of Maurice's class would be dead by 1918.

Cheltenham's routines and values took its toll on Maurice. For him to be described, in early school reports, as 'quiet' is literally astounding. No one who knew him in adult life would reach for that particular adjective. Clearly, he was somewhat cowed by his new surroundings, feeling his way and learning the tricks that would make him acceptable to those around him. His first school report suggested 'a fair start', but warned that 'much more sustained effort' would be needed 'if he is to meet with success'. Astonishingly, he was thought to be less promising than his brother.[77] By January 1911, however, his housemaster, with some relief, noted considerable improvement:

> I have tried to stir up in him interest in games. I can't say with much success so far, but we must stick to it. It will come in time. He is far more communicative than he used to be and not nearly so much absorbed in himself. I don't mean that in a bad sense, but he took time to make acquaintances and kept very quiet. Now if there is a little fun going on, he is almost sure to be in it.[78]

Reading between the lines of house-masterly prose, Maurice's first months at Cheltenham were miserable.

In June 1911, he came fourth in the College's internal examinations, and consequently entered the Senior School with a scholarship worth forty pounds a year. In this examination, he was asked to find the prime factors of 37975 and 155155, and to translate lines of English poetry into Latin. One wonders how he rendered 'Methought from the battlefields dreadful array | Far, far I had roamed on a desolate track.' From this point, his academic progress was uninterrupted, and there was never any doubt that the classics particularly suited his abilities. He could at least be grateful to Cheltenham for a thorough training in Latin and Greek. His texts for the summer term of 1912, for example, included Horace's *Odes*, Cicero's *Pro Archia* and *Oratio Philippica*, Euripides' *Heracleidae*, and Thucydides' *Retreat from Syracuse*. He claimed that, on leaving school, he had a working knowledge of all the works of these authors, together with a knowledge of Sophocles, Livy, Xenophon, Virgil, and Martial. More and more he allowed personality and precocity to have full rein. He read the syllabus and more than the syllabus. When he met Henry James at a party in London, in 1915, he already knew *The Turn of the Screw*, *The Aspern Papers*, and *The Princess Casimassima*. The great man gave him sixpence.[79]

Increasing academic success made life tolerable, but Bowra never subscribed to the public school ethos, which demanded a compromising of individualism. Of that he was incapable. His *Memories* record the inconveniences and irritations of school life. Rules and regulations governed every moment of the day. He was 'hemmed in by restrictions on every side. The authorities were so eager to keep us virtuous that they gave us very little opportunity to be ourselves.'[80] Beyond the classroom there was little to excite the mind or the imagination; 'no art, no handicraft, no music, no acting, no dancing with girls from the Ladies' College, and only very occasionally a lecture, preferably about travel or nature-study with coloured slides of sunsets, which always evoked loud applause.'[81] Bowra would remember this controlled and restrained world all his life, and determined to subvert its values wherever he met them.

In this unforgiving climate a boy either survives or sinks. Never the sinking kind, Bowra learned rules of engagement that could make life tolerable. First and foremost, he came to believe that the privilege of a private life was only possible in the company of a few chosen friends. It was a belief he acted on throughout his life. Most Cheltonians, like the world at large, did not share his values, but the trust and affection of a few friends compensated for this difficult fact. In his *Memories*, Bowra mentions Felix Brunner and Miles Rowden as two of these. They both possessed 'a sharp wit', read the plays of Oscar Wilde in secret, and 'disliked Cheltenham as much as I did'.[82] In the whole school, Bowra 'was very little interested in anyone else'.[83] Almost certainly, one of these friends is the 'charming Cantab.' referred to in letters in the early 1920s. He too had been 'at my bad school', and was always 'in literary, and artistic reaction to Cheltenham'.[84] Under Bowra's direction, this friend, the first of his protégés, also escaped Cheltenham's purpose.

Beyond this small circle, Maurice's defence against the outside world was humour. Early on he discovered 'that schoolboys will forgive anything for a joke'. Deliberately, he 'set out to amuse the other boys and by such simple devices as imitating the masters or inventing fantasies about their private lives I got myself accepted'.[85] He was a mimic of quality. Much in demand as a dormitory storyteller after dark, he told tales of the Orient, and mastered the lesson that a good story is not always a true story. Apparently, this invested him with a 'dark and sinister' reputation,[86] but it worked. A clever boy, who was bored by games, could be accepted by the manipulation of humour. It was a formula that Maurice would employ with devastating effect in many other contexts. School contemporaries remembered both his academic brilliance and his ability to raise gales of laughter.[87]

Cheltenham therefore gave Maurice the necessary grounding in the classics that would underpin a whole career. But it inadvertently gave him something more important. In letters of the early 1920s, he is talking of his 'system',[88] which had carried him through the experiences of school and war service. The system rested on two propositions. First, if you are vulnerable to the rules of English society, put on the armour of wit. If the clever man is amusing he is less threatening to the not-so-clever. If the wit is sharp enough, it keeps an enquiring world at bay. Secondly, if Bowra's England was a society in which the word intellectual was barely a compliment, and in which the word academic was synonymous with irrelevant, most people by definition were outside his range. Therefore the friendship of a few companions had to suffice. To seek them out and confirm them in affection was 'the system' he now referred to. On these terms he could survive and prosper. On these terms he could even come through the rigours of an Edwardian public school.

Predictably, he left Cheltenham with deeply ambivalent views about English attempts at education. In a poem of 1923, he satirized public schools as offering nothing but the Church of England, the British Empire, 'beef, beer, bacon and eggs, and rowing'.[89] Returning to these establishments occasionally was to be reminded of horror; 'The season of Speech Days is on me. I do nothing but give away prizes and wring the greasy hands of small boys. The wages of sin ... I had forgotten how horrible schools are, and it is useful to be reminded. I can't think how the poor boys survive at all.'[90] He explained to an American friend that the only aim of English schools was to produce 'character through suffering'.[91] He could also not help reflecting that, if the building of character was the whole point of these schools, looking at their 'bloody headmasters',[92] there was clear evidence that they had failed. Stories of schoolboy uprisings delighted him. When the pupils of Winchester tried to blow up their headmaster, Bowra reported the incident to Cyril Connolly as 'a nice, spirited action, if rather Balkan ... There seems too to have been an outbreak of homicide in the school. That is where the cult of Character leads.'[93] When a protégé became headmaster of Lancing, Maurice congratulated him on his promotion, and asked that he 'be kind to the boys and remember your own none too virtuous past. It saves one from hypocrisy.'[94] Public schools were full of philistinism, moral duplicity, and hectoring nonsense.

Given views such as these, it might have been anticipated that Bowra would have severed his connections with Cheltenham completely, but this was not the case. The links remained strong. Whatever his sarcastic remarks on headmasters in general, he kept up with his own. The Revd Reginald Waterfield had insisted that Cheltenham 'always stood for three things, flying high, going straight, and sticking together to the end'.[95] Despite this Maurice regularly visited him in the deanery of Hereford, to which chance and good fortune had brought him.[96] Visitors to England were taken to see 'the Perp. at my old school',[97] and nostalgia led Bowra to regret the abolition of Greek.[98] It was at Maurice's insistence that Day-Lewis went to teach at Cheltenham, and, most surprising of all, he served on the school's governing body from 1943 to 1965, in company with Dadie Rylands. He only retired from this post when 'a dear general' gave up the chairmanship, to be succeeded by an air chief marshal who was 'rather a come-down' and inclined to cronyism.[99] As a parting gift, he gave the school three hard tennis courts. Whatever Maurice thought of Cheltenham, the school eventually claimed him as its own. After his death, a Bowra Memorial Lecture was established.[100] No doubt the honorand would have been both gratified and amused.

Maurice was sixteen when the Great War began. He had lived through an exceptional childhood, half exotic, half traditionally English. It was an upbringing that fostered long-term consequences. Most importantly, ties of family came to mean little to him. Between 1905 and 1922, he had little contact with his parents and sisters and too much contact with his brother. When his father and mother were in England on leave, they were loving enough, but they were never near him for long, and, with the best will in the world, they could not share the academic preoccupations of a clever son. Alienation from family loyalties was so deeply ingrained in Bowra that it could not be overcome when his immediate relations at last became accessible.

In April 1919, Cecil Bowra, on leave from China, returned the family to its Kentish roots by buying the Dower House in the village of Ightham. It was the first settled home the family had ever had, and, when the Bowras retired there, in January 1924, they had their first opportunity to live together. It was a world of servants, Sunday church, and village gossip. When Elizabeth Longford was taken for tea, she found the atmosphere 'rather sort of gentlemanly ... it was simple and not at all snobbish, and I would say typical professional class'.[101] If he had not escaped abroad, Maurice would spend most university vacations in Kent until his election

as Warden of Wadham in 1938. He represented these weeks and months as
a kind of martyrdom. He lived in 'accumulated misery and utter boredom.
I am so emotionally debauched by Oxford that I detest being here, and that
is that, as Confucius would say ... Of my family the least said the better.'[102]

Life at Ightham was picturesquely described by Bowra to be 'like listening
to scales played by a little girl with red pigtails, one by one, next door'.[103]
Kent was 'terribly neat and well kept' by 'glum gardeners', who were
continually lectured by their employers. There were no opportunities 'to
talk about books or politics. The neighbours and relations are the main
topics.'[104] Using the language of prison, Maurice, in 1920, told a friend
that he had 'done nearly four weeks at home', which had brought 'my
depression' to an 'uncommonly low' level. He was made to play tennis at
the rectory, to take 'dull and hideous female cousins for picnics in the local
woods', and to play endless rubbers of bridge.[105] He even had to watch
cricket in Canterbury with a certain Poppity Evans-Gordon.[106] For Bowra
this was torture of a not very subtle kind. Predictably, all this led him to
behave badly, and his family loudly complained that he was unreasonably
'peevish'.[107]

Christmases were to be dreaded. Relations were everywhere and unavoidable. In his view, 'the prospect of the Christian god being born again'
seemed to make everyone even more impossible. 'Stale maidens from the
village' would appear for meals,[108] and the house would fill with 'dried
up creatures, jealous of each other and incapable of judgement'.[109] Worse
still were invitations to parties given by families with unmarried daughters.
Here, there was nothing but conversation with 'spare men and critical
matrons' and 'hushed breathless women intervals when I shall be expected
to have something to tell them'.[110] Subverting the machinations of the Lady
Bracknells of the Kent marriage market by introducing village worthies to
risqué games compensated only slightly for these trials. Christmas would
always be a problem for Bowra. Its religious challenge was unwelcome and
its social rituals were stifling. He was delighted that the Christmas of 1925
was enlivened by the disappearance of the butler with the family silver.
The joke was even more delicious when it transpired that the man was 'a
super-burglar wanted for murder'.[111] Rumours of homicide at least gave
people something to talk about.

Work and private reading were the only means of keeping the imagination alive. At Easter 1921, for example, he delightedly informed Sylvester
Gates that Maupassant had come to his rescue; 'It is easy French and

provides the lurid thrill to which I am so susceptible ... it is full of innocent old men in goal and stale English virgins soaking in salt sea ports.'[112] But even the simple act of reading was not easy in Kent. There were 'no books' in the Dower House itself,[113] and, in order to get on with the dialogues of Plato, Maurice had to turn down invitations to play mixed hockey and to attend the point-to-point of the West Kent Hunt.[114] All too often he was 'encumbered with aunts and cousins'.[115] He would inevitably be accused of anti-social behaviour.

Contact with his family for a few weeks merely confirmed how little they had in common. In term time, Bowra spent weekends with Ottoline Morrell at Garsington and Margot Asquith at The Wharf. In vacations he was at the mercy of the social lions of rural Kent. The contrast could hardly have been more stark. Letters of October 1927 make the point. One sister, 'agreeably childlike', had married against her parents' wishes. Maurice gave her credit for this spirited independence, but detested the ensuing turmoil; 'The Bowras are not at their best. My niece howls, cutting her teeth. My sister has heard no word from her husband for six weeks, and is on the verge of collapse. The baby has been ill and howls. Mrs Bowra has no servants and is flustered and querulous. The Mandarin has tried to drive the car, and has failed. True to his tradition, he wants to put the car in the wrong. Even this he cannot do, and for the first time in his life, he is experiencing defeat.'[116] In this domestic hugger-mugger, Maurice found himself and his priorities of no consideration or consequence. Even when he was offered prestigious Chairs, his family could not understand. In 1937, he told an American friend of his

> Oedipus complex which works like a dynamo the moment I cross the Bowra threshold. It has not been made any better by the presence of a sister, brother-in-law (Danish and very difficult) and two children. Noise, scenes, guilt, indigestion and colds are all much to the front. My parents, obsessed with the difficulties of house-keeping, have not troubled to ask me about the American offers. So even that small triumph is denied me.[117]

In reaction to rebuffs such as this, Maurice sometimes found solitude preferable, even though it was something he normally feared. Family life made working impossible and forced him to cope with the emotional demands of people who, for most of his life, had been strangers. He told Ottoline Morrell that he could not live in 'a crowded house, where the presence of others, let alone their demands, invades and scatters my thoughts at once'.[118] To be alone at home was a rare pleasure, even though it meant being looked after by the gardener's wife, who offered a diet of 'carrots, porridge and bread-and-butter puddings'. Such 'solitude in the home of my fathers' was still 'impressive'.[119] Stodgy puddings were a small price to pay for a freedom from obligations that seemed to suck all the oxygen from rooms. As has been noted, Bowra never lost touch with his family, but they had little influence on his development except by reaction. He was undoubtedly a man of a certain class and situation and could not escape all the assumptions of his order. But, in all that was essential to his character he was a self-made man.

One other important question arises from an examination of Bowra's childhood; just how English was he in terms of habit and cultural reference? Witnesses were sharply divided on this matter. For some Cheltenham and Kent had created an English gentleman who was even capable of patriotism. Peter Fraser pointed out that, although Maurice read many languages, he could not speak any of them with that fluency that establishes a second identity.[120] Aline Berlin agreed, recalling an occasion in Italy, when he had ordered ham with the word 'jambone'.[121] The fellows of Wadham were sometimes teased for taking too many foreign pupils. The Warden gave the impression of wanting 'the College to be British'.[122] When overseas students were asked to pay fees higher than those of their British counterparts, Bowra welcomed the proposal, for 'it means we shall have far fewer of them, and high time too'.[123] Based on testimonials such as these, it would appear that Maurice's mission was only to the British, and not to the gentiles.

But other witnesses saw things differently. George Seferis, in his diary, hailed Bowra as 'one of the few Europeans still left in Europe'.[124] Ernst Kantorowicz, one of Maurice's most intimate friends, insisted that the Mediterranean was the true home of both of them. His friend was only a 'nationalist with regard to the past, or to English tradition'. Otherwise, he belonged spiritually and psychologically to the Greek and Italian worlds.[125] One Wadham man noted in the Warden 'a distinct mittel-europaische or brachycephalic mien to the person that set him apart from Anglo-Saxons'.[126] Others, again, thought that he had never shaken off his Chinese origins. John Bamborough remembered that Bowra read poetry in a way that no English don would dare emulate. He read 'like a distinguished Chinese, marmoreal, distant'.[127] When the novelist Berta Ruck met Bowra for the first time, in Vienna in 1934, she thought she was confronted by something very familiar and easy to put in a pigeon-hole; 'a youngish man, solidly built, square-shouldered, square-faced, fresh-coloured, firm in the jaw, quick in the eyes, a typical Public School produced, ex-War Service Englishman.' Very quickly she came to see that this appreciation had been lamentably superficial. She 'began to see, behind the Anglo-Saxon façade, a Maurice with a leopard skin flung over his shoulder and a strong shoot of vine twisted in his hair'.[128]

Clearly, on this question as on so many others, Bowra presented different faces to different people. Some thought him an Englishman of his age and class; others detected alternative loyalties. How then did Bowra see himself? Always guarded in his remarks on this matter, he admitted that, on arriving at an English public school, he was immediately aware of how little he had in common with those around him. The future members of the English establishment were largely uncongenial. He unwittingly broke schoolboy codes of honour, and found the cheerful philistinism of his contemporaries puzzling:

> For a boy of twelve I had seen a lot of the world and moved too much among grown-ups. I was used to talking when I had something to say, and that was often. Nor had I the faintest inkling of the English convention that it was bad form to talk too much. I could ride a pony and skate after a fashion, but I had never played either cricket or football. I found myself flung among a lot of boys whose interests were not in the least like mine and whose upbringing had been in a single, severe mould, which made them regard deviations with suspicion. At first they looked on me with surprise, then decided I was not one of them and left me alone. This was not in the least unkind, but I was not ready to live on my own resources, and I felt abandoned by God and man.[129]

This sense of distance never left him. In letters, later in life, he would slip into the habit of referring to the English as 'they' or 'them'. In congratulating an American friend on her command of language, he reflected that 'only foreigners speak perfect, grammatical English like you and me'.[130]

More practically, it was a physical necessity to leave England two or three times a year to live under different skies and different rules. This not only allowed him to escape the rigours of Kent, but such travel provided a necessary antidote to a long residence in England generally. Returning from Italy in 1931, England was 'worse than ever'.[131] Its climate and inhibitions descended like a smothering blanket. Not the least awful aspect of the

Second World War was that it made overseas travel all but impossible. Returning to Paris, in May 1945, was personal liberation. As he reported to Cyril Connolly, 'The weather was wonderful and I had a great feeling of exhilaration at being at last out of the English cage.'[132] Maurice was indeed a vehement apologist for England in the abstract, particularly when challenged on these matters by an American voice, but residence in that country was unfulfilling unless supplemented by all that abroad could offer. At crucial moments in his career, he could show the exaggerated patriotism of someone who felt himself to be eternally at a tangent to the English. He had survived Cheltenham, but had never won the whole-hearted approval of Cheltonians. He would become a figure of great distinction in English academic life, but he would always be a person around whom suspicion could easily gather.

A personality is perhaps the construction of three forces; the conventions absorbed in the living within a particular family, the correction of attitudes offered by contemporaries, and, more nebulously, the assumptions inculcated by the habits of a particular society. Bowra effectively had none of these. Family life was, through no one's fault, closed to him. Most of his contemporaries saw him as a phenomenon or an oddity. England offered him something, but never attracted his whole loyalty. As a result, Bowra was thrown back on his own reserves much more than most men. His character would be determined by a process of inner, private discovery. The exploration of literature, particularly poetry, began the process of building his values, which were then moderated through the thoughts and actions of the ancient Greeks. They would be given practical expression in the Oxford of the 1920s and in the trenches of the Great War. It was a totally personal exploration. To talk of those who influenced Bowra is to omit the names of teachers, parents, or friends, and to concentrate on particular writers whose voices set up echoes in his mind. The robust originality of Bowra, on which both friend and foe agreed, had its roots in the fact that, unlike most men, the world he lived in was largely of his own making.

2

War, 1914–1918

It is difficult to write with precision about Maurice's life as a soldier. The War was clearly a determining experience, and yet the evidence which might describe it is sadly thin. Like so many others, he rarely talked of the War, when he so readily talked of everything else. Few letters survive, and the chapter in *Memories* which covers these years is a heavily sanitized account. The misery of what he saw and heard had to be blotted out. Instead, he recalled the moments of humour, the comradeship, and the boredom. Only very occasionally, to a close friend, would the mask slip. Late in life, he confessed to George Richardson that, to understand what the Great War was like, 'think how bad it could possibly be, and then be sure it was very much worse'.[1]

In April 1916, Bowra passed his eighteenth birthday. He was now liable to be summoned for military service at any time. Ever since the War had begun, the inevitability of this moment had been all too clear to him. Sitting in Cheltenham, he saw casualty lists that included the names of young men who had only recently been at the school. Everyone knew that his turn would come. Bowra's reaction to this fact was both cheerful and apocalyptic; 'I saw how small the chances of survival were and made up my mind that I was certain in due course to be killed. Once I had come to this conclusion I felt much better, since it meant that I could pursue my own line and read what I wished.'[2] His father was less phlegmatic. With Edward already in uniform in the spring of 1916, he could only see the future as 'dark and uncertain'.[3] Ethel Bowra returned to England, in January of that year, for one last meeting with her sons before they went off to war. It was during her visit that it was decided that Maurice should make one more tour to China before starting military service. According to the family journal, the boy 'was doubtful if he ought to leave England'[4] at such a moment, but parental pressure proved overwhelming.

One 8 May 1916, Bowra left for China. Avoiding the war zone, he and his mother travelled by way of Norway, Sweden, Russia, and the Trans-Siberian Railway. His passport for the journey survives, decorated with colourful visas and stamps. It records that its owner was 5'6" in height, and had the following physical features:

Forehead	Broad	Eyes	Blue
Chin	Round	Mouth	Medium
Complexion	Fresh	Face	Oval[5]

They arrived in Peking on 22 May. For Bowra, there followed a last sustained experience of China and a last summer to be enjoyed before the start of soldiering. There were long expeditions on horseback and visits to the Great Wall and the Ming Tombs. Since Cecil Bowra was now a very high-ranking official in the Chinese civil service, the family was attended by no less than thirty servants, among whom was a chef called 'the Great Eating Professor'.[6] They enjoyed having a cottage upcountry and a seaside villa at Peitaho. As an honoured guest, Maurice was given a ringside seat from which to view the funeral of Yuan Ski-Kai, who had helped to destroy the Manchu Empire. These summer months of oriental privilege, however, ended badly. On setting out for England on 4 September, every piece of luggage disappeared on the Chinese border and was never recovered.[7] Even so, with a war to contemplate, this mishap was taken in his stride. Maurice was 'painfully aware' that, while his 'older contemporaries were being slaughtered on the Somme', he and his family 'had been enjoying themselves'.[8]

On his journey home he spent nearly three weeks in Petrograd. He would later speak of this time as of incalculable importance to his emotional life. His host was Robert Wilton, the correspondent of the London *Times* in the city. In his company he went to tea parties where he heard stories about Rasputin and the Empress, referred to as 'the German woman'.[9] Equally sinister were the bread queues that formed daily under the brutal direction of Cossacks with whips. Wilton insisted that life in Russia was still relatively normal, but Bowra became more and more convinced that the whole system had 'come near to breaking down'.[10] As he listened to well-to-do people discussing the possibility, even the desirability, of a revolution, he 'felt that I was witnessing the last days of Byzantium before Mehmet the Conquerer broke through the walls'.[11] Watching the disintegration of the Romanov Empire was a first indication that a world of seemingly stable values was always at risk. He would see other regimes founder, as an eye witness, but this first example of fallibility was the most impressive.

It was not, however, misshapen politics that made these few weeks so memorable. There was an altogether more personal reason. Early in his stay, he fell in with 'an ensign in a Guards Regiment' who took him to dinner in an officers' mess. The food was good, although his host and others had the disconcerting habit of shooting out the light bulbs and thereby plunging the room into darkness.[12] The ensign had a sister. In their company, Maurice went to hear Chaliapine sing *Boris Godunov* and *Ivan the Terrible*, and to ballet performances that owed more to Petipa than Diaghilev. In *Memories*, these evenings are described in exaggerated language; 'to enjoy such spectacles in the most delightful company possible was so enthralling that I have never regained its delight.'[13] Quite simply, he was 'enraptured' by the Russian girl. She in turn 'became very fond of me, and we passed most evenings together, with or without her brother, whom we both loved'.[14] For all this to take place within the short space of three weeks is astonishing. On returning home, he corresponded with the girl, until her letters stopped abruptly in the spring of 1918. He later discovered that she died in the Russian Revolution.

Clearly something of importance had happened in Petrograd. Even so, this intense, emotional experience is only given a few lines on one page of the *Memories*, and he spoke of it very rarely. As a friend remembered after his death, Maurice 'hankered after a romantic ideal of happiness which he'd once a glimpse of, and lost. Did he ever speak to you of that month in Moscow? [*sic*] He did to me, but only once.'[15] There was an agreement among those who knew him best that, perhaps for the only time in his life, he had been privileged to know the possibilities of loving, if in a highly idealized way. There was less agreement about who was the object of his affections. Some accepted the story about the girl; some thought she was invented to disguise devotion directed towards the ensign; some believed that love was offered to both brother and sister in adolescent confusion. The slight and embarrassed account of such an important moment in *Memories* perhaps gives weight to the second or third alternatives but the exact truth will never be known.

The experience was so telling that it moved Bowra to poetry. 'Nocturne' is a silken and serene account of loving and being loved:

> Dim-shadowed in a silvery mist
> The city lies.
> The moon, as though to swooning kissed,
> Upon her dies
>
> The river from her source afar
> Is locked in rest.
> And holds a single trembling star
> Within her breast.
>
> Alone in perfect quietness
> I wait for thee,
> And soon shall feel thy loveliness
> Grow one with me.[16]

In 'The Dreamer', which almost certainly was written at the same time, the beloved object is ethereal and distant, living in a pure and uncontaminated private world:

> Beneath a blue unclouded sky,
> Beside a dreaming sea,
> She sits behind her lattice high
> And dreams of worlds to be.
>
> The laughing sunbeams dance and play
> Upon her golden hair;
> They pry into her room and stray
> Adown the shadowy stair.
>
> The scent of laden orange-trees
> Is wafted to her breast
> By every lazy, languorous breeze
> That stirs the midday rest.
>
> The fountain in the laurel grove
> Murmurs its drowsy lay,
> And soothes the slumbering boughs above
> With soft, caressing spray.
>
> But nought cares she who sits within
> For light or scent or tune.
> She knows not when the flowers begin
> Or when the nights come soon.

She cares not for the world's delight:
Behind her casement bars
She scales the fastnesses of night
And feasts among the stars.[17]

In these adolescent verses, love is pure, luminous, but somehow unobtainable and removed from all possibility of being grasped.

He discovered too that loving carried risk. Paradise was as easily lost as gained. The likelihood of being left looking ridiculous was real. For Bowra these were real fears. A dread of loving and losing surfaces repeatedly in his later life. When letters ceased to arrive from Russia, it is quite possible that their absence provoked the composition of a poem entitled 'Out of Touch':

I am too dull, too dull for pain,
My sickening thoughts grow cold
And all is too often told.
Better be deaf and blind
Than hear this throbbing refrain
That drums again, again—
Out of touch, out of mind.

Out of touch with the past—
That at least could be borne.
Do I find myself forlorn,
Careless of sight or of sound?
I never thought it could last
But knew it would vanish fast
To this, dull labouring round.

Out of mind with the world—
Contemporaries sacrifice
Easy to pay the price
Of neglect and solitude,
Now that all hopes are furled
And fantastic visions hurled
Back to the empty mood.

Now that a casual word,
Severing as secrecy,
Keeps you away from me,
Do I think it can matter much
That passionate anger stirred
And left me alone, absurd,
Out of mind, out of touch.[18]

The Petrograd experience had gone deep, and may have engendered these verses and many others. It had taught Bowra that a loved one could be a muse, an inspiration. When poets he admired talked such language, he understood what they meant. But to love was also to run the risk of being left 'alone, absurd'. The world would be free to comment on your foolishness. Rejection and rebuff in his emotional life were things that Maurice both expected and feared in adolescence and in maturity. Three weeks in Petrograd had given him a glimpse of what a great love could be. Inexorable circumstances had then, almost immediately, carried it out of range. With some justice, he noted in *Memories* that, as he left the Finland Station for home, he 'had much to think about'.[19]

Bowra's war service would begin in the spring of 1917. In order to prepare for it, he spent the autumn of the previous year training with the Oxford OTC. Long before he knew the city as an academic therefore, he knew it as a soldier. Written fifty years after the event, his *Memories* claimed to set out his thinking as he prepared to go off to war. First and foremost, its inevitability had hung over him for years. At Cheltenham, army parades became more frequent in 1912 and 1913. Field days were increased in number, and he seemed to spend many afternoons 'falling down in cow pats and sheep-droppings'.[20] Sermons preached by the headmaster became more militaristic. In one, he attempted to assuage tender consciences with the thought that, though Jesus Christ could not have been a soldier, he would certainly have volunteered for the R.A.M.C.[21] After the outbreak of war, Cheltonians were encouraged to sacrifice what comforts they had, in order to empathize with their brothers at the front. It all seemed that his generation had been given over to 'a monstrous betrayal by Providence'.[22]

Unlike many of his contemporaries, he claimed that he in no way relished the prospect of army life. He already 'knew too much about intending officers to think they would be very congenial'. Nor did he think that the war could be ended quickly. Instead, he believed that it would be a long, drawn-out affair, in which his own death would be an insignificant episode. When his former governess, Ella Dell, surmised that he was 'longing to get at the Germans', he could hardly find any words in which to reply.[23] The only consolation lay in the idea that a soldier in action might be more the master of his fate than a schoolboy at Cheltenham could ever be. England was right to fight in 1914, and everything followed from this one fact.

Gloomy forebodings never led towards pacifism. The War was to be faced, not avoided; 'I never thought of avoiding my obligation to do military service, and was never able to see how conscientious objectors could cut themselves off from their fellows … I thought that I should have to fight just because there was nothing else to do, and if my friends could face it, so could I.'[24] Throughout his life, he found it hard to forgive those who had been conscientious objectors. His attacking personality could not distinguish easily between conscience and cowardice. When E. R. Dodds was preferred over him for the Oxford Chair of Greek, professional disappointment was compounded by the knowledge that his rival had taken no part in the Great War. In revenge, he harassed him around Oxford with the question, 'What did you do in the War, Doddy?' Bowra was not the only soldier, who, having seen death and misery in the trenches, found it hard to forgive those who claimed conscience and survived. The issue was guaranteed to produce a vituperative response.

This account of his feelings in 1916, given by Maurice in *Memories*, is unexceptional and largely restrained. Contemporary evidence, as far as it exists, invites more colour. There had been greater emotion in all directions. The eighteen year old had shown more hope, more anger, and more cynicism than the later narrative would suggest. His first, extant poem, 'Mecanophilus', probably written for a school competition in 1913, applauds a new world in prospect. Science and the machine would abolish poverty and bring nations together. The fifteen year old gave his generation a new mission:

> To pick the weak out of the mire of servile labour and greed
> To stir up a noble desire where cankers of selfishness feed;
> To teach to the slothful races the lessons of duty and toil,
> The strong love which honour embraces, the courage defeat
>   cannot spoil.[25]

Here was youthful, unbridled hope. For the only time in his life, Maurice lauded the scientist and the engineer as the prophets of a new age.

Before they could go to work, however, there was much that had to be changed or destroyed. 'Gold Dancing in the Air' is a remarkable poem written in or around 1916. It depicts contemporary Europe as a casino whose verminous inhabitants have made money their god. Everything is gangrenous and without real value:

> Gold dancing in the air, and gold
> Thrown back from mirrors manifold

Down corridors of frozen light
Women are walking. Slim and slow
Shadows slide past them—as they go,
The candelabras strike their eyes
And strike the shadows to surprise.
Hard stones and clanging metals cling
To flesh as soft as clouds, and ring
With multicoloured interchange
Of harmonies occult and strange.
Like gulls floating on wings outspread,
The women drift with soundless tread.
Each glance miraculously planned
Responds to hints from head or hand;
Lips that leave sentences half said,
Curve of the neck that slants a head
In silence summoning desire,
Eyelids that droop but do not tire

  . . . . . .

Outside, mocked by the wall of glass
Multitudes pass and stop and pass.
For a moment lamplit faces stare,
Then fade upon the solid air.
Pallid as lard damp faces gaze
Fixt on illuminated baize,
Where twitching jewelled fingers lie
And turreted counters totter high.
Coarse faces full of blood that leer
Emptily round the room and peer
In corners with secretive eyes.
Hands buzzing round like greedy flies
In search of meat, fat hands that clutch
And fumble when they come to touch.

  . . . . . .

Old women under tinsel hair
Croak welcomes down the marble stair;
Dancers crooning a negro song
Mechanically drift along:
Bodies unmuscled, melting knees
Move as the mastering discord please,
Subservient in the brazen din
To automatic discipline.
The bloodshot eyes light up and stare

With hungry looks across the glare,
Devouring breast and arms, and gloat
In prospect on a velvet throat.
Outside no faces peer. The light
Of morning generously bright
Strikes dingy catacombs and calls
Workmen asleep by peeling walls.[26]

In this world of stained velvets and silks, the Europe of 1916 needs purgation. A world war might accomplish at least that. If so, personal sacrifice would be in order. In the faint echoes of socialism in some lines there might even be the hope of something better emerging from the slaughter. Perhaps European society might be jolted into a rediscovery of values, when, according to Bowra the poet, it clearly had none at the outbreak of war.

If the sense of mission was keener than Maurice later remembered, and the cynicism more bitter, so too was the feeling of exhilaration. For a young man to know himself in the face of death was an experience not to be missed. As he pointed out in a lecture on war poetry, 'A large paradox of the War is that it was actually welcomed by the great majority of those who found themselves caught in it.'[27] Three days before setting out for France, he wrote a letter to his parents in China, trying to convey his feelings. He was in London helping his brother to celebrate his twenty-first birthday, although, in the circumstances, there could not be 'much joy-making'. As Zeppelins bombed Piccadilly, he expressed contempt for those who scurried for shelter into the Underground, 'encamped on platforms and stairs with their wives and children, making a filthy mess and a still filthier atmosphere'. Clearly, the untried soldier had not come to associate war with squalor and smell. For him it still had perhaps a nobler aspect. He finishes with determination and fatalism; 'Aunt Mabel is in fairly good form but I am afraid she suspects hidden sadness where it is not. Anyhow she consoles with me in going out, whereas I go out in a purely callous mood of intense curiosity. Doubtless the second time I shall not be anxious to go, but I do want to see what I can do with the guns. It is a real job and even if it is a very small part, it brings a feeling of satisfaction with it.'[28] To go to war was terrible. Not to go to war, for a variety of reasons, would be worse.

He was called up for active service on 1 March 1917, one month short of his nineteenth birthday. Initially, he was sent to the Royal Army

Cadet School in St John's Wood, being intended for a commission in the
East Surrey Regiment. He arrived with excellent references. The officer
commanding the Oxford OTC testified that 'he can take control. Has
ability and confidence. Should make a useful officer.' His old headmaster
reported on his 'good moral character',[29] thereby taking a line that few
others would follow in later life. Maurice passed his medical examination
with grade A. His 'physical development' was 'good', and there were no
'distinguishing marks' on his body apart from '8 moles on his back'. This
first report also noted that the new recruit had no wish to join the navy,
expressing rather a great desire to become a gunner.[30] Bowra could only
have been very pleased, therefore, when he was commissioned in the Royal
Field Artillery on 29 July 1917. This preference was no affectation. He liked
the power of the guns and the spirit of the soldiers who manned them.
Whenever he approached the Artillery Memorial at Hyde Park Corner,
'the reliefs moved him a lot'.[31] In later life, gunnery became an unexpected
part of his conversational repertoire.

The months between March and August 1917 were spent in basic
training. This consisted of little but instruction in the handling of guns and
the perfecting of horsemanship. Field artillery still moved around battlefields
on carriages drawn by horses, and it may be that Bowra's experiences on
horseback in China guaranteed him a place in gunnery. At the barracks in
Handel St., Bloomsbury, the day began in the stables, 'mucking out with
hands'. In the indoor riding school, horses were ridden bareback, even
over jumps. To Maurice, it seemed more like preparation for a gymkhana
rather than a war; 'the business of war ... had very little to do with what we
now learned. We concluded that the army was run by lunatics and that the
wisest course was to humour them.'[32] Although life improved somewhat
when his unit was billeted at Lords Cricket Ground, this suspicion of the
army leadership would only deepen as the War went on. At this early stage,
the only officer he respected was a certain Major Brown, who entertained
his men by reading aloud from a book of pornography entitled *The New
Lady's Tickler*.[33] The Army would be his world until demobilization on
9 February 1919. He resigned his commission on April Fools' Day, 1920,
no doubt being aware of the irony in the date chosen.

Bowra arrived in France in the first days of September 1917, being attached
to B Battery of the 298th Army Brigade, Royal Field Artillery. The War
Diary of the Brigade gives a detailed account of when and where it saw

action.[34] On 2 November, he arrived on the Ypres front, first at St Momelin and then at Poperinghe. He found himself in trenches which had 'reverted to a bog, an unbroken waste of mud pitted every few yards with holes full of greasy, scummy, slimy liquid, and more often than not of decomposing bodies of horses and men'.[35] Quickly the numbing routine of an artillery officer was established. It was a matter of firing at an unseen enemy, bringing up ammunition, and going forward to establish observation posts, from which fire would be directed. Of these tasks, the last was by far the most dangerous and disgusting. Observation posts, if recently captured, might be full of dead Germans who had to be removed; 'I insisted that they should be dragged out and usually did it myself, stopping my nose and shutting my eyes.'[36] On one occasion, he directed fire onto Noyon Cathedral, which the enemy were in turn using as an observation post. In later life, he much enjoyed pointing out that, any qualms he might have felt about destroying venerable architecture were overcome by the remembrance that Noyon had been the birthplace of John Calvin. He would always take pleasure in shooting at puritans.

Between 30 November and 30 December, Bowra saw action in the third battles of Ypres and at Cambrai, near the villages of Havrincourt and Beauchamp. Here the problem was 'simply mud. It was this which made all advances so hideously slow and therefore murderous, which meant that even slight wounds might turn gangrene and kill, that supplies were ruinously hard to bring up, that morale was damaged by everyone being perpetually caked in mud, that sleep was never easy and often impossible.'[37] The early months of 1918 were quieter, but, in March, he retreated for ten days before the last, major German offensive of the War. Five months later, in August, he took part in the counter-offensive, in which he saw tanks in action for the first time: 'This was one of the few days in my military life when I felt the terrifying fascination of battle.' As the Germans retreated, success bred 'a wild exhilaration in which we conducted our duties with fits of laughter and uproarious jokes'.[38] The Armistice found him near Sains du Nord. When the news arrived, the Battery's sergeant major enigmatically muttered, 'Now that the war is over, we can get down to real soldiering.' More prosaically, the French produced hidden bottles of wine 'from middens and wells' to celebrate what was 'a royal occasion'.[39] To survive three major battles in just under a year justified any indulgence.

Of course, an official war diary gives little indication of what actually happened to the men involved. Details of troop movements, of plans being hatched and enacted, suggest a precision that rarely existed. Real war was chaotic, macabre, and just occasionally romantic. Certainly, Bowra's war involved all these elements. He saw and smelt death on a daily basis. He had grave doubts about the competence of the High Command, and shared the fatalism of those around him. Yet, even in the midst of so much misery, astonishing things could happen. Cyril Connolly cherished a Maurice story which related 'how an incredibly lovely young Prussian nobleman fell from an aeroplane into his battery in the war, and for 2 hours Maurice gave him drinks and stroked his hair, and the airman was touched and gave him books'.[40]

Less lyrical were Bowra's brushes with death. He came near to being killed on two occasions. In the battle of Cambrai, he was buried alive when a trench collapsed. By a bizarre twist of fate, he was saved, as he explained to an American friend, by the efficiency of German equipment:

> In the battle of Cambrai I was buried in a deep dug-out, and saw the end near. However, there was a telephone there; so I rang it, and in due course it was answered from above. I naturally said 'Bowra speaking', and my old friend Humphrey Campbell-Jones, killed in the second war, then dug me out, but not before I had passed into a heavy coma. It took time, as I was some twenty feet below the surface—the dug out, needless to say, was a highly efficient German one, which we had captured.[41]

The story was also confided to John Betjeman.[42] He had survived only by showing great presence of mind and by having astonishing luck.

His good fortune held in March 1918. He arrived back at the Front from leave a matter of hours before the Germans unleashed their last, great offensive of the War. As his father recorded, the onslaught brought hand-to-hand fighting, with Maurice dressed in not much more than pyjamas:

> His mess and quarters in the dug-out were destroyed by a direct hit from a 9′ shell and he lost everything but what he stood up in—his pyjamas and a 'British warm.' The Germans were upon them in the fog before they knew what was happening and there was hand to hand fighting around the guns. Happily, somehow or other, they were able to limber up and get away; and we had a letter from him, written just after the battle, in which he said he had been thirty-six hours in the saddle before he finally came to rest in a French farmhouse in the rear, where he had the sleep of his life on the kitchen table, and that he would not have missed it all for worlds.[43]

Somewhere in all this, he was wounded in the knee, and he carried 'His old (war) trouble' for the rest of his life.[44] The bravado in his letter home was no doubt sincerely felt. To have fought and survived was exhilarating. But he must also have known that he was lucky to be alive. Even as a child, Maurice had always entertained an attacking view of life. To have cheated death twice enhanced the zest for living.

Not surprisingly, Bowra was, for the whole of his life, fascinated by the problem of just how an individual survives the experiences of war, not just in a physical sense, but in how a character and personality is kept whole in the most trying of circumstances. He was clear that there was no single answer to these questions. Each man found his own way to survive.

> Those who knew of events only from hearsay could not imagine the incredible variety of battle, of the moods which it evokes. When a man is inextricably dependent on his circumstances every little thing in them makes a powerful impression on him. He must at all costs acclimatize himself to this strange and unaccountable world of war, and his moods will cover the whole range of which he is capable. There is no standard reaction to war; each man takes what comes, as it comes, in his own way.[45]

Some men went on from day to day only because to stop was to show cowardice and to let down fellow soldiers. There was something of this reaction in Bowra. In writing about the Greek poet Tyrtaeus, he approved his description of the soldier's lot as 'grim and self-denying. The pain must be endured because of the reward which it brings and of the shame which cowardice means.'[46]

But, in a terrible way, he also knew grandeur in war. After reading Evelyn Waugh's *Officers and Gentlemen*, he admitted that a 'dislike of the army' made it difficult for him to admire certain sections of the book, while 'his liking for war' enabled him to appreciate the battle scenes.[47] Warfare even contained humour. Bowra retailed with relish tales of idiocy and absurdity. There was the officer who recommended *Field Artillery Training* to him as a book 'written by a far cleverer man than you are ever likely to have met',[48] and the major with the disarmingly straightforward manner; 'Got a boil on your cock, old man, then crash along to the MO, who'll soon put you right with a Number 9.'[49] As these stories passed into his stock-in-trade, some friends were tempted to think that he enjoyed the War a little too much. Isaiah Berlin wondered why Cyril Connolly insisted that Maurice had hated the War unreservedly, 'when those who met him immediately after the war here in Oxford ... say he rather enjoyed some of it, and spoke of it with a kind of stoic ebullience'.[50] But it was a gallows humour. Bowra, with appropriate mimicry, ridiculed the more bizarre characters to be found in the officers' mess. He also once told Connolly about 'men having to laugh when their companions were burnt in the blazing grass as the only outlet for their feelings'.[51] In some circumstances, death itself was a matter for laughter.

War had routine, terror, humour, and grandeur, but it was, above all, awful in the full meaning of that word. Nothing that happened to British servicemen in the Second World War could compare with what he had experienced. Noel Annan once witnessed a stern rebuke delivered by Maurice to a bomber crew who were complaining of their lot:

> I saw him at a dinner party in Cambridge … turn on some gallant RAF officers, who were contrasting the luxury of the evening they were enjoying to the terror that lay ahead next night, when they would be bombing Germany and could well expect to be shot down by night-fighters. Bowra delivered a furious rebuke, asking them if they knew what it had been like to live in mud, shit and decomposing corpses. Had they ever watched an enemy shell destroy the headquarters one had left a few minutes previously, and then dug out the bodies of one's regimental companions?[52]

To survive, the soldier had 'to adjust his mind to death. He does so by treating it as nothing unusual, and in his topsy-turvy world he is not wrong.'[53] The real horror of war was to put life and death on a par. Both were to be equally anticipated and equally accepted.

In fact, the War made Bowra angry. His stories at dinner tables and the fatalism in his rare writings on the conflict come nowhere near to describing his true feelings. These were reserved for expression in poetry. 'Gold Dancing in the Air' is in three parts. The first described the corruption and diseased state of Europe. The second chronicles the War that had come out of that society:

> Bell-beat of wild duck overhead
> Vultures wheeling to pick the dead.
>
> A pile of peat to feed the fire
> Carcasses pinned on shell-shot wire.
>
> Siesta on a grassy mound
> Gas crawling over blood-drenched ground.
>
> Parapets stacked with mouldy dead
> To keep the wine in the wine glass red.

Boys bayoneted in the night
To keep official buttons bright.

Death on the ramparts, black with cold
Death in the squelching, watery mould.

Death dizzying in the riddled sky,—
Torn bodies left alone to die.

A people lashed to a wheel of fire
To satisfy a fool's desire.

Fields sliced to shreds and cities sacked
To keep a mothy creed intact.

Lithe bodies full of sap shot down
To gild the glory on a crown.

To slaughter pits the victims go
Gorging a ghastly triumph-show.

Bronze amour on the evening clouds
Shines in the face of muttering crowds.

Cold blasts that freeze the speaker's breath
Blow sharp as vengeance, cold as death.

Snow settling on the pavement stones
Wraps the flesh closer round the bones,

Freezes the vagrant, watery mood
Into an iron certitude,

Chilling the tongue that calls on Christ
For honour to be sacrificed.[54]

Someone was to blame. The wearers of the gilded crowns, the purveyors of 'mothy' creeds, and the owners of 'official buttons' had much to answer. Maurice was always unlikely to become a figure of the establishment. Too many of them were stupid and now too many of them were guilty. He lost respect for them and their claims to deference, as he recorded the gutting experience of the death of close friends:

The spring returned and made carouse
On shattered earth and withered tree;
But birdless were the broken boughs
And all the world was dumb to me.[55]

For a time he contemplated revenge of the most unforgiving kind. The
third part of 'Gold Dancing in the Air' is uncompromising in its demands:

> A king sits in a golden crown—
> Pull the man down, pull the man down.
>
> Obsequious lackeys hang around—
> Lock them in cellars underground.
>
> Women with jewels in their hair,
> Throw their pearls for swine to wear.
>
> A sleek financier clothed in fur—
> Hang him for a murderer.
>
> Bird-like youths upon the wing—
> Cage them up and make them sing.
>
> Powdered girls with ruby lips
> Learn to come to closer grips.
>
> Parsons bent on knees to pray
> Cheer Barabbas home today.
>
> Soldiers shooting with God's will
> Make game for other men to kill.
>
> Schoolmasters who trade in lies
> Tongueless try to moralize.
>
> Philanderers who dream and dope—
> The sharp kiss of the hangman's rope.
>
> Marionettes who dream and sup
> Machine-guns quickly fold you up.[56]

But this bitterness never in fact translated into a serious interest in politics.
Though always slightly left of centre, politics came very low in his order of
priorities. For a talented man to choose a career in Parliament was a waste
of abilities. He voted for Asquith in the election of 1918, because there
was no one else to support.[57] Nevertheless, the resentment was real. Roy
Harrod convinced him that the War had been completely unnecessary,
inducing a 'shock' from which 'I have never fully recovered'.[58] Looking at
the England of Stanley Baldwin, he could only wonder whether so many
sacrifices had been worthwhile; 'Mr Baldwin had begun his long tenure
of power and offered a sleeping insular peace built on social inequalities,
prolonged unemployment, and a distrust of any political thinking. This

repelled Hugh Gaitskell, as it repelled those of his elders who now began to feel that the war had been fought for no purpose.'[59] Anger and frustration would be channelled into poetic mission, however, not politics.

A distrust of those who set the rules of English life came easily to someone whose childhood had owed much to other cultures. His suspicions were confirmed by his experiences in the War, and came to be personified by the incompetence, snobbery, and philistinism of his brother officers. For the most part they were held in contempt, and in this proscription he included his own brother. A special loathing was reserved for generals, who repeatedly ordered frontal assaults, knowing that they could not work. Casualty lists seemed to have no impact on 'invisible commands who from a remote security order multitudes to a senseless death'.[60] The evidence is thin, but there are suggestions that he was disliked by his commanding officers. His battery commander found him 'slovenly'.[61] Lord Longford retailed a rumour that Maurice had actually shot an unpopular colonel in the heat of battle.[62] When reading Evelyn Waugh's novels about the Second World War, it was his description of bumbling, even psychotic, officers that particularly caught Maurice's attention.[63] If this antipathy was returned in full measure, it may explain why he emerged from the War undecorated, an unusual fact given the amount of action he had seen. When he dreamed about the War, which he did frequently, it seemed 'that the people he hated had been killed in the War and people he liked had survived. When he woke up, he found it was the other way round.'[64]

In seeing authority abused and mishandled, the lesson to be taken was immediate and obvious. Young people were always to be encouraged, rather than merely directed. As Noel Annan remembered, 'he was absolutely under, at various times, highly unsympathetic senior officers, who were very keen to put him in his place, and he was very keen, always, in his life, never to put young men in their place, always to encourage them even in outrageous conduct ... He might get angry, but he never put them down. Anything to do with snubbing them, totally not.'[65] By instinct, and now by experience, he would always sympathize with those who challenged authority. A strange by-product of this feeling is the space given in *Memories* to three Australian soldiers whose systematic irreverence delighted him. He remembered their names, Bourne, Marsh, and Freeman. They refused to salute British officers, were 'magnificently outspoken' when nonsenses were perpetrated, and knew how to break wind on parade according to regulations.[66] In battle, they showed both courage and common sense. On one occasion, in their company, Bowra came close to capturing Heinrich Brüning, the future Chancellor of Germany, a fact that he enjoyed retailing to Brüning when he arrived in Oxford as a refugee in 1934.[67] Henceforth, Maurice always associated Australians with insubordination, and liked them the better for it.

At the same time as he was losing respect for his own class, he was discovering merit elsewhere. As he put it,

> Before I joined the army I had lived in a very select and privileged class, knowing nothing and caring very little about the ways of other men. The war opened my eyes to the basic similarity of human beings and the absurdity of artificial distinctions between them. Even paternal care meant very little, for though it was my task to look after my men, it was usually they who looked after me, and were more capable of dealing with a sudden crisis than I was.[68]

The private soldier did his duty, and killed the enemy without hatred or rancour. Above all they showed 'a powerful desire to get their jobs done and to remain themselves in doing them'.[69] In war, different social classes inevitably rub shoulders, often for the first time. For Bowra this was an infinitely rewarding experience, showing him a world beyond Cheltenham and Kent.

Very quickly he subscribed to the vitality and earthiness of his new associates. Their argot, expressed in bawdy humour and song, pleased him beyond measure, and he would make large claims for it. He told a lecture audience that, with reference to the songs,

> though their form and their language are extremely simple, the states of mind which they record are not. Some of them are remarkable for their deep feelings and for a strong candour in dealing with them. Their peculiar quality is their fusion of self-mockery with self-pity ... It is the response of men to an intolerable situation which they see in all its odiousness but by which they refuse to be completely defeated. Through such songs they form an attitude that keeps them sane.[70]

Maurice had no voice at all, but a rendition of a First World War song became one of his party pieces. One of his favourites had the refrain,

> Send out the Army and the Navy
> Send out the ships upon the sea.
> Send out my brother, my sister and my mother,
> But for Gawd's sake, don't send me.[71]

Holiday parties toiling up Greek hillsides would be encouraged with verses from 'Keep the Home Fires Burning',[72] while in Sardinia, he once sang impromptu for Princess Margaret. She was so impressed that she reappeared later the same day with a tape recorder.[73] To sing with soldiers dignified their tribulations.

In later life, nothing would be too much trouble if the well being of a soldier was in question. In 1958, Bowra was asked to give a Memorial Address for Alick Smith, who had been Warden of New College when he himself was an undergraduate. Smith had enjoyed a colourful career and material for a speech was not lacking. It is interesting therefore that Bowra should have chosen to emphasize the care Smith had shown towards his soldier-pupils:

> Many of them were battered individuals back from the War, who were uneasily afraid that they were no longer what they had once been, and concealed under an affectation of hard-boiled indifference a nagging mistrust of themselves. Smith saw through the pretence and knew what the trouble was. With gentle, patient skill he set out to build them up, to make them believe again in themselves and their work. Nobody who came under his healing influence at this time can ever forget it or cease to be grateful for it.[74]

That Bowra was describing his own condition in 1918 is highly likely. His gratitude to Smith never diminished. In his turn, he offered the same care to the next generation. Servicemen coming up to Wadham after 1945 were his 'Returning Warriors', for whom all barriers should be levelled. For some he arranged an early demobilization, for others he found accommodation. It was of course absurd that such men should be subjected to any more rules. When one ex-soldier worried that his lack of Latin would exclude him from Oxford, he was reassured with the words, 'No matter, War Service counts as Latin.'[75]

Bowra's most important legacy from the Great War, however, had nothing to do with adjusting political or social attitudes. Rather, it was the discovery that survival in war, or in life in general, lay in the unfolding of an 'inner life' that could not be touched by any external forces. As he put it, in one tantalizingly brief reference in *Memories*, 'I found that in this life of action … it was both necessary and possible to maintain some sort of inner life.'[76] When a god-daughter explicitly asked how he had come through the War, Maurice replied that he had 'retreated into my inner life'.[77] In his view, all soldiers had to follow the same path. As war threatens to 'dominate' a soldier's 'being', 'most men struggle against its tyrannical claims and create some private refuge for their own thoughts and fancies and dreams. In this way, they assert their right to be themselves and, so far as lies within their control, they master their circumstances by refusing to surrender to them.'[78] No one must be allowed to penetrate this inner world, or its purpose would be defeated. Its private nature was all important. This may well have been why Bowra and other soldiers so rarely invited discussion of what war had meant to them.

In Maurice's case, this 'inner life' was encased in poetry. In later life, poetry would prove to be his main private and academic preoccupation. He would claim great status for the poet, and would assert that the honouring of such men was one of the principal characteristics of a vibrant civilization. In poetry, men found 'catharsis'. Written always in 'one's morbid moments', it brought calm because it had 'little relation to the routine of life'.[79] He had experimented with the writing of verse at school, but it was the War that confirmed the power of poetry over his mind. His gratitude to poets was immeasurable. They made articulate what most men could not put into words: 'They spoke for mankind in one of the cruellest ordeals to which it has ever been subjected, and their work was testimony to what happens when malignant circumstances obliterate the familiar landmarks of civilisation and rob man of his last assurance that anything in his existence is secure ... that articulation made it tolerable.'[80]

Poets affirm life, even in circumstances that make death something to be almost welcomed. This fact underpinned his deep friendship with Edith Sitwell. By an act of creative imagination she understood the pain of the soldier: 'Miss Sitwell understands the war-stricken with more than an ordinary woman's sight. In such a time there are many who feel that the struggle is too much for them and turn with longing to the thought of death ... the consoling darkness where all men are equal.' Knowing this, she yet asserted 'positive values in the fact of corruption and destruction'. Of course her poetry had a religiosity that Maurice could not share, but he responded powerfully to the idea that the physical world was not only 'powerful and life-giving in itself, but something else more powerful and life giving'.[81] There would be an ultimate healing and a kind of redemption.

The routine of life in the trenches was relieved by reading. Books were regularly sent from England, and these were supplemented by purchases made on leave. Naturally, he kept up his classical interests by working stead-ily through Homer, Virgil, and Tacitus. Then there were new discoveries in European literature. He claimed to have read all the novels of Anatole France in the war years. But three poets in particular were the supports of that inner life that allowed him to survive the war psychologically; Yeats, Eliot, and Hardy. As Maurice explained to Cyril Connolly,

> I was a little perplexed when you challenged me with making Hardy my god and not Eliot. In fact my god from 1917 onwards was Yeats and then Hardy—Hardy, because he alone expressed my cosmic despair as a young man, when I was flung into that war, which was plainly mad and absurdly horrible. I never talk of it, and put it out of my mind, but Hardy did a lot to heal my wounds, and that is why I forgive him his many inept and absurd lines and comical choice of words.[82]

In *Memories*, he specifically mentions Hardy's 'Moments of Vision', Yeats's 'The Wild Swans of Coole', and Eliot's 'Prufrock' as being of particular importance.[83] Very soon after the War, he came to know both Eliot and Yeats, meetings which gave him huge satisfaction.

These men could not, in any meaningful sense, explain the War. It would always be inexplicable. What they could do was to embrace it. As Bowra wrote, Hardy composed poems about the struggle 'with no trace of hatred'. Of course, he realized that 'there was something wrong with the scheme of things,' but such moments were endemic in the human experience. The War was neither right or wrong. It simply happened. Thomas Hardy thought it enough to admire 'the soldiers who go out to die because they believe that their cause is just, and that is enough for him'. One generation is blessed to live in peace. Another is tossed about and consigned to the abattoir. To call this unfair is pointless. In what goes on around them, 'men and women are hardly responsible for their own actions'. They could ultimately only control the life within.[84]

Sometime in the 1950s, a cruise ship carrying Maurice Bowra stopped opposite the beaches which had acted as landing stages in the Dardenelles campaign. As the passengers stood in silence, wreaths were cast on to the waters. The ceremony was too much for Bowra. Overcome with emotion he retired hurriedly to his cabin.[85] In fact, he never quite escaped the Great War. It had destroyed forever the sense of security that his childhood and school had fostered. It had undermined any lingering respect for the social system which had taken England into war and then mismanaged it. On the other hand, he had taken what opportunities there were to evade the restrictions of his class to profit by the company of new friends. Above all, he had learnt that the gods enjoyed sporting with mere mortals and did not feel inclined to justify their actions. The only defence against this caprice was that 'inner life' which even they could not reach. All else was a question that was pointless to ask, because it could never be answered. In a lecture on *Poetry and Politics*, Maurice, as he often did, turned to quotations from Thomas Hardy to express his own thoughts. The verse is taken from Hardy's reflections on the Armistice, 'And There was a Great Calm':

> Calm fell. From Heaven distilled a clemency;
> There was peace on earth, and silence in the sky;
> Some could, some could not, shake off misery:
> The Sinister Spirit sneered: 'It had to be!'
> And again the Spirit of Pity whispered, 'Why'?[86]

3

New College, 1919–1922

Maurice Bowra went up to New College in the spring of 1919, shortly after demobilization. He had been to Oxford twice before: once when, early in 1916, he had visited the city in order to take entrance examinations, and once in the autumn of the same year as a soldier in the local OTC. According to *Memories*, these short periods of residence were enough to convince him that the city had everything any man could wish for: the city 'laid its hold on me, and I formed a picture of it which I found comforting in the months to come'.[1] As a future tutor, professor, and vice chancellor, he would of course come to realize that, in many ways, Oxford would fall short of being paradise, but traces of a romanticized vision of the place would never leave him. It gave him nearly everything he required from life. As a stage for performance, its decor could not be surpassed. There would always be young people listening to stories and old people spinning tales.

Arriving in Oxford from the trenches was intoxicating. He was 'light in the head and pocket, but infinitely relieved and ready for anything'.[2] Simply to be alive was one thing. To be finally free of war and the prospect of war was liberating beyond all expectation. He was, after all, no callow youth, arriving at New College as a war-seasoned veteran of twenty-one. In retrospect, he thought this an advantage. Most undergraduates brought the problems of youth to university with them. By contrast, Bowra claimed that all such questions had been answered before coming up. As he told Cyril Connolly, 'You must remember that I was lucky in not coming up till I was twenty-one, when I had settled some at least of the hideous problems of youth.'[3] This claim may have been a little over-optimistic, but men just four or five years younger, who had missed the Great War, had every right to see him as of another generation.

Bowra arrived in an Oxford that was less a university than a collection of federated republics called colleges, and he delighted in the colour and variety that such a system encouraged. A favourite after-dinner game was to give each college the identity of a foreign country. His own New College was England, full of men in suits and totally uninterested in revolution; Christ Church was France, louche and amateurly bohemian; Balliol was America, dangerously energetic and pursuing everything new; Jesus was Yugoslavia, where strange tongues were spoken; Exeter was Rumania, trying to emulate France and failing to do so; Corpus Christi was Denmark, small and decent and easily ignored.[4] Each college was to some extent a closed community, in which friends were almost exclusively to be found. In Bowra's case, he found Philip Ritchie in Trinity and Bob Boothby in Magdalen, but it was the names of New College men that filled his letters in these years. Throughout his life, Maurice would vigorously defend the college system, even in some of its absurdities, in order to preserve the intimacies and diversity of his own undergraduate days.

When Bowra arrived in New College, its Warden was William Spooner, whose eccentricities delighted the University, and whose misadventures with the English language were keenly anticipated by any audience he was addressing. He once began a sermon to Wykehamists with the words 'All of you have hands horny with toil and some of you are mothers.'[5] As will be seen, Bowra was not completely uncritical of the New College of his day, but, as with Cheltenham College, he carried away a certain loyalty to any institution he had attended. In 1935 he joined the New College Society, protesting that 'I feel I owe so much to my old College, and especially to my tutors, Mr Henderson, Mr Joseph and Mr Casson, that it would be unfilial in me not to contribute my mite.'[6] In fact, he had thought Casson a fool and Joseph a monster, but these feelings never compromised a greater loyalty. During his wardenship of Wadham, that college elected so many New College men to fellowships, that it could be described as a colony of its grander neighbour.

To some extent this cheerful picture was justified. Some dons were both approachable and agreeable. Bowra held Alick Smith in awe, for example. As a tutor and mentor, he took infinite pains with his pupils, many of whom went on to become his friends. In 1948, Maurice was 'disgusted and appalled' that such a man should be denied the degree of D.Litt. The examiners had to have been at fault; 'I have no doubt that Weldon was largely actuated by malice, though of course also by his hatred of learning, which is becoming maniacal ... most annoying for you to be treated in this frivolous and malignant way.'[7] New College also enjoyed the towering presence of H. A. L. Fisher. He was both scholar and a man with an international reputation in current affairs. More important still, he never lost an opportunity of being kind to the young. When Fisher died, Bowra told his widow and daughter that he had been his 'ideal of the scholar', and that he owed 'a great deal to his unfailing kindness to me, especially in my younger days when it was a very great help'.[8] People are apt to remember with gratitude those who noticed them in their youth, and New College had its fair share of such men.

Outside New College, only one don sought Bowra out, A. S. Owen of Keble. Known as 'The Crab', Owen cheerfully accepted this soubriquet, and would greet undergraduates with the words, 'Call me Crab.' As a former schoolmaster at Cheltenham, he made a point of cultivating those whom the school sent on to Oxford. In 1941, Bowra was asked to write Owen's obituary. He remembered that Owen during the Great War had kept up 'an enormous correspondence with men at the Front'. Quite possibly, Bowra himself had been one of his correspondents. Owen owned a cottage in the Cotswolds, where weekends were spent in cycling, swimming, and walking. After dinner there would be 'elaborate paper games'. Maurice recorded the life of a man who had 'liked dons' and who had 'liked undergraduates'.[9] As a model for what Maurice himself might become, Owen offered many useful tips. He, Smith, and Fisher all demonstrated that the good don could combine intellect, distinction in academic or public life, and an interest in pupils that went beyond seeing them once a week for formal instruction.

If Bowra's Oxford had conscientious dons, however, there was also at least one ogre. H. W. B. Joseph was Fellow in Philosophy at New College and a man Maurice would come to loathe. It was a tragedy that the two men could not avoid each other's company. The Classics degree that Bowra was pursuing was divided into two parts. Undergraduates first studied classical literature for an examination known as Mods. Having survived this, they moved on to the history and philosophy of the ancient world, and their efforts were appraised in an examination known as Greats. Because Bowra arrived in Oxford at a relatively advanced age, he was advised to skip over Mods altogether, and to proceed directly to Greats. That decision precipitated immediate contact with Joseph. As a result, 'the wonderful summer of 1919' was passed in 'weekly visits' to

Joseph, which were 'increasingly dark episodes to be faced with fear and anxiety'.[10]

It was unlikely that Bowra would ever have found philosophy totally congenial. His thinking was poetic rather than logical. Playing with the precise meaning of words was no substitute for responding to their sounds and rhythms. Stuart Hampshire believed that 'he hated Joseph and he hated philosophy at that stage, but he put up with it later. He felt humiliated by it. He had no abstract mind like that at all. It was a memory of humiliation for him—a classical scholar who couldn't do that sort of Greats very well.'[11] According to Bowra, the primacy of Plato on the syllabus was inexplicable; 'I cannot bring myself to rezd [sic] all the twaddle he wrote. He was a very wicked man and not even consistent. He was a Joseph born out of time and very stupid too.'[12] Too much reading in Plato ran the risk of 'being josephian',[13] of losing the all-important imaginative faculty. Late in life, John Sparrow formally thanked Maurice for undoing the harm that Joseph had wrought; 'I don't forget—tho' I may seem sometimes to be unmindful of it—that much of the poetry (or the power of appreciating or enjoying that side of life) that HWBJ knocked out of me was put back by you, and lodged in me so securely that even Cyril [Connolly] couldn't extract or destroy it.'[14]

For a man of Bowra's temperament, every encounter with Joseph had the character of a nightmare. It seemed that every word in every line of every essay would be challenged for its precise meaning and its place in a logical sequence. As Bowra remembered them, Joseph's 'methods of controversy bore some resemblance to family croquet in which you invent the rules as you go on and accuse your opponent of breaking them'.[15] Stuart Hampshire agreed. As a tutor, Joseph had been 'a kind of wrestler, bone breaker … Joseph was a bad philosopher, not good at all but very good at tripping people up, heuristic.' Those with forensic, legalistic minds, like John Sparrow and Herbert Hart, enjoyed Joseph's company. They 'loved a scrap, but Maurice not'.[16] The situation was exacerbated by other aspects of Joseph's methods. Mark books would be left open so that pupils could easily read what had been said about themselves and their friends.[17] It was so much easier to deal with a tutor like Stanley Casson, whose ignorance of the ancient world allowed his pupils to invent completely fictitious authors and to introduce them into their essays.[18]

Joseph really frightened Bowra, and, worse, came close to undermining belief in his intellectual abilities. In a spoof last will and testament he wrote 'a Death song for myself. I have tried Joseph and failed.' God himself becomes nothing more than a logician, forgiving but rigorous:

> For God is a great logician
> And we may writhe and rend,
> But this great Methodology
> Will catch us in the end.
> And man is a minor premiss
> That wanders about in the cold
> But God the great logician
> Will take him back to the fold.[19]

For one of the few times in his life, Bowra sought security in surrender. The only exit open was to stop thinking for oneself and simply to adopt Joseph's views. He told Roy Harrod that 'I have predetermined re philosophy to become a good Josephite. It seems a safe way.'[20] It was 'the Creed', and for once Maurice would have to bow the knee.[21] He knew perfectly well that such a concession of his own thoughts was the antithesis of what the tutorial system should be, but there was apparently no alternative. Even playing safe would bring only limited rewards. To his dismay, he discovered that Joseph would be one of his examiners. He looked forward to 'the grim humiliation of a bad second'.[22]

In despair, Maurice began to regret his decision to go to university at all. Perhaps the Civil Service would have proved more congenial, as his father had suggested. 'Curse Joseph', he advised friends, denouncing his tutor as cold, inhuman, and a disastrous influence on pupils. The mere mention of the man's name or his works was insupportable; 'I can't endure the sight of Joseph's book; it is tied up with terrible memories of my first term, as my intellectual decay and incompleteness dawned upon me. I am not much enough recovered to be able to read it.'[23] All his friends agreed that Maurice's scholarship was never expressed with the same brio that characterized his conversation. On paper he was cautious, careful, even constrained. This timidity may have its roots in Joseph's teaching. Much decorated and applauded though he was, Bowra was never completely convinced of his credentials as a scholar. Joseph remained a demonic presence throughout his life.

Burying his old tutor was quite literally a great relief. When he heard that Joseph had been taken ill, in June 1943, Maurice's mood was unforgiving: 'Joseph has been very ill, but it [sic], I am sorry to say, a little better, though he still enjoys considerable pain owing to his scandalous refusal to do what his doctors tell him. I feel that he will not trouble us much more as he can hardly move.'[24] Unfortunately, from his point of view, he had to wait two more years for a funeral, but, when it came, it was thoroughly appreciated:

> Joseph's obsequies to which I have just been were very enjoyable. Sir Hugh Allen read the lesson (from Wisdom, not Wisden, as you might expect)…There was an interminable anthem, 'Remember Now Thy Creator', which, if I remember the Higher Criticism correctly, was rather unsuitable to the notoriously over-sexed deceased. Smith gave an address—very good and not without malice.[25]

Bowra always asserted that 'while there's death, there's hope'. The dispatching of an enemy and a good funeral were invigorating experiences. None was appreciated more than the departure of Joseph.

Under Joseph's tutelage, Bowra's academic career came close to collapsing. It was saved by a chance meeting with 'Crab' Owen in Holywell. The old man suggested that, instead of Greats, he should read Mods first. An entirely literary course would be much more to his liking, and would substantially rebuild confidence. Owen later told Bowra that this encounter had given him great pleasure; 'I always feel (and often quote) as one of the most fortunate accidents in my life my meeting with you in Holywell that day, when I persuaded you to go back to Mods. I hope that Joseph has repented in dust and ashes for the advice he gave you then.'[26] The point was taken. Bowra went back to Mods, secured a good First, returned to Greats, and won another First, though even now his history writing attracted better marks than his attempts at philosophy.

Bowra's academic career was now back on track, and the option of becoming a don reinstated, but he had known at first hand both the benefits that a good tutor could bring and the damage that a bad tutor could wreak. Smith and Fisher had built him up, and Joseph had knocked him down. He had the confidence to publish many books and papers, but he always feared that they would not be well received. Reviewers had a power that alarmed him, and he tortured himself with speculations about what other scholars said in private. At Bowra's funeral, Isaiah Berlin noted this trait in his character, and traced it to its source:

> The treatment of him at New College by that stern trainer of philosophers, H. B. W. Joseph, undermined his faith in his own intellectual capacity, which his other tutor in philosophy, Alick Smith, who did much for him, and became a life-long friend, could not wholly restore…His disciplined

habits, his belief in, and capacity for, hard, methodical work in which much of his day was spent, his respect for professionalism and distaste for dilettantism, all these seemed, in some measure, defensive weapons against ultimate self-distrust.[27]

Many who knew Bowra best thought that this Address 'could not have been bettered'.[28]

Even the securing of an Oxford fellowship could not wholly remove the doubt. In 1927, he told a close friend that he wondered whether he was a true scholar at all, and feared that he had nothing new to contribute:

> I have been trying to work and been signally unsuccessful. I should like to be a very good man of letters and find myself only a parodist. It might even be fun to be a very good scholar, but it is so damned difficult to say what has been said many time before by good Germans, and the labour is enormous for the smallest result.

These moods were not helped when his father told him that 'I ought to become a head-master and get out of my rut. There is just enough truth in it to be thoroughly irritating.'[29] In a sense, Joseph had the last laugh. To some extent perhaps, Bowra's exaggerated claims for Oxford and its values owed something to this suspicion that he was himself not quite clever enough to be there.

To talk of his New College years as a largely negative experience would, however, be very wide of the mark. If brushes with dons had left scars, his experiences with his fellow undergraduates were entirely positive. Through their eyes, he discovered that he was rather exceptional. Contemporaries began to mark him out as a future prime minister.[30] It mattered little to Maurice whether he acquired fame or notoriety. To be accused of either was regarded as a form of flattery.[31] Only Douglas Woodruff and Cyril Radcliffe could offer any serious competition in conversation, and they were handled with care. Everyone else became members of an unofficial court. As Roy Harrod remembered, Bowra 'had a sort of salon' at New College, for which he set the rules of engagement.[32] There was an inner circle known as 'The Five' and a wider society called 'The Brethren'. Members were ruthlessly recruited and just as ruthlessly excluded if Bowra found them wanting. One who failed to make the grade was Lindsay Keir, a future Master of Balliol. Maurice acknowledged him as a New College contemporary, but added that he had not been 'recognized in my set'. Keir was an 'illiterate Glasgow Scot'. His success at Balliol 'remains a mystery'.[33]

Bowra was already establishing the principle that membership of his circle demanded certain qualities, without which there could be no redemption.

Those excluded from the Bowra set naturally resented the fact. They became the victims of 'barbed shafts' to which they had no answer. To fail in Maurice's company could lead to serious introspection. One individual complained to Roy Harrod that his only defence against 'the Brethren' was simply to take the opposite view from any they proposed: 'I immediately dislike what they say—I dislike books they suggest.'[34] Even worse was to be within the charmed circle and yet feel far from the standard required. Eric Siepmann was one of the favoured, but it brought nothing but anxiety. In 1921, he joined a reading party with Maurice, Edward Sackville-West, and others:

> There was more talk than work. They were brilliant. Through shyness I felt out of it. We went to the Scilly Isles, and I remember walking across some rough ground on St Mary's and keeping behind the others because tears of frustration were pouring down my face. Timidity leads to megalomania. I made plans to dazzle by my success … in the 'outside' world.[35]

In the event, he tried the stage before settling for a distinguished career in psychology. Already Bowra was dividing those around him into sheep and goats. Already, those near him were either finding him compelling or a threat and a challenge.

Bowra talked and wrote about his 'brethren' in a totally proprietorial way. He set out to direct their reading and their thoughts. In letters to Roy Harrod, who was one of his closest friends at New College, he periodically reviewed his entourage. Some were making good progress. Others were proving a disappointment. He was 'bringing up' Miller and Deane-Jones 'very well'.[36] A man named Bull, on the other hand, was doing no work and was showing less talent than had been anticipated: 'Have I ruined Bull? Probably. I filled him and left him empty. He then noticed his emptiness … I don't feel up to keeping him on.'[37] As for Eddie Sackville-West, his first efforts at novel-writing were 'very good', though the style 'is a mixture of *The Young Visitors* and literal translations from the German'.[38]

He also claimed the right to approve and disapprove of the career options taken by his circle. It was grim to hear that Maurice Hastings, one of his protégés, was thinking of the Church, a profession which, perhaps, more than any other went against the Bowra code: 'I still resent the creeds and the dog collar but perhaps it is better than his father's office. Hastings flatters me; so I don't criticize him. I assume he is perfect.' Even more disconcerting was the news that a good friend was intent on a career in the City: 'I hear that Hew is to go into business. Poor brute, he will be incompetent and unpopular in the office and at home. Result of Virtue at School. See my Magnum Opus on this. His good qualities will never be needed or appreciated, and he will get increasingly extreme with advancing years and increasing plainness.'[39] These New College men were the first to learn the iron rules of being part of the Bowra world, which were inexorable and rather Darwinian. The neophyte had to be prepared to have his character and hopes held up to dissection in public. To embrace false values, among them organized religion and money-making, was to invite exclusion. Even at New College, it had become clear that Bowra's company was not for the squeamish.

The geographical centre of the Bowra salon was the New College Essay Society, a club which owned its own silver, in which mulled claret was served at its meetings every Saturday night. Papers were read and discussed. Maurice himself read essays on 'Prose as Fine Art', 'Theocracies', and 'The Comfortable Life', all topics congenial to his interests.[40] When John Galsworthy honoured the Society with a visit, he presided over the proceedings in the character of 'a more philosophical and less charitable Pickwick'.[41] For the most part, these evenings had a serious purpose. Topics were debated with a certain rigour. Inevitably, however, as the meeting went on, members descended, or rose, to the exhibition of mere wit and humour. No evening, in Bowra's view, should be without entertainment. Christopher Hollis preserved the memory of one of his earliest, undergraduate limericks:

> There once was a Fellow of Merton,
> Who went down the street with no shirt on,
> He would titivate shyly
> His membrum virile
> For the people to animadvert on.[42]

The other forum in which to display fine feathers was the reading party. In the 1920s, the most prestigious of these was led by 'Sligger' Urquhart of Balliol at his 'Chalet' in the French Alps. Though no intellectual himself, Urquhart somehow managed to attract many of the most talented undergraduates into his parties, and Bowra could not help being a little jealous of his success. In *Memories*, he claims that he was indeed invited to the Chalet, but declined to go, as its 'programme did not appeal to me'.[43] For a start, Urquhart was Catholic. A priest sometimes joined his gatherings, and Maurice delightedly started the hare that the Chalet was nothing more than a scarcely concealed plot to convert the future leaders of England to Rome. He could only be pleased when Cyril Connolly assured him that he had taken advantage of his few days at the Chalet to write rude words behind the many pictures of the Madonna and Child that festooned its interior.[44] Then there was the problem of the Chalet's Spartan credentials. According to Maurice, 'nobody ate or drank too much', a major problem since members of the party were required to take incommensurate amounts of exercise.[45]

Bowra's idea of a reading party was rather different. Of course, attractive countryside should provide the context. Beaches and hills should be on hand. Exercise was permitted, but ascents should be something less than vertical. Above all, the Bowra code allowed for no equation to be made between scholarship and asceticism. After a day of working and swimming, a dinner of quality became almost a birthright. A reading party at Llanthony Priory in 1922 was reported to be in good spirits, because of 'the excellence of the climate' and because the 'food is good'.[46] The soldier who had fired on the puritan association of Noyon Cathedral was now determined to enjoy life.

In all these social situations, Bowra aimed to be the arbiter of everything that was said and done. Throughout life, he was temperamentally incapable of playing second fiddle. As master of the revels, he could not tolerate rivals. Cyril Radcliffe would go on to be one of the most distinguished judges of his generation. At New College, he and Bowra, though they had once shared lodgings in King Edward St., were open competitors for the attention of their contemporaries; 'They seemed to be engaged in a verbal fencing-match. They coruscated wit. Most of us gazed at them with wonder touched with awe.'[47] Bowra recognized Radcliffe's powers, but found his personality too cold and unspontaneous. The man was irredeemably a lawyer rather than a poet. In public, the two men treated each other with a distant courtesy, which marked their relationship in later life. Each knew that the other could sting. In private, Radcliffe became a victim of Bowra versifying:

> Milord in the gloaming takes his ease;
> He hears his bloodhound bay,

And throned on a yellow pouf enjoys
The end of a perfect day.
Here is no labour, here is no blush,
No lips that lust and no eyes that kill.
A corpse is laid out in the bridal bed
To hold him close and very still.[48]

The two men barely kept up after their New College days were over. Quite simply, according to Bowra, 'something chilled' in Radcliffe 'years ago and has never come to life again'. There was 'no click' between them.[49]

Less of a direct, intellectual challenge, but still clever enough to need watching was Douglas Woodruff, the future editor of *The Tablet*. Bowra suspected that he was a Roman Catholic of the proselytizing kind, who therefore represented an immediate threat to his own flock. Maurice's response to religion was deeply ambivalent. He could not be described as simply agnostic or atheistic. But his distaste for Catholicism in all its forms was deep and real. If one of his friends converted, it was a betrayal on the scale of lese-majesty. As a result, he found himself trying to save souls from Woodruff and his kind. At one point, the two men found themselves in a pitched battle for the allegiance of Roy Harrod, a confrontation Bowra won but at a cost in terms of effort and energy.[50]

In retrospect, Maurice dismissed Woodruff's challenge and his Catholicism as symptoms of a major defect. Woodruff had 'a deep strain of envy and malice in his character'.

> At heart he could not bear anyone else to do anything, and he wanted to shine all the time. He solved the problem by reverting to Romanism, which gave him, so he thought, an unanswerable superiority over everyone who wasn't a Papist. I have only seen him two or three times in recent years, but none has been a success. He searches for my weak points, for which he has an excellent eye, and then biffs me on one of them. Also I cannot endure this inner world of mutually admiring Papists.[51]

Like Radcliffe, Woodruff spun away from Bowra into other orbits. None of these men regretted the separation.

Other Oxford contemporaries managed a modus vivendi with Bowra. Their wit was so sharp, that they had a licence to tease, but the penalty was that they were seen less frequently than others, and were, to some extent, kept at a distance. Sylvester Gates was already showing at New College that quality of mind which would give him prominence as a barrister. Maurice could only applaud the demonstration of pure intellect: 'In my

bath I occasionally think of you, flustering your Surrey neighbourhood as
"the clever Gates boy", or annihilating the selectist of select society by
the logical application of St Paul's maxims on morals.'[52] Just as able and
amusing, though untrustworthy and idle, was Basil Murray. His quick mind
and sharp tongue made his company exciting and his absences perfectly
congenial. He told Roy Harrod in a letter that, though he himself and
Maurice were not 'naturally cruel', they both inclined to jealousy, and
that this was 'the reason for Maurice's malice too'.[53] Significantly perhaps,
Maurice's close friends in later life were not drawn from his New College
contemporaries, on whom he had practised his arts, and by whom he
had sometimes been challenged, but from people of a slightly younger
generation.

Bowra's determination to lead in conversation and to dominate in
company was an entirely conscious decision. As letters to Roy Harrod
make plain, he had developed what he called his 'System' in order to cover
up deficiencies he felt in his own character. To know more than anyone
else in a room prevented assaults on what he called his 'cardboard exterior'.
Surviving at Cheltenham had taught him the rudiments of the 'System'. At
New College, he perfected these 'parlour tricks'. Layers of wit were being
laid down, like sheets of armour, against the possibility of being found out.
Somewhere at the centre of his being Bowra felt a weakness that had to be
hidden. Surviving the Great War and securing great academic success had
not brought confidence.

He lived with the worry that certain people would always see through
him. Roy Harrod was identified as the first of these, and Maurice begged
him not to give the game away.

> surely you see that my real complaint is that My System is useless once it
> is realized. The trouble is I don't *desire* to please consciously at any rate. I
> cannot help adapting myself to the entourage—chiefly because I am morbidly
> susceptible to any feeling of hostility, and find on the whole I can get over it
> this way.

With Harrod, Bowra feared that 'the Confidence Trick no longer works'.
His friend had 'undermined' his 'system' by 'consistently maligning' him.
How, he asked, was he 'to get on without it'.[54]

Once someone like Harrod had guessed that Maurice dealt with the
world from behind a mask, or a series of masks, he or she thereby achieved
a power that could be used destructively. In letters, Bowra begins to

complain of betrayal, claiming that Harrod was telling others that his performances were based on feelings of weakness: 'You have your picture of me, an automaton with parlour tricks, who politely repeats back in other words what is said to him and merely tries to please. You went around saying this … Would you like to be an automaton?' This particular letter goes on to explain his hurt and to ask for understanding:

> I am extremely jealous of Woodruff and your affection for him. I have at times felt supplanted by it … I regard my intimacy with you on the whole as a failure because I have never understood you. I never understand anyone intellectually, but with some people I can tell what they feel and know why they feel it. Your impermeability terrifies me, and makes me feel a failure. So I have to attack you to sustain my pride. This is another miserable confession. I know what you feel. I have tried for years to adjust my interior, but it cannot be done. So I have hidden it … Please don't make me feel a failure too often. You always do. Your insistence on weakness is unnecessary in my case. I know my weaknesses and I don't want them increased.[55]

In the event Harrod proved no threat. The two men remained on friendly terms throughout their lives. But there was always the fear that others might behave differently.

For a war veteran in his early twenties to talk so much and so often about weakness and failure is remarkable. It would surprise those of his friends who only knew him in later life, when every aspect of his character seemed to be energetic, robust, and affirming. By then, of course, the performance and the style had been honed and perfected. The mask rarely slipped. As a New College undergraduate he often had to adjust it, for the demons with which he had to struggle were already at their posts. One carried in his claws the suspicion, implanted or confirmed by Joseph, that Bowra's academic credentials were not quite of the best. In his classical writings, which were voluminous, he would willingly defer and refer to the opinions of other men. Another held the secret of his sexuality, which either had become clear in Petrograd or was becoming so in New College. These were matters best kept hidden and this could be done by dominating social situations and deploying 'the System'. A master–pupil relationship would be one he would always find easier than a friendship between equals.

Setting out on life on terms such as these carried a penalty. Only a few people could qualify to be friends when the bar was set so high.

There would always be a Bowra circle, but it would always be a tightly drawn group. Some people would not be open enough with themselves or with the world to appreciate the noisy assault on convention. Others feared being smothered by the Bowra personality. To take a sabbatical from Maurice's company was not unusual. In Anthony Powell's case, this therapeutic kind of separation lasted years. As a result, Maurice very much liked to be reassured by his friends that they would never leave. Too often in his life already, he had had the experience of affection being taken away from him for one reason or another. China had taken his parents away; revolution had destroyed the loved one in Petrograd; and death carried off those who came close to him, like Philip Ritchie and Adrian Bishop. Among his papers, there is an unpublished poem entitled 'Leavetaking', written in or soon after 1922. It is the work of someone who has already had the repetitive experience of loss:

> I never thought the blaze of light
> That shed its splendour on my soul
> Was but a phantom of the night
> Crowned with a treacherous aureole.
>
> That all the answers that you gave
> Were only meant for kindliness,
> A charitable plan to save
> My spirit from its deep distress.
>
> The comfortable words you said
> Have left a sharper wound in me
> Than if my secret soul had bled
> With unimagined cruelty.
>
> If only you had told me 'No',
> I should have courage still to live:
> Your kindness deals a double blow,
> I cannot hate you, nor forgive.
>
> You leave me with a friendly smile
> Pretending that you understand:
> You do not see that all the while
> My hope lies broken in your hand.
>
> You have new visions still to see—
> Go on your good and generous ways
> Unheeding, while you leave to me
> The bitterness of deceitful days.[56]

Against such terrors, Maurice required friends endlessly to reaffirm affection and loyalty. The spats, which peppered even his closest friendships, arose when his demands became too challenging.

Nearly all witnesses agree that, by the end of his New College days, in 1922, Bowra's personality had already taken on a final shape. Deeply self-aware, he had identified his strengths and weaknesses. The main themes of his life were in place. Three in particular deserve close attention. As a student of the Greeks he discovered an alternative and, in his view, a better set of values than those of the Anglo-Christian society in which he had been brought up. Secondly as a poet and apologist for high culture, he worried about the survival of his values, as many countries began to experiment with democracy in the twentieth century. Taken together, these two passions prompted a crusading spirit in everything he said and did. He was positive and robust in the affairs of the world, because a sense of mission gave him the confidence to speak and act. On the other hand, the weaknesses he had talked of as an undergraduate, and the 'System' he had devised to hide them, never left him, and became increasingly associated with doubts about the nature of his sexuality. In a life that was generally attacking, there were moments of fear and paralysis, when his private life was called into question. Two major themes in his life pushed him forward therefore and one held him back. All three require close scrutiny.

PART II

Fundamentals

4
Greece

Inner doubts did not immobilize Maurice Bowra or lead to inaction. On the contrary, his instinct was to meet the world head-on, with courage and determination. He liked a battle. Friends and enemies were always easily and clearly defined. The first were to be cosseted and the latter harried to destruction. In conversation and on committees he was an ally or a foe, and nearly every incident in professional life was a victory or a defeat. Every new friend or acquaintance was ultimately placed in one of two categories that brought on approval or disapproval. This combativeness was made necessary by the fact that he had a purpose in life, a missionary enterprise. He had the energy and attack of the preacher. As Isaiah Berlin pointed out in his funeral address, 'no less cynical man ever breathed—[Maurice] was a believer and a crusader for what he believed'.[1] Against all appearances, there was, under the wit and the clowning, a deep seriousness.

Central to this 'crusade' was his study of the civilization of ancient Greece. In Bowra's mind, classical values were not dead or merely academic. Rather, they still retained a relevance in the twentieth century. In fact, they were to inform the lives of himself and his contemporaries, if civilization, in any recognizable form, was to survive. Four months before his death, in almost his last public speech, he addressed an audience in the Cambridge Arts Theatre on the occasion of the one-hundred-and-fiftieth anniversary of the Greek war of independence. He took this opportunity to articulate once more what western Europe owed to Greece: 'Greece has done more than any other country to make men believe in themselves. She has established principles which later generations have often reviled and rejected, but which nonetheless thrive in our innermost thinking and in our conception of what a complete life ought to be.'[2]

In Bowra's view, the Greeks were the only people in the ancient world to make the individual and his dignity the centrepiece of all art and thought.

The essence of Greek political thought is that a man is an individual, who lives among other men in his own right and for his own worth, that he is entitled to be himself as he would wish to be, and that in this he realises natural endowments, which vary from person to person but are all the gift of the gods and not to be thrown away. The individual must be given the freedom to exert his full capacities, to be an end in itself, not a means for the use of others.[3]

This idea embraces the whole man, recognizing and accepting virtues and vices, heroism, and failure. Completeness in living necessitated each man being free 'to make mistakes, and he will make many, but he can follow his own star and his own soul, and find his full being both in his own likeness to other men and in his difference from them'.[4] Nearly everyone would fail in this strenuous endeavour, but the Greeks saw small heroisms in the striving.

Such a message could only have had the strongest possible appeal to someone who had felt isolated at Cheltenham College, who had been plunged deeply into introspection in the trenches of the First World War, and who had known private doubt and public success at New College. It must always be borne in mind that, when Maurice wrote about the Greeks, he was, in some sense, committing autobiography to paper. His experiences had already taught him that the individual fought hard to create his own world or was nothing. In his books, he was quite open about how closely the Greeks touched his own times and himself: 'The Greeks seem to bridge the centuries which separate them from us, and to touch on matters which we think to be peculiarly our own.' For him, 'the unchanging elements of human life' made connections over centuries perfectly plausible.[5]

When friends came to write about Maurice as a classicist, they could not fail to make the point about the scholarship and the personality being intertwined. In a draft review of *Landmarks in Greek Literature*, Cyril Connolly gave his opinion on how Bowra's mind worked.

What is this quality of mind? An extremely clear judgment: a gift of poetic imagination, respect, even reverence for his subject, and an intuitive knowledge of what the Greeks were like, based on an understanding of their beliefs and a correlation with his own. He has the quality which certain judges possess of cutting through the nonsense and assessing human worth; he is anti-fusser, an anti-bunker rather than a debunker, who wears his humanism like a bullet-proof vest.[6]

It is not unusual for academics to find topics for study that are congenial to their own characters, but, in Bowra's case, the ideas of the Greek world and the values by which he himself lived were nearly one and the same thing. Propagating them was both a personal and an academic requirement.

What then did the Greeks offer? To that question, Bowra would have answered, first and foremost, a world, which, if not god-free, was not god-focused. The Greeks had gods of course, but they made them in the image of man, and not vice versa. They made 'gods in the likeness of men at their most impressive and most beautiful'.[7] Like men, the gods were capricious and heroic, treacherous, lecherous, and vain. They had intercourse with mankind at every level. It was possible, like Achilles, to be half-man, half-god. In works of beauty or acts of heroism, any man approached the divine. And all of this was possible in one earthly existence. For Bowra, the Greeks speculated about an afterlife, but never really cared for the idea. Heroes were somehow wafted away to a paradise in the west, but most people would have to make do with less or nothing. As a result, life, rather than death, was the thing to be prized. It should be made as sweet as honey. The metaphor comes from a verse of Pindar's that Maurice was fond of quoting:

> Man's life is a day. What is he?
> What is he not? A shadow in a dream
> Is man, but when God sheds a brightness,
> Shining light is on the earth,
> And life is sweet as honey.[8]

For the Greeks, the hope of living such a life 'lay at the centre of their lives, and sustained them in all their misgivings that the generations of men wither like leaves and that impartial death waits at the end for all'.[9] Such a stance was totally distinctive in the ancient world. In Egypt and the empires of Mesopotamia, theocracy was the order of the day. Kings and emperors, doubling as gods, ruled with the assistance of armies of priests. But then, as Bowra put it, 'a people gets the gods it deserves'.[10]

In a man-made world rather than a god-made world, the individual did not live by divine regulations, but instead sought out his own values. Here was a challenge which demanded that no man be passive in the face of events. A Greek won his 'manhood through unflagging effort and unflinching risk', knowing 'that the prizes went to the eager and the bold'.[11] Man was autonomous spiritually and morally. If he met with failure, it was useless to blame the gods or the neighbours. If injured, 'it was useless to invoke the anger of the gods or the disapproval of men'.[12] At the age of thirty-five, Bowra claimed to have read all known Greek literature. In his view, 'the spirit that breathes through these works' was the notion that each individual had his own world to make.[13] One of his greatest strengths was that he was happy to take up this challenge.

It followed that Bowra would react intemperately to any suggestion that Greek values had been overtaken or superseded by later systems. None of them, and certainly not the Judaeo-Christian, could make such a claim. Normally a considerate reviewer of the works of young academics, he wrote a blistering attack on an unfortunate American who had concluded that the Greeks had no religion and were therefore free of the sense of guilt that played a part in all morality. To this argument, Bowra replied that 'where there is no sense of guilt, there may indeed be no virtue, but there may be something like innocence'.[14] Religions that dealt in guilt merely gave validation to those who wished to bully and persecute. Remarks such as this led some acquaintances, like A. L. Rowse, to the view that Maurice 'was really a Greek pagan'.[15] In elevating the Greek view of the gods above later, monotheistic systems, Bowra did indeed appear to approve of Pan rather than Jesus Christ, but this assessment would be too simplistic. The Greeks had a spiritual dimension and so did Bowra. He was not against religion as such, but rather against religions that constrained man unduly. In giving Rex Warner's translation of Thucydides a puff in *The London Magazine*, he set out his debt to the Greeks: 'They did something for intellectual life of which we are still enjoying the fruits. In the passionate integrity and the bold adventurousness of its thought, it dispelled the mists of superstition and barbarism, and proved that through his ability to express thoughts in words man realizes his own nature and finds his place in the universe.'[16]

A subscription to Greek values was more than challenge and striving, however. The Greeks also preached pleasure for its own sake. Maurice told Lady Longford that he regarded 'the happiness of the individual to be the only socially acceptable aim'.[17] In wine, in friendship, and, above all, in beauty, the sweetness of life was to be found. There was no mistaking that 'the whole idea of the beautiful was their discovery'. In the clear light of the Mediterranean and by warm waters, guiltless pleasure was prescribed for all. The pleasures 'which poets and artists interpret' were 'within the reach of anyone who has eyes to see and ears to hear'.[18] Even better was the thought that the Greeks refused to separate art from daily life as something special, nor did they restrict its delectation by social class. Contemporary England sadly fell into both these traps. By contrast, if Greek artists and writers were originally drawn from the aristocratic classes, by the fifth century the artist was a mere citizen, an unremarked detail in everyday life: 'The Greeks were not a nation of artists, still less of aesthetes, and the reason for this was largely that the arts played so large and so accepted a part in their lives, that they did not feel any call to apologize for them.'[19] Pleasure and the savouring of beauty were so closely entwined in everyday life, that the artist was as welcome and as unnoticed as the carpenter.

Notions such as these owed nothing to the Christian morality he had heard in the chapel of Cheltenham College. Bowra was acutely aware that, to most of his contemporaries, what he preached was hedonism and mere licence. The sad, benighted English were smothered in real and metaphorical fogs. He jokingly told Felix Frankfurter that, to be happy, it was necessary to put public school morality to one side: 'A good cigar is the grandest and purest of pleasures and would have appealed to Aristotle, whose views on pleasure are much sounder than Plato's. The concept of a "pure" pleasure is, I know, ambiguous, but not if you keep out English (or new English) notions of morality.'[20] Dolefully, the English could never disassociate pleasure from guilt. Their worries drained colour out of everything, leaving monochrome grey. In writing such words, Maurice was very aware that, once again, he stood at an angle to his countrymen.

The individual, who takes up the challenge of moulding his own world and who discovers pleasure in doing so, cannot afford conventional morality. In teaching the Greek world, Bowra was wholly subversive. His pupils described being in his company as a kind of liberation of the spirit. They were taught to pay no attention to the values that their public schools had peddled, and to reject the rules of the society in which they had grown up. Irreverence almost became a new creed. The uninhibited enjoyment of life was truly godlike. Men 'will never really resemble or rival the gods, but at unaccountable moments, they will know, if only for a moment, what happiness the gods enjoy'.[21] Inevitably, Aristophanes was a great favourite. As he put it, 'It is to be hoped that some Aristophanic satirist will arise and mock the bores and bullies of today. In the meantime we can get considerable comfort from the incorrigible and high-minded satirist, who cared little for good taste or respectability, and flung fine handfuls of mud at a number of unpleasantly self-righteous people.' Sadly, England honoured the wrong people: 'English education has taught us to attribute nobility of character to those who would repress and deny. To Aristophanes these men were crooks and cranks.'[22]

Of course, such teaching carried terrible dangers. To tell pupils that they must slough off the guidelines of convention, in order to fashion a world of their own, was to saddle them with a great burden. The challenge was immense and an individual's resources might not be up to the task. Failure was almost inevitable. Yet failure itself had elements of the heroic within it, and it was this feeling that led Bowra greatly to admire the works of Racine, a writer who should have been outside his range of interests. The heroes and heroines in his plays refuse to be the victims of circumstances or the playthings of designing gods. Instead, they assert themselves against the force of events, often at terrible cost. Their passions 'compel decision and action, which smash through the restraints imposed by society, and drive human nature to assert itself in primitive violence'.[23] No taboo, no convention was sacred. Racine's characters suffer 'agonies' at the hands of men and gods. They struggle to overcome intolerable situations, and it is the struggle that dignifies them and becomes the stuff of poetry: 'Without its [poetry's] transfiguring influence these events would be unbearably painful, but through it their horror is absorbed in an excited and exalted understanding.' Bowra insisted that all this was 'close to much that we know in ourselves'. Anyone who had experienced the brutalities of the Great War knew about unreasonable gods and the necessity of a deeply personal battle against the Fates.[24]

Offering each individual the dignity of a personal identity and the guiltless exploration of the pleasurable and the beautiful constituted a major element of Bowra's crusade. His own confidence in facing the world came from this source. But his claims begged one very big question. Was everyone able or willing to take on these tasks? In all his writings, Bowra assumed that this was the case. As he put it, his world was open to all who 'had eyes to see and ears to hear'. In private, however, he was not so sure. Perhaps only exceptional people who might be called aristocrats could cope with these heavy responsibilities. Perhaps independence of mind and perception was a function of great birth and financial security. He hoped very much that, as aristocratic worlds gave way to democracies, the people as a whole would accept aristocratic values as a valuable legacy, but would they? It was a question that would be settled in his own lifetime. Maurice was already twenty years old when universal suffrage was introduced into

Britain in 1918. There was an urgency in his proselytizing therefore. Greek precedents gave valuable clues of what could be won and what could be lost.

Bowra wrote books on Homer and Sophocles, but it is hardly a coincidence that his academic work is concentrated heavily in the period 550 to 480 BC. He is less interested in the heroic age or the democratic Athens of the later fifth century. In his chosen period, aristocratic government in city states was often giving way to more democratic forms. The analogy with his own times could hardly be missed. The poets of this period, his particular favourites, largely came from aristocratic families and 'sought to exploit the graces and the gaieties of an aristocratic existence'.[25] In his view, 'the poetry of Alcaeus and Sappho is, then, the special product of an aristocratic society'.[26] So is that of Xenophanes and Theognis. Above all, so was the work of Pindar, the poet Bowra admired most. Their poetry 'was not popular; it was the creation of small classes of educated men'.[27] All these writers felt under threat. Theognis saw in the attack on aristocratic values 'the wrecking' of 'what he honoured and loved'.[28] Pindar's odes, praising the athletic and mental prowess of young aristocrats in competitive games, was lauding 'the sentiments, the outlook, and the convictions of the Greek aristocracies, which were then so obviously threatened'.[29] With luck, the new democracies would appreciate what was valuable in the societies that they succeeded and hold them fast, but nothing could be guaranteed.

As political systems changed, so value systems changed with them. There was always the danger that the baby would be thrown out with the bathwater. Those who rejected aristocratic politics might carelessly discard the benevolent aspects of such societies as well. Bowra always showed great sympathy for men and women, who had been born into aristocratic values and security, but who then were dispossessed by historical floods. Wilamowitz was revered as a scholar, but was also pitied as a German landowner who had lost everything in the Great War. Piers Synnott, Billy Clonmore, and Elizabeth Bowen were members of an Irish ascendancy that had to learn new ways. Their equivalents in England, like Gerald Berners and Edward Sackville-West, often failed to adapt, and retreated into eccentricity and irrelevance. All historical change, even the movement from aristocracy to democracy, dispossessed some and undermined others. Examples were not hard to find among Bowra's closest friends.

In praising Pindar and his kind, Bowra was trying to describe exactly what he meant by calling some aristocratic assumptions valuable. There was the full expression of body and mind. There was the duty of state service, if necessary, at the cost of personal sacrifice. And there was 'the high value' that was 'set on friendship, loyalty and personal obligations'.[30] Pindar's aristocratic youths were complete men and complete citizens. In thought and action, they provided the model for all that was most remarkable in the Greek experience.

> Though the aristocratic life was confined to a few, it solidified Greek civilization and gave a special pattern to it. Those who enjoyed its liberties were expected to shoulder the responsibility for maintaining them, and their respect for individuality was guaranteed by the social frame which held it... This had indeed its own *douceur de vivre*, but it was built on firm convictions of a man's worth and possibilities.[31]

In the early decades of the fifth century BC, in Athens and other cities, this world gave way to more democratic forms. In Athens, there was no violent confrontation. Aristocratic families like the Alcmaeonids cooperated with those wanting change, thereby infusing the new democracy with some of their values. Their influence was, however, swept away in a generation or two. The politics of democratic Athens rapidly became more and more vulgar and more and more brutal. Exceptional men of independent character were turned into objects of suspicion and frequently faced ostracism. As Bowra put it, 'In the sixth century the oligarchies succeeded, despite considerable troubles, in providing a generous measure of dignity and honour at least to the privileged minority; in the fifth century democracies maintained their ideals in practice until they broke themselves in over-exertion and by asking too much.'[32] Athens destroyed itself in populist excess and meaningless wars. The surrender of the city, in 404 BC, was always for Maurice 'the end of the world'. After that date, he 'always fond [*sic*] something missing'.[33]

None of these concerns made Bowra a reactionary, or even a conservative. When he voted in elections, he supported the Left rather than the Right. Change was inevitable and change was necessary for the vitality of a civilization. He told Roy Harrod that, in a static situation, 'don't try to pretend that you are alive'. The constant threat of barbarian assault, domestically or externally, was energy and opportunity, because 'there is more life in the efforts of barbarians to become civilized than of civilized people to remain so'.[34] The trick was rather to manage change. Above all, there was the responsibility to ensure that the best in art and politics weathered all changes, safely transferring from one system to another.

The analogy with his own times was vivid, and the omens were not particularly good. In country after country, the writer and the poet faced persecution and exile. Bowra watched German democracy elect Hitler with terrible consequences for his friends. Democratic Britain elected Stanley Baldwin, pig-breeder not poet. America had many qualities, but McCarthyism was always close to the surface. In the late 1960s, he saw students burning books in Paris and Oxford. His world, like Pindar's, seemed to be crumbling. When Maurice voted Labour or Liberal, he probably did so with fingers crossed and a lump in his throat. Some friends thought he ultimately 'cared more about culture than democracy'.[35] His books on Greece were a plea. Its civilization, particularly the poetry of Pindar's generation, should instruct the new democracies of the twentieth century what to preserve and what to aim for. The Greek experience and his own experiences ran in parallel.

Bowra's voluminous writings on Greece were therefore unashamedly didactic in purpose. His mission was to encourage his readers to live like the Greeks and to embrace the freedoms he identified in their civilization. Many of his books are works of persuasion, proselytizing. Earlier in his career, he concentrated on articles of a severely academic nature. Between 1928 and 1940, he wrote thirty-one of these. They comment on fragments of lost plays and books, contribute to debates about the dating of Greek productions, and discuss the nature and purpose of myth.[36] Those who are quick to dismiss Bowra's capacity for real scholarship might well revisit these essays, with a view to moderating their opinions. Appearing within the chaste covers of academic journals, however, these articles were never going to reach a wide audience or influence their opinions. Increasingly, therefore, he turned to writing books with wider appeal. Books such as *Periclean Athens* and *The Greek Experience*, which introduced the Greeks and their ways to non-specialist audiences, gave him particular pleasure.

He was 'after the life expressed in Greek Literature'. According to Leslie Rowse, he once explained his objectives as follows: 'I thought that I might remove some of the obstacles which stand between us and the Greek poets, and, by placing them in their historical context, show more clearly what they were trying to do and how they did it. This was more history than criticism but I could not keep criticism out of it.'[37] If such books proved subversive of the values of the England in which he had grown up, that was so much the better. He knew he generalized too much and romanticized more than a little, but colour and clear lines of argument were essential to engage the attention of a non-academic audience. He thought *The Greek Experience* 'rather abstract and generalized, too many bogus ideas',[38] but, 'bless it', it might do good in 'corrupting the Xtianity of good English public school boys'.[39]

Inevitably, he was appalled by the gradual elimination of Greek and Latin teaching in state schools. It was tantamount to blinding people. Their eyes were literally being closed to the possibilities of life. When Oxford was considering dropping Latin as an entrance requirement, the change represented a shift of values that was hard to bear:

> There are three schools of thought. 1. The go-ahead young scientists, who think the subject is absurd and should not be compulsory for anyone. They talk about German, which they may know, and Russian which they certainly do not, as splendid alternatives. 2. The die-hards, who think that Latin should continue to be compulsory for all. They speak of the Unity of European Civilization, of the need to study Latin in order to write English etc. 3. The compromisers, like myself, who give up hope of teaching scientists but think Latin indispensable for any of the arts, including law and history, mod. Lang, and Eng. Lit. ... Cambridge have jumped the gun, and that is quite in character. They are the Business Man's University and know where the money lies. No rot about culture for them.[40]

To choose to lose contact with the ancient world was to impoverish present and future generations.

None of this was new. For a generation or two before Bowra, writers had worried that the oncoming democracy might be unwilling to take ancient worlds and their claims seriously. H. A. L. Fisher and Michael Sadler speculated on what sort of syllabus should be offered when education became available to all. Matthew Arnold, Walter Pater, and Gilbert Murray pleaded for the continuing presence of the Classics. Bowra was intellectually the heir of these men. His books are often written in the belles-lettres tradition of the late nineteenth century, rather than engaging with the textual criticism and sociological scholarship that was overtaking classical studies between the wars. In the debates which divided the Classics faculty on these issues, Bowra adopted a robustly traditional stance.

Of course he respected meticulous scholarship in others. J. D. Denniston was a reclusive figure in Hertford College, whose monumental work on Greek particles represented scholarship at its most painstaking.

Maurice could never have produced work of this kind, but he set out to promote Denniston's career in everyway possible, though he felt it 'a gross impertinence on my part' to compensate for his colleague's 'extreme modesty'.[41] Quite simply, he was so distinguished that 'few living scholars can rival him'. He had 'sound knowledge, untiring industry and faultless taste'.[42] A. E. Housman was also honoured for 'an ideal of impeccable scholarship', but neither he nor Denniston would ever extend an invitation into the Greek world that most people would want to accept. Housman's 'tastes were too narrow'. He pleased himself rather than opening up new worlds.[43] In Maurice's view, a precise text or the detail of linguistics were not enough:

> To make contact with a world so remote in time we require more than texts: we require interpretation and other aids by which this lost world can be brought to life, and this is where the historian of literatures comes in. He must indeed master his material and muster his facts, but he must relate them to some embracing scheme which gives them significance ... By such methods the ancient work is made relevant to modern situations and enabled to reveal its claim to our own very different society.[44]

A well-balanced Classics faculty should have people capable of fulfilling all these tasks. Increasingly, however, this balance was not being maintained. Instead, Bowra's style was more and more discounted. The Oxford Classics faculty seemed to be full of practitioners of the art which achieved the impossible; they actually made the study of the ancient world dull. Even when an undergraduate at New College, Maurice had complained that Ancient History was taught without 'passion or sympathy'. It was 'too exact and crabbed ... How is one to prevent the facts, which are essential, stifling a larger outlook? This is very serious and I have got to find it out. The moment I get into close contact with facts I am swamped. Perhaps the consciousness of swamping will get me out.'[45] Forty years later, the complaint was the same. Half the classicists were uninspiring, soaked in 'Philistinism' and 'more deplorable than ever'.[46] To kill interest in the Greek world by teaching it with pedantry rather than inspiration was a sin against the Holy Ghost.

No one was more sinful than Eduard Fraenkel. As a refugee from Nazi persecution, Fraenkel automatically won Maurice's sympathy, but his appointment to the Chair of Latin in 1935 was seen as a disaster. Bowra denounced Fraenkel's work as stultifying, and Fraenkel returned the compliment by describing Bowra's scholarship as shallow. In describing Fraenkel's 'best (and only) pupil', Maurice detected 'all the marks of the beast. A total Philistine to the point of illiteracy outside his immediate subject. Extremely conceited and proud of having done so well. Maddening at all meetings and committees. But in the end childlike and rather touching. The rudeness comes from thinking that other people don't exist.'[47] In return, neither Fraenkel nor Denys Page, a Cambridge professor and protagonist of the new scholarship, congratulated Bowra when he was awarded a knighthood.[48] The warfare between these men was real and unforgiving. What was at stake was the future of classical studies. Should they become more textually—and sociologically—based at the price of becoming accessible to fewer and fewer people? Or should they continue to be made available to anyone with a claim to education? Such stark options probably misrepresented the choices available, but Bowra usually saw controversies in manichaean terms.

Bowra's stance in this debate would have the most serious consequences for his own career. By the mid-1930s, he was visibly the standard-bearer for a kind of classical writing that was falling out of fashion. Embarrassments followed. In 1936, T. W. Adorno, one of the greatest representatives of the Frankfurt school of writers who tried to give new depth to literary and historical studies by relating them to new discoveries in psychology and sociology, was living as a refugee on the Banbury Road in Oxford. He had known Bowra by reputation and was now delighted to meet him: 'He is one of the most intellectual and cultivated men I know.' Adorno proclaimed Bowra to be very interested in social theory and in its application to classical studies. As a result, he was anxious that Bowra should be invited to contribute to a journal which his friend Max Horkheimer was editing in New York. Bowra's name would guarantee the journal prestige and support.[49] Horkheimer simply had to meet 'one of the most cultivated and amusing of men'.[50]

The invitation to contribute was extended and accepted, but when the essay arrived, both Horkheimer and Adorno were disappointed. Bowra wrote too much in the belles-lettres tradition, and showed too little acquaintance with the social theorists of the Frankfurt school. 'In fact, the piece presents a big problem. It is much too general and has only the tone of good journalism. Therefore it contains little that is new, and there is hardly any evidence offered, which we set great store by.' They thought Bowra used technical words without understanding their meaning and 'without relating them to the underlying social reality'. The whole article was shot through with 'naivety', which was really astounding for an academic of his learning. Bowra had tried to write in the modern German style, and had failed. The essay could not be published as it stood.[51]

A revised version of the contribution was eventually published by Horkheimer, and Bowra tried hard to meet the demands of these severe Germans. In it, he talked of early Greek poetry as the product of a particular society. It was context and background rather than pure colour and sound.[52] Horkheimer ultimately thought it would do, but added, condescendingly, that, if Bowra were fortunate enough to have more contact with Adorno and his friends, something might be done with him. 'He is certainly an intelligent, cultivated and accessible man. If one could have a more permanent contact, we could have a very productive influence on him.'[53] Bowra's brush with the cutting edge of German scholarship left scars. To him, these men were incapable or unwilling to make their great scholarship available or intelligible to a wider audience. The colour of Greek civilization dulled in footnotes.

Here was more evidence, if more was wanting, that Bowra was required to please two audiences. The poet and the missionary in him wanted to write about the Greeks for the enlightenment of the general reading public. The academic, and would-be professor, had to impress his fellow practitioners. When the latter sniffed at popular works, they succeeded in reawakening in Bowra all the doubts that Joseph had implanted. All his instincts told him not to bury the Greeks in Germanic theories, but these were now the prized playthings of Classics faculties. One way out of this dilemma was for Bowra to exploit a linguistic competence, which few of his contemporaries could rival. To write about epic or pastoral traditions in Italian, Russian, Spanish, and German poetry made him distinctive. One of his pupils believed that, by venturing onto linguistic terrain where others could not follow, Bowra found both distinction and safety from unwelcome criticism.[54] To write about the poetry of many languages and cultures was enlightening. It was also the kind of study that invited the perceptive generalization rather than the forbidding footnote.

He never, however, was free from concern about what others might think or write about his scholarship. All of his enemies and most of his friends noted an astounding discrepancy between the way he talked and the way he wrote. His conversation was all sparkle, full of pyrotechnics and uncompromising flare. His academic work, by contrast, is cautious and a little flat. Harold Nicolson said of one book that it was 'like a man writing luggage labels'.[55] Noel Annan believed he could explain the very different characters of the written and spoken word: 'I think he had a horror of not being taken seriously as a scholar. Had he allowed himself full rein, he would have thought he would have been written off by people.'[56]

Always battling with doubt, Bowra nevertheless published voluminously. He edited or wrote over thirty books, together with numerous reviews and articles. He worked methodically and to a fixed regime. Certain hours every day were spent at an increasingly battered typewriter. As Maurice, self-mockingly, described his working methods, it was all a matter of perspiration and akin to stamp collecting: 'My long and boring book goes on and on. There is a lot of nonsense about learning. It is really a substitute for stamp-collecting, but instead of coloured bits of paper one collects comic little facts in the faint, far hope that one day they will fall into a pattern. But of course they don't.'[57] He used nearly the same words to a goddaughter:

> I have begun work on a subject so obscure that I can't tell anyone about it. It is quite mad, and I have no qualifications for it. Not that *that* has ever hindered me. I collect bits of useless information and put them together. It is just as if, after fifty years, I had gone back to stamp-collecting. It provides what Tennyson calls 'the sad mechanic exercise', words most appropriate to what we dignify by the name of learning.[58]

Such denigratory remarks should not be taken too seriously. He never stopped writing. The imperative to vindicate poetry and to put the Greeks on display was too great. Doubt and criticism had to be faced down.

Nevertheless, he waited for reviews with anguish. To acquaintances he pretended that they were beneath his consideration; 'Can you endure the sort of rot that reviewers say? I find that the years do not make me less impatient with them and I still long to point out to them how silly they are.'[59] To close friends he admitted deep concern:

> I have just finished the first proofs of my long and pretentious Pindar book. I oscillate between thinking it very good and very bad, but the latter is more likely to be right. Anyhow nobody will read it, and those who will [will] say that I ought to have written about something else. 'But why so dull?', as dear Raymond [Mortimer] said to me about a previous work. The awful thing is that in a way I mind. I can't think why, but I get pains in the chest at hostile reviews. The old trouble of vanity, I fear.[60]

To soften the blow, he would himself think up 'in the bath' the most vindictive criticisms that could be voiced about his work.[61] What actually appeared was bound to be less painful. It was hard for Maurice to accept small criticisms, because he would always assume that they were indicative of larger doubts. An incautious publisher who wanted to suggest changes for the republication of *Pindar* was told he could have only 'an hour and a half on Wednesday morning'.[62]

Enemies could be relied on to wound when given the opportunity of reviewing a Bowra book. Denys Page would always be 'an unfair critic'.[63] Steven Runciman's critique of *Primitive Song* stung so sharply that Maurice wanted 'to pour a bottle of hot water' over him.[64] Raymond Mortimer, as Bowra complained to Edith Sitwell, simply never understood the academic's predicament:

> Raymond Mortimer writes in the press, and to me personally, that my work on poetry is terribly dull and that I should write as I speak. What can a man do? If I did what he asks, I should have twelve suits for slander at once, and I can't afford it. Nor do I think it wrong to try to get a thing right by thinking about it until it is properly digested instead of dashing off some gay, girlish paragraphs in blissful ignorance, as R. M. does. My relations with him can only be described as cold.[65]

To suggest a doubt about his scholarship was to penetrate Bowra's armour. In 1964, an American professor wrote to point out an error in *The Greek Experience*, adding the uncharitable words 'I believe such an error in a scholar of your reputation is inexcusable. If there is any rational explanation for this mistake, I hope you will communicate the same to me.'[66] The interesting point about this letter is not that Maurice received such a document, but that he kept it. It remains among his papers when much else was destroyed.

Criticism from supposed friends was even harder to accept. Questions of personal loyalties would be raised in a man, who always claimed that he was not exactly thin-skinned but that he had been born with one skin too few. Hugh Trevor-Roper was never quite forgiven for pointing out a mistake on a postcard which any porter or postman might read. Maurice just 'couldn't lose face in that way'.[67] When a pupil of John Finley at Harvard wrote 'a false and phoney' book in which he was taken to task, Bowra reacted with ruthless determination. A great friend had let him down. The author was demonstrably wrong at every point, and I have him quite cold. No errors this time, no howlers ... Now he is a close friend of Finley, to whom he dedicates the book ... This is serious. I am not prepared to let Finley off. He must have known what the book said ... Finley has been disloyal, both to me and to scholarship. I have written him a firm and not very nice letter ... I hope it has given him a few sleepless nights.[68]

Friends were expected to show affection by not allowing hurt.

Criticism was not only personally painful. It also compromised the mission of exhibiting the benefits of Greek living. Readers had to be caught by his words and had to believe them. The sneering of German professors and the sniping from other English classicists brought all this into doubt. The ghost of Joseph still walked. In classical studies, the essayist dealing with broad issues for a general readership was being overtaken by the technicians. As a result, Bowra ran the risk of being dismissed as old fashioned, and he knew it. One of his favourite, after-dinner games was 'If'. He would recite Kipling's poem and then ask guests to award themselves marks if they had all or any of the attributes that the poet associated with manhood. He only awarded himself three and a half out of fifteen. When he came to considering 'Triumph and Disaster', he commented, 'Can't say about Triumph. Never experienced it.'[69]

These tensions became gangrenous when Bowra failed to secure the Oxford Chair of Greek in 1936. To the outside world the matter was a storm in an academic tea cup. To Maurice it was of supreme importance. It raised questions of the deepest personal and professional interest. He regarded his failure to secure the appointment as one of the major defeats of his life. The academic world passed judgement on him and found him wanting. It was rejection of him and his approach to Greek studies. Maurice sometimes felt rejection when none was intended, but, in this affair, there was no question about evidence that was public and incontrovertible.

For a generation, the Oxford Chair had been held by Gilbert Murray, a figure of international repute. His translations of Greek literature were known to every schoolboy. In addition, his committed Liberalism brought him roles in national and international politics. At his home on Boar's Hill near Oxford, he entertained in plain, high-thinking surroundings. Bowra visited the house often, and was happy to see himself as Murray's pupil and protégé. He and Bowra, crucially, saw themselves as sharing a common purpose, that of finding in the Greeks 'a sane and generous ideal of what one ought to be'.[70] In a generous obituary notice, Maurice claimed that his mentor had belonged 'to an ancient and rich humanistic tradition, which believed that learning should be closely related to life and that the study of great masterpieces enlarges our vision and sympathy and understanding'.[71]

Then, too, each man recognized the poet in the other. Bowra praised Murray's translations as those of a man to whom poetry was always in the ear. Murray returned the compliment, telling the younger man that he would always write 'as if Greek Literature was a living thing'.[72] In his early career, Bowra published nothing without first securing the approval of his idol, and it was no coincidence that Murray helped to secure his admirer the fellowship at Wadham which made an Oxford career possible. For nearly fifteen years, Murray flattered Bowra that his approach to Greek literature was well founded and in tune with his own beliefs. As a consequence, Maurice stood in awe of Boar's Hill. It was only in 1934 that, at Murray's suggestion, he could bring himself to address the great man as anything other than 'professor'.[73] Bowra saw Murray as his model and inspiration in proselytizing about the Greeks: 'It is from your books and lectures that I begin and end.'[74]

Murray's successor would be elected in the summer of 1936. Many people thought that the Chair was Bowra's for the asking. Even the highly critical Adorno thought so: 'er wird wahrscheinlich Gilbert Murray's Nachfolger sein' [he is probably Gilbert Murray's successor].[75] More importantly, so did Maurice himself. He was only thirty-eight years old, but Murray himself had been appointed when still a young man. Between 1930 and 1936, he had published a series of books and articles, including *Tradition and Design in the Iliad*, which some consider as one of his best productions. Like Murray, Bowra had established a name for himself in worlds outside Oxford, even outside England. And most important of all, he believed himself to have been anointed by Murray as his successor. The great man had promoted his career at every turn, and had openly avowed common values. The Regius Chair was a Crown appointment. The final decision therefore rested with Stanley Baldwin, the prime minister. If Murray were consulted by his friends in London, there could surely only be one outcome.

Some of Maurice's friends were not so sure, however, and, knowing what value he put on the appointment, became alarmed for him. Isaiah Berlin reported to his mother a rumour that he had heard from T. S. Eliot: 'Mr Eliot doesn't think he will be professor of Greek after all. This would be a bad thing. For our own sakes he must become something grand soon.'[76] Berlin feared that Gilbert Murray was about to commit a kind of treason, abandoning the school of Greek scholarship in which he had spent his whole life for something more modern. In the process, he would be forced to abandon his protégé as well:

> Maurice himself (it is impossible not to start with him) is on tenterhooks about his professorship. I doubt if he will get it. Murray being himself a popularizer, has a naturall [sic] passion for austerity, rigorism etc., and suspects Maurice of slipshodiness etc. Lady Mary hates him. His faculty is a jealous body of men, full of resentment and secret hatred of their subject... He is still the most fascinating man I know, and infinitely responsive to every inflexion and accent. But somehow resigned to academic failure.[77]

The stakes could not have been higher. Berlin and Elizabeth Bowen among others feared being 'scorched by the reflected rage and dismay'[78] of Bowra if things went wrong.

Their fears proved justified. At the beginning of the process, Oxford assumed that there were only two possible candidates, Bowra himself and Denniston, to whom Maurice would dedicate his *Sophoclean Tragedy*. Although the University divided into 'Bowristas' and 'Dennistonites', both men knew and respected each other. To everyone's surprise, and to the horror of some, neither was eventually appointed. The Chair went to 'some man called Dodds',[79] of whom many in Oxford had barely heard. Gilbert Murray's influence had been decisive, and it had destroyed Bowra's chances. In June 1936, Murray told Baldwin that he had 'at last got some clear light on the problem of the Greek Chair'. Having heard Bowra in seminars and lectures, Murray had 'come reluctantly to the conclusion that his would not be a good appointment. It is not so much that he sometimes makes mistakes or rash statements. It is a certain lack of quality, precision, and reality in his scholarship as a whole.' In recommending Dodds, Murray admitted that he was trying to turn Greek studies 'back towards philosophy rather than poetry'.[80] He was well aware that his decision represented the repudiation of one kind of Greek scholarship, his own, and that Bowra would be the principal victim of the change.

In letters to Bowra, Murray claimed that his decision had been entirely based on soundings he had taken within the Oxford faculty. Understandably, he wanted to share the responsibility with others. But his letter to Baldwin makes no mention of Oxford opinion generally. The preference he expressed was his own. Bowra, with some justice, cried foul. The master who had taught him and others that the Greeks were to be found through poetry had struck his tents and slunk away. The appointment of Denniston could have been accepted, but the elevation of Dodds was inexplicable.

For a start no one had heard of him. Ernst Kantorowicz wrote from Berlin to ask who he was.[81] On closer acquaintance, he, like all Maurice's friends, found the new professor grey beyond all greyness: 'He is a Puritan who overcomes his Puritanism by Labor [sic] Party activity and Freud and "a mission in the world." Unfortunately he is not nasty; he is only somewhat dull.'[82] Dodds seemed to have an infinite capacity for draining Greek studies of all colour. Having heard him lecture in California on 'the psychoanalytical interpretation of Greek irrationalism', Kantorowicz found him incapable of 'visualizing a single Lebenspunkt'.[83] Dodds's Greeks never truly lived. For Isaiah Berlin too, the appointment had enormous significance. It was 'the triumph of Puritanism and the last embers of the dying twenties. 1936 has been the most horrible year on record.' Oxford was full of 'Baldwinite faces ... Cox, Boase, Maud etc.'[84]

To make matters worse, Dodds had been a conscientious objector in the Great War. As an Irishman, his reluctance to fight for the British Crown was understandable, but to Bowra it was unforgivable. He complained to Isaiah Berlin that 'Lindsay and Murray definitely did not count war service in one's favour—which was he argued correct of them, but positively against me, which was hard.'[85] The veteran of trench warfare could not tolerate the argument that principle prevented certain individuals from sharing in the common suffering. As a result, the Bowristas teased Dodds unmercifully and ensured that his reception in Oxford would be a cold one. When Bowra turned down the offer of a Chair at Harvard, he puckishly wrote to Murray to ask if perhaps Dodds 'would like it'.[86] Years later, Dodds wrote to Bowra to express his thanks for the way 'that old rumpus of 1936' had been treated in *Memories*.

> It worried me dreadfully at the time, and still nags a little ... I allowed my name to be put forward only to please Murray and on his express assurance that I had virtually no chance. I was horrified to find myself appointed, and was on the verge of declining—as I should certainly have done had I realised in time what the feeling was in Oxford. As it was, the next few years were the most unhappy period of my life.[87]

Predictably, the two men were never properly reconciled.

One great question perplexed Oxford: why had Gilbert Murray acted as he did? Perhaps his decision had been dictated by a genuine belief that the direction of Greek studies had to change. But some people believed that darker forces were at work, and that Bowra was being penalized for a private life that was a little too notorious. T. W. Adorno thought so. He told a colleague that Bowra has 'not been given Murray's Chair. That would not mean much, and it is not our business to console others about their academic careers. But it appears that he was denied the Chair on sinister grounds: for real or imagined homosexuality.'[88] Inside Oxford, Mary Fisher reported that Enid Starkie and Isobel Henderson, the one 'by guile' and the other accidentally, had informed Gilbert Murray about his protégé's private life. She herself did not think that Murray would be moved by such tittle-tattle, but the rumour mill was clearly working well.[89] Bowra himself never made reference to such gossip, but then he could hardly do so in public. If he felt an element of persecution, it would have to be coped with within the security of his own thoughts.

Inevitably, the relationship between Murray and Bowra was gravely impaired. In the aftermath of the appointment, the two men exchanged the sort of letters well known in academic circles, full of civilities that mean the exact opposite to what is said. Murray told his pupil that 'the whole business had made me very unhappy', that Dodds's references had 'just turned the scale', and that he had no doubt that Bowra would be 'a Hellenist of the highest quality, wherever you may be'.[90] In reply, Bowra combined politeness with casuistry:

> It was good of you to write. The whole thing must have been most difficult and trying for you. Please don't think that I cherish any sort of resentment. Of course I should have liked the job but in spite of appearances I am a modest man and I have always known that my faults and deficiencies were probably too many. Also I have a gift of exciting hostility among my elders, and this is no advantage. I am sorry to say I hardly know Dodds and I can't claim to be a judge of his work. He will (I fear) have a good deal of hostility to face. But if he is a good man, that will do him no harm.[91]

Maurice was playing the game according to the established rules, but there was no question of him forgetting or forgiving.

In fact, he continued to visit Boar's Hill, if only to enjoy the embarrassment of his hosts. At a lunch party in March 1937, he found Sir Gilbert 'full of guilt and very affable'. His wife, Lady Mary, was 'equally full of guilt', not least because her sister, Lady Cecilia Robarts, 'a fine, fat old thing', spent the entire meal berating her for not having supported Bowra's candidature more forcefully.[92] Maurice owed too much to Murray to exact a crippling revenge, but he could assuage his feelings with a little mockery in verse. The highminded and teetotal world, in which the Murrays moved, was all too open to satire. In 'Gilbert and Mary, an Eclogue', he wrote of Lady Mary hearing of her husband 'carrying a flask of port | And visiting a place of low resort' in the vicinity of Soho. Her retribution was swift and final;

> 'Gilbert, if you refuse to tell me right,
> I shall cut off your Horlicks from tonight.'[93]

The two men would remain on terms, but warmth of feeling had gone. Bowra saw Murray's rejection of him as an apostasy from that exposition of Greek values in which they had both once been engaged.

With undisguised relief, Bowra left Oxford to spend the autumn of 1936 and the spring of 1937 in Harvard as a Visiting Professor. In December 1936, news reached England that he had been offered permanent positions at both Harvard and Princeton, and that he was minded to take one of them. This suggestion threw the Oxford Classics faculty into panic. A flood of communications travelled across the Atlantic begging him to reconsider. Isaiah Berlin sent a telegram: 'Panic. Stop. Dundas Wade Gery Mynors profoundly upset. Stop. Entreat defer final decision until spate of letters this releases reaches you nobody able to face up to real facts. Surely highest disinterestedness on your part demanded in this crisis.'[94] Roger Mynors wrote to condole with Bowra about how 'unsympathetic' Oxford had been, adding that he 'wouldn't put this down on paper in the ordinary way, the English are an undemonstrative race, but if there is any question of your feeling that there is no gratitude in Oxford, then I must say my little piece for what it's worth'.[95] Even Eduard Fraenkel wrote. After the terrible disappointment he had just encountered, Bowra 'had such fun'[96] receiving insincere letters from enemies and warm entreaties from friends, all demanding that he stay in Oxford.

In fact there was no question of him staying in America. A new Warden of Wadham was about to be elected, and Bowra was an obvious candidate for the position. Theodore Wade-Gery, Wadham's ancient historian, had promised his best offices. Securing the headship of a college would more than compensate for the loss of a Chair. But even without this inducement, America and Maurice could not be long-term partners.

According to Isaiah Berlin, Americans would never understand him. They would only remember 'the most violently exaggerated characteristics (3 or 4 days later)'.[97] Ernst Kantorowicz, too, joined the chorus of friends who reminded Maurice that Oxford was essential to his well being: 'Be wise and contemplate life as an old stoicus, who knows that happiness is not to be found in power nor in money, but in good food and truth and wine.'[98]

The reaffirmation of loyalty and affection from friends always did more than anything else to carry Maurice through a crisis, but, even so, he returned to Oxford a somewhat changed man. Public rejection had been a dreadful experience. As Stuart Hampshire put it, 'the poor old boy had to reorientate his life'.[99] He continued to write about the Greek world, but, more and more, his interest turned to evaluating the poetry of his own generation. In *Memories*, written thirty years later, the drama is played down. Only five lines are given to Dodds, who is nevertheless hailed as 'an excellent choice'. As for himself, the only disagreeable aspect of the business was 'the publicity, which made it appear that I was an uppish young man who had been properly snubbed'.[100] In fact, time had dulled pain but had failed to cure. He continued to write. He moved energetically into new fields. But the repudiation of 1936 reinforced the doubts about his scholarship that he had always had. As he himself put it, 'I knew at heart that I was not a good enough scholar for so central a post.'[101] When Dodds retired, some friends suggested that he should offer himself for the job once more. The reply was emphatic: 'No, no good then, no good now.'[102] In personal terms he had been damaged. Worse still, Oxford no longer seemed to value his views on the Greeks and the benefits they could offer to the contemporary world.

The shifting of emphasis in his intellectual pursuits towards contemporary poetry in no way implied a diminishing interest in Greece as a living experience. Going there meant rejuvenation and emancipation. Wadham undergraduates would be told that it was essential to go below 'the wine line' every year. That invisible frontier below which vines could be grown should appear on every map. Only in such journeying could foggy English minds clear and inhibitions loosen. In 1952 for example, he found himself on Ischia with Robert Boothby, 'mountains, sea, sun, servants, a boat and a jeep'. It was therapeutic: 'I cannot have been sober for more than an hour a day and found my broken tissues joining up and the blook [*sic*] circulating among the grey cells as it has not done for many years.' Graffiti in Naples, 'American fag off', set off a merry train of thought: 'I had not hitherto realised the close association of "fag" with that other monosyllable used so frequently by our armed forces. This discovery throws a new light on such phrases as "the fag-end of the holiday", and the fagging-system at our great public schools—and what pray is a fag-master.'[103] All Mediterranean peoples thankfully ate too much and drank too much in the company of friends. Only the Portuguese were a little 'flat'. Maurice sadly speculated that they were too like the English: 'having conquered half the world and lost it, they both know that it was not worth having and feel worse for having lost it.'[104] With this exception, however, those who lived below the wine line had much to teach.

Inevitably, Greece had most to offer. It mattered little that he tore his 'feet to pieces at Actium and sprained an ankle on Ithaca'.[105] He probably visited the country for the first time in 1932, in the company of Martin Cooper, and returned repeatedly thereafter. These visits were not without embarrassments. Maurice only had 'snatches of Modern Greek'. When corrected for using ancient words which had no modern meaning, he simply declared that 'the language had gone downhill'.[106] On another occasion, while staying with his former pupil Rex Warner in Athens, he discomforted his host by loudly declaring that a group of unshaven Greek soldiers 'looked like Bulgarians'.[107] Twice, Greece nearly killed him. Serious road accidents in December 1952 and April 1961 left him shaken and momentarily filled with 'a slight sense of relief that the end had come at last'.[108]

None of these inconveniences mattered. Greece was to be visited as often as time and money allowed. In 1946, he went on a British Council lecture tour of the country, even though vigorous civil war had followed the German occupation. 'Greece was very much itself—even down to the brigands and the return of the king, like Pisistratus. I was foiled from getting to Delphi by the road being mined but got to Marathon and Sounion and Rhamnus ... what a delight to see those mountains and that sea again.'[109] He repeated the exercise in 1952.[110] More often, he simply went on holiday, frequently in the company of Ernst Kantorowicz, or stayed with friends. Barbara Rothschild's house on Corfu was congenial, as were the homes of Joan and Paddy Leigh Fermor on Hydra and Poros. He had an attachment to Joan Leigh Fermor which could be called romantic. Relations with her husband were more ambiguous, but, under a Greek sun, tensions eased, as Maurice cheerfully reported to Billa Harrod, 'I go off to Greece on August 1st, where dear, oh dear, Joan has got a house on an island. It sounds bliss to me. Dear Paddy will be there and I have decided to be angelic to him and treat him like a great writer...though of course one sees his toes more.'[111] In fact Bowra and Leigh Fermor held much common ground, as Ann Fleming noted: 'they both love Greeks, Greece, talking, war, medals and royalty.'[112]

For Bowra, intimacy with a country necessitated a knowledge of its poets, dead and alive. He had always admired Cavafy. In 1946, he met George Seferis, with whom he occasionally corresponded.[113] At some point, Kazantzakis was a guest in Wadham, 'an extraordinary old man', who 'refused to eat anything at all'. Nevertheless, Bowra, as 'an Old Believer...greatly enjoyed his novel *Christ is crucified again*'.[114] Cultivating acquaintances with Greek writers and poets gave Bowra an edge over other Oxford classicists. In this, as in so many other ways, no one could compete with him. Modern Greece was as alive to him as the ancient world. Indeed, he could be territorially aggressive if his sphere of influence was challenged. The Kenneth Clarks were two of his oldest friends, but when they discovered Greece for the first time and began sending 'patronising postcards', Maurice shamefacedly admitted that he felt 'somehow as if my privacy had been invaded by German tourists'.[115] Greece was as personal to him as a well-kept secret.

Of course, his ideas about links between the ancient and modern Greek worlds were somewhat romanticized. The mouthing of words familiar to Pindar made him all but unintelligible in the modern country, for example. But the light was the same, as were many of the sights and smells. Nothing could change the fact that it was the country where great deeds had been done and great ideas generated. It was not England. Accordingly, Maurice was pro-Greek in any crisis. When Cyprus demanded independence, he wrote letters and signed petitions urging concessions. In his view, 'it is no good trying to rule people who don't want to be ruled by you, and the Greeks regard us as just the same as occupying Germans in the war'.[116] To stay in Cyprus would simply mean that 'our young conscripts will be shot in the dark and we shall then hang a lot of schoolboys. And a lot of good that will do.'[117] The depth of his philhellenism was such that the Greeks must be given the benefit of the doubt on all occasions.

As a consequence of his views, Maurice could only regard it as a personal catastrophe when Greek democracy succumbed to a military coup in 1967. It was an affront to the Greek strands in his own personality. With 'those bloody men'[118] in power, he immediately determined on a boycott which cost him dear. He would never see Greece again. He never had the chance to stay in the Leigh Fermors' new house in the Peloponnese, but, as he explained to Berta Ruck, he could not go to Greece 'while these ghastly colonels attack and torture my friends and insist on that awful middle class sham Greek being taught and talked'.[119] In retaliation Bowra joined the resistance. Under the direction of his colleague George Forrest, Wadham was turned into a political cell. Refugees from Greece were sheltered and supported;[120] Helen Vlachos and Melina Mercouri were wined and dined; and pro-democracy newssheets were run up on a hand printing press in the front quadrangle. Somehow, Bowra knew of someone who could guarantee their safe arrival in Greece.[121]

This refusal to go to Greece was noble in that it came at huge personal expense. Democracy would only be restored in that country after Bowra's death. In the last years of his life, he looked in vain for worthy alternatives. As he put it, 'the world shrinks and there is nowhere to go'.[122] In 1967, he tried Sardinia but found it wanting; 'the landscape with no gods and no beauty, the towns deplorable, the High Life nauseating', consisting as it did of 'Italian duchesses saying how sad [it was] that there was no more British Empire'.[123] The cost was enormous, yet there could be no compromise with the perverted politics that controlled Athens. Shortly before his death, he insisted before a lecture audience that 'Those who love Greece must resolutely refuse to be fooled by the tittle-tattle of gullible tourists or self-seeking professors or cocksure agents of new imperialisms.' There was no doubt in his own mind that, sooner or later, the Greeks would re-establish their liberties. Everything in their history and in the air around them was an imperative: 'The Greek landscape enshrines the memory of many struggles for liberty, between the shadowy mountains and the echoing sea at Marathon and Missolonghi ... The gods of truth and justice are not mocked.'[124]

In his academic studies Bowra suffered the inconvenience of becoming old-fashioned. His way of writing was overtaken by new scholarly pre-occupations. Some of his colleagues became interested in the preparation of precise texts; others tried to bring into classical studies the insights of the psychologist and the sociologist. But Bowra could not, or would not, change. As close friends recognized, his Greek studies were so intimately entwined in aspects of his personality that they could not be easily read-justed. The Greek experience was a living reality to him, and one which he passionately wanted to offer to anyone who would listen. As John Finley observed, Maurice's books came 'from much of your life'. To write about the Greeks was part of a personal, larger whole. 'Surely everything went toward it, and you could not have written quite in this way without your long union of Greece, poetry, Oxford and Britain, the Aegean, friends.'[125] His scholarship was a function of his personality. It could not bend to changes in academic fashion.

Above all, the wish to impart a message never left him. He wanted others to find in the Greek world the sense of personal liberation that it had always vouchsafed him. Many pupils came to know this. Day-Lewis had been one of the first undergraduates to experience Bowra's teaching methods and objectives. In 'Hellene and Philhellene', he coupled the names of Seferis and Bowra as the two men who really knew what the Greeks had been about:

> And you no less, dear tutor of my young days,
> Lover of Greece and poetry, I mourn.
> To me you seem the exorbitant blaze
> Of Aegean sun dispelling youth's forlorn
> Blurred images; the lucid air; the salt
> Of tonic sea on your lips. And you were one
> Whom new poetic languages enthralled
> (After I'd stumbled through a Greek unseen,
> You'd take *The Tower* or *The Waste Land* from a shelf
> And read me into strange mysteries).
> You taught me most by always being yourself
> Those fifty years ago. For ever Greece.[126]

5
Poetry

L iving out Greek teaching was one of the main props of Bowra's personality. It also gave him a sense of mission that led him on to the attack in so many areas of academic debate. But whether it would have been enough in itself to sustain him is debatable. Most classicists, then and now, do not seem to have derived a sense of personal empowerment from their studies. In Bowra, classical studies were potent because they were linked to another preoccupation, namely the proposition that poetry and the poet were of supreme importance. Maurice had discovered in the trenches of the Great War that poetry could literally save a personality from disintegration. It gave clues to a beauty of living, a spirituality, that dignified everyday events. It suggested that life might have a purpose after all. The Greeks of course had known this, but the task now was to re-establish this truth in the England of his own generation. To embark on such an enterprise would involve struggle. English ears, particularly public school ears, were not easily attuned to the demands of poets. But, for Bowra, there was no choice. As Cyril Connolly remembered, Bowra 'saw human life as a tragedy in which great poets were the heroes who fought back and tried to give life a meaning'.[1] Bowra's favourite characters in Shakespeare were Hamlet and Mercutio.

Above all, Maurice wanted to be accepted as a serious poet in his own right. He regarded the greatest tragedy of his life to be the fact that his talents never reached these heights. He was a respected critic of poetry; he was the patron and friend of poets; he was an entrepreneur in the publication of poetry; but he himself would always be 'the poet manqué'.[2] Friends knew this. According to Connolly, Bowra's poetic ambitions were undermined by 'an intractable inhibition, a block resulting from some parental situation or possibly the trauma of the trenches'.[3] Kenneth Clark reported that Bowra's consciousness of his failure to write poetry

of distinction was 'his greatest failing'.[4] Stuart Hampshire saw his mentor
only as 'an inspired host—after that a poet'.[5] They all knew him to be
a passionate and emotional man, for whom poetry expressed what was
otherwise inexpressible. As Noel Annan observed:

> Deep seated as was his hatred of injustice and cruelty, the rule of his life
> by which he set most store, so it seemed to me, was to read poetry, to
> live by it and with it, to turn to it for wisdom and to pray that it would
> continue to replenish the springs of feeling which flow ever more sluggishly
> the older one gets. Above all to reverence the poets as men ... not only
> dead poets, but the living exponents of the European heritage. You realised
> that beneath the noise and the laughter was the conviction that unless you
> refreshed yourself by re-reading poets and letting them, if only for an hour
> or so, take command, you would inevitably become a castrated pedant or a
> dehumanised bureaucrat—and beyond redemption.[6]

When he was awarded public honours, Bowra joyfully accepted them as
'one in the eye for one's enemies', but, more seriously, hoped that they
were taken as a reward for his services to poetry.[7]

He would, however, never be a poet himself. Although he had begun
to write verse at Cheltenham College, in or around 1929, he abandoned
all attempts to write serious poetry. Henceforth, he retained the poet's
involvement with words but never shaped them. Day-Lewis observed that
Bowra 'had a long series of love affairs with words, which is the poet's
daily life', and that in these dealings he was 'as selfish and egotistic as any
other lover',[8] but for some reason these words would not be moulded
into verse. Perhaps, having met Yeats and Eliot, he realized that he could
never compete at their level. Perhaps, the experience of the Great War
had induced a sense of fatality that words were incapable of soothing.
Bowra once praised Apollinaire for being able to describe 'those moments
in war which show how helpless its victims are and how little their personal
wishes avail against the brute tyranny of circumstance'.[9] Whatever the
reason, Bowra ducked the challenge. For most of his life, he confined his
efforts to writing scabrous verses as a form of after-dinner entertainment
for his inner circle of friends. Many of these were clever parodies of others'
styles and thoughts, but they were far below what he himself had hoped for.

To fail in a long-cherished ambition can have one of two consequences;
either the aspirant turns his back on the whole enterprise, even to the point
of affecting disdain or contempt for it, or he admires with even greater
fervour those who succeeded where he could not. In Bowra's case, the

second of these options was emphatically to the fore. Even though he had to mouth the words of other men and women, he did so with real passion and conviction. He felt what the poets felt, even if he had not been able to speak with a poetic voice. He had an affinity with them, even when its clear articulation was beyond him. This failure therefore reinforced his commitment to them. Though he could not be a poet himself, he could fight their corner, and offer a kind of paternalistic protection. Inevitably, poets of distinction would figure prominently among his friends and correspondents, and Bowra would not have had it any other way.

Not to be a poet was a tragedy because, according to Bowra, the poet was the most blessed of all men. Endowed with special talents he is privileged to have special insights. Again and again Bowra returned to the story of Hesiod, a simple farmer who was invited by the Muses to the summit of Mount Helicon. There he was touched by an olive branch, contact which gave him 'the divine voice' of the poet. The gods spoke through poets, in order to warn, to instruct, and to edify. As a result an 'intimate connection between poetry and prophecy' was set up.[10] Poets acquired a unique wisdom, or 'Sophia', which turned them into prophets, seers, and magicians. As Bowra put it, 'the poet is wise because he has a special knowledge'.[11] Great writers experience 'a visitation' from the gods which might be called inspiration. This 'creates a state in which they see as a whole what normally they see only in fragments … It is not surprising that in such circumstances they feel that they have passed into eternity.'[12] In lecture after lecture, Maurice hailed poets as the only chosen race. It was his duty to point this out. As he confided to Edith Sitwell, he always wanted to speak 'on the prophetic element in poetry. Our great modern instances are Yeats and you. I think the subject is of importance if we are ever to get away from the depressing psychoanalysis, which so many think is the same as poetry. After all, poets and prophets have much in common, and it is high time this was pointed out.'[13]

If poets had special wisdom, all societies should honour their works. The Greeks of the fifth and sixth centuries BC knew this. Twentieth-century England did not. Among the Greeks, poetry 'had its honoured place, and from this fact it drew confidence and power'.[14] By contrast, the poets of his own day had no status and only a tiny audience. Worse, in Europe, poets faced persecution and harassment. Yet the voice of the poet was never more needed than in the first decades of the twentieth century. Reflecting on two world wars and the miseries of Nazism and Communism, Bowra was sure it could only be a tragedy that the poet should be silenced by such catastrophes. Everything should be done to bring about their rehabilitation, but there was no guarantee that this could be achieved.

Worryingly, the analogies to be drawn in politics between his studies of sixth- and fifth-century Greece and the decades of his own lifetime were close. In both periods, aristocratic societies were giving way to democracies. Aristocratic societies allowed a small number of people to live the life that the poets talked of. The great question was whether such values transferred easily, or transferred at all, to democratic systems. After all, poets, having a gift from the gods, could not by definition be like other men. Theirs had to be a separate world. If poets were not set up on pedestals in democracies, they had to seek other kinds of isolation. Bowra himself had too active a personality to live such a life, but he well understood the argument.[15]

The link between his preferred Greek poets and aristocratic values was undeniable. Alcaeus had been 'a passionate, uncompromising aristocrat'; Sappho represented the 'ripe development of the aristocratic age'; Xenophanes voiced 'the intellectual vigour and range of his class'; and Pindar, above all, was the 'product of the aristocratic age in Greece'.[16] The latter's lauding of aristocratic competitors at Olympic games was pleasing. He was

> more sublime than any poet in the world, sublime by sheer poetry without any artifice or even emotion than true aesthetic rapture … he liked a lot of things one likes—breeding and manners and splendour … The races were not like Doncaster (or Naas) but like a Yacht Race in Edwardian days at Cowes … Antique snobbery is hard to recapture, but it seems terrific ever to have made poetry out of it.[17]

All these poets sang as their world vanished in the new democracies.

Exactly the same experience seemed to be repeated in Bowra's own life time. In 1943, he told the readers of *Horizon* that the great poetry of '1890–1921' had been the gift 'of a highly educated and sensitive class. Its members had private incomes, lived in an extremely intimate and cultivated society, and wrote for others hardly less educated than themselves.'[18] Populist politics then destroyed them. Apart from Mayakovsky, 'the prince of yes-men', all the great Russians of his generation were killed, literally or imaginatively, by revolution. In Germany, the poets became the victims of Nazism. His Greek studies and his own eyes taught the lesson that a high culture, from which great poetry might emerge, depended on government by aristocracy, meaning not necessarily the best by birth but certainly the best in spirit. He went on to assure *Horizon*'s readers that he himself was convinced that poetry and democracy were perfectly compatible. He even looked forward to a renaissance of literature in Soviet Russia. Whether he believed his own words is debatable. Almost certainly, he was whistling to keep up his spirits.

Maurice was no reactionary, nor even a conservative. The democratic world was coming. Resisting its challenges would be absurd. Instead, they had to be fully engaged. Just as he had to tell his countrymen about the Greeks, he now also had to teach them to love the poets and their wisdom. Though a failed poet himself, nearly all his academic work involved writing about poetry. He would make himself an impresario in the field, seeking out talent and protecting it once found. The English would be introduced to the poets of other countries, whether they liked it or not. Steps would be taken to ensure that the best new voices found publishers, and poets would become his friends. The Greek model could teach a twentieth-century democracy how to live well, and the poets would tell how to live wholly.

If all this represented a mission to be pursued with passion, Bowra was magnificently equipped to take it on. His linguistic range gave him few equals in Oxford, albeit not in the spoken word. Friends enjoyed catching him out in conversations abroad, rather as schoolboys relish discovering their headmaster in error. Stuart Hampshire thought Bowra's spoken French was 'painful', though admitting that his German was 'goodish'.[19] Here was a weakness that Bowra himself admitted. In the introduction to *The Heritage of Symbolism*, he protested his limitations in the knowledge of languages to a degree barely credible.[20] But in terms of being proficient in reading languages, the situation was very different. Isaiah Berlin credited his colleague with Russian, French, German, Italian, and Spanish, in addition to Latin and Greek. Taken together, these skills allowed him 'a sense of world literature as a single firmament'. As he ranged across linguistic frontiers, 'it was all, for him, part of the war against embattled philistinism, pedantic learning, parochialism'.[21]

Being a citizen of Babel was greatly attractive to a man who had never found being merely English easy. As Noel Annan remembered, Bowra's name

> will never be associated with some great breakthrough, or some revelations,
> as it were, in the humanities, … but the breadth of his reading and his work
> was unlike that of any other person in England … And another thing, he

knew the poets, and they knew that he loved them and cared for their poetry, Quasimodo, Pasternak, Valéry, Sitwell, Yeats.[22]

Through Bowra's agency, Oxford would be introduced to the works of poets in other cultures, who would materialize for honorary degrees. He championed Stefan George and Paul Valéry in the twenties and Octavio Paz and Pablo Neruda in the sixties. He even introduced poets to each other. Edith Sitwell wrote to thank him for bringing Cavafy and Alberti to her attention, concluding her letter with the words, 'How often I wished I could be a boy of nineteen, and one of your students. What it would have been like to have started with such a grounding.'[23]

If the eyes of the English were to be opened, the art of translation had to be taken extremely seriously. Maurice translated a great deal and always took trouble. In offering Blok and other Russians to the English, he called in the services of Isaiah Berlin and Serge Konavalov. Boris Pasternak praised the end result. T. W. Adorno was equally complimentary about Bowra's translation of Rilke. A cousin of Federico Lorca wrote to praise an essay on his friend and relation.[24] In the last years of his life, Bowra collected doctorates and awards from many countries, all of whom felt that he had honoured their literatures. France admitted him to the *Légion d'honneur*. Germany awarded him the *Pour le Mérite*. Such distinctions allowed him to challenge Oxford's insularity and any tendency towards a feeling of self-sufficiency.

On paper, Bowra's range was dazzling. Any statement about poetry would be based on a knowledge of the literatures of many centuries and all continents. A collection of essays, published under the title *Inspiration and Poetry*, contained pieces on Horace, Dante, Gil Vicente, Milton, Hölderlin, Pushkin, Lermontov, Pater, Dario, and Shotha Rustaveli. In *Mediaeval Love Song*, a comparison is made between Provençal poetry of the twelfth century and comparable efforts in Persia and Georgia of the same period. When lecturing on the poetry of the Great War, Bowra chose to place English poets like Brooke, Hardy, Rosenberg, and Owen alongside the voices of all the belligerent nations: Ungaretti and Apollinaire, Blok and Bryusov, George and Trakl. Such lists are not exhaustive. Nor was he reluctant to make incursions into the territory of the anthropologist. *Primitive Song* involved a discussion of the songs of, among others, the pygmies of Gabon, the bushmen of the Kalahari, the Semangs of Malaya, the Veddas of Sri Lanka, and the Yemana of Tierra del Fuego. It was proper for him to undertake such studies, because the song of primitive peoples, like poetry, 'enhances the desire and strengthens the capacity to live'.[25]

Such an approach was of course open to criticism. Specialists complained about too much generalization and too much superficiality. No man could have the depth of reading required to cover so much ground with real scholarship. But such comments, while alarming Bowra, could not deflect him from his purpose. He wrote to inform his readers about poetry and its meaning. To do this effectively, he felt that he had to draw on all cultures and all practitioners, because there was a universality about the human experience that made national boundaries absurd. Of necessity the scholarship was not always profound, but the aspiration was compelling. Gods and politicians came and went, but the poet, as seer and prophet, had an enduring wisdom. Bowra's Greeks had known this and had honoured poets accordingly.

In Maurice's view, the Greeks of his own generation were the Symbolists, who found representatives in most European countries between 1880 and 1939. Like the Greeks, they endowed the poet with prophetic vision. Like the Greeks, they feared that their values would not be welcome in democracies. Like the Greeks, they imposed a sense of mission on themselves to teach what was best. Bowra's admiration for them was unqualified. He told John Sparrow that 'all the great poets of Europe from 1880 till today have been Symbolists (except Bridges and Jammes)'.[26] After all, the horrors experienced by Europe in these decades made the poet's role as seer, looking beyond events, of particular relevance. In a lecture of 1959 entitled *The Prophetic Element*, he talked of 'the prolonged crisis of our time' and of a world 'perilously poised on a flaming abyss'. Only the poet could give dignity and meaning to events that would otherwise be intolerable: 'these enormous catastrophes and menaces, these revelations of the fallen state of man, can only be interpreted by a seer who grasps them in their horror and is courageous enough to speak out about them when others are silent.'[27]

Sometimes mere words could not capture the significance of what was in progress. The poet's vision had to be expressed in Symbols. As Bowra explained, 'the Symbol is an object standing for something else which has so undefined and indeed so indefinable a character and such a wealth of implications that it cannot be expressed in ordinary abstract words without its essential nature being obscured, or misrepresented, or lost.'[28] In *The*

Heritage of Symbolism of 1943, he called the poet 'a shaman', who 'is no longer a man among other men'.[29] Rather, he was 'in touch with some superior order of things and ... his art is the ritual by which this is brought down to men'.[30] Mortals live and poets feel. In the intensity of feeling there is the possibility of a beautiful, spiritual calm that transcends any misery. The Greeks had held this secret, but it was then lost in the religiosity of the Middle Ages. The nineteenth century had dealt only in the dirt and squalor of realism. But, around 1880, Symbolists like Mallarmé had rediscovered the vision and the purpose. Bowra learnt the lesson in the trenches of the Great War. Readers of the poets should have 'the luxury of dream'. Since all poetry should strive to achieve 'a spiritual effect', they should feel no guilt about succumbing to the music of rhythms and the perfume of words.[31]

Friends recognized in *The Heritage of Symbolism* one of Maurice's best and most personal books. Edith Sitwell hailed it as 'the most important work of criticism of our time'.[32] Ernst Kantorowicz offered a very personal validation:

> Once in our honeymoon we agreed upon our love for the 'singing' verse; and when there is music there is charm or magic too. So we are lovers of enchantment, we are out for it, and we wish to be enchanted both for its own sake and because it stirs the vital ambitions, the forces of life proper, like a drug of vitality.

This letter ends with the sad reflection that, in the United States where Kantorowicz had taken refuge, 'there is no enchantment except ice-cream for which I do not fall'.[33] The book was, for Maurice, both a work of literary criticism and a personal manifesto. That 'inner self' that he had discovered in war, and which had so materially contributed to his survival, was fed and nurtured by the poets he wrote about. As another friend, the actress Irene Worth, put it, 'it's a wonderful book and Maurice is a wonderful man—his profound understanding, intellectual as well as emotional, of a hidden country of an artist's spirit, is one of the most moving experiences I have had in a long time.'[34]

Behind the Oxford grandee and the public figure, therefore, there lay a man of deep emotional responses. Bowra was someone who, while recognizing that the greatest poets of his day were Russian and German, sought the company of their British equivalents and treasured it. T. S. Eliot was an acquaintance and someone whose work was to be sincerely praised, but his commitment to revealed religion presented a barrier that Maurice could not cross. W. B. Yeats was in every way more congenial. According to *Memories*, the two men met for the first time in the Savile Club in 1917, when Yeats described for the younger man how the Dublin prostitutes had danced in the streets on hearing of the conviction of Oscar Wilde.[35] In the 1920s, they met again at Garsington weekends hosted by Ottoline Morrell, and in Ireland when Bowra spent vacations with Piers Synnott at Naas. Bowra was therefore privileged to hear Yeats declaim his own verse, and the mimic in him joyfully reproduced the great man's rhythms and cadences. Reading poetry in the style of Yeats became a party piece. In 1931, Bowra secured an Honorary Degree for his hero, entertaining him to lunch in Wadham together with Kenneth Clark, John Sparrow, Elizabeth Bowen, and Nancy Mitford.[36]

In return, Yeats took Bowra's claims as a commentator on poetry seriously. In May 1934, Maurice wrote about Yeats for the first time, and asked the poet himself for reassurance. The response was warm and flattering. Yeats thought that Bowra had been too hard on the writers of the 1890s, when in fact that had been a decade 'of very great vigour, thought and passion … breaking free from tradition'. He also thought that Bowra had allied him too closely with the French Symbolists when he had simply 'seized upon everything' in their work 'that at all resembled my own thought'. But, as a whole, the 'essay was excellent'. Humbly, Yeats thanked Bowra for introducing him to the circle of Stefan George: 'Ignorant of languages I have always had to get much of my knowledge from such books as yours. A single quotation is often an illumination.'[37] Yeats stayed in Wadham again, in September 1937 and April 1938, even though he worried that the buildings might be haunted. According to Bowra this was 'twaddle' but forgivable.[38] Yeats thought that Bowra and his friends 'had the right mouths for praise'.[39] Their comments stimulated new effort: 'I have not written verse for some months, and it may be owing to you and your friends that I am eager to write it.'[40] Bowra and Yeats were never close friends, but the poet in Maurice received a certain validation by being taken seriously by someone of Yeats's stature.

Real friendship was to be found with Edith Sitwell. In Bowra's view, she stood in the apostolic succession of prophetic poets. He once lectured to the English Association on 'the prophetic element in poetry from Hesiod to Dame Edith Sitwell'.[41] He had written about her before *The Heritage of Symbolism* was published, but it was the appearance of that book which prompted the opening of a correspondence in January 1944. Dame Edith noted that Maurice was now 'writing about my poetry', and confessed that 'it would be quite impossible for me to tell you how much pleasure that gives me'. It was 'great happiness' to have her poetry 'so understood—understood so richly and completely'.[42] These letters set up a twenty-year friendship. For Sitwell, Maurice was accepted as a critic and arbiter of real authority. His opinions were always canvassed before any new work was published. Among Bowra's papers are draught poems which had been sent to him by her for revision and editing. Together they promoted the careers of Sitwell's protégés like Dylan Thomas. At Sitwell lunches at her London club, T. S. Eliot often joined them to snipe at literary enemies such as F. R. Leavis and Geoffrey Grigson.

There is no doubt that Sitwell's acceptance of Bowra's literary credentials was genuine. For her, he was the foremost critic of his generation. As she told him,

> You are the *only* Englishman who can write about poetry constantly (Tom [Eliot], who says flashing good things from time to time, is often wrong-headed, and wears blinkers. You see widely as well as deeply) ... How true it is that 'the creative fit has something wild and unearthly in it', as you say in the chapter about 'The Odes of Horace.' What is the matter with most modern poetry is that there is nothing wild or unearthly about it.[43]

Such words could only have been heartening to the poet manqué in Bowra. Receiving them was tantamount to becoming a poet by proxy.

In return, Maurice worked hard to promote poetry he profoundly admired. In articles and lectures, Sitwell was hailed as someone who had 'set herself a hard task when she made up her mind to restore to English poetry the richness of texture which had been largely lost in the Edwardian and Georgian periods'. In undertaking this task, she had become 'a seer, a prophetess', warning against the 'deadly, meaningless, hopeless uniformity'. Her work appealed 'to the imagination through the ear and the inner eye'. There was music in the rhythms she used and in the positioning of words. Her poem 'Still Falls the Rain' was the finest to emerge from the Second World War.[44] He was happy to associate her with the best in the European tradition, greeting one volume of poems as a 'real *oeuvre,* such as Mallarmé and the great saints of poetry dreamed of ... In recent years I have felt that the only thing needed by the world is poetry and that it is the only cure for our sorrows, and here you have given it ... If this is not genius, nothing is.'[45]

Year by year, the eccentricities of dress, manner, and speech that Dame Edith famously displayed became more and more elaborate, but this fact merely confirmed her character as prophetess. Bowra had always believed that poets could not live as others did. One of the greatest bonds between them was the indulgence of, and enjoyment in, the foibles of other writers. In 1958 for example, she playfully recounted the story of how Jean Cocteau had inadvertently murdered a chameleon.

> Did I tell you that I hear that Jean Cocteau's pet chameleon has come to a tragic end? But perhaps you know this. Jean noticed that the chameleon seemed to be suffering from the cold, so when bedtime came he wrapped him up in a plaid shawl. Next morning his pet was found dead from exhaustion, having spent the night trying to adapt himself to *all* the colours.[46]

Apparently, the licence of artists to live without the restraints imposed by what might be called common sense extended to calamitous incursions into the animal kingdom.

As Bowra came to know poets, questions which had long troubled him gained a new urgency. To what extent would the language of Yeats, Eliot, or Sitwell be intelligible to most people in a democracy? Would their lifestyles be accommodated or would they be found intolerable? Was poetry in any form likely to survive in a period of mass taste, which was likely to discount the written word? No capitalist, democrat, or bureaucrat could be relied on as the ally of the poet. To survive, poets needed to organize, which meant finding new ways of pursuing a common purpose and fulfilling their mission. Bowra took this point very seriously, and since every instinct in his personality led him to favour attacking problems rather than passively accepting their consequences, he was more than happy to join in the search for the means of survival. In this endeavour, his European interests were invaluable, for, in Europe, there were models to follow. It was Bowra's duty to import them into England.

In the last years of the nineteenth century, the French poet Stéphane Mallarmé held court once a week at his home in the Rue de Rome in Paris. These occasions were half-lecture, half séance. Mallarmé, calling himself 'le Maitre', regaled an audience of acolytes with statements about the nature and purpose of poetry. Having been instructed in their mission, these disciples were then expected to carry the message out to a wider world. Bowra knew of Mallarmé and admired what he wrote, but since the Frenchman never produced what Maurice recognized as a masterpiece, he was open to criticism. Non-production was always the most venal of sins in Bowra's eyes. What was intriguing about the sessions in the Rue de Rome was the system they exemplified: a master with disciples pursuing a common purpose in art, to the exclusion of all other considerations. No distractions were allowed; politics was a vulgar diversion and the domesticity involved in marriage a nonsense.

Mallarmé's audiences were almost exclusively young and male, and there was the faint whiff of homoeroticism in the ideal of a dedicated brotherhood. One of the young men listening to the Master in 1899 was the German poet Stefan George. So impressed was he with what he heard and saw that when he returned home, he consciously recreated and elaborated Mallarmé's methods. The George Circle would become one of the most distinctive elements in German poetry in the first decades of the twentieth century. Contact with members of this group was exhilarating for Bowra, and gave him clues as to how the cause of literature might be forwarded. Of course it was all too serious and too German. George's precepts would have to be filtered through the fine mesh of English humour and common sense, but the underlying method was sound.

Three elements in the George creed were of importance to Bowra. First, the master–disciple relationship confirmed the view that there had to be a leader directing the talents of others. Disloyalty could not be allowed. Even dissent was questionable. George endlessly quarrelled with friends like von Hofmannsthal who rebelled against their subordination. Bowra's friendships, too, would have their stormy moments. Secondly, pursuit of the mission had to be single-minded, with no distractions, least of all marriage. George believed that 'marriage changes the intellectual horizon of a friendship and this would necessarily diminish the friendship'.[47] A marriage would always represent crisis for Bowra as well. Thirdly, and perhaps most importantly, George saw his mission as one taken over from the Greeks, and Bowra grasped this point. One of George's poems entitled 'The Hellenic Miracle' affirmed that Greek culture had been 'something incomparable, unique, and perfect'.[48] Bowra believed that George's poems 'are about the Greeks but they are also about himself, because he feels that he is like the Greeks in the simple stark issues which the creative life forces upon him'.[49]

No three points could resonate more powerfully with Bowra's own pre-occupations. The methods and claims of Mallarmé and George would be given a definite English character, but in heavily modified form, they found expression in his own life. By 1930, he too would be the leader—Master would be too pretentious a title—of a group of talented young men whose careers he would attempt to inform and instruct. There would be a Bowra circle. Like George, Bowra dismissed politics as a suitable career for his disciples and distrusted their marriages. He was also as insistent on the claims of friendship, with perceptions of disloyalty easily aroused. Since he had had a coterie of sorts at both Cheltenham and New College, these rules were to some extent his own invention. But contact with powerful, Continental equivalents must have been exciting and reassuring. Here were rules, Greek in origin, that offered some hope that the crucial values of the ancient world would not be lost and that poetry would always be a force in men's lives. A sense of mission could take organizational shape.

According to Kenneth Clark, it may have been Bowra's New College contemporary, Edward Sackville-West, who introduced him to George's works. Certainly, the two men shared a common regard for George and Rilke.[50] Whatever the origin of Bowra's interest in George and his disciples, frequent visits to Germany between 1928 and 1933 allowed him to come face to face with them. Maurice claimed that he never met George himself, although he was once briefly glimpsed in a Heidelberg street. But he certainly knew others, among them Kurt Riezler, Karl Wolfskehl, Kurt Reinhardt, and Lucy von Wangenheim.[51] The latter would appear in Wadham as a refugee from the Nazis in 1938. One of Bowra's books would be published in Berlin, in 1936, by Georg Bondi, who was also George's publisher. Ernst Morwitz helped with the translation.[52] Almost certainly no other Englishman knew the George Circle so well.

One friendship, however, stood out, that with Ernst Kantorowicz, who was commonly known as EKA. Kantorowicz, a classicist by training and inclination, had been an associate of George's since 1920. The Master had found him 'Lithe, yet of masculine firmness, sophisticated, elegant in dress, gesture and speech.'[53] In 1934, he appeared in Oxford as a visiting professor at New College, and a friendship was struck over a lunch in All Souls. A few years later, Bowra would go to Germany himself, in order to rescue Kantorowicz from the Nazis, and he would be instrumental in finding his friend a safe haven in an American university. They would become friends for life. They shared views about the importance of Greeks and poetry, and they shared holidays when circumstances allowed. Their correspondence is confidential and intimate. They may, at some point, have been lovers. Certainly, the friendship of Kantorowicz was among Bowra's most precious possessions. It was an association that allowed Bowra access to the inner sanctum of the George world.[54]

These contacts gave Bowra a unique position in England. Little wonder that he should be the man to tell Edith Sitwell and W. B. Yeats about people like themselves abroad. He was becoming an honest broker between different European literatures. Almost certainly, he was among the first to write about George in English. In October 1932, he told John Sparrow that he had the intention to 'amuse' himself 'by composing my chapter on George'.

> I am hampered by not being able to translate him or when able to see if he is good. It all seems much of a muchness to me. However, I have collected some 'interesting' if not 'curious' facts about him. I thought I would write to him and say that there is a circle of young man [sic] chosen for their looks who study his works in Oxford.[55]

The essay appeared in the *New Oxford Magazine* in February 1934, and would be refined and elaborated for inclusion in *The Heritage of Symbolism* nearly a decade later.

The mocking criticism in his letter to Sparrow is reproduced in the published work. George was too German for the English. He 'was highly educated, incurably intellectual, desperately serious, dangerously solemn'. At least Kantorowicz had a pronounced sense of humour. Then, too, George was so self-obsessed that he stifled as much as he liberated. He was 'a man who is so caught up in himself that, however much he may wish to be free, he is unable to break his bonds...he can never forget himself, never break into unrestrained song'.[56] And he was too autocratic. As Bowra put it, 'by imposing his imperious will and forcing his special notions on others, he denied their independence which is the lifeblood of all true art'.[57] Clearly, if Bowra was going to copy George's methods, such emulation would be undertaken on his own terms. A Bowra circle would resemble the George Circle in what it hoped to achieve, but otherwise there would be a distinct and separate flavour, enshrined in more humour and much less self-importance.

These criticisms were genuinely felt, but they should not be given undue weight. Bowra admired George and his methods. He saw in the Master someone who knew that the poet had 'to become a seer and a teacher'.[58] His was 'the voice of deliverance to a barren age'.[59] If his words were not immediately accessible, this was because they were said and written 'for friends in a narrow circle. The outer world has no claim to criticize it or even understand it.'[60] Like Blok, George was 'a mystic, a seer'.[61] Like the Greeks, he knew that 'in an enhanced life of the spirit lay the salvation of mankind'.[62] Like Bowra, George believed that 'Ein Volk ist tot wenn seine götter tot sind.' [A people is dead when its gods are dead.] With all his faults George embodied the synthesis between the Greek view of the poet as prophet and contemporary equivalents. These were precisely Bowra's preoccupations, too, and his freedom from strict Englishness allowed him the freedom to explore the views of strange Europeans who made poets gods. Bowra had more attack in his personality than they, more humour and more common sense, but he saw their point. He always knew in any battle who his allies were.

He also knew his enemies. First there were bureaucrats and politicians, who, consumed with self-importance, reduced the possibilities of life to agendas and programmes. The committee was their only community. Having little or no creative abilities themselves, they tried to censor talent in others. In 1959, Maurice joined others in signing a letter protesting against the prosecution of the novel *Lolita*. The letter baldly stated that 'Prosecutions of genuine works of literature bring governments into disrepute and do nothing to encourage public morality.'[63] He signed similar protests against the harassment of writers in Russia.[64] At the request of Desmond McCarthy, he became a vice president of PEN, but does not seem to have been overactive in its proceedings.[65] Public interventions of this kind did not come easily to Bowra. For him, to touch politics was to touch pitch. For the artist to become a politician or committee man was to endanger the soul.

The point is explicitly set out in a lecture of 1966 entitled *Poetry and Politics*. A poet in politics ran a real risk of making himself ridiculous:

> all his attempts to make events part of himself must be to some extent hampered by recalcitrant elements in them, which he does not understand or finds irrelevant to his creative task... On one side he may try to include too much and lose himself in issues where he is not imaginatively at home; on the other side he may see some huge event merely from a private angle which need not mean much to others.[66]

Protégés like Hugh Gaitskell, who decided on a career in public life, were a disappointment. Engagement with the worlds of the politician and the bureaucrat was only admissible in so far as it was necessary to facilitate the production of work by creative writers. The noise of politics 'impinges on the serene silence of his contemplation and their vulgar emotions spoil the delicate concentration of his vision'.[67] Patriotic politics represented the worst temptation for poets. In Bowra's opinion, there was 'not a word of truth' in 'Land of Hope and Glory'.[68]

Then there were the logicians, the dry-as-dust men, who wanted words only to have sequential meaning rather than colour or the power to arouse. The ghost of Joseph always loomed over Bowra's shoulder. When John Sparrow first published a work on poetry, in 1933, Maurice denounced his friend for following Joseph too much and his poetic instincts too little. He was too much the logician:

> Here I think the Joseph parallel is real. Think of him about morals. He may be acute or even serious, but has he really ever felt the importance of a single moral conflict? Have you ever really wondered whether after all Virgil has his faults and Auden his virtues? I don't mean wondered in the Josephan sense of sitting dumbly before the problem and answering it at the end as you did before, but making a painful effort of the imagination to see how far you may be wrong, and after all you may well be...Remember that no poet thinks as carefully as you do and that many great men have worked on theories which are logically untenable. There are many theories of poetry and most are wrong, but their interest is that they have been believed and therefore have had results.[69]

If Sparrow insisted on being a lawyer, no doubt Joseph's teaching in logic would prove helpful, but he had no right to import such ways of thinking into poetry. As Maurice put it, 'Personally the intellectual content of poetry means very little to me. I am content to be excited and can do without being informed. I feel there is an abstract universal [in poetry] which can be isolated theoretically from information, even if it can never be divorced from information in practice.'[70]

In the forces of Midian, arranged alongside the regiments of politicians, bureaucrats, and logicians were the legions of science. There were men who seemed to think that man could be redeemed by machines, who thought that spiritual fulfilment lay only in being warm, well fed, and healthy. In fact 'any civilization worthy of the name is much more than a technical application of scientific discourses and is of no importance unless it brings enrichment to our inner lives.'[71] Once, in the Victorian world, scientist and writer had shared a sense of mystery and awe. Now, in the twentieth century, the two were moving further and further towards positions of mutual antagonism. In 1959, Bowra told a lecture audience that

> the scientific and imaginative approaches to experience, which were even in the nineteenth century closely related, are growing more and more separate. This is partly due to a recognition that their functions are obviously different, but it has been aided and accelerated by the conviction that each must go its own way without paying attention to the other.[72]

Any writer who embraced science died to his artistic calling. Maupassant, Zola, Wells, Bennett, and Shaw had no merit in Bowra's eyes. It was one of his most serious jokes that scientists would eventually destroy his Oxford.[73]

It could be no consolation to Maurice therefore that the bureaucrat, the politician, and the scientist were becoming ever more powerful in his lifetime. There were more and more of them. They claimed the direction of more and more aspects of life. Together they represented the Establishment that regarded Bowra as a rebel and a subversive. They had been taught in English schools that had always discounted the world of the imagination. Their philistinism had official sanction therefore. As a result their taste was suspect and their range narrow. Could there be any comfort in the knowledge that the best-sellers of the interwar years were written by Dornford Yates, Sapper, and Edgar Wallace? As these people gained in status and power, the creative poet would be pushed to the margins. The prevailing mood 'cuts them off from many other men, leaving them in an isolation that might prove their undoing'.[74] They could literally become extinct. The Muses had covered their faces with veils before. Bowra's embattled view of life was therefore provoked by the belief that the enemy was formidable.

Worst of all, there was a fifth column within the world of literature itself. Too many poets seemed only too willing to abandon the role of the disinterested seer in favour of various forms of selfishness. The Futurists, for example, argued for the destruction of everything old and the worship of everything new, finding in machines a beauty of compelling quality. To break established rules for the sake of breaking rules was, according to Bowra, nothing but 'cocksure impudence'.[75] Writing a furious attack on Marinetti and his *Technical Manifesto*, in 1945, he denounced it as merely destructive. Marinetti himself produced no work of consequence. Poets of vision should recognize and venerate those who had been possessed of this gift in the past.[76] To reject nearly all that had gone before was childishly wilful. Guillaume Apollinaire signed up to Marinetti's *Manifesto*, but, for Bowra, he was worthy of consideration because 'he usually writes in the classical tradition of French verse'.[77] Bowra saw nothing wrong with alexandrines. If poetry 'breaks too violently with the past', it runs a real risk of harming itself, and he believed that 'something of this kind has happened in our own time'.[78]

Instead of destruction, there should be real respect for period and context. When translating poetry, an occupation to which he devoted much time, care was to be taken on both these fronts. He insisted to Stephen Spender that a translation should exactly follow the metre of the original, and that the words chosen should reflect the cultural assumptions of the period in which the poem was written.[79] In other words there should be a humility in dealing with the poetry of the past. For this reason, he was totally dismissive of Ezra Pound's attempts to translate Greek masterpieces. His 'colloquial language bears no resemblance to the artificial, poetical language of Sophocles', the varying rhythms in the lines had no Greek equivalents, and too many twentieth-century preoccupations were introduced into contexts where they had no place. It may have been good poetry in its own right, but it was not a translation. Bowra was 'too little acquainted with the colloquial American in which it is written to be able to judge its aesthetic merits'.[80]

Rebellion for rebellion's sake was merely one of the traps that led poets to prefer self-indulgence to the retailing of vision. Sadly, T. S. Eliot's talent was nearly swamped by immersion in religion. Bowra only came fully to appreciate his work when it became obvious that Eliot's verse was larger than his religious interests. As he told Cyril Connolly,

> Eliot hit me very hard, but I resisted it, because I could not quite believe that everything was so drab as he said, and I resisted the Christian part. But I now see that he was on the whole right, and that the Christian part is in fact hardly Christian at all, but really a plan for the inner life.[81]

Eliot survived in Bowra's estimation because he raised poetry above the recitation of creeds and the enforcement of ten commandments.

There could be no such reprieve for W. H. Auden. In Maurice's view, Auden was so obsessed with his own psychological state that he had nothing to say to the world at large. There was no vision here. Rather everything was earthy.

> Wystan's taste is too odd. He used to be a great Rilke-fan, and his present line is partly that of a lost love. He really likes rather second-rate authors,

and he has never had any taste or interest in high accomplishment. If he had had, his own work would have fewer ups and downs. He is enormously an *impure* poet.[82]

Maurice disapproved of Auden's election to the Chair of Poetry in Oxford, and attacking him became a standard theme in his correspondence with Edith Sitwell. Neither could understand why Cyril Connolly did so much to promote Auden's career: 'The effort to reinstate Mr Auden goes on. The Chevalier Connolly, as he now is, has declared that my dislike of Auden's verse is due to personal reasons, and that anyhow I am no judge. We are, it seems, to swallow the whole thing and call it genius.'[83] Auden, in fact, was clearly going 'to be a great nuisance in the future'.[84] He would teach the young that poetry was only about rumpled bedclothes. The poet-prophet had become ordinary.

Alongside poets, who had forsaken their mission, stood literary critics who refused to show them better ways. When Maurice called to mind that F. R. Leavis and Edmund Wilson were among the most respected critics of his generation, he could only expostulate, 'really, the age we live in'.[85] Leavis turned literature into dust. The joy of it was drained away, leaving only quasi-religious sermonizing. Predictably, he praised novelists who dealt in grime and disease. Dickens was one of his gods, but even then he felt happier talking about *Hard Times* than *The Pickwick Papers*. He was puritan in temperament and an enemy of life. In 1964, Maurice heard Leavis lecturing on Dickens, and reported his views to Dadie Rylands.

He had nothing to say, but the whole mystery was revealed. He is what our mothers would have called CHAPEL. The low, mousey voice, trailing into inaudibility at the end of each sentence, so suitable for the ministration of the Lord's supper; the quotations from scripture in the form of Lawrence and James; the moral themes, *Little Dorrit* above all *good*, Dickens stands for life (eternal no doubt), to deny it is *sin* ... above all the sense that if you sign with him on the dotted line, you are saved ... I can now understand why our miserable undergraduates brought up in Little Bethels and Mount Zions and Bethesdas feel at home with him as with nobody else, especially as his Salvation means a great deal less work than the ordinary methods of studying the subject.[86]

It was intolerable that such a man should be considered for the Poetry Chair at more than one election. His message was 'Methodism', suitable only for 'a Bank of Saints'. He was the most 'ghastly' of the 'new English know-alls'.[87] What he argued was 'meandering gabble'. His lectures were a debased form of theatre, using the tactics of the populist preacher. In one lecture, he 'took off most of his clothes to show how deeply he felt'.[88] Young people listening to his gimcrack views ran the risk of being locked up in a kind of nonconformist morality. Literature, which should be a great agency of liberation, would instead become a kind of prison, where Leavis would establish the rules. There was no vision here, only earthiness and morality.

Unfortunately, Edmund Wilson was just as bad. Here was a bitter, small-minded man who hated the English and their literature, because, Bowra joked, he had once gone with an English prostitute and caught 'a disgusting disease … The logic is a little obscure but the facts are beyond dispute.'[89] He knew nothing of the origins of poetry in the ancient world. He wrote as though he wanted to take revenge on a literary world that had never given him the respect he deserved. In short, he was 'a sour, shabby little man who thinks that nobody loves him. On this, if nothing else, he is right.'[90] Under his direction, young people would learn cynicism, not pleasure. He and Leavis had to be fought, and 'never allowed to rest in peace'. The preferred technique to counteract their influence would be 'continual prodding with a poisoned dung-fork'.[91]

In all of Bowra's many campaigns, he never had any doubt about who the enemy were. In the all-important battle to elevate the status and dignity of poetry, his opponents were clearly defined. There were politicians and bureaucrats, whose self-importance led them to ignore literature or try to censor it; there was the self-obsessed poet dissipating his talent in scratching private neuroses or in succumbing to the discipline of religion; there was the puritan and the pedant peddling platitudes from a great height. All these people denied the essentially life-enhancing possibilities of the written word. The list was a long one, but Bowra was never intimidated by numbers or the likelihood of becoming unpopular. This battle was much more than mere academic fisticuffs. Rather, it was part of a mission which grew out of what he called his 'inner self'. It was an energy that charged his whole personality.

Of course Bowra was never alone in his battle. If enemies were numerous, friends were always on hand. They were people who shared his visionary view of poetry. For them Maurice worked tirelessly. Their careers were to be advanced in every way possible. Conceiving of himself as a failed poet, he was yet a conscious impresario of poetry. By writing literary criticism, he promoted Dylan Thomas, Sydney Keyes, and Edith Sitwell. After experiencing academic failure, Betjeman looked to Bowra to save his career. The Bowra archive is full of letters from young poets asking for assistance. Sometimes he offered only constructive criticism and encouragement. Elizabeth Jennings was assured, for example, that her work had 'touched me very deeply', and just at a time when he feared that 'my arteries were hardening into stone'.[92] A young American was buoyed up with sincere praise: 'Too many books of poetry are just haphazard collections but yours is truly a Book, le Livre ... Your range is most remarkable, but you always make each piece a true poem with no bones sticking through.'[93] And sometimes he did more. At Edith Sitwell's request, he bullied Oxford University Press into publishing Quentin Stevenson, an act which was hugely appreciated by his friend. As she put it, 'it will be so useful to the boy to be talked about by Maurice'.[94]

As a patron, Bowra operated in large matters and in points of detail. In retrospect, Day-Lewis, for example, felt deeply grateful to his old tutor for three gifts. First, he was told that it was not silly to wish to be a poet. Tutorials would involve the declaiming of Yeats and Tennyson. Secondly, he was introduced to the important link between the Greeks and the moderns. As Bowra put it, reading the classics gave him 'a furlong's start on the wretched people who have to read English'. Thirdly, he insisted that Day-Lewis should never waste time in reading second-rate authors. Life was too short. 'Big Stuff Bowra', as Maurice was sometimes called, demanded that his pupils should never meddle with the mediocre.[95] Further Day-Lewis was found a job at Cheltenham College, Bowra's old school. When he insisted on selling the *Daily Worker* on Cheltenham's streets, thereby running the risk of summary dismissal, Bowra intervened to save his career. The only price to be paid for such lavish attention, a severe one, was that the pupil should not challenge the master. Maurice Bowra came close to being as sensitive as Stefan George on this point. In 1951, when he retired from the Chair of Poetry, Bowra took the extraordinary step of summoning Day-Lewis to Oxford in order to ask him to withdraw his candidacy to be his successor. When Day-Lewis ignored this request and pursued his campaign to a successful conclusion, Bowra was all sympathy and support, but the episode is instructive.[96]

Someone of Bowra's cosmopolitanism of course took the view that poets outside England needed his help. His sense of mission had an international dimension. In his lifetime, writers in Russia were among the most needy.

It was a language he had first heard as a little boy in Manchuria, and one for which he had a particular affection. He read it with some fluency, spoke it barely at all, and produced translations that were, at one and the same time, praised by Pasternak and denounced by Berlin for the occasional howler.[97] In his view, 'only Greek beats Russian as a language for poetry. Its syntax, stress-accents, liquid consonants, uncorrupted vowels all gave Russian strengths.' Starting with Pushkin, Bowra identified generations of poets who had understood and exemplified the prophetic vision. He and his successors had understood that 'the only reality is that of the spirit, and that the poet is specially gifted to understand it'.[98] Understandably therefore, the persecution of poets in Soviet Russia was of deep concern. As he told Sybil Colefax, 'poor Anna Akhmatova' and 'poor Pasternak' were always at risk: 'The Russians are really *too* bad. They overdo it, and I it [*sic*] is really distressing.'[99]

Never inclined to accept passively what was clearly intolerable, Maurice tried to help. It was at his suggestion that Isaiah Berlin sought out Anna Akhmatova on a visit to Russia, in order to bring her predicament to the attention of the world at large. The two men had already published some of her poems in translation. In 1963, they persuaded Oxford to give her an honorary degree.[100] Similarly, Bowra was instrumental in reminding the world of the existence of Vyacheslav Ivanov, a refugee living in reduced circumstances in Rome. Oxford's University Press was induced to bring out a volume of his poems in translation, and the two men came face to face in Italy in December 1947. Ivanov was hugely grateful for not being forgotten. He expressed his 'very great joy to have won, as poet, so much sympathy, comprehension and help'.[101] In his view, Bowra's translations came near to being poetry in themselves.

> It seems that it is difficult for you not to sing with those who sing, not to share the enthusiasms, even the follies of the poets you have to judge. The language of foreign symbolism is transparent to you, and more familiar to you than it is to their un-initiated countrymen. Your translations of Russian lyric poetry are as precise as they are musical.[102]

To be recognized as one of their own by what Bowra called 'the lost generation'[103] of Russian poets was payment in full for all his efforts. No doubt, these words represented, to some extent, merely polite formulas, but there were very few Englishmen to whom they could have been addressed.

In this context, Bowra's most important relationship was with the Pasternak family. In December 1945, Boris Pasternak opened a correspondence with Maurice in what he called his 'forgotten or never known English ... it will form a good comic-papers-stuff'.[104] Somehow, he had managed to find a copy of *The Heritage of Symbolism* in Russia, and had read it with pleasure: 'When I read in your beautiful Heritage of Symbolism your admirable lines about Rilke and Blok, when afterwards I saw your deep, exact and melodious translations, I dreamed. Would this man (this Bowra) ever hear of me, could I, some day, attract his high attention, and, perhaps, deserve his recognition.'[105] Six months later, as Maurice informed Edith Sitwell, another message was smuggled out of Russia, together with some 'unpublished poems' and a request that they should find a publisher. The documents had reached him 'by a somewhat underground route'.[106]

There followed a friendship between two men who could never meet. For Bowra, Pasternak became a cause, lecturing on his work in Oxford when holding the Chair of Poetry. Pasternak responded by 'saying it had been his life's ambition to be lectured on by Bowra'. Every year, Maurice nominated the Russian for the Nobel Prize for Literature. Quite possibly, the poet's step-daughter was released from prison in 1962 after Bowra brought her predicament to the attention of Yevtushenko on his visit to Oxford.[107] Of course the gruesome and grotesque literary policies in force in Soviet Russia very much limited the help that could be given, but Pasternak's gratitude was heartfelt: 'Handfuls, armfuls, heap of thanks to you. My gratitude to you is enormous ... You have invented me and gave me a renown, you made my life difficult and responsible by your overestimation.' With the completion of *Dr Zhivago*, Pasternak at last believed that he had lived up to Bowra's expectations: 'it seems me to be fit for my acquittal and to justify your exaggerations, I pardon you and turn your reproaches to thankfulness.' Maurice had become his 'dear and more than dear, thrice dear Bowra'.[108]

Pasternak's family lived as refugees in North Oxford. With them there was a steady interchange of dinners, lunches, and civilities. He genuinely enjoyed their company, but the friendship had a deeper purpose. It was almost certainly through the Pasternak family that Bowra came into possession of letters and poems smuggled out of Russia. In 1956 for example, Boris Pasternak warned his patron that 'my sister ... will hand you a dozen of my new verses of this autumn. I know your point of view in *Creative Experiment*, preserve it. Be absolutely free towards these sheets and dispose of them as you please.'[109] Gradually, Bowra became the principal ally of the Pasternak sisters in the delicate task of making their brother's work known in the West in a way that would not expose him to danger within Russia itself. In 1958, he had to bully the BBC into withdrawing a proposal to read extracts of *Dr Zhivago* on their Russian service. Such an idea had driven the Pasternak sisters 'into a fearful state', feeling that such an action would end in their brother going to Siberia. 'Really the mercileness [*sic*] of these institutions makes the blood run cold.'[110] By way of expressing their relief and gratitude, the sisters gave their friend a portrait of 'a great poet', painted by their father, Leonid Pasternak. It would hang in Bowra's library. He 'could not think of anything I would like more'.[111] Poets in trouble had an absolute claim on him.

Much of Maurice's work as impresario, critic, and patron had to be conducted in private. His most public activity in the field of poetry came every five years, when Oxford elected a new Professor of Poetry. To the outside world the process would resemble a pantomime. Oxford Masters of Arts, many of whom had never read a line of verse, returned to the university for a good lunch and the opportunity to pronounce on the reputation of poets. For Bowra, however, it was a matter of great seriousness. The Oxford Chair represented one of the few platforms in English life, from which the cause of good poetry could be pleaded. It was just possible that some spiritually starved undergraduate might hear something to his or her advantage. As a result, Bowra entered every election with vigour. It was, he thought, his 'job ... to help to find a man to whom the undergraduates will listen'.[112] He cared deeply about winning these particular battles.

His opponent in these elections was often Enid Starkie, the respected biographer of Rimbaud and others. An eccentric figure, she would parade through Oxford's streets in a costume resembling that of a French sailor. This led Bowra to describe her as wearing 'all the colours of the Rimbaud', but he respected both her scholarship and her attachment to Oxford's values. She wrote, he believed, 'in an imaginative way, not with that awful German heaviness which weighs on us all'.[113] They dined with each other from time to time, and, at the memorial service held for her after her death, Maurice paid her the ultimate compliment with regard to Oxford, that 'she had kept the faith'.[114]

But there were moments of tension in their friendship as well. As has been noted, Maurice entertained a suspicion that she had played a minor role in his failure to secure the Greek Chair in 1936. Worse, she could not resist, in his view, the temptation to turn the search for a Professor of Poetry into a game. Her Irish temperament simply overcame judgement. In 1951, for example, she was prominent in the contest between Day-Lewis and C. S. Lewis, although cheerfully confessing that she had never read a word of either candidate.[115] For Maurice this was a kind of academic treason. As he put it,

> The more than active interest which she displayed in elections for the Chair of Poetry was in the first place dictated by her belief in its civilizing importance for Oxford, but an Irish zest for politics ran away with her and her campaigns degenerated, as she herself admitted, into 'great fun'. They turned the elections into popular sporting events, and this was not what she intended.[116]

In the circumstances, these words represented quite a reprimand.

It was therefore a matter of considerable pride for Bowra that he himself should have been elected to the Chair, unopposed, in February 1946. The *Oxford Magazine* welcomed his success. He could, it asserted, 'criticize poetry in every language from Greek to Russian, and is as much at home with Rilke and Aragon as he is with Virgil and Milton'. The *Magazine* specifically wanted the new Professor to tell Oxford which of the 'moderns' were worth reading, how they related, if at all, to contemporary writers around the world, and to describe the direction that twentieth-century poetry had followed and should follow. Maurice was to pronounce, literally *ex cathedra*. He was Oxford's 'Dr Johnson'.[117] In this respect, the inaugural lecture worked well. Edith Sitwell was all praising:

> This Inaugural Lecture is a most exciting work. I hope you will not mind my saying that it is an amazing thing to me how the whole *vitality* of the history of poetry during the last eighty years or even more, I suppose a hundred years, could have seethed into this space. The lecture seems to me to clear away every mist.[118]

Thereafter, the elections did not always go so well. Bowra lost as often as he won. Robert Graves was 'a complete disaster', as Bowra had anticipated, because he was incorrigibly 'dotty'. He would insist on talking about 'goat-footed bards, Laura Riding ("all passions and bandages" as W. B. Yeats said of her) and himself. I fear he will deprave the young men even more than their present mentors do.'[119] At the end of 1955, the shadow of W. H. Auden was falling over the Chair. Inevitably, his candidature was 'being run by Enid'. Bowra was appalled. Auden was 'never a scholar or a critic and no longer a poet. I don't think Eliot or Betjeman would be any good at all. Eliot is too silly and Betjeman too mad. I want Helen Gardner, learned, excellent writer and lecturer, very presentable.'[120] To an American friend, Maurice described Auden as 'no friend of mine. Bad lecturer, bad scholar, bad man, drunk and dirty. He should get in.'[121] The man was full of 'slapdash, superficial judgments', 'sham psychology', and suffered from an unwillingness to take trouble.[122] In the event, Auden proved to be a successful and popular lecturer. Bowra was forced to rapidly revise his views and to give him a dinner at Wadham. To Maurice's surprise and delight, Auden proved 'quite excellent with undergraduates and talked to them as an equal'.[123] Even so, he had not voted for him.

Worse was to come. In 1966, Edmund Blunden defeated Robert Lowell for the Chair, a decision which seemed to Bowra to expose Oxford at its most philistine. It was simply 'painful'. Once again Miss Starkie was up to her old tricks, and there was the sinking feeling that 'you cant keep a second rate man down. The girls voted solidly for him, no doubt for his sex-appeal to which several divorces testify.'[124] The result had 'depressed' him. The campaign had degenerated to 'the level of the boat race'. Oxford electors had no feeling for poetry. They preferred 'Georgian slop, meadows, and cricket and smooth, easy lines. He [sic] young men were largely on our side, but they are not considered.'[125] Oxford had no feeling for poetry or its importance. The only consolation was that it could have been worse. At one point, Yevgeny Yevtushenko was being considered for the post, a man whom Bowra regarded as a fraud and little better than a collaborator with the Russian regime that persecuted his friends.[126] All too often, in Maurice's view, Oxford turned something of great seriousness into a game. It was perhaps the only way it could cope with having a responsibility towards poetry while knowing nothing about it. Sadly, the result was that the voice of the poet went unheard and his claims could more easily be sidelined.

Maurice never succeeded in turning elections to the Chair of Poetry from a campus frolic into something more serious. This fact spoke volumes for the way the English received literature. It had helped to form his view that poetry was dying with his generation. In one of his last lectures on the subject, he told his audience that the prophets and the seers had been killed off by science and an all-pervasive materialism: 'The decline of the prophetic attitude has meant a withdrawal from the wider horizons of the imagination, and in this we may see a diminution of power and grandeur.'[127] It seemed all too possible that democracies did indeed prefer the mechanical and the material to anything that the poet could give them. The same lecture, admittedly, ends with some lamely optimistic words: 'What counts is that life continues, for good or ill...and this is what concerns us...The old distances have receded out of sight, and we must look at the present moment and refuse to be dispirited by its menaces.'[128] He offered his audience the image of the poet and democrat advancing towards each other, arms outstretched in welcome.

Almost certainly, he privately believed not one word of this. Poetry and its claims had been one of the most dynamic forces in his life. To promote the poets of Greece and the Symbolist movement across Europe in his own writings had been a mission to be pursued with evangelical fervour. Some good had been done. Careers had been saved and persecution mitigated. European writers appeared in Oxford to receive honorary degrees. But nothing could hide the fact that what meant so much to him meant little or nothing to the vast majority of his countrymen. The English, seemingly, had no ear for the music and rhythms that had shaped his own 'inner life' since the Great War.

6

Sex and Sexuality

The promotion of Greek civilization and the defence of poetry were the two most dynamic aspects of Bowra's personality. They gave him a sense of purpose and presented targets, at which his formidable energy could be directed. On these issues, everything was positive and attacking. Yet they were balanced throughout his life by another theme that engendered only caution and negative responses, namely his sexuality. Bowra rarely talked about it, and he was never comfortable with any aspect of the subject. He regarded his sexuality as something that made him vulnerable. All the armour of wit and learning, so carefully pieced together at Cheltenham and New College, was no protection against assaults from this quarter. On this matter, he was open to ridicule or worse. As a result, he chose to suppress and hide his feelings, redirecting them into the production of scabrous verse. He quickly learnt that it was easier and safer to ridicule oneself before others had the chance to do so.

This was so hidden a subject that even his closest friends could not agree about where his sexual preferences actually took him. Some thought him exclusively homosexual; others believed him to be bisexual. No one really knew whether he had ever expressed love in a physical sense, whether his proposals of marriage were to be taken at all seriously, or whether he had made such offers to one woman or to five. Friends found it easier not to dwell on the topic. Maurice was to be loved and admired as a rather asexual character who stood outside these matters, mocking and caring for the relationships of others. To worry too much about Maurice's sexuality was somehow to miss the point. He was to be considered as sage, jester, or ringmaster, but not as lover.

On one point friends did agree. Maurice was always troubled by his lack of physical stature and by his appearance in general. Early in life, he seems to have come near to convincing himself that no one could possibly find him physically attractive. Well below average height, he suffered sallies on this point that really stung. While undergoing officer training in 1917, riding lessons would be punctuated by sergeants shouting, 'Come on, Shorty, hang on, hang on.'[1] When the taller-than-average Guy Chilver complained that a new bed might prove too short for him, Maurice answered only, 'Go on, rub it in.'[2] While giving evidence in a magistrates' court, he was asked to stand up to answer questions. Bowra sulkily informed the court that he already was standing up.[3] The episode left him looking 'Napoleonic and angry'.[4] In private, some undergraduates cheekily referred to him as 'Little Maurice'.[5]

A lack of inches was not the only problem. Even as a young man he was acutely aware that the absence of a well-defined neck meant that a square head sat on top of a compact, rectangular body that rounded with age. Some thought that his legs were too short to carry such responsibility. Everything about the physique was muscular and solid, but there was always the danger of ridicule. The wife of a Warden of Keble thought that he resembled Humpty Dumpty.[6] In a game of charades, Maurice once incautiously appeared as Queen Victoria, and, to one witness, 'it was a giveaway, because that was what he was really like'.[7] According to Stuart Hampshire, Bowra thought of himself as 'Ba Ba Black Sheep',[8] an oddity.

Almost certainly, this self perception set limits to his emotional development. To quote Hampshire once again, Bowra 'was a sort of joke figure. He thought he was anyway. I think that affected his sexuality and his emotional life a lot. He was very nervous about anything to do with—he was frightened of women.' If he went off in a homosexual direction, it was merely 'a turning away' from what he regarded as the inevitable rejection by women.[9] According to Hampshire, Maurice may have been homosexual by instinct, but he was certainly homosexual by circumstance. Lady Annan agreed. For Maurice there 'was no chance of intimacy', and this was an almost intolerable situation for someone who was naturally 'loving' and 'all spontaneity'.[10] Ann Fleming told Evelyn Waugh that, emotionally, Maurice was 'an island'.[11] Many friends could, to some extent, fill the vacuum, but, in sum, they were not a sufficiency.

In the 1920s and 1930s, Bowra tried to express love but was defeated on every occasion. These experiences scarred him. Affection meant humiliation in the end. So sure did he become of this that he acquired the habit of precipitating the outcome. As he confessed to Noel Annan, 'I create rebuffs before I am rebuffed.'[12] In his view, he had no right or expectation of ever being the most important person in someone else's life. What he could hope for was a shared affection, and as a poem of 1928 makes clear, he would be grateful for that:

> I honour you because you mock at ease
> And walk the world with such a conquering air,
> Deserving better company than these
> Poor fanatics who track you everywhere.
>
> Thinking this rare possession is all his own,
> Each suddenly is drunk and stupefied
> To find a crowd, who thought himself alone,
> Sharing his triumph and his secret pride.
>
> Yet such enchantment does your beauty hold
> That none at such discovering loses heart.
> Each knows his secret ecstasy untold,
> Unreckonably private and apart.
>
> Nothing diminishes the gift you make:
> Endless division cannot make it small.
> A multitude may share, but cannot take
> From each the glory of possessing all.
>
> Giving yourself so carelessly you give
> Confidence to the broken and the cowed,
> Teaching the unconsidered how to live,
> The garrulous to be serene and proud.[13]

Expecting affection only in small doses left Bowra much moved by acts of unexpected kindness.

A belief that the offer of affection would always end in rebuff and embarrassment meant that Bowra was not an easy man to know well. Verbal ambuscades and entanglements kept people at bay. Early in their friendship, John Sparrow came up against these defences and found them daunting.

> The more, and the more intimately I get to know Maurice, the more I like him; I do not think it would be possible to like anyone more, and I am more dependent on him and influenced by him than I have ever been by anyone ... I wish I did not feel that his perpetual dislike/distrust/fear of affection leads him to despise it when he knows it to be genuine. But perhaps I am misled by appearances.[14]

For Bowra, to be surrounded with friends was both totally necessary and potentially threatening. He once admitted to real fear after reading a short story by May Sinclair called *Where the Fire is not Quenched*. Based on a verse in St Mark's Gospel, the story tells of a woman who finds initial exhilaration in an adulterous *affaire*, which then turns into habit and boredom. The lovers both die and are condemned to spend eternity in each other's company.[15] When people came too close, their presence became quite literally hellish. In these circumstances, sexual encounters of an anonymous and transitory character might almost be preferable.

Quite possibly, therefore, Stuart Hampshire and others might be right in thinking that Maurice's dealings with the homosexual world before 1939 were dictated by a reluctance to consider alternatives that he believed could only end in humiliation or boredom. Certainly, these dealings were real and of importance. In convivial moments, he would proudly proclaim to his disciples his membership of, or even his leadership of, what he called 'The Immoral Front', 'the 69th International', or 'the Homintern'. As Noel Annan bluntly put it, 'Let's get it clear, he was the centre of the great homosexual Mafia if you like to call it, of the twenties and thirties.'[16] In these years, homosexual behaviour, real or affected, was almost the fashion in certain literary and intellectual circles. Rejecting the moral rigidities of the Victorians had a purpose of its own. Most of the men involved went on to more or less successful marriages, but, for a time, they experimented with alternative lifestyles. The 'Homintern' therefore was a club which had both permanent members and many others who renewed their subscription from time to time. In this small, necessarily secretive world, Maurice was an acknowledged luminary.

It was not always a comfortable position to hold. The disgrace of Oscar Wilde was still very much a living memory. Allegedly, Bowra had once met Lord Alfred Douglas and had found him thoroughly disagreeable.[17] Great fun could be extracted from John Sparrow's being 'very up on the whole thing, and will soon have autograph letters from Charlie Parker, bits of sheet from the Savoy, and unpublished sonnets of Robbie Ross',[18] but the fact remained that homosexual activity of any kind constituted a criminal offence. In Bowra's lifetime, Earl Beauchamp, Lord Montagu, John Gielgud, Alec Guinness, and many others fell foul of the law, and discovered that the penalty was a fine, imprisonment, or exile in France. Homosexuals who were too indiscreet or unlucky would be happy, in Bowra's view, only 'till the inevitable crash' came.[19] In addition, beside the lawyer who pronounced homosexual behaviour illegal stood the clergyman who called it immoral and the doctor who equated it with mental instability. Of course the Greeks had taken a different view, but they could hardly be quoted in a twentieth-century court. In this aspect of his life, Maurice had to learn caution.

Equally importantly, the homosexual world of the interwar years was not of one mind or character. Groups within it suspected and disliked each other, as much as the outside world disliked and suspected them. In 1926, Frances Partridge was sharing a house with Ralph Partridge and Lytton Strachey. For one weekend, Dadie Rylands brought Bowra over from Oxford as a guest. As the men talked, she noticed that they were 'so fussy about how they were described. Some preferred to be called "queer", which seemed to me very nasty.'[20] In this respect, Maurice was completely 'masculine in manner and appearance',[21] so much so that A. L. Rowse concluded that he was bisexual.[22] Maurice admired people like Lord Boothby, who had a robust and amused approach to the whole question. He found Boothby 'dashing', and turned him into something of 'a hero'.[23] In the same vein, he described one of his greatest friends, and possible lover, Ernst Kantorowicz, as 'one of the best men in the world, with no element of shame in him, a real *Mensch* in our sense of the word'.[24]

Such men could turn the worries and complexities of the sexual situation into the most enjoyable talk. They perfected witty gossip that shocked the puritan and penetrated all but the thickest skins. Bowra, too, liked to shock. In his view, it improved the circulation of an Englishman's blood. It was one of Cyril Connolly's more endearing qualities that he was so ready to share accounts of his escapades on Dartmoor or on the Embankment in London.[25] In the same spirit of openness, Maurice would enjoy teasing friends with the assertion that homosexuality was in fact 'the natural' state of things for anyone with a claim to intelligence.[26] In a sense, these men turned homosexual inclinations into a kind of game, with rules of its own. How often that game was actually played can only be a matter of conjecture, but they talked about it often.

Predictably therefore, Bowra detested the camp and effeminate. He loathed being called a 'carefree bachelor', because it suggested someone of exclusively homosexual inclinations.[27] What he characterized as the self-obsession of feminized men appalled him. One such visitor was dismissed as follows: 'Not a very nice man, nor very interesting. The real homosexual, vain as a woman. Touchy and suspicious. He talked tiresomely of his lovers—how dull and silly other people's lovers seem, and how numerous. I hope he won't come again as he depressed me a good deal. He seems to have no other interests.'[28] Such people were so consumed with their own predicament that they never achieved anything worthwhile, dissipating talents to right and left. It was even worse when 'normally-sexed' people like Goronwy Rees occasionally played 'the pansy', in order to bemuse and bewilder their friends.[29]

Bowra avoided such people as though they carried the plague. In the Oxford of the 1920s, he avoided men like Harold Acton and Brian Howard, who led the aesthetes against the hearties. Walking around the University wearing facial make-up and green bowler hats was absurd. They made 'a great deal of fuss' about the smallest details of their private lives.[30] Worst of all, they were talented people who produced nothing of consequence. Evelyn Waugh's association with this world meant that he only came to know Bowra after the publication of his first novel. As a statement of faith, Maurice dismissed the literary god of the aesthetes, Ronald Firbank, as 'too pansy'.[31] It was an aversion that remained with him throughout his life. In 1940, as an act of charity, he took in Lord Berners as a refugee, but the arrangement only lasted six months. Maurice found the man spectacularly 'useless' in a time of war. To his dismay, his guest went on trying to throw parties 'in a slightly Decameron sort of way'.[32] Some time later, Bowra occasionally found himself in the company of Guy Burgess, whom he simply found unclean. There were unpleasant things under his fingernails.[33]

Nor should membership of the Homintern compromise scholarship. Nothing made Bowra angrier than what he perceived as the homosexuals' ambition to claim every historical figure of note as one of their own. He took great delight on correcting a man who had been taken in by a story, maliciously circulated by Somerset Maugham, to the effect that Hugh Walpole had once slept with Henry James. Since Bowra admired James profoundly, he rode to his defence with a will.

> In about 1949 I met Maugham at Amalfi, and he spoke disparagingly of the Master [James] because of his lack of sex-life. Not a word about Walpole, who had been dead for years … The Master liked young people of both sexes, and was often fascinated by them, eg Rupert Brooke, who did a great public school act for him. But I don't believe that was ever on the bed. It is a relief not to have to accept anything so absurd.[34]

Trying to give homosexuality a certain respectability, by retrospectively claiming men like James as member of the clan, was inexcusable. It was an introverted and defeatist tactic used by men who defined themselves too narrowly by their sexual orientation. Bowra preferred to mix with people who never allowed such considerations to undermine their talents, and who based their whole life on hard fact rather than comfortable fantasy.

Unfortunately, Maurice could not always live up to his own pretensions. He lacked the devil-may-care attitude of a Boothby, who slept with the wife of a Tory prime minister and leaders of the London underworld, while daring the public to comment or act. Maurice was always more cautious. He worried that academic enemies like Hugh Last and Sandy Lindsay were 'sneering at him' for conducting an irregular private life. It was rumoured that Lindsay refused to send Balliol men to Bowra for tuition on the ground that he was 'an evil man' whose influence on the young was malign.[35] Such attitudes confirmed a suspicion in Maurice that, even within Oxford, his sexuality made him 'an outsider figure'.[36] He feared that the prospects of promotion within his profession were being put at risk by innuendo.

Certainly, there were moment of crisis. At a party in the late 1930s, a working-class undergraduate from Glasgow convinced himself that Bowra had propositioned him, and was barely reassured when friends suggested that he had merely misread Oxford's codes.[37] Similarly, just before the Second World War, the arrest of a German friend sent Maurice into a panic. For some reason, he believed that this event might lead to his own prosecution, in which case he would, as he confided to Isaiah Berlin, contemplate suicide.[38] In fact Berlin himself asserted that 'Maurice did not corrupt any young man, as far as I know.'[39] The ice was sometimes a little thin, but the ice held. Indeed, there was even a measure of surreptitious humour in the situation. As a Christ Church man recorded in his diary, on 2 May 1939, 'I rushed to Blackwells for warmth. There I found Hugh Trevor-Roper, Shiah [Berlin] and Maurice. We raged on about Maurice's recent mishaps having to turn round anxiously every minute to know if we were being overheard. It was all splendidly parochial and Trollope-like.'[40] Even so, the nerves had been severely tested. Two years later, Bowra made a point of warning John Sparrow against a too-liberal enjoyment of the opportunities presented by army life.[41]

Worries of this kind imposed a quite uncharacteristic reticence on his behaviour. Fearless in the defence of academic and artistic values, he hid from public view when homosexuality was the topic of debate. Of course he favoured the abolition of oppressive law. As he observed to Sparrow, 'I can't really see why "you know what" should continue to be outlawed etc.

There were, as you say, times and places when it was OK enough, and these might recur to the benefit of many.'[42] He also followed the campaign for a change in the law with interest. Noel Annan, who had just benefited from what he called 'the Life Peer racket', reported the strange fantasies of those resisting liberalization: 'What a curious world Maxwell-Fyffe and Goddard inhabit? How many do we know who have been corrupted by buggers' clubs? I thought the young went to them because they already enjoyed, or were longing to enjoy those particular delights of the flesh.'[43] Even so, apart from signing round robin letters to newspapers on the subject, Maurice remained silent, and that must have been a sadness for a man who spoke out on everything else. Sadder still was a decision to decline Leonard Woolf's invitation to write an introduction to a volume of Cavafy's poetry. Shamefacedly, Maurice pleaded that a Warden of Wadham could not be associated with such sexually explicit material. His pupil, Rex Warner, took his place.[44]

Saddest of all, because it constitutes one of the few examples of cowardice in Bowra's life, was his refusal to associate in any way with André Gide. In 1947, Enid Starkie put Gide up for an honorary degree, reasonably claiming that he was one of the greatest living writers in French. Maurice refused all assistance. Gide's homosexual activities were well known across Europe and North Africa, and as a result 'the degree would be refused on moral grounds'.[45] When, to his surprise, the degree was granted, Bowra refused to act as host for any part of the proceedings. According to Enid Starkie, he even stayed away from the Degree Ceremony itself, and she found it hard to account for such behaviour: 'I do not understand what has been actuating Bowra... Maybe it was caution. Yet he has nothing now to fear or lose in Oxford.'[46] This became the standard account. John Sparrow told Hugh Trevor-Roper that Bowra had been 'at pains to be out of Oxford for the occasion, fearing that a display of cordiality towards that questionable character might damage his reputation'.[47] In fact, although refusing to walk in the official procession, Bowra had slipped into the Sheldonian to watch the ceremony from among the crowd of onlookers. According to Rosamond Lehmann, he had found Gide 'a noble-looking old-boy'.[48] Compliments apart, his behaviour had hardly been glorious. Gide was apparently left wandering around Oxford asking, 'Who is this Maurice Bowra that everybody asks me have I met?'[49]

Maurice's reaction to the Gide visit had been so extreme and so odd that friends were led to speculate about what could possibly have caused it. They simply could not 'fathom M's behaviour over it all'.[50] Rex Warner thought that his old tutor blamed Gide for having had a disastrous influence on his great friend, Adrian Bishop. Rosamond Lehmann wanted someone to have 'a show-down' with Maurice. She admitted that Oxford was 'always full of spying eyes and ears', but was inclined to put the incident down to 'jealousy'. Perhaps Gide had somehow managed to 'snub' Bowra; 'if G ever showed lack of appreciation of M's importance. That would be enough to account for it.'[51] Enid Starkie came up with the preposterous idea that Bowra was anxious not to offend the Soviet Union, whose government had just denounced the Frenchman.[52] It was simply baffling that a man who took such pride in his European contacts should weave and dodge in this way.

The real answer was basically quite simple. Publicly to raise questions about his sexuality was one way, possibly the only way, of occasionally reducing Bowra to silence. Using this tactic, an opponent could defeat him. Such considerations imposed caution on an otherwise ebullient personality. His was a generation for whom homosexuality was a matter of hidden codes and secret meetings. An open expression of it was simply impossible for someone, who wished to be taken seriously as the promoter of other causes. To be forward in some campaigns, he had no choice but to be reticent in this one. The sadly compromising response to the Gide visit was the sort of penalty that had to be paid.

Bowra's own emotional life was hesitant, uncertain, and even muddled. It involved advances to both men and women, all of which were unsuccessful. No one friend seems to have been privy to all its details or aware of its variegated nature. The only point on which they agree was that his models in homosexual behaviour were to be found in Cambridge. In King's College, John Sheppard and Dadie Rylands, among others, were at the centre of homosexual circles, with which Maurice seems to have come into contact in the early 1920s. Parodying a popular song, Bowra described the situation of many King's men as being that of 'Yes, sir, that's my Dadie. I'm your Dadie now.' In fact Rylands became a friend for life. Visits were conducted on a regular basis, and the intervals between meetings were filled with a correspondence that bristled with Oxbridge gossip.[53] There was real affection as well. Two years before his death, Bowra received a letter from Rylands which simply said, 'This is really a farewell in case I am stabbed during the Rio carnival, and to say I love you very much, and shall be for ever and ever grateful for all you have done to educate me.'[54]

Among the protégés of Ryland's was a certain Adrian Bishop,[55] who, according to *Memories*, first crossed Maurice's path in 1921. The book is silent on the enormous impact Bishop would have on his new friend. From the beginning, Bishop was one of the very few people in whose company Maurice was listening rather than talking. As Bowra put it, 'He was used to dominating any group in which he mixed, and in this, as in other ways, he resembled Oscar Wilde, who came from the same layer of Dublin society.'[56] The reference to Wilde was not chosen at random. Bishop and Wilde not only shared the same physique and sexual tastes, but they also shared patterns of speech. Bishop's humour, like Wilde's, was epigrammatic, often relying on simple word inversion or punning to achieve its effect. This style, according to Steven Runciman, he handed on to Bowra, giving his diction a faint echo of the 1890s.[57] Like Wilde, too, Bishop would not obey the rules. Usually without employment, he had to leave Ireland in order to avoid prosecution for immoral behaviour. After collapsing with encephalitis on Battersea Bridge, he underwent some sort of epiphany, which led him to become an Anglican Benedictine. Henceforth, he would be referred to as 'Brother Tom'.[58]

But Maurice owed Bishop far more than the turning of linguistic tricks. According to Stuart Hampshire, Bishop was the only close friend who could be called 'bohemian'. By example and 'palpable vitality', he taught that life did not always have to be led within rules that others prescribed. He introduced Maurice to brothels, although the experiment 'wasn't a great success'.[59] As Bowra describes it, travelling in Bishop's company was 'terrific, and I felt like Robbie [Ross] looking after Oscar abroad. You should have seen him standing drinks all round, and as for his bathing dress words fail. We sang a great deal, ate a lot, and had the usual round of fun.'[60] To hear Bowra and Bishop talking at the same time 'would be rather like, not like the Marx Brothers exactly, because it wasn't wise-cracking, but competitive play upon words of a really intoxicating kind … playing tricks with words and with literary allusions'.[61]

To honour the man, whom he acknowledged as a kind of mentor, Maurice wrote the poem, 'Old Croaker'. It describes the louche, Berlin world of the late 1920s that Bishop knew so well: 'Brown shorts, brown necks that encumber the Metro | Sidelong glances down Unter den Linden.' The homosexual bars—the Silhouette, the Bohème and the Cosy

Corner—became the necessary backdrop for Bishop's adventures. He, 'Like Little Jack Horner | Sat in Cosy Corner | Pretending to be pi.' After a night of debauch, his progress home was told in a parody of a famous line by Cardinal Newman: 'Lead, blindly tight, amid the revolving room'. Basically a pastiche of 'The Wasteland', the poem also refers to the work of Milton, Yeats, Coleridge, Rimbaud, Byron, Kipling, Swinburne, Tennyson, Joyce, Shakespeare, Al Jolson, the Bible, Marie Lloyd, and many others. It is a masterpiece of literary humour nestling on the edge of pornography.[62]

Normally, Maurice suspected any man who wasted his talents. Bishop was the only friend who was forgiven over and over again for this and other delinquencies. He was always without funds. Staying in Wadham in 1940, he ran up debts that he had no chance of ever repaying.[63] Even his death was irregular. Having once worked for an oil company, he was moved to the Middle East during the war, almost certainly as some sort of intelligence-gatherer. In June 1942, he reported to Maurice that he swam in 'the shit-coloured Tigris which keeps me semi-sane, and I have a very nice Staff which averts suicide'.[64] But shortly after this letter was written, he fell to his death from the third floor of one of Teheran's smartest hotels. Officially, his demise was attributed to alcoholic over-indulgence, an explanation Maurice angrily refused to believe: 'as if drink ever made the slightest difference to the old man's steadiness of movement.'[65] Instead, he offered the view that Brother Tom had been murdered: 'Poor Adrian. I miss him enormously—all that noise and vitality ... I think he was murdered, as the Axis press announced his death at once with a cock-and-bull story that the Free French had killed him with a bomb.' It was a consolation that Bishop had been very successful as a spy, even if his methods were hardly textbook: 'I am glad the old boy brought it off at the end. One of his strokes of genius was running boys' clubs for Irakis, at which he found out all sorts of things, no doubt by his own special, intimate methods.'[66]

Bishop will always remain a very elusive character. His surviving letters are few, and the exact nature of this friendship will almost certainly never be known. But what is clear is that his influence was profound. He taught Maurice what conversation could be. More importantly, he set an example of how free an uninhibited homosexual could be, if he chose to defy the world and live for long periods outside England. His career also demonstrated the price to be paid for such freedom. Bishop lurched from one job to another, interspersed with flirtations with religion and brushes with the law. Charitably, this pattern of life could be called eccentric. In cruder terms, it was the taking of one bromide after another, each less successful than the last. It was a style that Bowra usually abhorred. For Bishop to have commanded his long-term loyalty therefore demonstrates the power of personality. He was just too clever and exciting to ignore. For Maurice, Bishop was an inspiration and a warning.

The other influential example of homosexual living in Bowra's life was Philip Ritchie, at one point the lover of Lytton Strachey, although there was no great distinction in that. In many ways, he was like Bishop, but in a minor key. He was 'a most engaging, amusing, fanciful, and self-indulgent man',[67] whose attempts to find a purpose in life included a brief period in the Communist Party, an *affaire* with Molly McCarthy, and prodigious gambling. Having made at least one suicide attempt, it may have been something of a relief to die at twenty-seven, as the result of a botched operation for tonsillitis. Like Bishop, he was quite open about his sexual preferences, sometimes to the point of boring his audience. As Dora Carrington once observed, 'He is rather tedious because he talks of nothing but B—y…very seriously as if it was a public duty.'[68] But such talk was not heard in family circles in Kent, and Bowra found it emancipating. For him, Ritchie was 'the young idealist'.[69]

When Ritchie died so suddenly, Maurice wrote to Molly McCarthy as follows:

> This terrible news about Philip must have hit you hard. It is quite intolerable and there is no kind of satisfaction or comfort for any of us, but I am afraid it will have hurt you almost more than anyone…he was in a way my best friend though I only saw him at long intervals and his friends were not mine.[70]

Cyril Connolly believed that the matter went deeper still: 'I sympathize with Maurice more than Molly for the latter had a silly mainly physical love affair, but to Maurice he was a confessor and an ideal, and his death must seem as a kind of treachery.'[71] Even his death had been a kind of selfishness, for, in *Memories*, Bowra recorded that, despite the love of friends, 'he did not wish to live'.[72]

Both Bowra's models in homosexuality failed in living. One gambled, the other drank. One tried monasticism, the other Communism. Both died absurd deaths. By the force of personality, they could dominate any company in which they found themselves, but they were too far from the mainstream to be able to do anything constructive. Without an anchorage of any kind, they could be of little assistance to any other human being or even to themselves. Their lives were waste. Bowra had more common sense. Bishop and Ritchie were friends who were to be admired, but he was always prepared to compromise with the world in order to achieve positive ends. As someone with homosexual tendencies, he was anxious to learn what the limits of acceptable behaviour were. The English set rules in this as in every other aspect of life. It was merely a question of learning them and, occasionally, of bending them.

On several occasions, Bowra took the risk of offering affection to someone else, and every time he met with failure. To some extent, Bishop, Ritchie, and Kantorowicz must have filled this emotional void, but all of these men either inconveniently died or lived thousands of miles from Oxford. Attempts to find a permanent relationship nearer home, with a man or a woman, came to nothing. As Maurice himself predicted and feared, all his expressions of regard would be rebuffed. His first adventure would set a pattern for all the others.

Piers Synnott went up to Balliol in 1923. He came from a long-established Irish, landowning family. His correspondence with Bowra runs from 1924 to 1931, and these letters suggest a love on Maurice's part that was not, and probably could not be, reciprocated. On the face of things, the relationship was potentially controversial. Bowra was a don and Synnott an undergraduate. But only six years separated them in age, and it was therefore an association between two young men. From the start, Synnott was simply dazzled by Bowra's personality: 'Maurice talks quite magnificently here and keeps everything under his wing... really Maurice is amazing... He jokes in six languages so that Sligger [Urquhart] cant understand.'[73] Equally, Bowra found Synnott's company a necessity. To be separated from him was intolerable. In November 1925, the two men had gone to Venice on holiday, where Bowra had worried that he might have bored his friend with 'all these damned sights... they are always indigestible and worrying to the mind at first'.[74] They then had to go their different ways for Christmas, and to Bowra this was deeply painful: 'I have been in a dead state since leaving you, thinking and doing nothing. I wish you were not so far away, but whenever I think of you I feel happier. Dear Piers, you made last term far, far better than any term before.'[75] The fear of losing Synnott turned him into a 'gibbering fool'. He made 'several decisions not to see you', but 'simply could not hold to them'.[76]

It was a difficult situation for any young man to find himself. To be subjected to the full impact of the Bowra personality required a certain resilience. Embarrassments of one sort or another were always in prospect. In January 1925, for example, Synnott joined Bowra, Sligger Urquhart, and Cyril Connolly for a reading party in Minehead. Here, Bowra and Connolly competed for Synnott's attention by showing off with displays of quicksilver wit. Connolly thought Maurice's behaviour was demeaning. As he informed Patrick Balfour, Synnott's greatest friend,

> It is funny to hear him [Bowra] using arguments in favour of it being the beloved's duty to sleep with the lover etc. so as not to cause pain, and then pretending he does not want to sleep with Piers, but Piers sees through it pretty well—Maurice has simply got on my nerves qua wooer.[77]

A few days later, while Bowra was entertaining the company with music hall songs, Connolly crept away to write to Balfour again. In this letter, he describes Bowra as in a kind of 'slavery', which left him 'fearing a rebuff' and laughing 'inordinately all the time'. He seemed to be 'less illusioned about Piers but more gone on his body'. The whole effect was 'rather nauseating'. To make matters worse, Maurice sang 'badly but with confidence'.[78]

Quite separately, Synnott also wrote to Balfour, describing the process by which Maurice's 'jealousy' had led him to 'the abuse of Maurice', for which he now felt regret. Using the argot of 1920s Oxford, it was sad that Bowra should now feel 'humillers and embitters'.[79] Balfour, who must have been both amused and bewildered by these reports from Minehead, carelessly left these letters lying around in his Balliol rooms, where Bowra, on a visit, read them. His reactions were predictable. To Synnott he apologized for being overbearing, or, as he put it, for 'suffering from the unforgivable fault of "good form" ... Crashing'.[80] On Connolly he visited his wrath. With biting irony, he informed him that

> I read, in Patrick's rooms, your letters to him from Minehead and enjoyed them a lot, though I cut a figure of fun in them. I was amused to hear that Piers had seen them before they were sent. It was comforting to think that one has helped to make drama, if only for sketches in the Casino de Paris.[81]

In Maurice's view, his attempts to show love had been turned into a music hall joke. Equally, Connolly knew that a Bowra anathema was something to be feared in Oxford. He wrote hurriedly to assure Maurice that he had 'never tried to make bad blood' between him and Synnott, and he expressed the hope that Bowra would not go in for 'too much goose-cooking'.[82] His hopes were in vain. It would take nearly a decade for the friendship between Connolly and Bowra to be resumed.

The friendship between Synnott and Bowra somehow survived Minehead. They again went to Italy together, so that 'Piers will be able to look at the moon.'[83] Synnott was even accorded the rare privilege of being invited to spend time with the Bowra family in Kent.

> Piers came here for the weekend and was an unqualified success. He played tennis well, did not support the Roman Church, said his family was Norman, and talked about fruit to my father. My father said, 'Nice fellow that. Good style of man. I should stick to him if I were you,' and my mother said, 'Has he got pretty sisters? He has such a charming face.' She is a woman of discernment.[84]

But winning praise from the senior Bowras was enough to engender suspicion in Maurice himself. He began to worry that Synnott might 'soon marry and become a drunken Irish landlord, venturing into Irish politics'.[85] Nor had his reactions to Italy been entirely cosmopolitan. He had 'had constipation all the time and complained of the heat, the food, the people, the hardness of the beds, the drink and the insects'.[86] From 1927 onwards, the intensity of the friendship began to cool. By 1931 it had ended, not in acrimony, but in the dribbling away of mutual interest.

The *affaire* with Synnott had been unsatisfactory and deeply painful. The firm rebuff that Maurice had received in Minehead was known to Urquhart, Connolly, and Balfour. If they knew, Bowra could be sure that the whole of Oxford would soon be in on the story. His humiliation would be a matter of public knowledge. Jokes would be made behind his back. The *affaire* proved what he had always feared, that his sexuality made him vulnerable if it was expressed too openly and too near home. He wished that Synnott would always be 'nice to me', if only out of 'habit' but realized that time and circumstance would probably make even that impossible.[87] In February 1928, he confessed to Synnott: 'God I wish you were here. It is damnable without you. I walk the streets and know that you are not at the end of any of them.'[88] Inevitably, lessons were learned from this awful experience: first, a man like Bowra must never make a firm, emotional commitment without being aware that he was courting another defeat; and secondly, the pursuit of sexual adventures might be better undertaken abroad, where the mocking laughter of Oxford would not follow.

There was one further consequence of this wearing experience. In 1928 or so Bowra abandoned all attempts at writing serious poetry. As the friendship with Synnott faded, so did Bowra's poetic ambitions. Given the importance he attached to poetry, this was the heaviest of prices to pay. In April 1927, he composed 'Anxiety', the first verse of which reads as follows:

> Today a sudden fear has troubled my mind,
> That you have gone and will not be back again
> Till time has changed you, so that all our pain
> To fasten our companionship and find
> An unassailable confidence will seem
> Irrelevant words flung in the teeth of chance.
> What right have we to cry challenge to circumstance,
> To defy defeat with an insolent, idle, dream.[89]

A year later, he sent Synnott a poem entitled 'Separation'. It expressed nothing but hopelessness:

> I am so used to you being far away,
> To wondering when we shall meet again.
> So sick with waiting day to day,
> That though I try to keep my thoughts at bay
> I think of you instead
> In retrospect, and count all we have done
> As though you might be dead.
> Then half-hearted echoes of familiar tone
> Would still beat in my brain
> As now they beat, and still
> The same familiar contours of your face
> Hang diamond bright before me on the air.
> So tired am I of waiting for a word
> To come from you, and change
> This cold memorial into living grace—
> If once your voice was heard,
> Your presence in my room, the strange
> Stare of your eyes back at my wondering gaze!
> The dull days pass, and not a word from you,
> Your memory turns to stone,
> Rigidly fixed in lineament and hue;
> I keep the past alone.[90]

This poem could stand as an epitaph on Bowra's emotional life.

If love was out of the question, then mere sexual fulfilment was the alternative, and, like so many homosexuals of his generation, Bowra looked to Weimar Germany as the country where it could most easily be found. Here lived a few doctors and psychologists who refused to define homosexuality as the expression of mental illness, poets with whom he found himself in sympathy, and lawmakers who favoured toleration of dissidents. In other words, Germany was not England. From the late 1920s onward, according to Lady Harrod, Maurice 'never had *affaires* in England. Only abroad. It only happened abroad.'[91]

Berlin was visited for the first time in September 1928. Accompanied by John Sparrow, Bowra travelled armed with 'addresses and letters of introduction' provided by Bob Boothby, who described the city and its nightlife as 'Paradise'.[92] Even so, the logistics of the expedition were complicated. Sparrow was consulted on 'an important point'.

> Do we have a room with two beds or two rooms. For the first, it is cheaper and more intimate. One makes good jokes going to bed which are lost in the separation of separate rooms. For the second, it might be better if we were to introduce guests late at night. But perhaps one takes them elsewhere.[93]

Exactly a year later, he went again, once more accompanied by Sparrow. This time Boothby and Duff Cooper were on hand as guides to the ways of 'the wild, curious Hun' and 'the night life of Berlin'. It was altogether 'lots of fun', not least because Christopher Sykes went with a woman 'who later he discovered had caught VD from a Herr Klapper'.[94] In retrospect, Maurice thought that the expedition had been an unqualified success, even if Duff Cooper and Harold Nicolson had demonstrated too many 'ties with respectability'. It had been 'a succès fou, and its Berlin for me at the New Year'.[95]

Visits to Germany became a fixed feature of the annual round, for 'now that I find it so easy to fly, it is really no worse than going to Cambridge from Oxford or to Wimbledon from Paddington'. In August 1930, Duff Cooper went with him. In Berlin, they met up with Adrian Bishop, who was 'most generous in the matter of boy friends'.[96] A year later, once more in the company of Sparrow, he found Berlin 'incredibly amusing'. Bishop had been on top form, there had been 'night life of great fun', Sparrow caught 'an extraordinary disease', and the Germans had been 'very nice and serious' about sexual encounters.[97] In May/June 1932, it was Martin Cooper's turn to keep Bowra company on his annual pilgrimage to the German capital.[98]

The coming to power of the Nazis, in January 1933, could not stop Bowra visiting Germany. Indeed he went with astonishing regularity throughout the 1930s. But Hitler closed the bars and clubs that Maurice and his friends had come to appreciate, and Germany's homosexuals became just another group to suffer Nazi persecution. Nevertheless, for four heady years, Bowra had mixed in a world that barely existed in England. His closest friends knew this. His hope was that no one else did.

Germany was not the only country to offer sexual opportunity, but in Bowra's mind, there seems to have been the clear idea that each country has its own menu fixe. It was Germany for the homosexual and France for the heterosexual. Maurice sampled both. Lady Longford remembered that

> as he reached middle age, Maurice didn't want to be pigeon-holed as just 'one of the queers', ... apart from his besieging women, I remember Maurice telling me that he used to dash over to Paris now and again for 'a French tart', and I looked rather surprised and he confirmed it. I was rather amazed.[99]

Evidence for this and allied activities is necessarily thin, but a letter to John Sparrow of December 1929 is suggestive. In it Maurice reported a visit to Cannes with Maurice Hastings, a New College contemporary: 'We visited an interesting establishment kept by a Madame Clou. You would not have enjoyed it, but I did my duty like a man and found my psychology admirably adjusted.'[100] Almost certainly, Bowra was not exclusively homosexual, but the exact disposition of his preferences matters little. He was simply one of the many Englishmen between the wars who regularly slipped across the Channel to take advantage of opportunities that the rules of England did not allow.

It is not hard to understand why the world of the bordello should appeal to Bowra. For someone who believed that the offer of affection would always lead to rebuff and humiliation of the kind he had experienced in the *affaire* with Piers Synnott, the anonymity of Berlin and Cannes was ideal. Here he could not be snubbed. Since he would have regarded it as cowardly to deny pleasure and live as a monk, he had to make his own rules for living. Such behaviour carried risks. The mills of gossip and rumour were always in motion. Their malice could only be contained if the Homintern never confronted the sensibilities of English society directly. Europe had its uses.

With this background, Maurice, not surprisingly, came to see marriage as a kind of cage. How could two people of intelligence and spirit so merge their wills, that companionship for forty years or more would be sustainable? It was inconceivable that Bowra himself could have surrendered so much. Cyril Connolly was not alone in thinking that at Bowra's core was a privacy so deeply buried that no other person could ever be allowed access to it. As a result, Maurice mocked the institution. For him, marriage was simply a matter of 'cockles and Fuckles, alive, alive O'.[101]

The marriages of others, however, could not simply be dismissed with ridicule, for they represented a real threat. For Bowra, the loyalty of friends represented his most important, emotional resource. The marriage of one of his friends necessarily involved a renegotiation of the terms on which friendship was conducted. Some friendships would survive the change, but others would end abruptly or slowly fade. For Bowra, there was always the threat of losing something precious. In 1922, for example, he wrote to congratulate Ethel M. Dell on her engagement. She replied with comforting words to her 'dear Maurice': 'I assure you that I should be very sorry indeed to think that I was losing any old friend by getting married, and I hope that we shall still meet sometimes in the future.'[102] But they almost never did.

Apprehension could lead Maurice to act without much consideration for the feelings of others. He openly disapproved of Elizabeth Harman marrying Lord Longford, because it removed her from 'his court'.[103] When Joan Leigh Fermor married, he worried about who would be 'the new friends of old friends'.[104] When a new wife was in prospect, he would nervously ask, 'Is she one of us? Is she one of us?'[105] When Kenneth Clark married, Maurice regarded it as 'mere insanity. I feel quite sick at the foolishness of it. Love perhaps, lust certainly, but marriage? ... We shall never see him again, as his wife will suspect us of wanting to bugger him—all wives suspect it.'[106] Women who married into the Bowra circle were given what amounted to a form of positive vetting over lunch or dinner. When they passed whatever tests were laid before them, the relief for both them and Maurice was palpable.[107] To avoid such encounters, he thought himself justified in prescribing the conditions on which his friends should marry. Roy Harrod was told that Maurice was 'strongly in favour' of his marrying, 'provided 1) It is not into the upper classes 2) she has money 3) you are prepared to go through will [sic] the revolutionary changes it means in your life. Write me a full account at once.'[108]

The marriage of friends often produced an epithalamium, penned by Maurice to relieve his feelings. Such verses combined affection and indecency in equal proportions. His 'Prothalamium' for the Kenneth Clarkes started as follows:

> Angels of St James's Park,
> Make the bed for Kenneth Clark.
> Make it when such loves are sealed
> Broad as any battlefield.
> When he strips him for the fight
> Help him in his work tonight.[109]

Noel Annan's new wife was encouraged with the couplet, 'Come, O come, O Gabriele | Rescue, poor repressed Noel.'[110] The supposed innocence of the Betjemans in the ways of the flesh was satirized in the thought that perhaps they should be taken to witness stallions mounting mares in order to take on one or two tips. No one should marry simply for 'dear old sex'.[111]

Great was the rejoicing when a new wife or husband turned out to be not merely acceptable, but someone who joyfully accepted Maurice and the conventions of his world. Billa Harrod turned out to be 'a good sort, rather Vile Bodies, likes staying in bed and drinking sherry'.[112] Jill Day-Lewis was welcomed into what Maurice called 'our circle'.[113] Best of all, the marriage of Isaiah Berlin to Aline Halban was welcomed by 'the old foundation members of the Immoral Front'. She was 'extremely intelligent, pretty, warm-hearted, rich and devoted to Isaiah as he is to her. I look forward to a House of Gentlefolk in Headington, with Isaiah shooting partridges and lots of indeterminate relations staying in the house for months.'[114] Amidst the rejoicing, however, Maurice still felt that he was 'losing an old friend...but he is so loyal that he will not be lost, and it is a great comfort to know that he will really be settled happily'.[115] It could have been so much worse.

Nervousness, slight resentment and an irrepressible sense of humour combined to make Bowra a caustic observer of the marital contortions of his friends. They were productive of endless good stories, retailed in uncompromising verse and after-dinner conversation within his own circle. The emotional convolutions between A. J. Ayer, Stuart Hampshire, and the woman who married both of them, represented an opportunity for much good copy. 'Mrs Ayrshire' had, as he put it, a way of making 'herself felt, if you will pardon the expression'.[116] He was equally delighted to hear that Quinton Hogg's wife was rumoured to be having a wartime *affaire* with a Free Frenchman, but thought it a pity that the lover was not General de Gaulle himself.[117] But the Betjemans offered the best opportunities for teasing. Penelope Chetwode was 'a peach', but her Catholicism, love of animals, and addiction to the countryside meant that she could never be a fully paid-up member of Bowra's court. She was the sort of girl who enjoyed 'putting dead dogs in your bed'. Maurice advised Betjeman not to marry her. Instead he should 'have an occasional grummitt with her', because 'it will do your reputation good'.[118] Bowra loved to think of her 'among all the livestock'. He equally appreciated the story that, when Field Marshal Chetwode heard of his daughter's pregnancy, he described Betjeman as a 'plucky little fellow'.[119]

To modern ears these remarks might sound blatant, even cruel, but that would be to misunderstand the period and the context. Jokes such as these were made within a circle of friends only, the 'us' or 'we' so often referred to in Bowra's correspondence. They were definitely not for public consumption. Friends relished the reinforcement of their friendships by the deployment of humour of this kind. It was part of their code, and they were happy to direct it against themselves. Those who knew and liked Maurice recognized these jokes as one of his most important devices. Such poems and stories sprang from a nervous affection that was fearful of being put aside.

Although Bowra was largely homosexual, he was never a misogynist. Indeed, undergraduates at Wadham in the late forties believed that he 'had a mistress in France and in Greece and that they were all separated by the war—and the post-war reconciliations failed'.[120] This account was too romantic and too flattering. Instead, Maurice always had a number of female friends for whom he felt real affection. But he demanded educated and amusing women, as he demanded educated and amusing men, and these were not plentiful in the interwar years. Too many women were taught the social graces and not much else. After dancing with a sister of Elizabeth Longford in Paris, in 1928, Maurice reflected that 'she was charming—trim and manageable. Also she doted on me (very pleasant that is). Her conversation was pretty limited. School talk for girls is as bad as for boys. They had better go back to paint, play the piano and talk languages.'[121] Even worse were women who thought that they were educated and intruded this delusion into social life: 'I went to London for the day and had lunch with J. Maud. It was spoilt by his woman being there. She is a bore—the sort of woman who wants to impress and be thought infinitely subtle.'[122] In fact he demanded female friends that had the same qualities as his male protégés. They should be people with a sense of loyalty, an amused and amusing approach to life, a genuine regard for literature, and a willingness to let him be the centre of attention.

Consequently, educated women should be prized, particularly in Oxford. He was amused to hear that one of his predecessors as Warden of Wadham had voted against the introduction of a degree in Politics, Philosophy, and Economics, on the ground that it would only be suitable for women, who 'may sometimes be respectable but are always troublesome'.[123] In 1925, Maurice joined Margery Fry in protesting against a decision to limit the number of women in Oxford. In his view, the decision was 'unjust and offensive … a nasty blow to my ideal of the University'.[124] Even so, he never could reconcile himself to the idea of colleges becoming coeducational. In this respect, he probably reflected majority opinion among Oxford men and women of his generation. For someone born in Victoria's reign, the social consequences of such a change were simply tiresome. If, for example, female guests were allowed at dinner, Fellows would either bring their wives or their mistresses. The first was vulgar and the second brazen. In one case, they would have nothing to say to each other; in the other they might say too much. Both eventualities disrupted the normal, conversational patterns.[125] In voicing such views, Bowra was of course rationalizing the nervousness he felt in the company of women he did not know and trust, but many contemporaries understood the point he was making.

Women certainly had to work harder than men to win Bowra's trust. This was an inevitable consequence in these decades for someone whose sexual experiences had been largely homosexual. But, as close friends knew, none of this ruled out the possibility that Bowra might marry. As Cyril Connolly remembered:

> He loved several women profoundly and spoke of them in terms of deep devotion. They were all above the ordinary: characters in their own right: and they too were generous and brave and loyal, the qualities he most admired almost more than brains or beauty. He had thought of marrying but I think his genius demanded an inner privacy which would never have tolerated the wear and tear of proximity.[126]

Certainly, Maurice's views on the subject were distinctive. Often he thought of marriage as something he ought to undertake, rather than seeing it as something to be desired in its own right. Often too, he talked of it in terms of offering companionship and a chance to achieve a respectability that had hitherto eluded him. In a rather Proustian way, the desire to marry seemed to precede the appearance of a possible wife.

Nevertheless, Maurice approached the altar on a number of occasions. In 1927, at the same time that he was involved with Piers Synnott, there was a dalliance with Aileen Craig, the daughter of Lord Craigavon and the future wife of Basil Murray. Maurice described their meetings in highly romantic terms, mixing hopes of becoming 'the average man' with the usual fears about being rebuffed:

> I have been posturing before strange audiences and cutting a strange enough figure in my frenzy to become the average man. I have resumed my pursuit of Miss Craig, taking her to the New College Ball ... my romantic feeling for her was sealed by our dancing an old-fashioned waltz together to the tune of 'Der blau Donau.' I shall probably never see her again. But compared to my exquisite feelings [John] Maud's passion is an appetite from the stews and Miss Hamilton a dairy-maid. She even wrote to me on coroneted note-paper in a large hand which sloped backwards, breathing, I hope, gratitude, though I do not dare hope for affection.[127]

He began to dream of dancing with Miss Craig, although their efforts in the ballroom in these dreams were interrupted by Maurice himself being overcome by waves of vomiting.[128] This sad fact led him to conclude that his girlfriend 'was only a symbol after all'.[129] In other words, he was not really in love, but merely wanted to be in love. Nevertheless, some people thought that he had been genuinely smitten, among them the next woman with whom he would become seriously involved.[130]

This was Elizabeth Harman, by general consent one of the most beautiful and accomplished undergraduates of her generation. She would ultimately marry Lord Longford. In 1927, she had been taken to one of Maurice's parties by Hugh Gaitskell, and came out reeling from 'the stunning impact of Maurice's personality', which 'obliterated everything else'.[131] His company 'changed' her life: 'I got into a totally different set. It was the picture Maurice painted of his wonderful world.'[132] She changed to Classics and became his pupil, whereupon the necessary catechism began: 'First question when he took me for a walk was "What do you think of Oscar Wilde", and all that, and I said wisely "Oh I think it's all right". And he said, "Oh I'm glad you've said that because otherwise we couldn't have proceeded any further." '[133] Once this test had been passed, Elizabeth

Harman was easily accorded the title of 'one of us'. Her tolerant spirit was evident. She just assumed that Maurice was sexually 'ambidextrous'.[134] She had no inkling of the existence of Piers Synnott.

On Bowra's side there developed real affection. Miss Harman could have been just a little more clever, but this hardly seemed to matter. As he confessed to John Sparrow, 'I must tell you in confidence, I summoned up my courage and gave Miss Harman tea at the Ritz. She affected me a good deal, and I hummed all the way home in the train. I *like* her a *lot*. She flatters me and makes me boast. Also her appearance exalts me.'[135] He began to think of marriage, and Piers Synnott was let into the secret. By thinking of marrying it 'keeps my mind off myself. Not that that is the real reason for marriage. It abolishes those moments of lonely exhaustion before bed, or at 4 pm when one sits in a chair with melancholy thoughts of desertion and lost opportunities.'[136] A month later he wrote again: 'I am thinking of getting married. Is it a good idea? I think it would make me less bored with myself, though I know of no suitable woman … I want your serious views on this. The thought possesses my mind, and I am probably getting hysterical about it.'[137] He was after all approaching thirty.

If these letters are taken at face value, the desire to marry preceded any decision to propose to Elizabeth Harman. His affection for her simply fitted in chronologically. This being so, the courtship was predictably curious. First, there was a knightly wooing with poems and books 'with chaste dedications' being despatched by post. Then came a formal proposal at the end of a tutorial. No tutorial was supposed to finish in this way, and Miss Harman 'was absolutely staggered'. There had been moments, when she had been inclined to love him. Asleep in a train, he had looked as cuddly as 'one of Beatrix Potter's pigs'. He was also an academic god: 'Everything he said about the classics and the ancients was gospel.' But when the moment came, there was never any doubt that her answer would be a grateful refusal. 'It never occurred to me to say yes … [but] I can remember vividly taking a joyride around Oxford in the bright sunshine and repeating deliriously to myself, as I swayed and swooped from one side of the road to the other, "Maurice has asked me to marry him."' Mature reflection on the incident led her to perceptive comments on her would-be suitor: 'My own postscript would be that he liked to think of sex as earthy, funny, absurd, while love had to be romantic, tender, poetic. Marriage was not for him, in which these two incongruous ideals could live happily together.'[138]

When the proposal was declined, it was probably a relief to both parties, and, in the event, the outcome was happier than any marriage could have offered. Bowra and Elizabeth Harman remained friends for life. He cheerfully accepted an invitation to her going-down party, dressed 'in his canonicals' as Proctor, where he 'drank cocktails and then went to dinner with the Bishop of Worcester'.[139] Thereafter, he was a regular visitor with the family, and acted as godfather to one of the Pakenham boys. It was probably an ideal resolution of the incident.

Some eight years later, Maurice approached the fire again. In September 1936, he told Felix Frankfurter that

> I have made a new set of plans and want to get married in December. Of course cold feet and all that may break the whole thing up, but that is my hope. The arguments against hurrying are a) a house has to be found b) hurried marriage is construed by colleagues and parents as evidence for pregnancy and 'shooting before the twelfth', c) it will give the poor girl time to get out of it if she wants to—not that I shall encourage this.[140]

The girl in question was Audrey Beecham, niece of Sir Thomas, and described by Isaiah Berlin as 'a young, earnest, impulsive, feministic anarchist'.[141] She was also reputed to have lesbian tendencies. When this fact was reported to Maurice, he philosophically replied: 'Oh, that's all right. It makes that side of things easier.'[142] Allegedly, he also suggested that 'buggers can't be choosers'. The whole business was a little strange. Bowra was thirty-eight, Miss Beecham several years younger. Both of them enjoyed shocking by word and action. Some friends thought that Maurice was only marrying to make himself sufficiently 'respectable' to win the Chair of Greek. Whether an alliance with Miss Beecham would bring respectability, however, was an open question.

They were together for a year, from the summer of 1936 to that of 1937, separated only by Maurice visiting Harvard for a semester. They gave dinner parties together, which he described as a 'Domestic evening, dear, domestic evening'.[143] Miss Beecham was also introduced into the codes of the Bowra circle, learning that a thick skin was an absolute prerequisite. Maurice cheerfully reported, on one occasion, that 'Cyril ragged Audrey for her more pompous and prefectorial opinions. It does her a lot of good, and she quite enjoys it.'[144] All in all, Maurice declared himself to be 'very much in love'.[145] In August 1937, they went to Paris together for three days, where they had 'quite a time... visiting the usual night-boxes'.[146]

Playing at being engaged was clearly agreeable, as far as Maurice was concerned.

Soon after returning home, however, Miss Beecham began to have doubts as Bowra sadly reported to Cyril Connolly:

> Since getting home Audrey has been having cold feet, revulsions, and jitters, and has taken against the idea of marriage. So I doubt if it will come off. She objects, reasonably enough, to being a don's wife, where she will have to entertain other dons' wives and live respectably. I feel there is really no answer. It is after all like marrying a curate, and I can't very well get out of my job now without starving... The alternative for her seems to me pretty grim at some underpaid job in London and losing her looks in a racket of lesbians and nancies.

Her rejection genuinely hurt him: 'I must admit that the whole thing has got me down, and that I curse my luck which robs me of the few things I really want and prevents my few good actions.'[147] As it happened, Audrey Beecham had been one of the few women 'to get' him 'below the belt'.[148] Here, once again, was public rebuff and humiliation. Answering letters of commiseration from friends inside and outside the Homintern was a grim business. If left him 'depressed and humiliated'.[149] Writing 'The Late Lorn Lesbian' hardly relieved his feelings:

> Strange are the tricks of the purblind blender,
> Who planted thus
> Some dark Oedipus
> In a breastless bosom, and will not mend a
> Shuddering horror of male pudenda.
>
> Nay, in your sex are some like me.
> Choose your Nancy
> And pay your fancy
> Till both the sexes are mixed may be,
> And none can tell if it's he or she.[150]

Oxford looked on with bewilderment. Isaiah Berlin had sympathy for both parties in what had turned into a 'sheer disaster'. Maurice was too childlike and unknowing in such matters, being completely unaware of how intimidating it was for someone to have the full force of his personality directed at them.[151] He was not surprised that Miss Beecham described her situation as sitting on a carousel that was spinning round faster and faster. She repeated the metaphor to Lord Boothby, who bluntly told her to get off it. Others were even less generous. Mary Fisher's strong common sense was offended by the whole episode. Audrey Beecham had been 'a goose' to become so entangled and Maurice had simply used her to experiment in heterosexual affection.

> Do you not think that Mr Bowra is doing what our mothers w'd call taking advantage of Miss B's highly romanticized picture of herself as a generous, untamed, untameable, chivalrous character? We all know that romantics are a nuisance, but the truth about Mr Bowra is that, however considerable his general style, there seems no reason to suppose he will behave like a gentleman in particular circumstances.[152]

In truth, there had been an element of theatricality about the *affaire*, in both its comic and tragic representations, but real feelings had also been engaged and badly bruised.

After the Second World War, there would be more close relationships with women. According to Stuart Hampshire, Maurice had 'a short fling', whatever that may have implied, with Barbara Hutchinson and Joan Eyres Monsell.[153] He was certainly very fond of both these women, and stayed with them often. Then there was Ann Fleming, the widow of James Bond's creator, who entered his world through the good offices of Hugh Gaitskell. Maurice once asserted that he had actually gone down on one knee in order to make this lady a proposal of marriage. Whether his age and physique would have allowed such acrobatics is to be doubted, but the story registered the depth of his feelings.[154] Isaiah Berlin acknowledged all these relationships, and even felt confident about ranking them: 'M's love of her [Ann Fleming] was greater than for Barbara: second only, in my time to that for Joan Eyres Monsell, who, I suspect, was the greatest single love of his life, of either sex, and who (in some senses) loved him too.' There is some evidence that this last relationship may have been more than Platonic.[155]

No one will probably ever know the detail of how such friendships were conducted, and such detail matters little. What they powerfully suggest is that, even if marriage was out of the question, Maurice liked the company of many women, and probably loved some.[156] His complicated sexuality encompassed many varieties of theme. In return, he could inspire deep feelings in women. At his death, Joan Eyres Monsell wrote a letter of condolence to one of Maurice's goddaughters: 'I feel exactly as you do, and it seems as if some tremendously good and vital force had disappeared from the world as well as one's oldest friend.'[157] She and others recognized a Don Quixote quality in their friend where women were concerned. Maurice was a romantic, who was always inclined to separate the pure emotions of love from the physicality of sex.[158] As a result, he was often out of his depth in such matters, often hurt, and sometimes close to inviting ridicule. But then the same could be said of his relationships with men.

Increasingly, the price of respectability and renown was more and more caution in sexual matters. Some friends doubted if he ever had a physical relationship with anyone after becoming Warden of Wadham in 1938. It was not exactly that the poacher had turned gamekeeper. Maurice watched the antics of his friends with more humour than disapproval. It was rather, as Noel Annan put it, that Bowra had become 'the non-playing captain'[159] of the Immoral Front. England could not deny him distinction, but even he had to abide by some of the rules that others lived by. In private, among his courtiers, he could continue to set the tone, but in public, the authority that his voice carried could not have survived too much scandal or rumour. Bowra and the English idea of establishment came to an arrangement.

This significant concession on Bowra's part was made more bearable by him becoming increasingly bored by the whole topic. As he grew older, he complained about how foolish the pursuit of love was. Rosamond Lehmann, for example, kept him tied to the telephone for hours as she dissected her own feelings and those of everyone around her. It was intolerable. As Maurice confided to Edith Sitwell, 'if she had *one* more *affaire*, he was going into a lunatic asylum or was going to shoot himself, because he couldn't stand being kept up all night while Rosamond examined her and everybody else's motives.'[160] When her 'band of lovers' began to diminish, he regarded it as a blessing.[161] Equally tiresome was the tendency of ageing people to slip into moralizing. For obvious reasons, Maurice never took the high moral tone, and much disliked those who did. When John Sparrow was inclined to censure the behaviour of a mutual female friend, Bowra reprimanded him by writing that 'You and I, John, have never taken a risk in our lives. Our only course is to love and support her.'[162] With age, he came to see the demands of sex and the pursuit of love as tiresome. They had always carried the risk of humiliation and ridicule. Now they were simply boring. The only recourse was to turn the whole nonsense into humour. Typically, late in life, he dismissed 'buggery' as being merely 'useful for filling that awkward time between tea and cocktails'.[163] Not surprisingly, when Cyril Connolly came to put together material for an obituary notice for his friend of forty years, he had to admit that there were many areas of Maurice's private life about which he could barely pronounce at all. He, like all Bowra's friends, only knew some stories, even if they suspected others. It was all rather muddling. He had certainly loved men and had probably loved women. From both quarters he had demanded intelligence, loyalty, and a subscription to his values. Even when these conditions were met, he would find it difficult to move on from friendship to something more intimate. The risks were too great. The rebuffs, to which he referred again and again, were always just around the corner. It was easier to observe, make jokes, and perhaps, to seek out more anonymous forms of sexual fulfilment. Bowra recognized that this was hardly a satisfactory arrangement. It left him alone too often, and solitude was fearful. It also made him a demanding friend, since he was always expecting to suffer the loss of friendship. Connolly and others met patches of rough water. But he was ultimately prepared to forgive supposed slights for new realignments. He guessed that Maurice's personality was too large to be confined within one relationship, and his soul too private to be shared.[164] A doubtful sexuality was identified as the only inhibiting factor in a personality that was otherwise entirely directed towards attacking strategies.

PART III

Action

7

Oxford, 1922–1938

In 1925, Wadham College, of which Bowra had been a Fellow for three years, sold valuable property within Oxford, and was suddenly in funds. One of the senior Fellows, Reggie Lennard, no friend of Maurice's, formally canvassed views on how the money should be used. Bowra's reply was robust. Lennard's suggestion that some new science should be supported was first dismissed out of hand: 'I dislike your attempt to improve the position of Science … As you admit that you know nothing about science … your attempt to improve its position looks like vote-catching.' Instead, Bowra wanted something which confirmed that 'the object of education is not the accumulation of knowledge but the training of the mind to think'. Science, in his view, just involved 'facts, facts, facts. Is that education? I doubt it.' The answer to Wadham's dilemma was, therefore, to establish a post for 'an active History scholar', preferably one with a classical training.[1] Given the imperatives in his character, such views could have been predicted.

When Bowra talked of training the mind, this was no platitude. He meant every word. He believed that his generation had unparalleled opportunity. The constraints of Victorianism had been dispersed. It was now possible to think freely, as the Greeks had advocated. In retrospect, Maurice would agree that many of the opportunities of the 1920s had been lost or misused. Opportunities always are. There had been too much silliness and some self-indulgence. But in establishing the principle that everything could be talked of and nearly everything done, the twenties had opened gates that would be hard to close. He told a lecture audience, in 1967, that this decade had allowed men and women to see a new vision of themselves.

I am sure that this is the thing the young value most—that they know that their own personalities are too serious to be badgered and pushed about by

a lot of silly rules they do not agree with, or understand, or approve of;
they want to be civilized members of a civilized society getting as much out
of each other and everybody else as they can. There the Twenties laid the
foundation, and we ought all to be grateful to them.

Those of his generation who had survived the Great War found the
mere fact of living intoxicating: 'we did not eat and drink for tomorrow
we die, but because yesterday we died.' Life was simply too wonderful to
be confined within a moral corsetry designed by others. If some thought
the Twenties immoral, they were only closing their eyes to the fact that
people were now saying and doing things openly, which their parents and
grandparents had said and done in secret.[2] The decade created 'a new sense
of human worth'.[3]

As a result, battle was joined between those with the largeness of spirit
to welcome new possibilities and those who suspected them. In Oxford,
there was no doubt about who captained the new wave. A. J. Ayer and
others were clear that Maurice was 'by far the most influential'[4] don
in the University. According to Elizabeth Longford, he was 'Voltaire and
the Sun King rolled into one'.[5] His court was the most talked about, the
most admired, and the most suspected in Oxford. In a sense he came to
personify Oxford's values. Without him, the place was 'a mutton sand-
wich without the chutney'.[6] What he represented was much more than
wit and wordiness. Rather he was seen as leading a crusade to make
the Oxford experience quite different from what had gone before. Before 1914, dons occasionally and distantly retailed their knowledge to
undergraduates. Bowra, too, would conscientiously teach his subject, but
he did much else. Each pupil would be invited to express his personality to the uttermost, to live as the Greeks and poets had lived. This
was his system. It made him famous and infamous. Mary Bennett, in
a perceptive remark, always regarded Maurice 'as a concept rather than
as a person'. Seeing him striding down the Broad, she thought, 'There
goes Maurice. There goes what he stands for.'[7] Bowra, of course, had
many talents, not least 'a talent for best-sellers and administration',[8] but
it is as a liberator of the personality that he invited admiration and
controversy.

When the young men who came to inhabit the Bowra circle wrote
or spoke of their mentor, the word 'liberation' recurs again and again.
To them Maurice directed his attention. He once advised Lady Quinton
'not to waste time on the old'.[9] The middle-aged and elderly had either

discovered a personality or never would. With the young, by contrast, there was everything to play for, and the English young were particularly in need of help. The system of education they had endured had taught them to attribute nobility of character to those who would repress and deny.[10] In Bowra's view, this teaching was pernicious. Instead, he encouraged them to laugh with Aristophanes, who enjoyed 'mocking the great', most of whom he found cranks and crooks.[11] Young people should be taught to see through the posturing and self-importance of those who liked to exercise power. Not surprisingly, when he heard *Fidelio* for the first time in Berlin, the chorus of prisoners, as they emerged from confinement into light, 'moved' him 'to the depth of my being'. The experience was the more compelling because it was followed, the next night, by 'four hours of hell at Meistersinger'.[12]

Testimonials to Bowra's influence on a set of talented men are easy to find. It was rather like being caught in a gale. Boys, trained in middle-class morality at public schools, were suddenly confronted by raw energy. Day-Lewis remembered that Maurice chose people 'with pretensions to brain'. On them, he would unleash 'the full force of his personality—as flesh and paradox, its challenging, testing, sometimes merciless edge'.[13] Kenneth Clark acknowledged that Bowra had been 'the strongest influence in my life ... I was timid, priggish and inhibited. I was not even a scholar, and "scholarly," repeated several times, was one of the first words of praise in Maurice's vocabulary.' He had been the man responsible for 'disinhibiting' him.[14] Bowra simply said 'all the dreadful things one was longing to hear'.[15] Combined with an unmistakable warmth of personality, the tuition was irresistible: 'he hated indifference. "A cold fish" was one of the worst things he could say of anyone. He hated tyrants. He hated hypocrites, sycophants and place-seekers. He had no use for conventional values. All this disqualified him from public life.'[16]

Many others had the same experience. After a dinner in Wadham, David Astor felt that he had been 'given a shove' to challenge every idea he had ever had.[17] Cyril Connolly, for all his warring with Maurice, admitted that his friend had 'saved' him as a writer.[18] Bowra 'burnt out pretension' in John Betjeman,[19] and taught John Sparrow 'zest and a catholic appreciation of the arts; how to enjoy life with freedom of mind; and in society not to play the prude or the hypocrite more than is necessary'.[20] Less piously, Noel Annan simply learnt what laughter could do. Once Maurice's conversation was so humorous that sitting upright in a chair became uncomfortable.

Lying on the floor was the only possibility.[21] Importantly, this humour invited young men to see the words of parents, headmasters, and clergymen for what they were worth.

Perhaps more than anyone else, Isaiah Berlin returned to this theme of liberation over and over again. As he recalled, 'parents trembled about the wicked influence he might have on their children', and Bowra 'was emotionally with the poachers, even when he officially crossed over to the gamekeepers... he never did join the pompous establishment, the majority'.[22] Berlin struggled to find words to express his gratitude:

> As you know, I take a low view of myself and all I do and friendship means more to me—and always has—than anything else at all; any evidence props me up for a little ... as you know, it is not merely love and admiration for you that I feel, though these emotions are genuine enough; but I owe you a transformation of my entire mode of life and attitude towards it. It is a trite way of putting it perhaps, but you did 'liberate' me. Whether you had any such purpose—whether I should have been less of a nuisance in chains—is something else. At any rate I am very clear that what is free, generous, life-and pleasure loving, warm-hearted, and intellectually anti-prig front, anti-Eliot, anti-solemn, anti-Balliol, everything that makes one not merely a *de facto* but a conscious member of the immoral front, all or most of that I owe to... your influence ... I do not for a moment suppose that you were aware of the strength and emancipating power of your mere presence, but if I am anything to anybody the ... responsibility is largely yours ... I have always longed to say some of this to you, but direct statement is impossible ... even now I don't begin to say all that I want.[23]

Such a testimony would be re-echoed by many others in his own and subsequent generations.

Education, Bowra style, was to be conducted inside tutorials and outside tutorials, in university terms, and in vacations. Promising protégés were taken on holiday at Maurice's expense. When he took John Sparrow to Italy in 1927, the younger man was simply told 'to pay as much as you like'.[24] That same year he travelled to the Adriatic with Hugh Gaitskell, who was 'kind and will respect the pageant of my bleeding heart, as I take it from "Venise, sur l'affreuse Lido", to Wien and Belgrad'.[25] The future Labour Leader, 'devoured by all kinds of bugs' and lacking 'regular bowel movements', was subjected to museums, historical sites, and the full force of Bowra's conversation.[26] Such journeys were not necessarily undertaken with ulterior motives. They were the last whispers of the arrangement by which young gentlemen undertook the Grand Tour. Dons would continue to undertake them in the 1950s.[27] As concentrated educational experiences, their impact was considerable.

But the College dinner party was Bowra's preferred method of supplementing the pedagogic opportunities of the tutorial. Anthony Powell was introduced into the Bowra 'monde' in the summer of 1924. Fifty years later, his memory of such parties was still vivid. A group of six or eight men would sit down to the sort of food and wine that undergraduates had barely encountered before. There was too 'a slight sense of danger', by which Powell meant the fear of displaying ignorance or saying something wrong. At table there was nothing that could not be said. Bowra himself always knew how far he should go in this respect, and then made a point of going a great deal further. Undergraduates were encouraged to do the same.[28] There were rules, but they were of Bowra's own making. Intoxication was vulgar, and vomiting so gross that it could bring on excommunication.[29] Cruel remarks that were funny were admissible, but comments that were only malicious were 'bad form'. Jokes simply 'prompted by a desire to shock rather than to illuminate were pointedly ignored'.[30] In other words, manners, as Maurice defined them, mattered.

Inevitably, Bowra talked most, not least because he was always in possession of marvellous copy, 'but he controlled conversation in a way that no one ever felt excluded'.[31] He told stories that demolished the pompous and brought heroes down to size. He also talked freely about sex, a topic of conversation that had, seemingly, been absent from English dinner tables since the French Revolution. Its vagaries were dissected with the same wit and irreverence with which he talked of everything else. When Cyril Connolly announced that he had, temporarily, given up 'the Maurice creed', he meant that he had enjoyed 'three months of perfect chastity'.[32] At the end of one dinner party, Christopher Sykes was given a drawing of a nude by Matisse, and Maurice was, shortly after, delighted to hear that his present had caused a moment of crisis between the young man and his mother.[33] As sacred cows were slaughtered evening by evening, undergraduates learned that life could be about what was possible, rather than what was allowed.

Such dinners often ended in games. Guests would be invited to name all the nice characters in Proust, the joke being that, in Maurice's view, there were none. Alternatively, they would be presented with the titles of famous novels in Finnish or Slovak, and then asked to provide English equivalents.[34] Entertainments such as these were merely an extension of how the dons themselves spent their evenings. Bowra was, for example, a member of the Composition Club of seven classicists, who translated works of English literature into Latin or Greek. On one occasion, Maurice was impressed by the facility of Denniston of Hertford in turning a mystery of Dorothy Sayers into Platonic Greek. It was 'certainly Plato, but it was also Miss Dorothy Sayers'.[35] In inviting his student-guests to play the same games, therefore, Bowra was at once flattering their abilities, and suggesting that they could inhabit the same world as their revered elders.

Linking food, drink, wit, and games was what Anthony Powell called the open 'worship of Pleasure'. They were exposed to 'the whole bag of tricks of what most people think, feel and often act on, yet we are ashamed of admitting that they do, feel and think'. Such occasions were to be approached with 'apprehension', but ended in a great 'sense of release'.[36] Invitations to Wadham were keenly appreciated. New College undergraduates put new words to the popular song 'Daddy wouldn't buy me a bow wow':

> Oh, I do want a Cecil Maurice Bowra.
> Oh I do want a Cecil Maurice Bowra.
> You can have a Maurice Plat
> And be satisfied with that,
> But I'd rather have a Bow-ra-ra.[37]

Maurice once asserted that one of the central tenets of his Oxford creed was that 'the boys should be entertained like no how'.[38] Among many others, John Betjeman was grateful for this, and memorably described the experience in 'Summoned by Bells':

> Dinner with Maurice Bowra sharp at eight—
> High up in Wadham's hospitable quad:
> The Gilbert Spencers and the Campbell Gray
> Bright in the inner room; the brown and green
> Of rows and rows of Greek and Latin texts;
> The learning lightly worn; the grand contempt
> For pedants, traitors and pretentiousness.
> A dozen oysters and a dryish hock;
> Claret and *tournedos*; a *bombe surprise*.
> The fusillade of phrases ('I'm a man
> More dined against than dining') rattled out
> In that incisive voice and chucked away
> To be re-used in envious common-rooms

By imitation Maurices. I learned,
If learn I could, how not to be a bore,
And merciless was his remark that touched
The tender spot if one were showing off.
Within those rooms I met my friends for life.
True values that were handed on a plate
As easily as sprouts and aubergines:
'A very able man' 'But what's he like?'
'I've told you. He's a very able man.'
Administrators, professorial chairs
In subjects such as Civics, and the cad
Out for himself, pretending to be kind—
He summed them up in scathing epigram,
Occasionally shouting out the truth
In forceful nineteen-fourteen army slang;
And as the evening mellowed into port,
He read us poems…
King of a kingdom underneath the stars,
I wandered back to Magdalen, certain then,
As now, that Maurice Bowra's company
Taught me more than all my tutors did.[39]

Of course such evenings were also testing grounds. Bowra was always anxious to recruit new members of his court. There was a continual search for the right people, by which he meant people with the talent and personality to understand his Greek and literary objectives. Lady Longford once noticed that, having reduced a roomful of undergraduates to helpless laughter, Maurice's own face was 'stern' and full of observation.[40] Similarly, Enid Starkie observed that Bowra 'notices what one does, even every yawn'.[41] According to one of his closest friends in the classical world, 'Many people are made of pulp and warm water. Maurice was made of fire covered over with ice.'[42] Like Stefan George, Bowra was always keen to find new friends who would also be disciples.

Such initiates needed thick skins. Maurice's company was not for the faint hearted. No area of private life was considered sacrosanct. No long-held conviction or cherished belief could not be ridiculed. Often those laughing around the table found that they were laughing at themselves. Spontaneity was everything, and no one was allowed to put up barriers. The teasing of friends in stinging verse was a practice Bowra had started with respect to his circle in New College.[43] In later life, he perfected the art. These poems circulated among his friends, where they read of their sins and shortcomings in parodies of Yeats and Eliot.[44] As after-dinner entertainment, they were unbeatable. Stephen Spender, reflecting on these descriptions of 'our common friends', found it 'amazing' that 'they should be circulated and read by his friends, that he should have given them to the wife of the editor of a great newspaper, and that they should actually be known to members of the Cabinet'.[45] This was dangerous behaviour for someone like Bowra, who always believed that he 'had a skin too few'. Retaliation was always possible. But even so, the method of undermining nonsense with ridicule was never moderated.

In order to destroy inhibition, uproot prejudice and obedience to unthinking convention, disciples were not allowed areas of private retreat. Betjeman's Anglicanism may well not have been untouched by a Christmas card which read, 'Dear Barnacle, Merry Syphilis, Clappy New Year, Gleetings.'[46] Nor might he have enjoyed his architectural passions being used to describe a new girlfriend; 'Polychromatic is each tit | To them must Keble's glory yield | Her Early English nipples fit | Like gargoyles carved for Butterfield.'[47] Isaiah Berlin's hypochondria was another obvious target. Maurice insisted that his repeated visits to hospital were 'nothing more than welcome returns to the womb'.[48] Nor was his Jewishness sacrosanct:

> But in the bluest blood of Riga
> Pulsates a stronger, redder wine.
> In Palm Beach suiting, solar topi,
> Isaiah rides to Palestine.
> Solomon's temple rises for him,
> The minions of the Mufti fall.
> The new Messiah stands conducting
> Beethoven by the Wailing Wall.[49]

More prosaically, Bowra was 'happy' that Evelyn Waugh divorced his first wife, and thought that he should be fixed up with Elizabeth Harman.[50] In short, everything that middle-class, English sensibilities regarded as private was on open view within the Bowra circle.[51]

In all these scamperings, Maurice called the tune, and no one in his lifetime questioned his right to do so. Close associates recognized that he had 'his own way of cutting friends down to size',[52] but also recognized why he did this. First, it offered protection to Maurice's own vulnerabilities. If he directed the revels, he was safe. Secondly, he dug spurs into the flanks of his friends, not to inflict pain, but to make them go faster than they had ever thought possible. For example, Isaiah Berlin could worry himself into illness about the demands of lecturing, and it is with that in mind that Bowra could report that, 'Isaiah has had a great success in Washington lecturing on art. Rather a new thing for him, especially as he has never looked at a picture in his life. But that of course enables him to talk with an open mind.'[53] For a friend to overcome an inhibition that threatened the expression of talent was to be welcomed unreservedly.

This was, however, a kill-or-cure training. Not everyone could accept the rough elements and some rebelled. Mary Bennett, as a young woman, 'couldn't see the gold for the brass'.[54] Later in life, as Principal of St Hilda's College, she discovered that Bowra was 'the only person whose advice I wanted',[55] but earlier she had not enjoyed being labelled 'a nice, amusing, bad, scheming girl'.[56] Others solved the problem by taking sabbaticals from Maurice's overpowering presence. Anthony Powell's lasted decades. Day-Lewis, too, thought that his old tutor was 'best taken in small doses'. He was to be compared to 'strychnine—a tonic in small doses, but, if one took too much, one bent into a hoop and died'.[57] For Cyril Connolly, 'slander seems the keynote of existence, and only in absolute seclusion, fugitive and cloistered, does salvation lie.'[58] None of these people, however, had the sort of retiring personalities that could bear withdrawal for long. Maurice's court was too exciting to reject for simpler pleasures.

Through all this wining and dining, Maurice was a recruiting sergeant for his private army of those who could be brought to share his preoccupations and who would fight the common enemy. There were few neutrals in his world. Everyone was potentially 'one of us' or not. As Noel Annan remembered, every issue took on a manichaean character:

> His letters speak of a world in which the Legions of Darkness are in perpetual warfare with the Children of Light. He saw university politics as a ceaseless struggle against the enemies of freedom, vitality and the intellect: they are the *bien-pensants*, the trimmers, the advocates of the sound and the safe, not to mention clericals, technocrats and progressives ... one feature of his face never smiled: his eyes. They were pig's eyes, fierce and unforgiving, unblinking, vigilant. They were inspecting the enemy's dispositions. Lucid as his prose was, his universe was Heraclitan and Dionysiac.[59]

There could be no quarter given to anyone identified as an opponent in Annan's categories, or to any collaborator with them. A. D. Lindsay was condemned on several counts, and therefore Maurice could only sadly report that 'The Master of Balliol has been ill, but unfortunately is getting better. Otherwise deaths have been poor for the time of year.' An incompetent Vice-Chancellor was dismissed as someone who split infinitives, 'until the floor was covered with them'.[60]

Every job in Oxford, from College porter to Vice-Chancellor, could be taken by a friend or foe. Every election, therefore, was a battle that had to be won. Maurice was clear that everything was fair in love, war, and Oxford politics. To defeat the philistine, it was perfectly acceptable to cut corners, exploit weaknesses, and fix appointments. Isaiah Berlin even believed that 'integrity was an empty concept to him. He lied like a trooper, to win, to enhance life, to humiliate an enemy, to do good to a friend, to get out of a corner.'[61] According to this testimony, Bowra's sense of right and wrong was determined by the passion with which he pursued his crusades. What advanced them was right; what hindered them was wrong.

In Maurice's view, Oxford in the 1920s was full of enemy targets. They came in every shape and size. Leslie Rowse could not be a friend, because, as Bowra told him, 'Social life—not your thing.' Rowse found 'all that eating and drinking, wining and dining, loud and boisterous', rather 'vulgar', a view which the Bowra circle could only dismiss as suburban.[62] Equally, Harold Acton and Brian Howard could only be enemies. They were posturing aesthetes who squandered their talents and produced nothing of value. Worse still, their baleful influence nearly ruined Evelyn Waugh. In their company, Waugh had been 'drunk the whole time'.[63] Nor, later, would W. H. Auden ever find favour. Here, in Bowra's view, was a man who had reduced poetry to a kind of introspective masturbation, and who had come near to undermining the more genuine talent of Stephen Spender. He also thought that Auden might be a moralist in disguise, giving him the nickname of 'Martin Tupper'.[64] This exclusion hurt Auden a good deal. He had 'dearly wished'[65] to be numbered among Bowra's troops. Listing people of note who were rejected as friends is as illuminating as naming those who were accepted. Mere celebrity was not enough. Instead, there had to be a willingness to live as full a life as possible and a profound, underlying seriousness.

Senior Common Rooms around the university harboured many ex-amples of unsatisfactory forms of human life. In Magdalen, there was T. S. R. Boase, whom Maurice denounced as an intellectual poseur, a snob, and, worst of all a born collaborator, bending before every fashion and pressure:

His topsail is trimmed to all winds that blow,
Low to the high and high to the low;
To him the envious Graces yield
The juiciest fruits from the Potter's Field,
And carpet his path on the windy Lea
With blossoms from the Judas-tree.[66]

It was simply extraordinary that Magdalen should have elected a man 'of no public virtues and no private parts'.[67] All assaults on such a creature were in order, even those which depended on the accident of his having a lazy eye. Friends were warned about the magical powers of his 'Beaux Yeux'.[68] In Balliol there lived Ronnie Knox, who not only filled the heads of undergraduates with religion, but also specifically warned them against consorting with Bowra.[69]

Worse still were dons who had the effrontery to set up salons of their own. Such assemblies all too often pedalled views that challenged the Bowra creed. Colonel Kolkhorst, for example, held court on Sunday mornings, offering a diet of aestheticism and High Church Anglicanism, which, in Maurice's view, had come near to undermining the natural talent of John Betjeman.[70] 'Sligger' Urquhart in Balliol gave parties that were 'restful and relaxing'. Bowra dismissed him as 'a nice old nurse', adding that he himself liked to 'disturb undergraduates more'.[71] Urquhart was also the possessor of a chalet in the French Alps, to which Bowra's protégés, but not Bowra himself, were invited. Here the cult of fresh air and lots of exercise as the answers to life's problems was promulgated, with, according to Maurice, a Roman Catholic chaplain in residence fishing for souls. No establishment could have been more sinister.[72] To counter Sligger's influence, Bowra thought, at one point, that he would have to buy a property abroad, as a counterpoint in good living.[73]

Kolkhorst and Urquhart represented various forms of high-mindedness, a kind of Bloomsbury in Oxford. Just as Maurice would have doubts about the Woolfs, so he had doubts about them. He was too short for the high moral tone. As a result, he preferred dons with a more robust attitude to life. He much approved of Marcus Dick, whom he identified as the new type of don, who 'gave tutorials with a bottle of whiskey by the armchair and a girl in the bedroom'.[74] The monkish academic was a physical embodiment of defeat rather than victory. When told that one of his Fellows had established a reputation as a womanizer, Bowra replied that he hoped that the girls in question 'were foreigners. They would be rather in his line. I hope they are not his pupils. I find that boring.'[75] It was not a tutor's function merely to confirm the public school morality of his pupils.

For undergraduates were sorely in need of help. Between the Wars, they came from the middle class and the public school. In the mass, they would be dismissed as 'the foul host of undergraduates', who looked 'pretty beastly'.[76] Too many of them substituted sport for life. They seemed to find comfort in its rules and regulations. Such submission was no part of the Bowra code. On one occasion, he asked a girlfriend of Christopher Sykes to leave the room after she had suggested he might take up rowing.[77] Games players too often missed the joke, according to the Warden, being content 'to love athletically and socially. I am not in sympathy with the ideal.'[78] Maurice had been a useful rugby player at Cheltenham and continued to appear on the tennis court. As Dean of Wadham, in charge of College discipline, he attended sporting dinners, and understood what was required. At one Bump Supper, he bought in a quantity of second-hand furniture, so that 'a bonfire satisfied the undergraduate thirst for destruction without any damage to College property'.[79] But it was largely an act. He could play the part of 'a hearty among hearties', and even sometimes feel 'colossally hearty',[80] but his preferred company lay elsewhere. When he wrote 'beautiful poems on topical themes—chiefly indecent', they were only 'appreciated by the selecter souls'.[81]

So the Bowra creed could not be for everyone. Very few scientific undergraduates would know him well, for example. The Greek imperative in him drove him to foster an aristocracy of talent; aristocratic in its sense of separateness, and talented in what it produced. It was an elite in that it consciously excluded those who could not meet its standards, but it was not snobbish. Entry was open to all those who had what Day-Lewis called 'a pretension to brains', and who were prepared to use them in ways of which Bowra approved. Following the tactics of Mallarmé and Stephen George before him, Maurice would assemble a circle of acolytes who, in their writings, would carry the message further.

In Oxford, they would be known as 'the Bowristas'. Their social formation is perhaps best described in astronomical terms. Maurice sat at the centre of the constellation. Around circled others, some close in and some further out. All were kept in fixed positions by the power of his personality. Mallarmé had been 'le Maître' and George 'Der Meister'. Bowra never used such terms, but he was called 'the Great Headmaster', giving 'term reports' on his friends: 'all good points were assessed with judicious approbation—such weaknesses as there were glanced at, not with discouragement.'[82] He was only five or six years older than his acolytes, but they were a crucial five or six years. He had had to fight in the Great War, and they had missed it. As a result, he was in every way more adult. John Sparrow referred to him as 'Old Maurice' or 'the Old Boy'.[83] In return, Maurice's letters to Sparrow are full of peremptory instructions: 'Come to lunch on Monday without fail'; '*Why* have you not written to me? Are you staying with Crossman? Write at once'; 'Don't lose your passport or miss the train.'[84] According to George Huxley, one moment of coldness in the relationship between the two men was caused by Sparrow's wish to create a similar circle without having the necessary force of character to hold it together.[85]

A friendship with Maurice therefore always had a strong strain of the master–pupil theme within it. Bowra always 'wanted to be on a different level'. There was 'an element of ipse dixit' in his conversation. Like Stephen George, Bowra did not much relish being contradicted by his pupils or friends. Friendship for him was expressed in protecting, promoting, and teaching those whom he liked. It was probably easier for him to express affection along the axis of the master–pupil relationship than in conversation between equals.[86] But that affection was none the less real for finding outlets in this way. He called his friends 'the Old Contemptibles', fellow-warriors in all his important battles. An evening in their company was much prized: 'All the Old Contemptibles were beaten up and I found myself pleasantly able to lose myself in the crowd and laugh at other people's jokes.'[87] Bowra set the terms for his friendships, just as he set the agenda for conversation, but the offering of affection was genuine.

In assembling 'the Bowristas', between 1922 and 1930, he demonstrated an eye for talent that was enviable. Among the inner circle were John Betjeman, John Sparrow, Isaiah Berlin, and Kenneth Clark. Orbiting at a greater distance were Day-Lewis, Stephen Spender, Cyril Connolly, Rex Warner, Osbert Lancaster, and Henry Yorke. Evelyn Waugh and Anthony Powell enjoyed what might be called country membership. Much later, Noel Annan, Stuart Hampshire, and A. J. Ayer came into view. Some of these men divided their loyalties between Bowra and other magnets; some rebelled and then made atonement; none escaped without moments of difficulty. But, as a group, they represented some of the greatest talents that the Oxford of his day had to offer.

Only Bowra had the force of personality to attract talent and hold it in some sort of formation. His body was all authority. Though he was short of stature, one compact square formed the head and another compact square the body. Even when he grew stouter with age, no one would ever call him fat. His was a granite figure, made for the offensive. A Provost of Queen's was reminded of the appearance of Toad in *Wind in the Willows*,[88] but the analogy is a weak one. Bowra showed Toad's exuberance, but he had a greater sense of purpose. Maurice dominated any company he was in, not only by wit, but by sheer physical presence. Exercise was despised as boring and redundant. When an American friend suggested the expedient, Bowra's answer was firm: 'Exercise? Out of the question. I gave it up thirty years ago and felt rid of a terrible burden, and anyway there is no time for it in a full life.'[89] Somehow the conviction apparent in everything he said and did gave his body muscle.

Out of this body issued one of the most distinct voices of the twentieth century. It rose and fell in totally distinctive speech patterns, and many Bowristas consciously adopted elements of it into their own utterances. It was a bittern-booming voice, 'with the carrying power of the Last Trump'.[90] To receive a telephone call unexpectedly was to be rudely awakened. On one occasion, Stuart Hampshire 'nearly dropped it because I was blown backwards by the bounce and vigour in his voice; no one who has been in a London office speaks like that; I only know how tired and flat I and the people to whom I normally speak are when I talk to Maurice.'[91] With volume went distinctive rhythms. Bowra spoke at speed. His words had the quality of 'rapid musketry'.[92] A rattle of words would swoop down to a long-held vowel, before the sentence would end in a snap. Talking to him was, according to Hugh Lloyd-Jones, like confronting 'a machine gun'.[93] Isaiah Berlin, whose own speech patterns defied mimicry, observed that 'the words came in short, sharp bursts of precisely-aimed, concentrated fire as image, pun, metaphor, parody, seemed spontaneously to generate one another, in a succession of marvellously imaginative patterns, sometimes rising to high, wildly comical fantasy.'[94] It can hardly be a coincidence that so many witnesses fall back on the imagery of field guns to describe their friend's verbal accomplishments. Protégés flattered the Master by attempting the style. According to Evelyn Waugh, 'Maurice had formed the habits of speech of a whole generation.'[95]

'Bowraspeak' was not only a matter of accent and inflection, however. There was a private language that united the Bowristas. 'Presentable' suggested someone who could cope with their company; 'able' or 'able I'm afraid' meant someone who was just tolerable; 'upright' described a decent man or woman who could never subscribe to the Bowra creed; while 'nice, stupid man', 'shit', and 'shit of hell' delineated the several levels of wickedness. Disloyalty to friends might lead to periods of silence known as 'no speak'. Part of the fun of life was 'to cause pain' to enemies, or to 'make bad blood' among them.[96] Such penalties should be inflicted on people like Richard Crossman, denounced as 'Double Crossman', or on the Japanese professor with whom Bowra once had to share 'a long and interesting silence'.[97]

To modern ears, such language may sound a little unkind, but context is all important. Political correctness had not yet neutered conversation. For Bowra, the crusades in which he was engaged, were of such importance that there was no time to be fastidious. Enemies had to be mocked to bring their claims down, and friends had to be teased to keep them up to the mark. Since, with the latter, everything said was known to be spoken within the context of great affection, all could be forgiven. Everyone who knew Maurice was aware that going too far was part of the performance. As Noel Annan observed, 'I am bewildered by how to make people who never knew Maurice understand that the brutality of his comments on life didn't really matter at all, given his warmth and generosity.'[98] Equally, Anthony Powell was aware that, in dealing with Maurice, he was confronting 'a man quite different from any met with before'.[99] Quite simply it would have been absurd to expect him to follow conventions, verbal or otherwise. The leadership of the Bowristas could not have been accepted on any other terms.

Central to the Bowra creed was the insistence on hard work. He himself had a need to push himself into writing. He regarded such activity as the scholar's 'bulwark against morbidity'.[100] Without it, he would be lost. As he confessed to Alice James, 'I need work of this kind to keep me straight! I fear it comes from not having a family, but I have never dared to ask the psychologists.'[101] Periods, in which work proved difficult or in which words would not come, induced something close to panic. As early as 1924, he told Roy Harrod that 'my chief terror is weariness. I have never before realized how distressing it is not to be able to work. I gnaw the ground in anger sometimes because I can't think.'[102] Only in hard work could he fulfil his responsibilities to the Greeks and the poets, and bring their values safely into the new democracy. He and his friends had to work. Not to do so was personally corrupting and a betrayal of sacred causes.

Understandably therefore, to squander talent in idleness or superficiality was intolerable. In Bowra's creed, it was the sin against the Holy Ghost. When consulted about the possibility of Tolkien being offered the Companion of Honour, he wrote 'a forceful letter' against the proposal. No recognition should be given to someone who had published so little academic work, 'but only children's tales'.[103] When W. H. Auden's idleness ended in a Third Class degree, Maurice declared himself 'delighted'.[104] Early in life he had seen how unexpressed talent could send gangrene through a whole personality. A very promising contemporary at Cheltenham lost the chance of becoming a Cambridge don through idleness. He had to settle to being a schoolmaster in the provinces. Bowra saw his situation as a tragedy: 'This distresses me as I love the child and consider him quite unfit for so harsh and shattering a job.' Helping the talented out of inertia, goading them into a more fruitful life, was a burden willingly shouldered. His friend became 'another of the people I shall have to make work'.[105]

Maurice became a Fellow of Wadham in 1922. Clearly, with views such as these, his pupils were in for a taxing time. At the start, he found the College 'a bit diminished' academically, which was in itself 'a powerful incentive to get something done'.[106] He taught up to eighteen hours a week. His pupils were, inevitably, a mixture of the very gifted and the 'dullards, who were very difficult to teach, since they treated every attempt to help them as an affront to their dignity'.[107] He was equally conscientious about preparing lectures, and had a lifelong contempt for academics who did not take similar trouble. Such people offered 'unhappy undergraduates' nothing 'that might be called ideas', and left them in a kind of intellectual drought.[108] Pupils were instructed with a ruthless professionalism, couched in 'the full blast of his mocking cynical way'.[109] Inevitably, some undergraduates were put off. The method was too immediate and too challenging. Others, however, prospered. They discovered that it would be vulgar to laugh too much if Bowra declaimed Pindar's *Pythian Odes* while wearing a top hat to impersonate Zeus.[110] Pupils were provoked by his personality to compete. Rex Warner was delighted to receive more alpha marks in Honour Moderations than Bowra had received, even though the effort nearly brought on a nervous breakdown.[111] The traditional picture of Oxford in the twenties, a collage of drunkenness, idleness, and teddy bears, was unrecognizable in Bowra's rooms.

If Wadham undergraduates were pushed hard, pressure on the Bowristas, the chosen ones, was predictably even greater. Letters to and about them take on the tone of end-of-term reports. All too often they would be found wanting. The 'Old Boy' turned easily into 'the Headmaster'. As usual, some of the class performed well and some worked far below their potential. Kenneth Clark was a model pupil, producing book after book that invited the general reader to share the values of high art. Staying with the Clarks was always instructive and pleasing: 'We had a long and interesting talk *à deux* on the Sunday evening when everyone else was televisioning. He is very excited and pleased with his lectures, which will in time turn into another splendid book. So that is just what we want.'[112] Here was a fine example of the mission being carried forward.

But others would not, or could not, keep up, and this was Maurice's idea of committing offence. Cyril Connolly's problems all stemmed from the fact that he had 'ceased to read some twenty-five years ago', and was now indulged by an 'harem', who, after cooking and scrubbing, 'are allowed in after dessert to have a cup of coffee and listen respectfully while the Master talks. For this they are grateful.'[113] Noel Annan was given little sympathy when confessing to 'a sad state of Minko', a German colloquialism for an inferiority complex. Instead, he was told that 'Hard work, my boy, is what we expect from you. A good book—it is much needed—no one is writing and our civilisation is going to pot with books on "Planning for God" etc.'[114] Equally, the young Betjeman was a cause of concern. He did so little work that Bowra told him that he 'flatly' refused 'to appear as witness to character, if or when the crisis comes'.[115] As predicted, Betjeman was eventually sent down for failing examinations, and Bowra thought his behaviour 'contemptible'. He complained to Piers Synnott that Betjeman had 'been going to the dogs for a year. Sin getting the better of him and making him a bore where he used to be a comedian. It is a loss as his enjoyment of architecture is an enormous asset. He will certainly become a parson.'[116] In fact, Bowra went out of his way to rescue his protégé's career,[117] but the whole episode had been irritating.

Even when a Bowrista published something, the book would be read and marked with some severity. Maurice was pleased with Isaiah Berlin's study of Karl Marx and thought it 'an excellent work', but he also wished 'it had been written in English'.[118] Paddy Leigh Fermor certainly had 'a flow of words', but his reputation rested on the fact that everyone else in his type of literature was 'so dry and empty'.[119] No protégé was allowed to escape the consequences of producing shoddy or underweight work. For this there was a price to pay. In 1949, for example, Rex Warner returned to his old college in order to address its Poetry Society. Bowra, his old tutor, presided, and, in the presence of startled undergraduates, the following exchange took place:

> Warner—your book on Milton—page ?, line ?—following spelling and punctuation mistakes.
> Warden—printer's error!! printer's error!
> Oh, usual excuse, usual excuse.[120]

Metaphorically, Maurice filled the margins of his friends' books with head-masterly comments in red ink. Members of his court not only had to work hard, but they also had to work well.

In this respect, the most intractable problem was represented by John Sparrow. Bowra spent a lifetime trying to coax or bully this talented man to produce something of real quality. Letters from the 1920s contain sentences of uncompromising admonition: 'You ought to be working' and 'I *do hope* that you are working. Indeed it is my main anxiety.'[121] Unfortunately, when Sparrow finally produced *Sense and Beauty* in 1934, Maurice was unimpressed. His protégé was simply too ignorant on the subject of poetry, and, worse still, seemed to think that the writing of verse was a matter of logic rather than feeling. Sparrow the lawyer blinkered Sparrow the would-be critic.[122] His *Independent Essays* of 1963 was an improvement, but it still attracted from Bowra the sort of comment that might be found at the foot of an undergraduate essay: 'your method of close analysis, examination, and coming to a conclusion is delightfully orderly and first creates a curiosity and then satisfies it.'[123] Not surprisingly, perhaps, Sparrow retreated into minimalist studies of Renaissance Latin authors, a field in which Bowra himself had little expertise and could not therefore follow him.

To make matters worse, Sparrow perversely wasted his talent in triviali-ties. In 1962, for example, he achieved a certain notoriety by publishing an essay, which attempted to define exactly what Mellors the gamekeeper did with Lady Chatterley in D. H. Lawrence's novel. For Bowra, no exercise could be more futile, and he told Sparrow of his opinion;

> I am at a great disadvantage in that I cannot read *Lady C*, and that I have not read the account of the trial. However, I admit at once that the vital passage you quote on p. 38 calls for explanation, and you certainly give one. I have, however, a doubt. I don't believe Lawrence knew much about sex,

though of course Frieda in her Boche way tried to instruct him, and I think it possible that he does not mean anything very much. You in fact hint at this, and I feel your uncomfortable feelings about his cowardice, but I think the real explanation is that, in the last resort, he is just talking rot—not describing a real sexual act but some imaginary, impossible satisfaction.[124]

It was irritating that a favoured protégé could be taken up with such nonsense. He told Berlin that Sparrow's article was 'not merely trivial and mad, but ill-argued and inconclusive'.[125]

Such unremitting criticism made the friendship between Bowra and Sparrow difficult to maintain at times. When Bowra made his first will in 1940, Sparrow was appointed his literary executor, and he held this position of trust at his friend's death in 1971, but there were still periods of considerable coolness. In 1934, Isaiah Berlin bluntly told Maurice that he was pushing Sparrow too hard. This comment brought an apology of sorts, but, in asking for forgiveness, Bowra could not resist listing further defects in behaviour.

> Berlin, whose judgement I trust, tells me that I am often cruel to you, and I have thought it over and decided that he is right, and I am filled with shame and humiliation, because I can't feel that real cruelty is justified except towards the wicked, and I don't like to think I show it towards my friends … For this I am deeply sorry, and would like to think that it will not occur again. If it does, you must tell me at once. I definitely find your attitude to life too ethical … I feel that you have lots of moral standards which I do not share … in regarding morality as a set of rules, whereas what I like is a good man, a unique individual who is plainly good irrespective of rules.

The same letter ends with a complaint about Sparrow's academic 'muddling', and his tendency to be always late in keeping appointments.[126]

At the end of his life, Maurice could still not escape the feeling that his star pupil had failed him. In company, Sparrow was, of course, 'still infinitely agreeable', but 'alas for the way he spends his gifts. It is a kind of death wish. He longs to do himself in somehow, and to do quite of lot of others in at the same time.'[127] Six months before his death, Bowra was still worrying away at a problem that had puzzled him for years. He identified in Sparrow a 'terrible guilt about the way he has not used the gods' glorious gifts, and after all they gave him a packet. That is why he is so proud of his looks. Those at least he has kept, like Dorian Gray.'[128] As Sparrow and all the others would repeatedly learn, securing and keeping Bowra's approval was a labour for Sisyphus.

Not fulfilling promise was the most severe infringement of the code of the Bowristas, but it was not the only one. In advocating hard work, Maurice referred exclusively to academic performance. The vindication of the Greeks and the poets was a matter for books and lectures. Everything else was a distraction. Once again, his views followed precedents set by Mallarmé and George. Cyril Radcliffe, who earned Bowra's anathema for initially enticing Sparrow away into the law, was acutely aware that for 'dear Maurice ... the only true intellectual life is the academic calling, distinguished occasionally (should I say occasionally?) by the signature of joint letters to The Times.'[129] At the Bar, clever men dissipated their talents in making rich men richer. Equally, a career in politics only offered the illusion to men of ability that they could influence affairs. It was a terrible disappointment when Hugh Gaitskell chose this path. As for the Civil Service, there was nothing to be gained except a certain pomposity among the paper clips. When John Redcliffe-Maud left Oxford for bureaucracy in 1929, Bowra reminded him that 'not everyone that saieth Maud, Maud, shall inherit the Kingdom of Heaven'.[130]

In Maurice's mind, these careers constituted an establishment whose values should have repelled a true Bowrista. When a figure from this world died, Bowra was pleasantly surprised before sadly reflecting that it 'won't do any good, won't do any good—always more of them'.[131] For someone who had always seen himself at something of a tangent to his countrymen, the established world of lawyers, politicians, and civil servants represented so much of what was amiss with England. For talented men to waste their abilities in following its conventions and chasing its honours was depressing. Real life had more to offer. In Bowra's view, those who dismissed the Oxford life as one lived in ivory towers, irrelevant and complacent, said more about themselves than about Oxford. They simply had no idea what they were missing.

Criticism of each other and each other's work, however, could only be made within the privacy of the Bowra circle. To the external world, Bowristas had to show unswerving loyalty to each other and to Maurice himself. The word 'disloyal' was one of the most severe and most bitter in the group's vocabulary. Acts of disloyalty could range from an incautious sentence to the promotion of an inappropriate author. Bowra's fear of emotional rebuff demanded loyalty, and so did participation in his crusades. So strict was this rule that Bowra's friendships were often punctuated by spats with friends, who, for one reason or another, had not held the line. Transgressions could be great or small. John Bamborough was sentenced to a period of 'no speak' for refusing to support the idea of giving an honorary degree to Charlie Chaplin.[132] When Isaiah Berlin and Noel Annan found the company of Edmund Wilson agreeable, one of Maurice's greatest bêtes noirs, they wrote about their escapade, like errant schoolboys, who had successfully defied a headmaster: 'I secretly see Mr Edmund Wilson with whom (don't tell Maurice) my relations are becoming quite warm.'[133]

The most startling consequences of showing disloyalty were visited on Anthony Powell. For most of his undergraduate career, he had passed all Maurice's tests. So much so in fact that he was invited to spend a few days in Wadham. But disaster struck when he confessed over dinner 'how little I liked being in Oxford, and how I longed to get it over and go down … It took some thirty-five years for my relationship with Bowra to recover from that evening in Wadham.'[134] For an undergraduate to speak ill of Oxford was insupportable. It was to demonstrate a complete lack of understanding of Maurice's crusades for Greeks and poets, who would surely, in Bowra's view, have recognized Oxford as among the holiest of cities.

Inevitably, some of the more determined spirits among the Bowristas found this degree of subordination impossible to sustain. Cyril Connolly entered a lifetime of snarled relationship with Bowra because he could not control his determination to mock. At Minehead, as has been noted, he held Maurice the lover up to ridicule, in a way which his victim found 'very adroit and sheds light on Cyril's capacity for treachery; it is indeed greater than I had dreamed. I once thought that while he liked one he was fairly loyal; this is not in any sense true … Another year of his offensive venom would be too much for me.'[135] War was declared, which in turn led Connolly to complain:

> I hear you have begun an offensive against me again. Can't you manage to leave me alone for a moment, for, after all, it must be nine months since we last met, and as we are so little in each other's way, I don't see how a reopening of your former crusade will do you any good. I have made a point of not making bad blood about you, but you can't expect me not to retaliate, and, between us, we will only succeed in making a great many people dislike us … I realise that to you absence and failure are unforgivable sins, but I am neither wholly absent, nor completely failing … but if you want to go on quarrelling, this time I shall quarrel too—though I shall always acknowledge the intellectual debt I owe you.[136]

Connolly was almost certainly the first person to be on the receiving end of the remark 'Up-and-coming young man; hasn't come yet.' He would not be the last.

Between 1926 and 1945, the two men only met at infrequent intervals. Elizabeth Bowen was not the only hostess to 'not quite know if it would do' to have them as guests in the same house.[137] Sometimes Bowra would apologize for his 'unguarded and thoughtless talk about Connolly',[138] but such moments were rare. A real rapprochement between the two men only took place in the 1960s. Then the strangeness of the world around them reunited people with the values of the Twenties. Connolly was delighted to be back in Wadham, as a prodigal returning: 'ringing your bell, and seeing you was the best. I felt like Adam re-admitted to Eden as an old boy. One reason I have kept away from Oxford is that I can't bear it unless I stay with you, and if I stay with you I am afraid I will get on your nerves.'[139] He would be touched by Maurice's decision to leave him all his copies of Yeats, which the poet himself had inscribed. 'Perhaps', he wrote, 'we have forgiven each other.'[140]

To read of grudges held over decades by men who, on the face of it, ought to have known better is to invite explanation. To Bowra, these contests of will were of supreme importance. Not only was his emotional life always in need of reassurance rather than challenge, but there were also larger issues at stake. To mock him was to bring into ridicule those causes with which his personality had become completely entangled. Men and women who understood the points he was making about Greeks and poetry should have understood that he had to lead. It was simply frivolous for Connolly and his type to behave as they did. They remained Bowristas because they saw Maurice's point, and both Powell and Connolly came back into friendship late in life, but their difficulties only gave evidence of what moved Bowra to implacable behaviour. He cared for certain things too much to be able to do anything else.

After all, many men were so incapable of loyalty to any cause or anyone that there could be no question of them being admitted to the Bowra court. Goronwy Rees, for example, should have been an obvious candidate for the Immoral Front. He had wit, high intellect, and a liking for the good life. Yet Maurice disliked him intensely. In his view, Rees was incapable of being loyal to anyone. In 1936, a violent disagreement took place between the two men, the origin of which is obscure. It may have been provoked by Rees's decision to abandon an *affaire* with Elizabeth Bowen, in order to begin one with Rosamond Lehmann, while her husband was fighting in Spain. Maurice reported the tale to Marian Frankfurter:

> Rees is very much about, having a flaunting affair with Rosamond Lehmann, while her husband is driving a lorry in Barcelona. She is grey-haired and childish, but Rees sits on her chair-arm and makes goo-goo eyes at her. She does not like any joke at her expense and thinks I am very cruel to him because of my policy of keeping him on the run. He had dedicated his new book 'To E.B.', which will do just as well for Elizabeth Bibesco as for Elizabeth Bowen or my mother or anyone else. Very clever of him. The Bowen still sees a lot of him and always weeps after it.[141]

With Elizabeth Bowen, Maurice enjoyed a longstanding and untroubled friendship. The episode was unedifying and seemed to prove that Rees was 'a known non-loyalist'.[142]

After the War, Bowra despised Rees for the pursuit of the Cambridge spies, who had once been his friends. For Bowra, loyalty to individuals was at least as important as duties to a state. Governments, after all, liked having secrets for the sake of having secrets. As he casually observed, 'I can't really mind spies. After all they believe that knowledge should not be locked up in secret boxes, as our Cabinet loves to do, and in peace they can't do much harm, and in war anyone else can do quite as much.'[143] But Rees was accused of something much more serious than putting civic duty before personal friendship. It was obvious to Bowra that he took pleasure in the hunting down of men. When Rees denounced Anthony Blunt without producing substantial evidence, Bowra described it as 'a witch-hunt'.[144] Similarly, although Maurice disliked Guy Burgess, whose raffishness repelled him, he was not prepared to join the chase that Rees had helped to instigate. He simply told Rees to 'Go hang yourself from a judas tree.'[145]

Such views may be thought eccentric. In the early years of the Cold War, the Cambridge spies did incalculable damage. Lives were certainly lost as a result of their activities, and therefore Bowra's views could be called irresponsible, particularly because he had no liking for any of the men involved. However, there was a visceral reaction in Maurice to the spectacle of the state bearing down on an individual. His American friends told him of the terrifying impact of McCarthyism at the same time that the Cambridge men came under attack. Establishments in both countries seemed to relish their duty to persecute and prosecute. If a friend became caught up in such misery, then of course help should be offered. So paramount was the idea of loyalty in friendships, in Maurice's mind, that it should above all show itself when friends were most in the wrong. Those who shared this view, like Cyril Connolly, remained on terms. Those to whom it meant nothing, like Goronwy Rees, were despised.

Clearly, to be a Bowrista was emotionally and intellectually wearing, but the rewards were commensurate. In the 1920s, clever undergraduates like Day-Lewis and Rex Warner would be taken to Ottoline Morrell's Garsington for weekends in the company of Aldous Huxley, D. H. Lawrence, and Bertrand Russell.[146] When George Huxley set out on a tour of America, he was fortified with letters of introduction to Arthur Schlesinger and Felix Frankfurter.[147] It was always a Bowra function to introduce the promising young to those whose reputations were already made. What Day-Lewis called 'far flung intrigues'[148] secured him teaching posts at Sherborne and Cheltenham, and protected him when he was denounced to the governors of the latter school for lecturing on the merits of collective farming.[149] Betjeman was set up as a critic of architecture,[150] and even Cyril Connolly, the blackest of black sheep, was not completely abandoned. At critical moments in his life, when doubt about his abilities was at its most acute, the reassuring letter duly arrived. He was told that he was 'too critical and too clever'[151] to be cast down by supposed failure in a world where lesser men set the rules.

A friendship with Maurice was therefore hard on the nerves but infinitely rewarding. There was nothing shallow about it. Periods of turbulence were inevitable, but no experience of 'no speak' was without term. An old friendship, grown however chill, could always be warmed into life. Membership of the Immoral Front could be renewed. As he grew older, the gap between the master and the pupil perceptively narrowed, as it always does. Maurice could be addressed more and more as an equal, not least because, as he needed more and more to be looked after in old age, the power structure in his friendships changed. He depended on the Clarks and the Annans to bring him through the many threats of Christmas, against whose festivities he had no defence.[152] In the summer vacations, it was the turn of the Berlins or Leigh Fermors. For over thirty years, Betjeman overcame problems arising from Bowra's inability to drive by acting as chauffeur. As late as the 1960s, undergraduates were able to observe the two men in complementary, battered trilby hats, setting out for an assault on Oxfordshire's architecture. Consciously or unconsciously, when a Bowrista accepted Maurice's shilling in the 1920s or 1930s, he was making a commitment for life. They owed him the liberation of their personality, and this was repaid in affectionate gratitude.

The rules by which Bowra governed his court raised large questions for all those involved. For his protégés, his company was universally acknowledged to be enriching and liberating. Quite literally, they would have been different people and led different lives had they not known him. On the other hand, to be captivated by a commanding personality can be to risk being smothered. There would be the fear that no work could ever quite reach the standard that Maurice expected. It is possible that people like Connolly and Sparrow would have produced more criticism and scholarship if they had worked under a different configuration of stars. Kenneth Clark, who escaped into art history, about which Bowra knew relatively little, thought that Connolly was wise to leave Oxford: 'Maurice, though he encouraged him to read, also encouraged a disastrous vein of malice and a very tiresome taste for sex as the only topic of conversations.'[153] In 1925, Connolly the undergraduate found it difficult to establish his own view of the world, because he was 'so impregnated with Maurice that the consciousness of his hostility warps my outlook as much as his friendship did—I mean I can only see myself through his eyes now as an uncouth menial at Oxford, a deceitful bitch in vacations.'[154] In periods of disfavour, Connolly would 'wake up in the middle of the night and seem to hear that inexorable, luncheon-party voice tearing him to pieces. He once made Lord Eccles cry.'[155] But Connolly's criticisms end with the reflection that Maurice mellowed into 'a rock-like friend and counsellor'.[156]

There was the same ambivalence in John Sparrow. He never felt that he had come up to Maurice's expectations, and was grateful for any mark of approbation. When the two men met in London, in 1934, Sparrow was relieved that Bowra 'was very nice … He noticed me occasionally, and was not rude.'[157] Mutual friends toyed with the idea that Sparrow's notorious refusal to publish was, perversely, the only way he could define himself against Bowra. As Maurice Hastings put it:

John has a most secret sense of inferiority. And in regard to *Maurice*. When first a Fellow of All Souls, he used to draw me aside and tell me *preposterous* tales of how Maurice was always snubbing him. I assured him that there was nothing in it—he knew what Maurice was like! But I think it has grown worse. He is determined to assert himself against Maurice and NOT doing anything is part of it. He won't be bullied into anything—he feels! It is purely childish and very unfortunate.[158]

Isaiah Berlin, recognizing that he and Sparrow were privy to Maurice's 'inner pathos', asked his friend, 'How much are you prepared to pander, and for how long? I am, quite a lot; for quite a long time. But why? Affection? Habit? Gratitude? Can you answer?'[159] Almost certainly, Sparrow would have found it hard to reply.

Demands for endless effort, and for subscription to causes defined by himself, were rules that caused difficulties for Maurice himself. The question arises of whether he ever had many friends, if friendship is described as an emotional commitment among equals. Only Dadie Rylands was an exact contemporary. Everyone else was younger, with minds to instruct, talents to be brought out, and careers to be assisted. If friendship was to be achieved, a master–pupil relationship had to be dissolved in favour of something more equal in nature. Bowra found this transformation difficult, when his every instinct told him to lead. But having few equals is a lonely business, and being alone was fearful. As early as 1922 he told Roy Harrod that 'I have been abroad. I loathed most of it as I was alone. I found myself—a horrible discovery. I have been trying to lose myself ever since.' Mercifully, he had found a new undergraduate who had to be 'saved from bad friends'. The boy 'fills the gap which I always have to get filled'.[160]

In theory, no friend was closer than Isaiah Berlin. With a commanding intellect and the broadest of cultures, he was totally congenial to Bowra. Yet even he was kept at arm's length, as a master maintains a distance between himself and a pupil. In September 1935, they travelled to Portugal together, and Bowra's account of the excursion to Elizabeth Bowen is instructive.

> The fact is that Shayah [Berlin] was an indispensable part of the scheme, and I felt that I did not want to be intimately with him for a long time. Much as I enjoy his company, I find that somehow he invades my personality and hampers me, chiefly by his enormous curiosity, but also by his lack of subtlety on small things.[161]

To travel alone was an uncomfortable experience; to travel with a great friend was not much better. Not surprisingly, Lady Berlin was sure that although Isaiah would endlessly worry about 'what would Maurice say?', it would be a mistake to describe him as 'an intimate friend'.[162]

Almost certainly, Maurice found the emotional claims in strong friendship as difficult to manage as those found in marriage. Both exposed the individual to attack and uncovered vulnerabilities. Protégés were safer. There was always the risk of disloyalty and desertion, and there were bound to be periods of turbulence, but if he always led, his 'inner self' would be secure. To be caught up in his system was at once the greatest of privileges and something of a burden. The Bowristas were rightly envied. In Maurice's company, there always seemed to be more oxygen in the room. The liberation of a personality is a matter of some importance. Like Mallarmé's circle and George's Kreis, the Bowra court was a very distinctive feature of first Oxford, and then national life. But as in all friendships, there was both benefit and cost.

8

Bowra and the Wider World, 1922–1939

Maurice was without doubt the most famous or notorious Oxford don of his generation. To the outside world, he was often mistaken for Oxford. No other academic enjoyed the range of his European connections, or claimed membership of so many circles outside the University. By sheer force of wit and personality, he was transfigured into a kind of totem. Symbolic stories, passed on from one generation to another, which allegedly illustrated the characteristics and vagaries of donnery, were told about him as gospel truth. Wadham men found it 'pleasant to hear all the Jowett stories being told about you'.[1] There was the story about young academics trying to out-manoeuvre a polymath Head of House by collectively reading an article on Persian pottery, which would then form the basis of High Table conversation. To their horror, they then discover that the article had been written by the man they were trying to catch out. Another tale concerned Parsons' Pleasure, a bathing establishment in which dons swam and sunbathed naked. On one occasion, a boatload of ladies came by, and men hurriedly tied towels around their waists. One man, however, put the towel over his head, arguing that it was by his face that he was known in Oxford. These anecdotes were told about Bowra, as they had been told about others before him. There is not the slightest evidence that they concerned Bowra himself. Quite simply, they were oral myths intended to define what a great academic might have done. Bowra was a great academic, and therefore became the focal point for traditional stories. The Oxford tribe found a reassuring continuity in retailing them.

The same anthropological device was discernible with regard to Oxford wit. Maurice was undoubtedly the master of the genre. His epigrams and command of irony circulated freely around the University. But his reputation was such that every funny story was attributed to him. During the student troubles of the late 1960s, for example, it was rumoured that one Head of House solemnly informed a rather startled student leader that his Senior Common Room included one VC, four experts in karate, three specialists in chemical warfare, and an Olympic fencing champion. No less a figure than Senator Fulbright was delighted with this story, and told America that the Head of House in question was Bowra. It could be no one else. Stuart Hampshire was, in turn, amused by this outcome: 'The truth of the matter is that it is an amusing invention, which was put to the credit, quite falsely, of Sir Maurice Bowra, just because he was a well-known Oxford wit, who might have said something of this kind.'[2]

Another compliment to Bowra's pre-eminence was that he was a target for teasing, in the way that schoolchildren secretly mock headmasters. Such acts combined affection and insubordination in a healthy mixture. Osbert Lancaster, who had been a member of the Bowra court as an undergraduate, frequently represented the distinctive features of his mentor in cartoons. Hugh Trevor-Roper, while staying in Bangkok, was delighted to read in a local newspaper of a certain Maggie Bowra, a nightclub singer, who had just come to the attention of the authorities in a rather unsavoury manner. The lady had apparently resisted attempts to arrest her with some spirit. Sending a copy of the article to John Sparrow, Trevor-Roper also included an imaginary letter from Maggie to her 'uncle Maurice', which announced her imminent arrival in Wadham, and which suggested that she might earn her keep by entertaining the undergraduates. She thought she would be 'popular among the boys, and perhaps I could cheer up Old Souls too'.[3] Such jokes were the equivalent of writing something slightly rude on a blackboard.

Even more remarkable was the fact that Bowra's powerful personality proved irresistible to the novelist in search of good copy. No Oxford academic has been so frequently portrayed in literature. But, importantly, misattributions are just as common. Any depiction of a wit or polymath in a novel was assumed, often mistakenly, to be Bowra, because he so dominated the field. Isaiah Berlin assured Felix Frankfurter, for example, that Maurice had been 'teased' as a character in Virginia Woolf's *Night and Day*, and that the portrayal had been disturbing.[4] In fact, Bowra only met the Woolfs some years after the book had been written. Berlin's mistake stemmed entirely from the assumption that his friend had no rivals in suggesting to the outside world what an academic was like.

Genuine representations of Maurice are not hard to find. Twice, he was put into a detective story, though, surprisingly, never as murderer or victim. Day-Lewis, writing under the pseudonym of Nicholas Blake, created the character of Philip Starling, Fellow of All Saints, who was 'the foremost authority in England on Homeric civilisation and literature'. Starling was short of stature, and had 'an exaggerated candour [that] was appallingly infectious, and had led three generations of undergraduates into the most wholesome exposure of their private lives'. As bodies pile up around him, Starling claimed to 'relish the seamy side of life. But one sees so much of it in the Senior Common Room that there is no need to associate with professional criminals.'[5] In *Operation Pax*, Michael Innes introduced readers to Mark Bultitude of St Bede's, 'whose form was globular and his legs were short'. He was Oxford's 'most completely civilized being', and was so convinced about the evils of exercise that he referred to the slight incline in Beaumont Street as a hill. Under layers of verbal affectation, however, lay a deep seriousness of purpose, and Bultitude is given the honour of helping Inspector Appleby to solve this particular case.[6]

With only slightly more gravity of purpose, Lord Berners used Maurice as the model for the Provost of Unity College in *Far from the Madding War* of 1941. Berners had recently spent some months as a refugee in the Lodgings at Wadham but this experiment in living had not been a success. Maurice had found him a job in the Taylorian Library, which he had found boring, and had insisted on receiving assistance in growing 'edible matter' in the Warden's garden, which had offended his sensibilities.[7] Inevitably, therefore, the portrayal of Bowra by Berners contained equal measures of truth and malice: 'In his own house he had people more or less at his mercy,' and there, 'in spite of a pronounced disregard for the feelings of others, the Provost concealed beneath a certain spikiness the sensitive and kindly nature of a hedgehog.' His rudeness was 'a sort of anti-aircraft barrage against the insidious attacks of sentiment'. All in all, 'with his malicious understanding of human nature, his irascibility and his impatience of bores, [he] could never have settled down into being a dear old man. He was therefore inclined to welcome the reputation that had been thrust upon him, and he knew that eccentricity covers a multitude of sins.'[8] In penning this description, Berners was not so much an imaginative artist creating a character, as a sharp-eyed critic giving a point of view.

In periods of 'no speak', portraying Maurice in literary form was easier on the nerves than confronting him in person. While in exile, Cyril Connolly created the character of 'Mr Bogey', an Oxford don with no redeeming qualities at all;

> A little round man, Mr Bogey stands on the pavement in an ulster, a very ambitious man, he is thinking about Blenheim and how to stop other professors from going there ... [He said that he] saw other dons in ulsters, taller than me, desiccated, middle-aged, low-born, and I dislike them for reminding me of my appearance, of who I am. I can't bear my contemporaries or my equals, though I have to keep on the right side of those who can elect me Professor of Greek. My taste in literature is vulgar and rhetorical. I can't write but nobody knows that. I propose to earl's daughters after going to stay with their brothers. I have a right to the good things of the world. I am a magnificent talker, a wit who cauterises everyone, myself included.[9]

To mix truth with falsehood is an effective form of propaganda. The one gives credibility to the other. Maurice was, for example, certainly ambitious, but never a social snob. To be accused of so much indirectly underlines the scale of the target that Bowra presented to those who wished to praise or vilify. He could not be ignored.

The most serious and reflective representation of Maurice in literature was provided by Elizabeth Bowen. The two had met in Ireland, and had become good friends in the early years of the 1930s. It was a friendship that was less troubled than almost any other that Bowra took on. He chivalrously defended her against what he took to be the emotional depredations of Goronwy Rees, and there was an interchange of visiting that clearly gave pleasure. In *To the North* of 1932, Elizabeth Bowen created the character of Markie, which, almost certainly, described Maurice in his thirty-fourth year. All the usual attributes are in place. Markie, 'having no neck ... veered bodily from the waist, which gave one an alarming sense of his full attention'. His wit was 'incisive, spectacular, mordant'. His 'recollections' were 'entirely vindictive'. Since he looked 'like the Frog Footman', he repeatedly proclaimed that he was 'not the sort of person anybody could marry'. He was a man of 'shocking reputation', who, on entering a room, was always 'delighted to see himself'. In the novel, Markie is completely honest about his inability to love, because his self-doubt was too strong. Despite this, he attempts to have an *affaire* with a young, impressionable, and inexperienced woman, with catastrophic results.[10] The story is told with sympathy rather than malice, and found favour with Maurice's friends. Isaiah Berlin told the author that 'Markie is wonderfully unhorrifying and even sympathetic.' He was a character that Berlin was 'prepared to defend always and against anyone'.[11]

In the hands of literary friends, Maurice became a model for the eccentric don, the ambitious don, and the emotionally impaired don. He was the stereotype for donnery in all its forms. This totemic quality was achieved through a breadth of reading that few could match, an attacking personality that few would want to challenge, and a caustic wit that few escaped with impunity. If something was funny, it had to be said. In Bowra's view, it would have been pathetic to restrain language for fear of hurting. Language was, after all, a weapon, and always had been. Someone moving in the Bowra circle could not cry foul if he or she suddenly found their own personalities held up to scrutiny, but some people, with thinner skins, were led to protest. Stephen Spender, in later life, rather regretted 'the caddishness of that period of English social history, in which Maurice—in all his aspects—undoubtedly fits'.[12] Bowra's humour was unscrupulous and compelling.

His enemies, of course, provided the main targets. Sir Ifor Evans of Cambridge was 'the Fake's Progress'. David Mathew, the Roman Catholic divine, was the 'Prime Example of the Word made Flesh'. Renée Hampshire was 'the Voice' or 'the Influence under which was her husband'. T. S. R. Boase of Magdalen suffered from 'Cerebral Thromboasis'. The endless loquacity of Tommy Balogh produced 'Monologue, Dialogue and Balogh'. Such epithets were not only an amusing playing with words and sounds, however. They also captured something of the victim's personality, and exposed it to public view. Friends fared little better. The fluffy dressiness of Rosamond Lehmann led to her being labelled 'the Meringue Outang', a phrase which allegedly kept Edith Sitwell 'happy' ever after.[13] Noel Annan was said to feel things 'only sin-deep',[14] while a would-be acquaintance was dismissed as 'one of my more delible memories'. Betjeman's religion was mocked in letters by exhortations to 'prey on us now and in the hour of our death',[15] while a rowing enthusiast became the link between homo sapiens and the Neanderthals. Maurice entered a room 'like a naval vessel'[16] with all the guns run out.

This was not the wit of the Senior Common Room or High Table. It worked best at private dinner parties and in salons. In its epigrammatic nature, it owed much to the Wildean style of the 1890s, as Stuart Hampshire and many others noted. Developed at Cheltenham College as part of a 'defensive carapace',[17] it was polished by contact with Adrian Bishop and Philip Ritchie. Playing with words was power in the highly literary sort of world that then dominated social life. They could sting and they could amuse. With close friends, words turned into games. Ernst Kantorowicz and Bowra much enjoyed inventing names for new additions to the Hilton chain of hotels: 'eg the one in Pisa will be called the "Tilton Hilton" that in Baden-Baden of course "the Hilton Hilton", and for the one in Moscow we found "the Comrade Hilton".'[18] Paradise would have a 'Milton Hilton'. Just occasionally, the wit would be turned against himself. When he heard of a best-seller entitled *Lost Identity*, he thought the author 'clever', because 'I'm doomed to be with my identity forever.'[19] In general, however, keeping up with Maurice in conversation was a matter of always being on the qui vive, of always being willing to take risks.

In all his utterances, there was a conscious desire to startle. In 1950, he agreed to speak to Eton's Literary Society on the topic of 'Unwritten Masterpieces'. A clearly puzzled schoolboy attempted to take the minutes. After explaining that

> the chief merit of 'unwriting' lay in the power to prevent others from undertaking the same project, Maurice proceeded to give examples. Karl Marx, in his view, should have published his promised life of Balzac rather than *Das Kapital*, for then 'the Capitalist classes would have been shown up in their full villainy [*sic*] and Père Goriot's death attributed to the ruthless pressure of economic forces'.

If the Etonian audience was able to unravel so many layers of irony successfully, question time brought more challenges. Here,

> he related Balzac and Lewis Carroll to the railway depression of the seventies; he compared Sherlock Holmes to Falstaff as the character who was not allowed to die. He asked a distinguished Colleger whether he belonged to a Swiss Society called 'Les Amis de Charles Morgan'; he deprecated the results of a competition held in Vienna for the completion of the Unfinished Symphony.

The schoolboy secretary had done his best, but the concluding sentence of his minutes suggests that he had been treading water on the evening in question. Bowra 'was obviously a most interesting man, and it was a pity he did not choose a more interesting subject'.[20] Those not on the Bowra wavelength would always fall back on this sort of remark.

The Bowra style made him a welcome guest in many of the salons around which English intellectual life gathered between the Wars. Women of wealth and character hosted parties with the deliberate intention of introducing the talented to each other. Guests drank the house wine and subscribed to the menu of ideas that the hostess thought important. Such gatherings were ideal arenas for Maurice's performances. He 'liked clowning'; and here he 'could slash at windmills'. Here, too, people knew that 'Maurice never means what he says', which was a compliment to his irony and understatement, but which, on the occasions when Bowra spoke truth, exposed the speaker to yet more risk. The game simply became more complicated. As early as 1923, he was aware that all this attention fed the vanity in his personality, but he rarely declined an invitation.[21] At these long weekends, Bowra met the powerful from London, and became in their minds the personification of Oxford.

In those decades, social relationships and reputations were moulded by talk, and good talk, to an extent that later generations might find hard to understand. An American visitor noted without embarrassment that 'we all talk about each other all the time, don't we?'[22] Talking, for Maurice, was 'an opiate' dulling 'absurd but real fears about dying, dying in poverty, exposure of private life'.[23] If discovering a social difficulty, he 'boomed it away'.[24] Theatre managers found him a difficult patron to deal with, because his habit of commenting loudly on the play during the performance irritated other members of the audience.[25] By contrast, moving around salons where he was expected to speak was much more congenial. Sadly for Bowra, therefore, few salons survived the social and financial consequences of the Second World War. In this, as in many other ways, the post-War world was more intimidating than the one he had known. But between 1922 and 1939, he had time to establish a reputation in circles outside Oxford that would be his for life.[26]

In only one coterie, in fact, did Maurice experience almost complete failure. Most of the denizens of Bloomsbury could not cope with him, though it is not clear from the evidence who exactly rejected whom. According to Isaiah Berlin, Maurice had been 'snubbed by Bloomsbury ... so brutally',[27] that he had been forbidden their company. Jeremy Hutchinson agreed.[28] On the other hand, Stuart Hampshire believed that Bowra could never have been 'a natural denizen' of Bloomsbury, which he characterized as 'a rather pretentious society talking about pictures'.[29] He was 'too noisey'[30] for Bloomsbury sensibility, and his taste for high living would unsettle Bloomsbury digestive systems. Almost certainly, neither wished to have very much to do with the other. In 1927, Maurice expressed a clear preference to John Sparrow: 'In London I alternated between Mr Hastings' champagne dinners and suppers at the Berkeley and some dim garrets in the … circle of Bloomsbury. I realized that Bloomsbury is like the early Church—fanatical, dirty, persecuted, jealous. I preferred Mr Hastings champagne at 45/- a bottle.'[31]

Almost certainly, contact had been made with leading Bloomsberries through the good offices of Dadie Rylands in Cambridge. Maurice certainly knew the Woolfs, and as has been noted, he had spent weekends with Lytton Strachey and the Partridges. These experiences convinced him that there was something wrong with them. It was true that they had greatly contributed to the overthrow of Victorian morality, and for this they should be applauded, but it was all so rational and so cerebral. Their experiments in sexual coupling seemed to stem from a sense of duty. There was little warmth or spontaneity anywhere. To Bowra, their candour was 'odious', because it was 'cold and puritanical'. For all their emancipated language, he thought them the ultimate moralists. According to him, they 'kept asking themselves what they'd done wrong—no good aesthete ever did that'.[32] Not surprisingly, he dismissed Virginia Woolf's novels; 'I find her a bore, dislike her imagery, suspect her psychology.'[33]

Worse still, having destroyed the stifling conventions of Victorian England, they set up conventions of their own, from which no deviation was allowed, and hence Bowra's analogy between the set and the early Church. For example, the championing of modern French art seemed to necessitate the condemnation of established masters. Maurice liked both. As it happened, the young Kenneth Clark preferred Raphael and Michaelangelo to Derain and Matisse, and Bowra thought he had every right to such an opinion. Later, Clark reflected that this was one of the reasons 'why he never got on with the Bloomsberries'.[34] Their high thinking and plain living sat comfortably with a tendency to persecute other dissenters. In trying to describe Bloomsbury to an American friend, Maurice reflected on 'how absurd the Bloomsbury circle was, with its ridiculous little philosophy about beautiful states of mind'.[35] They were cold and small scale. Bowra preferred his friends to have more red blood in their veins.

There was no shortage of this liquid at Sutton Courtney, where Margot Asquith held court at The Wharf. The house was only a few miles from Oxford, and The Wharf's guest books make it clear that Maurice was a regular visitor through the 1920s, but particularly between October 1922 and February 1924, and again between December 1928 and July 1929.[36] Here he rubbed shoulders with E. M. Forster, Desmond McCarthy, L. P. Hartley, and the Princess Bibesco, who could give him a direct link with the world of Proust. As for politicians, he shared the house with Asquith himself, Winston Churchill, and grand old men of the Liberal Party, like Haldane and McKenna, who had served their apprenticeships under Gladstone. Collectively, it was a much more congenial company than anything Cambridge could offer. Mercifully, the Asquiths liked 'a good dinner', and had no objection to 'making bad blood' among enemies.[37] One Asquith cousin, Katharine Tennant, 'very unAsquithy—much more honest and kind hearted',[38] became the object of a brief flirtation. Even though there was, on occasion, too much 'splash and snobbery'[39] at The Wharf, the atmosphere was worldly and always interesting. At one such weekend, he was introduced to the first Russian woman to be elected to the Duma after the Revolution, and 'she endeared Lenin to me by saying that he enjoyed hunting cats. He is human after all.'[40]

For Margot Asquith herself he had nothing but praise. Her tongue was sharp and her view of life unsentimental. He also discerned in her a loyalty to those she liked. Staying at The Wharf a matter of hours before Asquith died, he saw her in grief: 'Lord Oxford has joined Hardy and Haig. I dined at The Wharf 36 hours before his death. It was terrible. Margot, white with watching by his bed, flitted in and out of the room like a ghost and refused to eat... The old man did well by refusing to be buried in the Abbey.'[41] Eighteen months later, her resilience in widowhood was admirable: 'I spent an agreeable day at The Wharf today. Margot was in terrific form. She has quite recovered from the old man's death, and delivered a great attack on Lord Lonsdale, on the grounds that he was no good in the hunting field.'[42] In sum, she was a vital force in a way that Virginia Woolf could never be. It was true that there was, inevitably, too much politics in conversations at The Wharf, but the literary element in the mix was always compelling. After a weekend with the Asquiths, Maurice could return to Oxford with stories, contacts, and information that was available to few other academics.

For the most congenial company, however, Maurice visited the Garsington of Ottoline Morrell. Her home was only five miles or so from Oxford, but accessibility was only the least of its attractions, for here was the literary salon par excellence. In her company, he met T. S. Eliot, W. B. Yeats,

Aldous Huxley, and Bertrand Russell. With some justice, he told her 'how delightful your friends are—and how different from the dead sensualists of Bloomsbury or the loud activities of the rich … an atmosphere of literary controversy [is] surely one of the best things in life.'[43] At Garsington, he was shown 'The Waste Land' in manuscript, which he described as 'a marvellous type-written poem of TSE on living corpses'.[44] At Garsington, Ottoline Morrell became for a time a kind of muse. Maurice's attempts at poetry would be submitted to her for comment and approval: 'I enclose some more verses—only by hard practice that [sic] one can become only better. The days of distant inspiration are over and one has to work instead.'[45] Through Garsington he was emboldened to send in verses to T. S. Eliot for possible publication in The Monthly Criterion: 'Really they are not the right sort of thing for him, not only too incompetent but [they] have an old-fashioned sentimental air which hardly suits this hard-bitten age. I suppose it is the same old fashionedness which makes me dislike Mussolini and still believe in the Right of Man.'[46] To some extent, the literary lions of Garsington took Bowra's poetic pretensions seriously, which, for him, would be the greatest compliment that could be paid.

Little wonder therefore that Maurice 'felt quite at home' at Garsington. It was a house where he 'talked freely'.[47] His unconventional hostess, whose exotic dress and behaviour had shocked and excited London society for years, encouraged that liberty of speech and action which was so much part of Bowra's own creed. Ottoline Morrell was a woman after his own heart. It was simply splendid to hear W. B. Yeats tell James Stephens over tea that 'life should be a beano'.[48] Of course Maurice could only agree. Further, Ottoline encouraged Bowra to bring his protégés out from Oxford for a little polishing in her company. As a result, undergraduates like Henry Yorke would sometimes find themselves 'shaking gloomily among the peacocks'[49] with apprehension, or taking tea with Walter de la Mare, who 'talked of friendship with other poets'.[50] Maurice deeply appreciated the fact that his hostess shared his belief, that one way for a culture to be preserved was to bring the talented young into the presence of established distinction. When the house closed, Bowra felt the loss keenly. He remembered 'all the fun we had there', and wished that 'someone we knew had bought it. But the rich never do anything like that, and all our friends are too poor.'[51]

Bowra's debt to Garsington, was considerable. After one visit, he tried to describe his sense of gratitude:

The beauty of the country today was beyond belief—the meadows more
gold than green and the chestnuts in full leaf. There can be nothing in
the world more beautiful. It goes to my head and fills me with a riotous
happiness. Also the sun clears one's mind, don't you think, and removes
those odd panics which grow in the winter.[52]

To talk literature and sexual liberation was a refreshing change from the
stilted, confined conversation found in Senior Common Rooms. Maurice
was under no illusions about his benefactress. As a worker of magic, she was
'an old witch' or even 'a fiend.' Her bizarre taste in clothes made her look
like a 'baroque flamingo'.[53] Her *affaires* were unfortunate, and she could
all too easily become the object of ridicule. But she was larger than life,
colourful, and flamboyant. Her manipulation of talented men on the lawns
at Garsington was a public service. Provoking conversation and fostering
talent demanded an energy above the average. Such an attacking view of
life could only recommend itself to Bowra. It so much resembled his own
modus operandi.

Crucially, Bowra's excursions into the salon world came about either as
an extension of Cambridge friendships or because the Asquiths and the
Morrells lived so close to Wadham. He was never in any sense a London
figure. Just occasionally, he found himself at lunch with Emerald Cunard
and Cecil Beaton, where he was hailed as 'the lion of the party'.[54] Equally
rarely, he went up to London to please a hostess like Sybil Colefax or
Patricia Hartwell. But, overwhelmingly, he only met such figures on his
own ground, namely in Oxford or in one of the salons he favoured. In
his view London talked about politics too much and about literature too
little. Its leading figures were, in Bowra terms, barely educated at all. As
he joyously described to Felix Frankfurter, Isaiah Berlin had abandoned his
attempts to educate Lady Hartwell after his promotion of Kant had only
left her looking 'very demure, as if she had just come from a gym class
at school'.[55] In short, Bowra met London on his own terms or not at all.
Mere social or political power had no interest for him.

Maurice's rare appearances in London so disturbed the social geography
that seasoned hostesses became nervous. Lady Hartwell, for example, had
to ask Isaiah Berlin if his friend could be seated at the same table as
leading Tories. It was so difficult to accommodate 'that strange thing that is
tucked away in his body/character/tummy of wanting to be loved, petted,
flattered, cosseted'. In the event, the dinner party went off reasonably well.

Prompted by Quintin Hogg, Maurice launched into unforgiving imitations of Lloyd-George and Lord Curzon, which caused the jaws of Lord and Lady Waverley to 'hang open all the time'. The Home Secretary [David Maxwell Fyfe] 'made an occasional interruption, but was not allowed more. I had the impression that Maurice was a great surprise to him, and that, whatever he had expected, it was nothing like the reality.'[56] Tory grandees were not the only London figures to find Maurice's style baffling. His humour was too oblique, too literary, too referential for comfort. Conversing with him was akin to crossing a minefield. When a politician banally remarked, 'I hear you are the funniest man in the world', Bowra sharply replied, 'Never made a joke in my life.'[57] The performance was for Oxford and Oxford's outposts alone.

In Maurice's view, those who became enmeshed in the social round in London ran the terrible risk of wasting whatever talents they had. Bob Boothby was a case in point. Epicurean to his fingertips, Boothby had enjoyed Bowra's esteem since their undergraduate days. Occasionally, they took holidays together. Boothby had many of the qualities that Maurice always admired in other people: ebullience, wit, and a disregard for convention. But, for Bowra, too much London living and London politics had coarsened his friend, and had ensured that his talents would not be fruitful. He seemed to suffer from 'a jilt complex … one never knows what is going to happen next'.[58] Worse still, his reputation became so tainted that his influence for the good was undermined. To be involved with the Kray brothers and Lady Dorothy Macmillan at the same time was going too far. As Maurice regretfully reflected, 'When Dadie [Rylands] comes into a salon in London, everyone says "Ah". When Boothby enters, all say "Whew!"'[59] This particular rake's progress was proof enough for Maurice that he should only go where the ground was firm underfoot.

As an enemy of promise, the London world had few equals. In 1964, Bowra read with interest a new biography of Rupert Brooke. He had known Ka Cox, 'plain and stooped' with 'rather a bossy, governessy manner', and Violet Bonham Carter, two of the most important women in Brooke's life. On finishing the book, Maurice found that his opinion had changed: 'I always rather hated the idea of him—much too English, and Rugby and patriotic, but he plainly wasn't at all. Nice and tough and marvellously efficient, and sometimes quite funny.' Even so, it was just as well that he had died young. Violet Bonham Carter would have 'bagged' him in the end and ordered him into politics, where his poetic talents would have atrophied. So 'perhaps he was well out of it'.[60] Such cautionary tales merely confirmed the obvious point that to meet London figures in or near Oxford was one thing, but to follow them on to their own turf and play by their rules threatened both sensibility and intelligence.

Rubbing shoulders with figures from the wider world, so untypical behaviour in a don of his generation, led Bowra to be accused of snobbery by enemies within the University. Notoriously, some thought that Evelyn Waugh may have taken him as a model for the oleaginous Mr Samgrass in *Brideshead Revisited*, haunting great houses and fawning on great names. Significantly, both Christopher Hollis and Christopher Sykes were quite sure that Bowra and Samgrass were one and the same.[61] Maurice, too, feared the vitriol in Waugh's pen, and paid him the compliment of endowing him with enough spite to be dangerous. As he told Cyril Connolly:

> Of course we all know that though he was servile enough to our faces, he was beastly about us behind our backs, both in his books under assumed names, and in interviews and so on with the Press. He found it impossible to be generous and he was really devoured by envy of almost anything—money, birth, talent, looks, health, success, etc. etc. I suppose there is a great deal of his unpublished records—the thought makes the blood run cold. He really was possessed by a demon, but it was an extremely powerful and creative demon. One of his troubles was that he thought (knew?) that he was not a gentleman, and he tried to get over this by snobbery of an absurd kind.[62]

Friendship with the novelist sometimes resembled 'the war to end Waughs'. When the novel was published, Waugh sent Bowra a copy of the first edition, and his friend counterattacked by declaring the book 'Brilliant!, Brilliant!, perhaps too brilliant! Perhaps too much of the wedding cake style about it, but a remarkable achievement for all that. I hope you spotted *me*. What a piece of artistry that is—best thing in the whole book.'[63] He then went on to belittle the novel by declaring that Cecil Beaton found it impossible to put down, and that Cyril Connolly's 'funny imitation' of Lord Marchmain on his deathbed was the talk of London.[64] Allegedly, Waugh was unhappy with this response. If Maurice himself was only too aware of the attempt to link Samgrass and himself, their common friends missed the point. Samgrass was not clever enough, nor witty enough, nor independent enough to be the Bowra they knew. If Waugh had intended to bring the charge of snobbery, the case had been too crudely presented for the average reader to take the point. When Waugh died, Bowra could afford to be forgiving: 'I miss the old boy very much ... I never thought him a *nice* man, but he was wonderfully generous and amusing and faithful. My only bad moment was when he told the press that I was "lucid and learned but dull", but I said nothing and recovered from the blow.'[65]

Waugh's poisoned dart missed its target, because it was all too obvious that Bowra's world and the London of the Bright Young Things were miles apart. Even when he found himself on their territory, the result was only embarrassing. At Rousham, on one occasion, he had joined his host in taking pot shots at the private parts of statues in the garden, but his aim had been so defective, that he 'did his Oxford reputation no good'.[66] In fact, Bowra's snobbery was intellectual not social, and in this he was brazen. He preferred clever people to stupid people. The only entry qualification into his court was intelligence. Membership was therefore open to all, irrespective of social background. In his generation, such views would have been called meritocratic or elitist, without carrying any of the opprobrium that the latter adjective now bears.

Mere social snobbery was a bore, and, worse than that, yet another threat to talent. When Henry Yorke married, for example, it was worrying that the bride 'seems a dim society woman used to guardsmen, and I am afraid she will drag Henry round to parties and play on his snobbery ... I only hope she does not interfere with his work.' It was the more galling for Bowra, because he had only just succeeded in rescuing Yorke from the influence of a father who was 'a bore—a clever man gone wrong, with the dull ideas of a banker and the worst sort of moral obtuseness'.[67] Equally, claims based on social pretension alone should always be exposed as hollow and worthless. Bowra enjoyed the hospitality of Kenneth Clark and his family at Saltwood Castle Christmas after Christmas, but had no compunction in reminding them that he took pleasure in their company, because they were intelligent and not because they were rich. According to Ann Fleming, at one dinner party, 'he had subdued his host and hostess by telling them that no matter how many castles they owned, they would always remain bourgeois, and took over the direction of the evening'.[68] As Warden of Wadham, Maurice was delighted that his College, after the War, should have been among the most welcoming to the grammar-school boy.

Any attempt to establish a link between Bowra and the kind of snobbery that oozed from every pore of Mr Samgrass's body would have to concentrate heavily on the years between 1922 and 1931, when Maurice was indeed, from time to time, a guest in great houses. But, in every case, what motivated him to accept these invitations was a close intellectual or emotional friendship with a member of the family. Samgrass was never on such terms with the Marchmains. In addition, certain houses contained people of intellect and interest. Bowra could be seen at Knole, 'that large, lovely house',[69] because Edward Sackville-West had proved to be one of the most colourful and promising of his New College contemporaries. He went to Hatfield House because Lord David Cecil was an academic colleague. True, Hatfield was sometimes Proustian in its arrangements—'the talk is very like Oriane's and quite easy to do'—but formidable Cecil uncles set a standard in 'judicious and unprejudiced conversation'[70] that Evelyn Waugh's creations would have found intolerable. On leaving Hatfield, Bowra travelled to Nottingham to spend time with Hugh Gaitskell, who was living in 'appalling squalor'.[71] Here, he found himself frying onions and making beds. Quite simply, the demands of friendship and the search for good company could lead Bowra anywhere.

Several times in the 1920s he visited Naas in the Irish Republic, where it was amusing to 'live the life of 1870, including walking to Church among curtseying rustics and attending a Christmas Tree for the tenants' children'.[72] But what took him there was his deep involvement with Piers Synnott, whose family owned the house. Once again, Maurice accepted invitations, not for the social advantage they might bring, but for the friendships they might confirm. In this case, it was a bonus that the Irish capital was so near at hand. As Maurice reported to Molly McCarthy, to meet 'the Dublin notorieties', including Yeats who, in 'a new suit of bright blue and his hair...like driven snow', was 'very pleasant'.[73] To meet his hero at Garsington was one thing, but to hear him declaim on his own ground was inspirational. After one such visit, he actually had a dream in which Yeats appeared, in order to inform him that his best poem was 'The Wild Swans at Coole'.[74] Visits to Naas allowed the mimic in Bowra to perfect an imitation of Yeats reading aloud, which would become one of his best party pieces.

Undoubtedly, Maurice played a full part in the social round of the 1920s, and, by doing so, became the figure that represented Oxford. However, he chose his venues with care. The mere opportunity to upgrade social status had little attraction. If he had wanted this London would have figured more prominently in his routine. Instead he looked for houses where the conversation had a strong literary bias, and which were full of people he liked. So he spent time at The Wharf and in Garsington rather than in

Bloomsbury. He went to Knole rather than Blenheim. In doing so, he acquired acquaintances and a fund of stories that were out of the reach of most of his fellow academics. As a result, he was admired, feared, and envied. To label him a snob no doubt eased frustration, but it was unfair. Evelyn Waugh was annoyed by how few people saw a connection between Samgrass and Bowra, but perhaps he should have known better.

In line with this thinking is the fact that Maurice's brushes with monarchy left him amused rather than fawning. When crowned heads appeared in Oxford, they were appraised critically. The King of Afghanistan had the look of 'a murderer turned preacher',[75] while the portly Juliana of the Netherlands struck him as 'every ounce a Queen'.[76] In discussing the advantages and disadvantages of a monarchical system, he was always keen to make a distinction between the institution itself and the often depressing individuals who occupied thrones. A classical scholar could hardly do anything else. The shortcomings of the many kings and emperors in the ancient world made it difficult to be too gushing about their representatives in the twentieth century.

On the plus side, monarchy, particularly the constitutional variety, represented stability and continuity, was less corrupt than many presidential systems, and, as pantomime, cheered people up. Maurice defended the institution vigorously in letters to Americans. In 1953, he was invited, as Vice-Chancellor of Oxford, to attend the coronation of Elizabeth II. Although he found himself sitting in the Abbey from seven in the morning until three in the afternoon, the spectacle was described to Alice James in Boston as 'magnificent … most deeply moving and exciting and exalting'. There was 'Winston wrapped up in the Garter robe like a bath towel, rather unsteady but very old and grand.' There 'were nice little Malays in silk clothes with small turbans, a tremendous Fuzzy-Wuzzy with a mop of hair … and even old dons in scarlet gowns and medals. Everyone dressed up to the nines, but dignified and genuine and not at all Fancy Dress.' He also noticed that 'Several duchesses were carrying sandwiches in their coronets.' After the ceremony and still 'all dolled up', he helped the police to direct visitors to Victoria Station. All in all, it had been enormous fun: 'I think it did good to everybody, set us all up, and proved that we can still do some things as no one else in the world can. So forgive this rambling account. It comes straight from the heart.'[77] The rare appearance of Bowra as patriot could be glimpsed in his interpretation to foreigners of Britain's institutional life.

A year earlier, he had had the opportunity to meet the new monarch when he was required to present the University's Loyal Address on her accession. He found Buckingham Palace 'a pretty house'.[78] In it lived 'a poor little queen', who was 'perched up on a platform and not allowed to sit down for two hours while she listened to speeches and delivered replies to them. She is rather pretty and much less vulgar to look at than most of her family.'[79] The new queen seemed to be a distinct improvement on the old King. When he had knighted Bowra, in 1951, his face looked as if it had been 'enamelled like good Queen Alexandra, and [he] was as bored as one could imagine he would be'.[80] But this early promise was soon dissipated. In 1963, he attended a dinner at the Palace in honour of the King and Queen of Greece, which was ruined by the Queen looking 'sulky' throughout and by the incessant playing of bagpipes.[81] At a private audience just before his death, the monarch was in better humour and talked knowledgeably about student revolution, but only because 'Prince Charles gives her the dope, so she says.'[82] All in all, for Bowra, 'the Queen Mum' was 'by far the best of them'.[83] To preserve respect for the institution of monarchy, it was probably best to keep meetings with its living representatives to a minimum.

Royalty was even less satisfactory when encountered outside an official context. Then its human frailties became all too obvious. Twice, for example, in the 1960s, Maurice stayed with Ann Fleming on Sardinia. Twice, he had to share the island with Princess Margaret. As a result, although Maurice and Mrs Fleming had been 'great pals'[84] from their very first meeting, these holidays were not a success. Sardinia, Maurice thought, was 'a horrible place. Very ugly. No mountains, no olive trees, no cypresses, but lumps of rock and scrub. On this is planted a top bogus town, which would just do as the stage setting for *Carmen* in Costa Rica.'[85] To make matters worse, he had had to meet Gore Vidal, whom he thought 'unsavoury'[86] and 'the English rich—Princess Margaret, American queens, lots of Austrians with Australian passports, Roman duchesses complaining about the disappearance of the British Empire. Not again.'[87] To another friend, he reported an island 'full of smarties from Princess Margaret up and down. Not at all my world—they drink your blood and you cant help being polite to them.'[88] He was out of his depth with the wrong sort of audience.

The princess herself was a mixed blessing. There were occasions when she behaved like 'a shopgirl but rather jolly'.[89] But, more often, she proved to be something of a disappointment.[90] On being introduced to Maurice for the first time, she had made the mistake of asking, 'What do you do?'[91] In her presence, the style and content of conversation had necessarily to be moderated. The usual 'Bowra noise'[92] had to be cut down. There could be 'no general uproar—topic—the seven deadly sins'.[93] As a result, Bowra's final judgement was that the Princess was 'a tremendous blood-sucker, and, like her sister, a bit of a sour puss'. Among the many consolations of growing old was the thought that he need never do many things ever again: 'Sardinia heads the list. Royalty comes jolly nearly as high.' He complained that the Princess had given him mumps.[94]

Fawning on royalty was therefore a sin, according to the creed of the Bowristas. John Betjeman transgressed in this respect over and over again, and had to be held up to correction. In *Prize Song*, Maurice took the poet's own metres and rhythms, and turned them against him:

> Green with lust and sick with shyness,
> Let me lick your lacquered toes.
> Gosh, oh gosh, your Royal Highness,
> Put your finger up my nose,
> Pin my teeth upon your dress,
> Plant my head with watercress.
>
> .   .   .   .
>
> Let your sleek and soft galoshes
> Slide and slither on my skin.
> Swaddle me in mackintoshes
> Till I lose my sense of sin.
> Lightly plant your plimsoll heel
> Where my private parts congeal.[95]

In short, Bowra liked monarchy but was an imperfect courtier. His tongue was too sharp, his eye for comedy too open, and his back too straight.

If Bowra's involvement with the world beyond Oxford was determined solely by a desire to talk literature and find amusement, it followed that politics held little attraction. Once again echoing the prejudices of Mallarmé and George, he was sure that parliament was for lesser men. He dismissed the Honour School of Politics, Philosophy, and Economics as 'uplift studies'.[96] The heirs of the Greeks and the poets had better things to do. It was simply 'stupid'[97] that talented people like Hugh Gaitskell and Bob Boothby should waste their time playing such games. On this subject his views never changed. Only six months before his death, he wrote to Colette Clark to express the hope that her brother would not consider politics as a career: 'He manages his life better than anyone we know, but I rather hope he does not go into parliament. I think it would bore him stiff, and, with his splendid, old-fashioned views, he would become a public joke. Not easy to tell him this.'[98] He was not even sure that politicians should be given honorary degrees. When Edward Heath was so recognized, Bowra decided to 'stay indoors and I hope not to be disturbed'.[99]

As far as he had any politics of his own, his views placed him on the centre-left, where he could best be described as an Asquithian Liberal who sometimes voted for the Labour Party. His anti-establishment prejudices, evident since his Cheltenham days, made him an unlikely Conservative. Noel Annan correctly thought 'he was, in fact, ever so faintly to the left of centre'.[100] Only in the immediate aftermath of the Great War did he experience a spasm of real radicalism. Two poems from this period survive in the Wadham Archives, one entitled 'Workers' and one, a fragment, with no title at all. In the context of the Russian Revolution and contemporary British politics, their language is millenarian and of the Left in inviting members of Bowra's own class to embrace new possibilities:

> What have you lost? Have you lost anything?
> A piece of bunting and a jewelled star.
> A clockwork engine with a broken spring
> Flung on a bonfire with an old guitar.
>
> A better morning lies ahead, and earth
> Rocked through a thousand centuries to sleep
> Awaits the ecstasy of second birth,
> Bursts with new harvests for new men to reap.
>
> Put off all private arrogance and join
> The great fight which calls for us. Beware
> Lest echoes of old music flood your brain
> And leave you gaping.[101]

As late as 1967, he told an audience at London University that the intervention of the Western powers in the Russian Revolution had been 'by far the worst thing that happened at this time ... They hated us, and out of it emerged communism.'[102]

Such youthful radicalism contrasted oddly with the New College parties and Ightham tennis afternoons of the same period. Not surprisingly, it never betokened a serious interest in socialism or communism. For

Bowra, they were systems that suppressed the individual as effectively as the Victorian codes they had supplanted. Communists like Guy Burgess were contemptuous of Maurice's pale words. Bowra claimed 'to *feel* awfully left',[103] but the collectivism of these options repelled him. Such a determined individualist could never follow orders. He had never been a teamplayer at school, and he would not be a party member, even under the pressures of the 1930s. When his friends the Longfords took to Labour Party politics, they could not even be sure of his vote in the Oxford constituency, but Lady Longford understood the reason. Maurice's 'cruelty to Frank's and my work in politics' was explained by the fact that 'Labour in those days was not concerned with the happiness of the individual.'[104] Party politics involved disciplines and compromises that Bowra would have found insupportable.

One friendship above all kept Maurice's sympathies indistinctly on the Left, namely that with Hugh Gaitskell. The two men had met in the winter of 1924–5. Almost immediately, Bowra recognized a potential Bowrista in terms of talent and sensibility. Twice, the undergraduate Gaitskell was taken on holidays to Europe. Bowra remembered with pleasure that his new protégé 'liked to talk not only because it engaged his faculties but because it cleared the air of convention and cant, and, if a party was more than usually convivial, there was always a chance that the talk would be freer and more honest than at other times'.[105] In return, Gaitskell liked Bowra 'to be on tremendous form', even if 'it was a trifle exhausting'.[106] Friendship between the two men was interrupted by the Second World War, but, at its conclusion, Bowra met him again, 'on 31 December 1945, and we picked up our relations just where the war had broken them off'.[107] As house-guests of Isaiah Berlin or Ann Fleming, they always found each other's company very congenial.

Predictably, Maurice watched his protégés 'rise to power and fame with gratitude and admiration'.[108] But there was also bewilderment. The Gaitskell whom Bowra knew read books and quoted poetry, so why should such a man devote himself to politics? It was 'odd' that he should have become 'important' at Westminster, when his Oxford friends suspected that his skin was not thick enough to withstand the rough-and-tumble of that world.[109] Here was a paradox, which Maurice tried to explain to Felix Frankfurter:

> The great point about him is his great warmth of heart—his lasting affections and loyalties. They make him at times fall in life, but he does this with

his usual tact, and he is extremely happy with his wife and children. He is absolutely without airs or pretences, and deeply sincere in his political beliefs. I think he is usually right, and, though he is too nice to the government, that is part of his nature. What he needs is an eloquent thug to do dirty work for him, but he has not got one, and would not use him if he had ... When tight he quotes poetry, and he knows a pot [*sic*] about pictures. I think he would be an excellent Prime Minister, and I wish he would get in, but I don't think he will. We shall have another five years of Conservatives, who will revive and extend flogging, kill a lot more Cypriots, and have a lot of our own young men killed too.[110]

A Bowrista in politics was a rare phenomenon, and, somehow, inexplicable. Nevertheless, when Gaitskell became leader of the Labour Party, Bowra wrote to congratulate him, suggesting that he 'drive Sir Antony [*sic*] [Eden] to a loony bin as soon as you can, before he drives everyone else'.[111]

Gaitskell's early death was, for Bowra, as much a personal tragedy as a political loss. It came

as a bitter blow to me ... Of all the public men I have known he was the least affected or spoilt by it. He never put on a public face or talked bromides or laid down the Moral Law or paid no attention to what you said (gifts all too amply displayed by Harold [Macmillan], our Chancellor, on every occasion, especially in Oxford), Hugh was really very simple—affectionate, loyal, courageous, profoundly honest. He did not understand very complex people any more than Gladstone did, but it did not matter; what counted with him was the cause on any occasion, and this he mastered and understood from all sides. It is indeed a bitter blow ... instead of him we shall have either far less good Labour people or that stuffed walrus Macmillan. I shall miss Hugh terribly.[112]

Gaitskell's biographers all claim that their subject greatly influenced Bowra's own politics, and they are almost certainly right. For someone who worried about the difficulty of the arts surviving in the new democracies, Gaitskell's presence was reassuring. If socialism or social democracy was the coming thing, in the figure of Gaitskell it was something that Bowra could deal with.

The General Strike of 1926 was the first of many crises on which it was impossible to retain a lofty neutrality. According to Christopher Hollis, Maurice's interest in the problem was 'only fitful', and entirely dependent on the influence of Gaitskell. Allegedly, he helped to collect signatures in support of the Archbishop of Canterbury's appeal for a negotiated settlement, but, otherwise, he told a friend, 'I stayed here and went on with my work.'[113] He told *The Times*, forty years later, that the strikers had been wrong to challenge an elected government, but also that the miners had been treated disgracefully.[114] He could not share the passion that animated both sides in the dispute, but he acted robustly at the behest of friends. When the rooms of his New College contemporary Deane Jones were attacked by a mob of Tories, Bowra appeared with forces sufficient to raise the siege.[115] Under Gaitskell's influence, he acted as Honorary Treasurer of the Oxford University Miners' Wives and Children Fund.[116] With Frank Pakenham and G. D. H. Cole, he later collected money to fund camping holidays in Wales for the unemployed. In a letter to *The Times*, the three men insisted that 'those of us who have never known what it is to be without hope of employment or a decent life have a duty to those who know it every minute of the day'.[117] None of this activity was heroic or passionate. Bowra's Edwardian Liberalism could not sympathize with the more brutal aspects of capitalism or militant trade unionism. It was, however, entirely comfortable in assisting the victims of either.[118]

In the 1930s, there was the more challenging threat of Nazism in Germany, the consequences of which Bowra witnessed at first hand.[119] He was also acutely aware of the persecution of poets in Soviet Russia. Together, these were numbing experiences. Clearly, there was no place for Bowrista individualism in the monolithic orthodoxies coming to dominate so much of Europe. In the Spanish Civil War, he supported the Republic against Franco, but it had not been an easy choice to make. Franco, on the one hand, represented that military thuggishness that Maurice had seen too much of in the Great War. But, on the other hand, the Republic was far from pure. Its socialist, communist, and anarchist associations were unappealing. So was its tendency to talk nonsense and tell lies, but, in the end, libertarian instincts left him no choice. The Republic had to be supported because 'we all talk balls, but what matters is that we should be allowed to talk balls'.[120]

The impact of the war on Bowra was significant in that it confirmed his deep suspicion of Catholicism. The Roman Church had been Franco's ally, and this came as no surprise. For Maurice, Francoism and Catholicism both stressed authoritarianism and hierarchy at the expense of individualism. The war created a permanent division between Bowra and those Oxford Catholics who, like Ronnie Knox, supported Franco.[121] When the leaders of French Catholicism collaborated wholeheartedly with the Pétain government at Vichy, and by implication with the Germans, Bowra was not surprised. It was all of a pattern. Those who demanded obedience in one context mirrored the psychology of those who sought it in another. When a Catholic writer attempted an apology for Vichy's existence, Maurice denounced him to Christopher Hollis as 'a charlatan'. ' "Anything else?" I asked, "No" he said, it's a full time job.'[122]

Bowra's natural aversion to politics was confirmed in the 1930s by the fact that, as Europe embraced various forms of totalitarianism, there was very little ground on which an Asquithian Liberal could stand. Contemporary options were all unattractive and, apparently, unstoppable. Even Oxford undergraduates were not immune to these siren voices. People at all levels seemed to be looking for creeds that offered final answers in return for unthinking loyalty. It was difficult for Bowra to understand why Oxford was full of politics and religion. As he explained to a friend, he felt stranded and out of place:

> It is very dull here. All the young men are interested in politics. The Christians have become communists and the others fascists. Where are the aesthetes of yesteryear? Dr Buchman absolves them from the sin of Onan and they walk out, confessing decorously and without enthusiasm to spectacled undergraduettes. There is much madness about, but that is to be expected. The naughty twenties are far behind and we are in the full flood of the regenerate thirties. I feel like a man of 1780 plomped [sic] down among Napoleon's marshals. The world gets worse and worse. The £ falls daily. It will soon be impossible to travel anywhere, what with accidents and revolutions. Even the kind French have gone astray.[123]

Where, in this new configuration of politics, could a man who knew doubt and loved pleasure find a home?

All a man of Bowra's temperament could do was to help friends and to fight nonsense in his own parish. In November 1938, a by-election which became an ad hoc referendum on the recently signed Munich agreement was held in Oxford. Predictably, Maurice had regarded Chamberlain's desertion of Czechoslovakia as an act of cowardice. Accordingly, he supported the candidature of the Master of Balliol who stood on an anti-Munich platform against the official Conservative nominee, Quentin Hogg. Maurice had little hope or expectation of success, not least because his candidate would insist on addressing bemused crowds of Oxford voters in theological terms. One election address began 'You will remember the Collect for today.'[124] In defeat, Bowra could only reflect that he should be prepared for many more disappointments. He was not Communist,

Socialist, Fascist, Catholic, or Conservative. He was out of the political fashion.

Matters hardly became easier after 1945. True, his eminence in academic and literary life was now so great that his signature at the bottom of a letter of protest was worth having. He was now numbered among the great and the good. Joining many of his friends, he signed petitions against any delay in implementing the decriminalization of homosexuality, the prosecution of Nabokov's novel *Lolita*, and the continued practice of capital punishment.[125] All these issues would be congenial to a libertarian temperament. More surprisingly, he moved outside his usual range to comment on international politics, at least to the extent of signing a letter to *The Times*. He protested against the Russian intervention in Hungary, American policies in Vietnam, apartheid in South Africa, and, of course, the overturning of democracy in Greece.[126] It was comfortable to make such gestures in the company of friends.

The production of such a list might lead to the view that Bowra had matured into a political figure, or that he had changed his opinions on the importance of politics, but this was not the case. Almost certainly, he lent his signature to oblige friends. In private letters, he mocked those who signed letters as a kind of profession, in the belief that dictators would go pale at the sight of their names. A particular bête noir in this category was Canon Collins of the Campaign for Nuclear Disarmament. In 1959, he and other professional dissenters sent a letter to *The Times* under the grandiloquent title of a *Writers' Christmas Declaration on Racial Discrimination*. Its appearance moved Bowra to write to Evelyn Waugh.

> I greatly enjoyed the letter to which you refer. One of the worst written, even by our intellectuals, that I have seen for a long time, and rich in inconsistencies and contradictions. I have not got a full list of the signatories, and wonder who wrote it. Collins? He is an ambitious ex-don from Oriel, with whom I have been more than once entangled in making protest against this or that. Not at all a nice man by any standard.[127]

To be 'entangled' with such people was an uncomfortable experience. Maurice rightly described himself as an innocent in politics. In 1928, while staying in Ireland, he heard for the first time of the atrocities committed by the Black and Tans a decade earlier. It made him 'sick with shame to hear of it'.[128] Thirty years later, he nervously signed letters protesting against apartheid, while admitting that he 'knew nothing' of 'South African affairs'.

He joined in because a friend, Harriet Cohen, asked him to perform.[129] Politics was just not his game. He always had other priorities.

In fact, after 1945, only one event, apart from the military coup in Greece, seriously moved him, namely the Suez Crisis of 1956. It brought back memories of the futile Western intervention in the Russian Revolution. It was the action of bullies. It would have compromised British standing in the entire Arab world. On 5 November 1956, the *Oxford Mail* carried a letter of protest signed by 350 senior members of the University. Bowra's was the first of thirteen Wadham names on the list.[130] Two days earlier, *The Times* had printed a similar statement sent in by Maurice and many of his friends which denounced 'the action of Her Majesty's Government in launching an attack against Egypt in defiance of the United Nations, against the principles of international morality, and in violation of the dictates of common prudence'.[131] On this occasion, Bowra's public statements directly corresponded to opinions expressed in private letters. In these, the Prime Minister, Anthony Eden, was consigned to the lowest circle of Hell. He was 'a stuffed dummy' who had led Britain into 'another war to end war'. Someone should initiate 'impeachment proceedings'. Bowra's only consolation was that Eden was reported to be staying with Ann Fleming. There 'the plumbing is very bad, and with luck he will catch some hideous disease'.[132]

The Suez adventure produced savage divisions of opinion within Oxford. Maurice was appalled that an old friend like Roy Harrod could think the invasion of Egypt justified. On this issue, there could, however, he no compromise. As he reported to an American friend:

> National events have rent the University in twain. Suez was without parallel in my lifetime. Quarrels and non-speak with old friends and accusations of coward, traitor, formalist, prig and so on. As a disciple of Mr Gladstone I know where my duty lay and said so firmly. I am somewhat embarrassed by kind Americans apologizing for letting us down. Not at all. I welcome even Mr Dulles on the issue. Thank God Eden has gone. I fear his beautiful wife, who is an old friend of mine, no longer loves me. I am getting past it.[133]

Suez was that rare issue in politics which engaged Bowra's full attention. He felt that he could fully understand it and knew the context. To invoke Gladstone's name was to recall other protests about the bullying of small nations. To call up the glib phrases of politicians in the Great War about 'a war to end war' was to associate Eden with those who had led Europe into misery in his youth. For once, contemporary politics touched his own memory and sensibilities.

By 1939, Bowra enjoyed fame or notoriety far beyond Oxford. In the salons of women he admired like Margot Asquith, Ottoline Morrell, and Ann Fleming, he found a good dinner, conversation with the giants of literature, and an appreciative audience for his performances. The dowdy world of politics and administration could offer nothing comparable. Of this world he was content to be an observer, unless friends requested assistance. To the end of his life, he hugely enjoyed seeing the posturings of public men being blown apart by scandal. In 1963, for example, the Profumo affair gave endless pleasure. It was 'a great joy':

> Mr Marples is said to be next for it, as he is a keen transvestite, and Mr Sandys, who was photographed in bed with the ex-Duchess of Argyll, but without a head,—odd but so they say. Poor Dr Ward comes to the end of the trial today or tomorrow. I can't see that he had done anything wrong, except of course to make some people's lives more enjoyable, and that must count heavily against him. As yet, fucking is not against the law here, though I can't understand why. It will be soon, on grounds of security. I look forward to a series of such scandals. They are excellent for the morale, and not at all good for Mr Macmillan, whom I can't endure. He now looks like a mixture 50/50 of the Walrus and the Carpenter.[134]

Such antics were not new, of course, but merely variations on themes that were the stuff of politics. Little wonder that Maurice should invite Bowristas into cynicism:

> Come let us mock at the great,
> That had such burdens on the mind,
> And toiled so hard and late,
> To leave some monument behind,
> Nor thought of the levelling wind.[135]

Unfortunately, the style of salons and hostesses barely survived the Second World War, and Maurice railed at the gods for 'attacking my world'.[136] For good or ill, status was passing from the literary man and academic to the bureaucrat and politician, and, as a result, Bowra was acutely aware of just how fragile his distinction was. The worlds, in which he was regarded and feared, were falling away before new ideas of celebrity. As a result, he affected to be ambivalent about how much success he had in fact achieved. Almost certainly, Bowra was grading himself too low.

In the first half of the twentieth century, he brought Oxford and its claims forward in a manner that demanded attention. The University's values were as substantial as any that could be found outside its walls. He himself was sure that Oxford mattered. His astonishing network of friends and acquaintances were squarely told that this was so. Wherever he went, Oxford went. Whenever he spoke, the University was in a manner vindicated.

9

Germany and America

B owra was a cosmopolitan. By instinct and upbringing, national borders meant little to him. In his promotion of poetry and the claims of the Greeks, he offered arguments free of national preferences. However, he knew two countries well, Germany and America. He was attracted to the first by a deep admiration for certain aspects of its culture; he was drawn to both by the opportunities they offered for testing one of his major concerns, namely the future relationship between democracy and culture. One of his darkest fears was that the new political order was actually inimitable to Bowrista values, for the omens did not appear promising. Germany had been one of the first European countries to institute universal male suffrage, and yet Bowra personally witnessed democracy crumble in that country, involving the systematic persecution of people like him. In America, there was less persecution, even allowing for McCarthyism, but Bowra found its culture hopelessly derivative and increasingly debased. Americans had vitality, optimism, and a brash sense of fraternity, but they often, quite literally, could not understand what he was saying. A style of conversation based on understatement, irony, and literary reference could not cross the Atlantic. In Germany, people like him were shouted down; in American they were met with an unnerving silence. In one country, democracy surrendered its cultural heritage to barbarism; in the other, culture dribbled away, as mass taste was economically exploited.

Such gloomy spectacles should have led him to find consolation in France, but, oddly enough, this was definitely not the case. The French flirtation with democracy predated such experiments in Germany and America, and yet its cultural life flourished. On so many grounds, Maurice should have responded to the spontaneity, high culture, and pursuit of pleasure that France offered, and he was indeed not entirely immune to this appeal. He wrote enthusiastically about Valéry and Apollinaire. He would become a member of the *Légion d'honneur*. Above all, he went there occasionally. In the summer of 1939, he joined the Connollys for a holiday on Cap d'Antibes, where he enjoyed 'three delicious weeks... Sun, sea, complete idleness, French food, French drink and the kind of good French all round.' He was spared a visit from 'our neighbours the Windsors', and saw 'very little of Marlene Dietrich, who is not at all beautiful'.[1] He had the same enthusiasm for Paris. The problem of Christmas was sometimes solved by staying with Nancy Mitford in the French capital. The city was 'heavenly'.[2]

Yet, there was something not quite right about the French. The reference to 'good French' implies the existence of less commendable examples. Too much of their literature was still Catholic in inspiration. Significantly, Bowra never wrote about Claudel or Mauriac. Possibly, Bowra had been unimpressed by the French performance in the First World War. He was certainly disgusted by the collapse of France in 1940. Their inability to fight effectively seemed to prove that the French elite were not very parliamentarian, and that there was a kind of gangrene running through French society.[3] The nation had both democracy and a great culture. But the democracy was a shambles and the culture at war with itself. As a testing ground for the questions that Bowra wanted answered, France was too muddled and too opaque.

In *Memories*, Maurice carefully set out the dates of his visits to Germany; he 'passed through' in 1909, then visits were made in 1922, 1929, 1930, and 1932. This account sounds reasonable, but is inaccurate. Bowra knew Germany much better than he was prepared to admit. In addition to the visits he recorded, he also made the journey in 1928, at the invitation of Harold Nicolson, in 1934, 1935, 1936, 1938, and 1953.[4] In a period when most people never had owned a passport, this degree of travelling was remarkable. Even odder was the fact that it should all be focused on one country. Before 1939, he knew Germany better than Greece. No doubt, the sexual adventures that could be encountered there, in the company of Adrian Bishop or Ernst Kantorowicz, were an important incentive. But these journeys also reflect a genuine fascination with German culture, and its relationship with the democracy of the Weimar Republic in its last days.

For some reason, Maurice was always reticent about his deep interest in things German. Perhaps to protect his private life, perhaps to hide guilty feelings about finding his enemy in the Great War so intriguing, Bowra systematically played down the scale of his involvement. He even concealed his familiarity with the language. Close friends like Lord and Lady Quinton and Lady Annan, herself German, had no idea that he had any degree of fluency.[5] Of course, his essays on Rilke and George were in the public domain, but people who knew him well still failed to make any connection between Maurice and the spoken language, or to see German themes in his conversation. The fascination with Germany was another aspect of Bowra's privacy. It was a kind of awful indulgence that he wished to keep hidden. In this, as in so many other ways, Bowra would only expose those aspects of his character which he was happy for his friends to see.

Before the Nazis became a serious threat, in 1929, he was full of sympathy for Germany as a defeated country. The camaraderie of the Great War extended to those who also suffered the miseries of trench warfare but were called the enemy. It was right to kill German soldiers, but not in hatred. As he tried to explain to a lecture audience, fighting men have a different view of the enemy than that being offered at home: 'Living in his own isolated world of the trenches, he feels that the enemy is closer to him than many of his own countrymen, and especially than the invisible commanders who from a remote security order multitudes to a senseless death.'[6] As a result, he deeply deplored calls for vengeance in 1918, and listened with approval when George Lansbury visited Oxford to preach the idea that Germany should not be unduly punished.[7] By the same token, he loathed remarks made by the Archbishop of Canterbury in St Mary's, Oxford, which suggested that, in the Treaty of Versailles, 'Truth and Righteousness have kissed each other.'[8]

For some years after 1918, Bowra would find himself in arguments with an older generation of dons who had not fought in the War and who wished to treat the vanquished with the utmost severity. Warden Wells of Wadham, for example, refused to speak to those who had been conscientious objectors, and wanted the Kaiser hanged.[9] Such views could not be shared by someone like Maurice, the grandson of a Garibaldino, who, as he put it, had been 'brought up on Italy'.[10] Young nations like Germany and Italy had liberal origins and should be given a chance. At the same time, these were not popular opinions, and when he read the pacifist works of E. D. Morel, he did so in secret, as though indulging in a kind of pornography.

On his first visits to Germany, in 1922 and 1927, he found that the Germans had much to recommend them. He agreed with Hugh Gaitskell that 'both the Germans and the Austrians' were 'honest democrats struggling to keep their countries alive and free, but hampered by the statesmen of France and Great Britain'.[11] He told Ottoline Morrell that he found the peoples of the German world 'gentle, humorous and sympathetic'. He added that 'the intellectual pleasures they provide are enormous'. It was simply 'hard to believe this was the people we were so busy killing'.[12] To Piers Synnott he was even more expansive.

> I got back from Germany refreshed and wiser. It is a very good country—pictures, barock [sic] buildings, magnificent early Greek sculptures and gold work, lots of cafes with beer and bands and dignified, humorous Germans. The climate is foul, but the life is good...We visited Night Resorts...Some are most interesting. The old (60 and over) are the most successful as all young Germans are gerontophiles. But the atmosphere is very friendly. They sit at tables and talk quietly and smile gently. A great people. They should be given the world to govern, and all would be well. I shall go to Berlin again soon. It is not at all dago. Very clean, everything punctual and the traffic controlled without police by a system of lights, which can be worked only by God.[13]

In addition, German scholarship and German literature were compelling. Bowra found the writings of Wilamowitz on the Greeks 'emotional and moving'.[14] Long before Maurice discovered in the Stefan George Circle ideas and concerns that ran parallel with his own, he had read widely in German literature. In 1925, he had finished Goethe's *Faust*, which had been 'a struggle', but infinitely worthwhile: 'The ideas are interesting and superbly well-expressed, and I rather like the curious Teutonic humour. I think Housman got his style from German. Goethe has the same sort of clanging effect with his rhymes and crisp consonated words.'[15] Two years later, he enjoyed *Jew Süss* as 'a good bad book'. Very soon, the novel would become notorious when it was taken up by the Nazis to propagate anti-Semitism, but, in 1927, it could be read in all innocence. Maurice found it 'exciting, highly-coloured and ironical. It is very moving about the Jews.'[16] Before Hitler came to power, it was even possible to make the suggestion, as a joke, that the book might particularly appeal to Harold Nicolson, who looked as though he had 'a Yid strain in him'.[17]

Appreciative remarks about the German world were not, however, intended to include Austria. By Germany, Bowra usually meant the protestant north, with Berlin at its centre. By contrast, Vienna was an airless city. Maurice once asked Adrian Bishop, 'How is horrible Wien?

Smelling of Kunstdung, I suppose, and full of those boring, tall Austrians talking about their relations.'[18] When visiting Vienna in July 1932, he attended dinner parties where the only topics of conversation concerned the 'various types of cottages to be found outside Vienna, or what kinds of roof-tiles were manufactured in Austria'.[19] Significantly, Bowra always judged a society by its literature. Music and painting were not nearly as important. As a result, Austria had, in his view, little attraction. Its Catholicism stunted all literary growth. It was simply 'dull'. In the spring of 1934, Bowra found himself contributing money to a fund for the maintenance of friends experiencing persecution in Vienna.[20] It would come as no surprise to discover that Hitler himself was Austrian.

Before 1929 therefore, Maurice was more than happy to embrace the language and culture of Berlin. After that date, however, politics darkened, and vitality became barbarism. On his later visits, Maurice saw Nazism at first hand, and was predictably repelled. From April to June 1932, he lived in the German capital, in order to perfect his German, under the guidance of a certain Frau Meyer, a former governess in the Asquith household.[21] He heard speeches by Brüning, and would remind the ex-Chancellor of these occasions when he met him in Oxford in 1934. More significantly, he also attended a Nazi rally, at which Hitler spoke.

> Hitler's meetings were superbly staged and directed at exciting the audience to the highest degree of frenzy ... Hitler looked just like all the pictures of him—the lock of hair dangling on his forehead, the preposterous tooth-brush moustache, ... he had a very harsh, strident voice with an ugly Austrian accent, and barked rather than spoke his sentences. The face revealed some violent emotion which I could not define ... Hitler put such a spell on his audience, that they interrupted only when they were so carried away that they could not restrain themselves, and then they burst into maniacal demonstrations, shouts and yells, umbrellas opened by women, hats thrown in the air by men, daggers slashed from their sheaths by young Nazis. At the end the confusion was appalling ... But neither Adrian nor I were in the least moved by him, and we slank away as unobtrusively as we could from the raving rabble.[22]

For someone who worried about what a future based on mass politics might hold, experiences such as this must have been deeply alarming. The democracy in Germany had voted Hitler into power, and so perhaps democracy itself had no solidity to it. The 'kind' and 'humorous' Germans of the 1920s had been so easily led astray. As a result, the culture of people like himself was either subverted or perverted.

Returning to Berlin, in the autumn of 1932, Bowra was shocked by how far the situation had deteriorated in a few short months: 'One evening, I found a battered body in the side-street near my lodgings and called to a policeman to help. He was very unwilling to do anything, and when at last I got him to move, the man was dead.'[23] At some point, he and a party of journalists were given an audience by Hitler where they were treated to an harangue on the theme that the unity of Germany would not be political or economic, but spiritual.[24] It was on this occasion allegedly that Maurice replied to a salutation of 'Heil Hitler' with a spirited 'Heil Bowra'. Unfortunately, there is no truth in the story, though it circulated widely and, as Maurice put it, 'brought me nothing but credit'.[25] What in fact happened was more prosaic. Bob Boothby was greeted by Hitler's secretary with a 'Heil Hitler', to which he responded 'Heil Boothby'. Later, as he remembered, 'the story was attributed to Maurice Bowra, who asked me whether I would mind if he did not contradict it. I said I would be delighted to share the honour with him, because I knew that if he had been in my place, he would have done the same.'[26]

On returning home, Bowra read an 'unexpurgated' copy of *Mein Kampf*, which convinced him finally, if further proof was wanting, that Hitler was in deadly earnest.[27] He was now sure that Europe faced a great evil. As he told Ottoline Morrell, 'The German madness is the most appalling thing that has ever happened—worse in some ways than the war. I don't know which is the more appalling, the persecution of everyone or the enormous campaign of lies.'[28] It was heartening, as late as 1938, to hear Berlin 'people like chemists' assistants and barbers talk with open dislike of the Leader and tell gruesome stories of barbarities',[29] but there could be no doubt of what the outcome would be. Nazism would conquer if it was not fought.

From the start, his German friends were in trouble. Bowra heard at first hand how their lives were first subject to constraint and then threat. He knew too many Jews, academics, homosexuals, and writers. All these categories were marked out for persecution, and Maurice felt the awfulness of their situation keenly. To face a direct attack was one thing, but to live with the slow strangulation of rights was somehow worse. Not knowing what was to happen next was the most refined of tortures. In the autumn of 1935, Bowra told Elizabeth Bowen that he intended to stop in Germany on the way [to Hungary] and have a last look at my poor friends before they are entirely driven underground or locked in a Ghetto. I find it very odd that politics should really alter people's lives and make them feel hunted...I can imagine a sudden violent act, like an attack, but to...have more and more insults and restrictions is curiously horrible and unreal.[30]

In letters to American friends, he tried to describe 'the Hell' that Germany had become. Kantorowicz was 'being watched by spies', and there was no possibility of any effective opposition to the Nazis:

The Liberals and educated people are few and quite powerless. The army has been squared with promises of more pay, more weapons, more medals, and bigger and better wars, and the Communists, who are incredibly brave have no weapons against 500,000 men now under arms. Meanwhile, Hitler has fits of temper twice a day, in which no one can speak to him except his cook. He had young girls to dinner and makes a forty minute speech to them afterwards: then they are sent home intact. He may go mad, but if he does they will kill him off, stuff his body, and use it as a wireless machine, through which Goebbels will address the nation. I met no one who liked the Nazis, but equally nobody can turn them out till they start killing each other.[31]

On his last visit to Germany before the War, in the autumn of 1938, the priority was firmly 'to do something for various friends who were plotting to leave the country', activity which gave him 'an excellent conscience'. With the help of the Frankfurters, the poet Kurt Riezler, a survivor of the George Circle, was allowed to leave Germany for a job in New York. The wife and children of Felix Grafe, the Czech poet, arrived in Wadham as refugees, when Grafe himself disappeared into a concentration camp.[32] But these were small victories. There were so many 'others', who were 'in a much worse way, as they seem to have no jobs open to them abroad. What can one do for instance with an ex-judge or an ex-diplomat?'[33] Bowra's letters now steadily record the imprisonment or death of German friends.

Inevitably, Maurice's condemnation of Nazism had a particular bias. In his view, Hitlerism had destroyed the most fertile strains in European literature. Alongside visible human misery was the inescapable fact that Nazism was also a cultural disaster. After 'a painful and depressing visit' to Germany, in September 1936, he reported to Gilbert Murray that militarism had destroyed the chances for the young to think freely: 'The extra year of conscription gives almost the final blow to their educational system, which will now be one of the worst in the world.'[34] Equally grim was the knowledge that German politics and French neuroticism were drying up sources of literary inspiration, upon which the English themselves depended.

> The worst of it all is that England is getting more and more isolated from the intellectual life of Europe than is right or healthy. It is curious to find no important books coming from Germany, and the French are in such a state that they can only write out of their hysteria. The result is that we too are cut off and stewing in our own juice. This never really suits the English, and it is liable to have pernicious results, especially a detached, ignorant and hard-headed callousness about what may happen elsewhere.[35]

Bowra was not convinced that, in cultural terms, England could stand alone.

For Bowra the anti-intellectualism of the Nazis was almost their most appalling characteristic, and one that threatened the whole European cultural tradition. State-sponsored philistinism, book burning, and exhibitions of so-called decadent art were the worst examples of what populists could do. Mass politics, in either democratic or authoritarian form, was the fashion. Observing them closely, Maurice had to wonder whether men like himself could survive in either system. Ernst Kantorowicz felt the same. In October 1938, he wrote to Bowra in words which Maurice could have used himself: 'our future biographers will appreciate our letters of consolation and condolence as sign [sic] of the dangers which we passed through. Yet it is all frightfully funny...peace or war...both mean the end of the old Europe.'[36] The language of the letter makes it clear that he regarded Maurice and himself as old Europeans, people holding values that had no future. German democracy had failed to protect them.

Cultural nemesis was given physical form in the persons of Stefan George's protégés, like Kantorowicz himself, who now faced persecution or worse. The Circle, which Bowra had so much admired, was broken up and brought to silence. All that could be done was to ensure their personal safety. As has been noted, Maurice played some part in sending Kurt Riezler to New York. He was even more instrumental in saving Lucy von Wangenheim, the half-sister of Woldemar von Uxkull-Gyllenband, to whom Kantorowicz had dedicated his famous biography of the Emperor Frederick II, one of the very few women to be found among George's disciples. In the spring of 1938, she was already a refugee, working for the writer Henry Ziegler's anti-Nazi campaign in Czechoslovakia.

1. Ethel Lovibond, Maurice's mother

2. Maurice and his brother Edward,
c.1903, when the family returned to
England

3. The Bowra family; Cecil, Ethel, Edward, and Maurice, photographed
between 1903 and 1905

4. Maurice hosting a fancy dress dinner in the late 1920s

5 Presiding at a Wadham Boat Club Bump Supper, 1939

6. On the beach

7. At Garsington, as a guest of Ottoline Morrell, talking with Sylvester Gates, Igor Vinogradoff, L. P. Hartley, and Kyrle Leng

8. At Garsington with Princess Elizabeth Bibesco

9. At Garsington with Virginia Woolf

10. In the library of the Warden's Lodgings in Wadham

11. In the country, visiting College estates, *c.*1955

12. With Charlie Chaplin and an unknown admirer at Encaenia, 1962

According to Mary Wesley, she was also in the pay of British Intelligence. When the German threat to Czechoslovakia became menacing, Ziegler, already a friend of Bowra, announced that he 'would give the Baronin to Bowra' for safekeeping.[37] She duly appeared in the Warden's Lodgings as a long-term guest, bringing with her the most up-to-date information. One undergraduate was flattered to be told by 'Frau Wangenheim in perfect English ... of the monstrosities of Hitler and the comic tragedy of Chamberlain, at Godesberg. She got all this from her daughter who lives there.'[38] It was little wonder that Bowra should be so opposed to the Munich Agreement and to the politicians who had signed it.

Most worryingly of all was the fact that Ernst Kantorowicz was still in Germany in the autumn of 1938. Jewish and liberal, he had lost his university post and was living on the charity of friends. The necessity of caring for an elderly mother[39] seemingly made it impossible for him to leave Germany. In letters to 'My dear old Maurice', he admitted, however, that he was 'very worried', and had breathed 'a coward's sign of relief' when news of the Munich agreement reached him. In September 1938, he formally asked Bowra for help with his decision to go to America.[40] Maurice went into action immediately, but even he could not initially do much to overcome bureaucratic obstructionism. In October, Kantorowicz complained about 'the waiting, waiting, waiting', while thanking his friend for sending a photograph that proved that Maurice 'must have been extremely handsome in your "buggerable" days'.[41] During the anti-Jewish riots of November 1938, Kantorowicz only survived by hiding in the house of Albrecht von Bernstorff, a former Rhodes Scholar who had been known to Bowra since 1934. It seemed that no country was prepared to offer shelter to 'owners of a passport signed with a huge red J'.[42]

Kantorowicz eventually left Germany on 6 December 1938. The details of how the escape was effected remain obscure. According to Bowra's *Memories*, another George pupil had married a woman who was also the mistress of one of Goering's adjutants. In return for obtaining a passport for Kantorowicz, the complaisant husband continued to turn a blind eye to his wife's infidelity.[43] The George disciple in question may have been von Bernstorff or someone codenamed 'Prince Hal', whom Maurice had lobbied on his last visit to Berlin in the autumn of 1938.[44] One way or another, Kantorowicz believed that Bowra had saved his life. He stayed in Wadham from 6 December 1938 until he left for America on 28 January 1939. Thereafter, the two friends continued to correspond by letter, giving each other news of the murder or imprisonment of common friends with pet names like 'Woldi', 'Dietrich', and 'Baby'.[45] Not surprisingly, by 1939, Bowra in talking of Germany had seen 'too much of the country to wish to see it again'.[46]

When Kantorowicz died in 1963, Maurice's tributes were unqualified. As a free spirit he had taken it philosophically when, in the Great War, he had been sent from the safety of Turkey to the hellish battle for Verdun, as a result of conducting an *affaire* with the wife of Liman von Sanders. He had known Stefan George well, and shared The Master's crusades. He had made no concessions to the Nazis. Above all, as friend, and possibly as lover, he had enriched Bowra's life.

> he was a true critic of life, noticing everything and knowing what mattered, from poetry to politics ... My own debt to him is incalculable. He stirred my intelligence, bolstered my morale, amused me with dazzling paradoxes and intuitions and formulations. It was these qualities, in addition to his learning, that made him so good a teacher ... Pupils were all devoted to him ... He broadened their minds and set their imaginations to work without their noticing it, and of course knew all the details of their private lives and saved them from being too pompous about them.[47]

At Kantorowicz's request, all Bowra's letters to him were destroyed, but his executors reported that the three photographs on his bedside table were those of his father, Stefan George, and Maurice himself.[48]

Bowra's entanglements with the miseries of Germany also led to embarrassments in England, none of which were more long lasting than the von Trott affair. To the day he died, he was forced, from time to time, to confront his behaviour in the incident and justify it. The story began with Adam von Trott's arrival at Balliol College, as a Rhodes Scholar, in the last years of the Weimar Republic. Good-looking, charming, and endowed with more self-confidence than was strictly necessary, von Trott easily penetrated the mysteries of English social life. Maurice accused him of having 'sex appeal', and using it as a weapon.[49] David Astor took von Trott to Cliveden to meet Chamberlain and Halifax.[50] He enjoyed the friendship of Isaiah Berlin, and became the darling of the ladies of Lady Margaret Hall. On returning home to a position in the German Foreign Office, he kept up with many of his Oxford friends, appealing to 'this European cultural solidarity'[51] that united them all. Such letters often ended with a request that his regards or love should be passed on to Maurice Bowra.[52]

In the spring of 1937, von Trott was becoming alarmed by rumours suggesting that 'some English friends considered me as moving more and more to the Nazis'.[53] He was particularly concerned about Bowra's views, in that he regarded him 'as very nearly a real friend'.[54] Such worries were well founded, and David Astor was only partially right in asserting that Maurice 'liked Trott and Trott adored him'.[55] In fact, Maurice was impervious to aristocratic charm in either its German or English manifestations. In later life, he talked of von Trott as an 'unreliable, upper-class Hun', whose métier in life was 'to dupe' his friends.[56] Few letters between the two men survive, though more were undoubtedly written. After Trott left Oxford, they met only rarely, once in Berlin in 1935. For some reason, Bowra had a visceral distrust of the man. Perhaps his many German contacts allowed him information about Trott which was denied to his other Oxford acquaintances. Whatever the reason, by 1937 he had written him off as politically untrustworthy. In recommending an Italian to Felix Frankfurter's good offices, he described the refugee as 'very charming, neurotic and over-educated. Not at all like Trott. He is very anti-Fascist.'[57]

At some point in the summer of 1939,[58] von Trott suddenly appeared in Wadham, bearing a tale that must have seemed the stuff of fantasy. Proclaiming himself to be the representative of a vibrant opposition movement in Germany, von Trott asked Bowra to convey to the British government the news that war was absolutely unnecessary. Given just a little more time, Hitler would be removed by the Germans themselves. However, since the army would be required to move against the Nazis, national pride and political necessity made it essential that the Sudetenland and Austria should remain within the Reich. At the suggestion that Germany should be allowed to keep some of the fruits of aggression, Maurice smelt appeasement, exploded with anger and, unceremoniously, 'chucked him out'.[59] It was inconceivable to him that such a high-ranking official as von Trott could be travelling freely without Nazi permission. It was equally absurd to talk of an opposition in Germany. Bowra knew many Germans who hated Hitler, and also knew their powerlessness. Oxford was full of refugees who told him the same thing. Shortly before von Trott's visit, Helmuth von Moltke had sadly confessed to Lionel Curtis in All Souls that he and his friends were helpless. Hitler 'has been enabled to clear the whole of Germany from any possible inimical movement. When there was a chance for a change a year ago, there is none now.'[60] Bowra had some reason to react to Trott's claims with deep suspicion.

In fact, he not only refused to help Trott, but he also took positive steps to thwart his mission. He knew that the German was going on to America to retail the same story in the hope of persuading Roosevelt that his country had no need to become involved in another European war. Maurice feared that Trott could make a serious impact in America, for, as he told an American friend, 'You know my line about the Americans and the Germans—that all that blonde hair and hygiene and hard work take in your countrymen, and they listen to stories of injured innocence with tears in their eyes.'[61] Accordingly, he tried to warn Felix Frankfurter about Trott's arrival. Frankfurter had met Bowra in Oxford in 1934. As a Justice of the Supreme Court and a member of Roosevelt's inner circle, he was an effective channel through which Bowra's warnings could reach the right ears. For reasons that remain mysterious, this letter was intercepted by British Intelligence,[62] and never reached Frankfurter. Almost certainly, however, it had some influence in an unintended quarter. When Trott attempted to make contact with British Intelligence, in 1943, he was rebuffed.[63]

To ensure that Trott would be unsuccessful, Bowra opened a second line of attack. His Wadham colleague Professor Lindemann was one of Churchill's most trusted advisers. Through him, a meeting was arranged in Washington between Frankfurter and Churchill in July 1939. Bowra was deeply grateful and relieved that his views had finally reached Frankfurter, if by a rather circuitous route: 'Thank you very much for your kind and successful offices in bringing Winston and Frankfurter together. F enjoyed it enormously and will be able to give a good report to the President of the US, who is almost our only friend in the world and worth cultivating.'[64] One way or the other, Trott was discredited. His reception in America could only be described as cool, and David Astor was sure that it was all Bowra's handiwork. He had 'finished Trott' in the opinion of the Americans. In particular, Eleanor Roosevelt, who had known and liked the German for some time, was brought to change her mind.[65]

The Trott story of course ends in tragedy. As a participant in the conspiracy to assassinate Hitler in July 1944, he was arrested, tortured, and finally murdered in a particularly gruesome manner. His heroic death seems to prove that he had been no Nazi, and that the claims made in the summer of 1939 had been sincere. Publicly, Bowra expressed regret. In *Memories*, he wrote that his treatment of Trott had 'led to much unhappy searching of heart', and that 'my rejection of him remains one of my bitterest regrets'.[66] Some of Trott's English friends attacked Bowra for callousness, reporting that he often expressed the opinion in Oxford that Trott had been 'one of the few Nazis to be hanged'.[67] Others were more sympathetic. Sheila Grant-Duff told Isaiah Berlin that Maurice 'does not in fact regret anything he did, and I should not think needs to'.[68] Even David Astor, Trott's untiring apologist, was ultimately forgiving: 'Bowra reacted violently. But I think quite understandably. What Trott was saying was, can't you do more for peace, give up all your strengths ... and something will happen, but we won't tell you what.' Bowra's had been 'a wholly reasonable mistake'.[69]

In fact, whatever regrets were expressed in *Memories*, Maurice almost certainly never changed his mind about Trott. He seems to have taken the view that the German had undergone some kind of personality change. The outgoing Balliol man had become, if not a Nazi, then an unrepentant German nationalist whose objections to Hitler were less that he was a tyrant, than that his policies threatened the destruction of Germany. When Christopher Sykes set out to write a biography of Trott, Bowra's contribution was to emphasize 'the element of vanity and of vain ambition' in his subject's character.[70] When the book was published, Maurice described its contents to an American friend uncompromisingly: 'It is about a German Rhodes Scholar who was eventually hanged, but not before he had done a great deal of harm. I played a part in it—which I still think was perfectly OK, but was not approved by the Astors.'[71]

All in all, the episode was, for many people, messy and confused. Since Trott died a martyr in the anti-Nazi cause, any mistreatment of him looked inexcusable. But in the summer of 1939, a few months after the destruction of Czechoslovakia, matters had had a different aspect. Bowra's many German contacts told stories that destroyed any belief in the possibility that an opposition movement existed on the scale that Trott claimed. The rejection of Trott was a terrible experience, but the man was, consciously or naively, peddling tales that had done terrible harm. In any case, Maurice knew of many Germans who were more deserving of his sympathy, namely friends who now found themselves in concentration camps or living the life of refugees. In these circumstances, an unsentimental choice had to be made, and, without too much reluctance, Bowra took a line.

Given this close involvement with Germany, it was deeply depressing for Bowra to find that the vast majority of his countrymen were indifferent to events in Europe. He told no less a person than Adam von Trott, in 1936, that pacificism was everywhere:

> The real factor which will prove decisive is the overwhelmingly pacific feelings of the average man. There is a minor trade boom going on for the bourgeois and they don't at all want to be let in for a war. The young have listened to speeches from the League of Nations for years and regard the idea with horror. It is a very different world from that in which I was brought up, which inculcated bigger navies and the splendour of adding to the Empire, so that even if one disliked the idea, one still regarded it as inevitable. The breaking of the Locarno Treaty has not made a great impression as I should have thought. People think it is part of the Versailles Treaty, which most countries, England included, have already broken. Against the extreme dislike of the idea of war and a rather cynical desire to patch up some sort of peace, one must put a real fear of war which seems to me to grow every day. Most people one meets speak of it.[72]

Worse still were those who positively admired the Nazis, one or two of whom Bowra had met. In Venice, in the 1920s, he had been introduced to Oswald Mosley by John Strachey. Maurice was amused to discover that, although Mosley professed socialist opinions at the time, he still had an army of private gondoliers, dressed in white uniforms with blue sashes.[73] Through Nancy Mitford or Roy Harrod, he had also come across Lady Mosley, who, while imprisoned in Holloway during the War, had read and enjoyed *The Heritage of Symbolism*.[74]

Bracing brushes with Nazi sympathizers became part of social life in the late 1930s. At a dinner party given by Kenneth Clark, Bob Boothby brought with him, 'as a tease', an admirer of Hitler and Franco. Different accounts credit the man in question with being either an English civil servant or a German professor. After listening for a while, 'Maurice rose to (should I say) his full height—and said, "I know what you are, and I'll tell you what I think of you. You are a Nazi." He then added that he looked forward to using the Nazi's skull as an inkpot.'[75] All accounts agree that Bowra 'let out a stream of abuse in sergeant major language'.[76] There was poison at work within English society as well. In such circumstances, he could not be surprised by the concessions made at Munich. He protested about them in the Oxford by-election; he signed a letter to *The Times* condemning the betrayal of Czechoslovakia; and he may have joined a campaign to persuade Neville Chamberlain to take Churchill into his Cabinet.[77] But such actions could only be consoling rather than effective. Bowra knew well that, in England, intellectuals rarely shake governments.

Even those within the University of Oxford could not be completely trusted. More aware and more informed than the country as a whole, academics should have known better, but this was not the case. Provost Lys of Worcester greatly admired Mussolini, and put him up for an honorary degree. Many Oxford figures approved of the Röhm purge, on the grounds that 'if you find a lot of buggers, you should kill them'. To counteract such influences, Bowra shared public platforms with Bertrand Russell, Richard Pares, and Tom Mann.[78] When Mosley and his Blackshirts hired Oxford's Town Hall, Maurice went to the meeting and saw Bernard Floud and Basil Murray being manhandled for trying to ask Mosley embarrassing questions. He walked back to Wadham with Alan Bullock, vowing 'to fight these devils'.[79] To his further dismay, he discovered that the Chief Constable of Oxford had decided to prosecute Floud and Murray for causing a disturbance, rather than the Blackshirts. Both men were heavily fined in a magistrates' court presided over by Lady Townshend, the doyenne of Oxford Conservatives. When the sentence was pronounced, Maurice stood up in the court and shouted 'miscarriage of justice', before being escorted outside.[80] This episode, and others like it, seemed to prove that too many in authority in Oxford were suspect. Only in May 1937 did the University make a public stand by refusing to attend celebrations marking the foundation of a university in Göttingen. But even this decision was only taken after a great deal of 'wavering'.[81]

If the University refused to exert its corporate influence, all Bowra could do was to join like-minded academics, like Gilbert Murray, in organizing relief for persecuted colleagues in Germany. He led a campaign to obtain the release of Theodor Neubeuer from a concentration camp.[82] He played some part in bringing the classical scholar Eduard Fraenkel to Oxford, though his arrival rather proved the maxim that no good turn ever goes unpunished. Fraenkel, a very prickly man, insisted that German scholarship was infinitely superior to anything found in Oxford, and frequently said so.[83] But one way or another, Bowra 'saw a large number of refugees', and was 'well conversant with their problems'.[84] He helped where he could, but such acts of kindness to individuals were pitiful when set against the prevailing mood of indifference.

Bowra never forgave Germany for its Nazi episode. His experiences of it were more than enough to transform a Germanophile of the 1920s into the most complete Germanophobe. After 1939, he vowed that he would never set foot in the country again. Two generations of democracy had not prevented the Germans from voting away their liberties and their culture to a populist barbarism. Nazism, in his view, had not been the work of a minority. Too many Germans had voted for it, connived at it, or put up with it. Too many good Germans, among them his friends, had been murdered. It all pointed to something gangrenous. As he told a lecture audience, in 1952, 'the gangster politics of the Nazis triumphed by their appeal to some deep disease in the German character. Even if they did not believe their own propaganda, the German people did.'[85] Everything humane and 'decent' had been destroyed. He could only agree with Kantorowicz, who, from exile in America, believed that 'all that survives in Germany belongs to la crapule'.[86]

The only recognition that Germany deserved, after 1939, was the honouring of those representatives of an older and culture-conscious country who had actively opposed the Nazis and paid for their courage with their lives. Not infrequently such men, like Albrecht von Bernstorff, came from aristocratic backgrounds. In 1951, Lionel Curtis was awarded an honorary degree by the University of Cologne. The honour was to be conferred at a ceremony in All Souls. Bowra, as Vice-Chancellor, had no choice but to attend and speak. Since the audience included many Germans, including the widow and children of the murdered von Moltke, it would prove a difficult assignment:

> It is hard for me to speak of Germany with ease or without emotion. Twice in my lifetime I have, like millions of others, seen Germany drench the world with blood in an insatiable lust for power. I have naturally had bitter and hard feelings about Germans, and of these I will not speak. But even at the darkest moments, even when the Germans seem to have forfeited all regard from civilised men, I have been conscious, and gratefully and gladly conscious, that among them have been courageous and honest men, who have resisted the brutal spirit of their rulers ... Many had paid for their efforts with the terrible price of prolonged suffering and hideous death.[87]

With von Moltke and his kind excepted, however, the Germans deserved no sympathy. After the War, the miseries of German civilians were dismissed as 'odious self-pity and sorrow for their lost lace curtains. Surely the villages of the Ukraine must be looking a bit odd with their wristwatches, lace curtains, and Biedermeyer fittings. I have a sneaking desire to go there and tell the Germans in a long speech how much they are hated by the whole world.'[88]

Revenge in any form was to be relished. In 1951, Konrad Adenauer, the German Chancellor, visited Oxford, and it fell to Bowra's lot to entertain him. As 'a Germophobe', he set out to make the occasion as uncomfortable as possible. In 'rusty Deutsch', he gave his visitor a totally misleading description of how Oxford worked. Adenauer was under the impression that a college was a kind of monastery or convent in which religious observance had become somewhat lax. Using 'all kinds of subjunctive', Maurice confirmed this view. In addition, he offered the Chancellor 'not ... a good lunch' with 'only a few old shits like C K Allen, G N Clark, Dean Lowe etc.', for company.[89] Adenauer left Oxford in some bewilderment and Maurice had enjoyed himself.

Bowra's resolution to keep the German world at arm's length held until the very last months of his life, but, in 1969, he became a member of the Order, Pour le Mérite, Germany's highest academic honour. It was received only because it was awarded by German scholars and had nothing to do with the state. Scholarship, free from politics, had no frontiers. It was a great privilege for an academic to be honoured by his kind. Even then, the Germans could not bring the incident off without embarrassment. At the presentation ceremony, in the German Embassy in London, the ribbon to which the cross of the Order was attached, was found to be too short to envelop Bowra's bull-like neck: 'the German occasion ... was wonderfully German, except that the dinner was quite first-class. The photographs are quite horrifying, especially one in which I am clearly being strangled by that Wagnerian dragon, the cultural attachée.'[90] A few months later, as the only holder of the Order in Oxford, he had to represent the University at celebrations in Germany to mark Hölderlin's bicentenary. There was, too, the prospect of setting up a German cultural centre in Oxford. In the event, the visit passed off reasonably well, because 'the Huns were very anxious to please, and I found myself forgiving them'. Even so, in Bad Godesberg, he stayed in a hotel, which had once been a favourite of Hitler's, and there were 'nasty ghosts around the place'.[91] He never went again.

This last visit confirmed Bowra in the view that the Nazi experience and the Second World War had destroyed everything in the German tradition that he had once so admired. Its scholarship was in ruins, its politics revolved around apology and caution, and its literature was only a shadow of what it had once been. Stefan George's acolytes were dispersed or dead. Their mission to preserve and edify the status of the poet was now meaningless. For the first thirty years of Maurice's life, Germany had been the contemporary inspiration that closely complemented many of his classical preoccupations. Populist politics had undermined all this promise. Democracies in the ancient world had elected demagogues from time to time. Their modern equivalents seemed fated to repeat these mistakes. In such upheavals there were many losers, principally among them people like himself. His friends, his culture, had been destroyed by Nazism. In his search for a model of popular politics and high culture living harmoniously side by side, Germany offered no consolation. He would have to look elsewhere.

As Germany dipped below the horizon of his consciousness, so America rose. The most powerful democracy in the world, and one of the oldest, had to be investigated. On his first extended visit to Harvard from the autumn of 1936 to the spring of 1937, the impact was immediate. The variety of experience offered by America made all generalizations impossible. He was in Wonderland. New York was all bustle and noise and everything that was agreeable. He particularly enjoyed the floor show at the Cotton Club.[92] He told Elizabeth Bowen that 'New York makes me feel like a god.'[93] In Utah, he discovered forms of religion that were new to him. Sending John Betjeman a postcard of the Great Tabernacle in Salt Lake City, he jokingly reflected that he was very 'lucky to have seen this and heard a recital on the biggest organ in the world. The Mormons disapprove of coffee as well as of other things. So I shan't become one.'[94] The houses in Newport, Rhode Island, looked like 'Compton Wynyates leaning up against the Grand Trianon'.[95] In San Francisco, at a dinner given by distant cousins, each place setting had a photograph in which Bowra's head had been superimposed on an animal or fish. The total effect was 'thought very chic'.[96] Everything positive in Bowra's character responded to American energy and American optimism. It was so refreshingly un-English. As he put it to Isaiah Berlin, 'Talk about foreign countries! Nothing comes odder than this.'[97]

Further, America, like Germany, provided him with important friendships, most notably with Felix and Marian Frankfurter. They had met in Oxford one or two years before his visit, and had discovered common interests in gossip purveyed epigrammatically, liberal politics, and the promotion of literature. For Bowra, the association with the Frankfurters gave pleasure and opportunity. As a Justice in the Supreme Court, Frankfurter knew the ways of Washington. Through him, Bowra was introduced to President Roosevelt, 'a most delightful man',[98] and through him, some German friends reached the safety of America. A lifelong friendship was kept alive in the writing of letters that consciously set out to amuse and to inform. For over a quarter of a century, the friends kept each other abreast of the scandals in their respective villages, and took pleasure in looking after their own. When John Sparrow first visited America, he was recommended to Frankfurter's care as 'an old friend of mine, as they say at Cambridge, Eng., to avoid further discussion'.[99]

In Harvard, there were inevitably yet more agreeable people. Alice James and her husband, William, a nephew of Henry James, ran one of Boston's most distinguished salons. Briefly, Maurice became one of the social lions in their circle. His meeting with the great novelist, while still a schoolboy, no doubt helped to establish his credentials. He and Alice James would correspond with some regularity until her death. At the same time, narrower academic interests brought him the friendships of John Finley and other Harvard classicists, many of which stood the test of time. In people like these he recognized his own preoccupations. All of them belonged to that 'large liberal tradition which was both American and European'.[100] He expected people of like mind to foster friendships across frontiers. It would not be an exaggeration to say that, when Maurice talked of his liking for America, he was in fact talking of three cities only: Washington, Boston, and New York.

Not surprisingly, given this narrow geographical range, all his close friends were Democrats. In November 1936, he cheered Roosevelt's re-election enthusiastically. According to Marian Frankfurter, 'On election night, sitting by the radio, he would say, "What of Arkansas? We've had no news from Indiana." '[101] In America again during the election of 1948, partisanship led him to place a substantial bet that Truman would carry the day. When his man unexpectedly did win, Maurice delightedly reported that he had 'made a packet'.[102] In the company of Harvard Democrats and Frankfurter's pupils, Bowra found 'a haven of enjoyment', because, in their company, he had no 'need to make concessions to American susceptibilities'.[103] He could, in this context, say anything, in his usual style, and be understood. In Washington, Marian Frankfurter reported him to be 'an enchanting guest', and a great social success 'floating on the tide of his own fervour'.[104] Deprecatingly Maurice himself attributed his success to the fact that Americans 'never know when they're bored'.[105] To be made much of on the East Coast, shortly after being rejected for the Chair of Greek in Oxford, must have made the offer of Chairs at Harvard and Princeton very tempting. Just possibly he could make his home in America.

Good friends, however, knew better. For a month or two, Bowra's originality had given him, in certain American circles, an instant notoriety, a *succès fou*. But Harvard and Washington were not America, and the rest of the country would find it hard to understand the irony, the purpose, or the man himself. In the same letters in which she recorded Maurice's triumphs, Marian Frankfurter also noted limitations. She thought 'the American backdrop' had proved too 'alien' to Maurice. Because the country lacked 'colour', Maurice's distinctiveness was 'the sharper'. Being on an eminence and having no competitors was a heady experience for a time, but would ultimately translate into loneliness.[106] In addition, the conventions governing American conversation were different to those of an Oxford Common Room. She enjoyed the spectacle of Bowra rather wobbling on his pedestal, on being repeatedly asked why, as a man of forty, he was not yet married.[107]

English friends who had known him longer agreed that the suggestion of taking up permanent residence in America was preposterous. Thomas Higham reminded Maurice that 'you might not like moose and the simple souls who stalk them'.[108] Roy Harrod, presuming on a long friendship, was more peremptory: 'Well, now, Maurice, don't be naughty. We can't have the whole world tumbling about us like this. I have just heard that you are toying with the idea of staying in America. Really this is too much.' In the first place, he was needed in Oxford, as 'the *one* person who saves us from complete petrification'. Secondly, Americans 'are not good material for you to work on'.

> I don't believe that their type of mind will appreciate what is most subtle and best in yours … You may interest them for a moment, but they are already alive and awake to all sorts of other things to which they will return. Whereas, when you inspire a young Englishman, you are giving him the one thing he wants, because he comes to you in the first instance suppressed, un-self-expressed, unventilated. Will you find that over there? I doubt it.[109]

Almost certainly, Bowra took very little persuading that Harrod was right. He was acutely aware that the American idiom was not his own.

But it was flattering, for a month or two, to be cosseted by people in high places. At the beginning of the War, Bowra put President Roosevelt up for an honorary degree in Oxford. In reporting the initiative to Frankfurter, he was obviously pleased that he idea had come as 'a surprise' to 'the other old boys who are not in touch with world affairs'.[110]

Bowra's second, extended visit to America was once more based in Harvard, in the autumn of 1948 and the spring of 1949. The lectures he gave on this occasion would become *The Romantic Imagination* in due course.[111] Overall, this second excursion was hugely enjoyable. Once again, Maurice dazzled and bewildered to such extent, that when Isaiah Berlin followed him to Boston a year later, he modestly described himself as 'the best' Oxford 'could do' to find a successor to Bowra.[112] Once again, Californian architecture was a fund of pleasure: 'I went to California for Christmas. The domestic architecture is very ingenious, and I was particularly pleased with the happy blends of style in the Hispano-Dutch and Sino-Swiss styles. There are also some excellent examples of Old Heidelberg, and of course, a lot of Stockbroker Tudor, with the beams nailed onto the stucco.'[113] Here he met Ernst Kantorowicz for the first time in over a decade, and heard 'all sorts of Europeans... talking their own languages'.[114] Once again, 'the fast set' around the Frankfurters were his principal interpreters of America and its ways: 'The Fast Set have lots of cocktails and one can say anything in front of them... I have of course gravitated to the Jews, and found a charming doctor with a delightful, handsome and intelligent wife. She is decayed New England and very much my sort of girl.'[115] Despite again being lectured 'on the duty of getting married',[116] the whole experience was familiar and warming.

As in 1936–7, the martini-shaken worlds of the East Coast and California met Maurice in mutual appreciation. But this time, in Bowra's letters home, praise is mingled with more criticism. The noise on a bustling, American campus made sleeping and working 'difficult'. To wish for quiet was considered unvirile. In addition, the food was 'quite appalling'. At breakfast, for example, you were 'lucky... if you get hominy and not a warm, wet pancake soaked in Lyle's golden syrup, or a thing of corn-beef hash, which is an all time low'. After queuing for all meals, he found himself usually clutching 'a brown paper platter, greasy with yesterday's synthetic gravy'. He speculated that suffering such rude conditions might be the reason why some American students showed such a keen interest in poetry, and why 'some of them, alas, try to write it'. It was some consolation that his lectures were well attended, but they had the air of a carnival rather than a university occasion: 'My lectures are attended by large crowds, who have a reverential look as if they were in church. The girls knit, the boys look at the girls. At intervals, elderly ladies come in, stay for ten minutes, and then go out. Small boys come from the street, playing hide-and-seek.'[117]

Worst of all, this time, Maurice took a more careful look at the leaders of American, academic life, and was not impressed:

> The boys were very kind to me and I liked them. So were the young tutors, and among them I have perhaps made a friend or two,. Also a wife here and there, but with the older people, the professors and the bosses, I feel that I failed...They plainly thought me a nice old thing, coming from a ruined country and therefore of no great importance. And, alas, I was not impressed by them. Somehow they all seemed to have missed the bus, and to be flapping their wings about without knowing where to go next. It is very different from here [Oxford], where people are a little sour and cynical but not aimless.[118]

Not for the first time in his life, Bowra found establishment figures arid and run through with self-importance. Too much of their work was spoilt by trying to impose personal agendas on to their scholarship. As Maurice put it, 'I have decided that none of them know what literature is, and pursue it for irrelevant reasons like patriotism, homosexuality, ambition, persecution mania, but not from love.'[119] Seemingly compounded of these elements in varying combinations, Harvard dons could not be liked or respected.[120] In 1936, Isaiah Berlin had warned Maurice against any idea of settling in America; sixteen years later, Bowra returned the compliment. To give 'two seconds to such a suggestion was simply not...worth it'.[121]

When establishment figures become lifeless and oppressive, or when professionals sank under the weight of their own ambition, Maurice's instincts always led him to seek out the company of the young. Junior faculty members and one or two undergraduates of promise might offer alternative insights. As he reported to a friend,

> Everyone works day and night and I am hard put to it to find conversation. I have found a cache of excellent brandy, and bribe the younger tutors from their duties with it. They are much persecuted and very congenial. They can be sacked at a moment's notice, and are treated like dogs by the professors, who think themselves very grand, though I am glad to say that I have found a lot of secret hatreds among them.[122]

His methods in Harvard mirrored his methods in Oxford. In a short time, he created a court that would resound with irreverent views. Among those attending his entertainments were Howard Hugo, the future musicologist, and McGeorge Bundy, who would become National Security Adviser during the Kennedy Presidency. When Hugo married, he was rewarded with an epithalamium, which for once made no reference to the language of the barrack room.[123] Bundy did even better, being invited to spend part of his honeymoon in the Warden's Lodgings in Wadham.[124] American Bowristas did exist, though with different colouring and form.

On 2 April 1949, Maurice set out for home on board the *Queen Mary*, 'a much overrated ship', whose captain was 'a poltroon'.[125] The journey was made tolerable by the fact that Winston Churchill was a fellow passenger. The two men had met at the Asquiths in the 1920s, and now had time to renew their acquaintanceship. Common ground was found in their joint opinion that the Nuremberg trials and executions had been a terrible mistake. It would have been better 'to put these criminals on an island, surveyed ceaselessly day and night by destroyers at sea and aeroplanes overhead, and let them stew in their own disgusting juice'.[126] Bowra claimed to have found Churchill 'easy and jolly', even when he had incautiously suggested that the only hope for Randolph Churchill lay in his applying for the post of butler in a New York household.[127] In the company of someone like Churchill, Bowra's style of talking could be once again uninhibited, as American sensibilities faded behind them.

To return to Oxford was pure pleasure. He described his recent visit to Alice James as a journey undertaken at the behest of Peter Pan: 'I felt like one of those embarrassing characters in a play by Barrie, who disappear to some Never Never Land, and then come back without warning to trouble their relations.'[128] His stay at Harvard had been 'a sojourn in the Beyond'.[129] Maurice in England was no patriot. So many aspects of his character put him at odds with English society. But he never felt more English than when in America, or when he had just returned from that country. He then thought that England was 'more steady and more solid than the US. I don't quite know why, but perhaps it is that we have had the same problems for longer, and have more experience in dealing with them.'[130] He could, in this mood, even wax lyrical about the English spring.[131] New doubts about America were confirmed when, four months after returning home, he was invited to tour the *USS Missouri* in Portsmouth Harbour. The ship had 'unintelligible devices for destruction', but there was no alcohol on board and everyone was called Smith.[132] Priorities were hopelessly and symbolically out of kilter.

After two lengthy visits to America, pre- and post-War, it was time to take stock and draw conclusions. On the positive side of the balance sheet was the American capacity for optimism and their liking for an attacking view of life. Maurice affected to admire the films of James Cagney, 'in which people don't shake hands on meeting. Strike each other in the face immediately.'[133] On the debit side, however, there was recorded a long list of criticisms, which might be summed up in the noted complaint of Kantorowicz that the United States had 'no enchantment except ice-cream, for which I do not fall'.[134] There was simply not enough cultural oxygen in the atmosphere to sustain life as Bowra knew it. In the heartlands of America his language was barely spoken. Outside certain circles on the two seaboards, 'the sensitive man without money must have hell. The only amusements are cocktails and women. No wonder they are so empty, poor dears.'[135] It was pleasant to be lionized in Boston and New York, but Bowra suspected that America's true values were set elsewhere in the country. He knew of English talent that had evaporated into American air. His former protégé Henry Yorke was reported, in 1951, to be 'decomposing rapidly. American influences, I fear.'[136]

With these views, it had been 'lowering' to be lectured in a 'very dictatorial manner' on the proposition that England was the past and America the future. He was told that 'we are all wrong—too much past when we ought to be studying the FUTURE'. One professor even accused Bowra of having 'English good manners. I really ought to call him out for that.'[137] Inevitably, Bowra had too much interest in the humane achievements of the past to be over-impressed by a future predicated on business methods and machines. America had a literature but it was noticeable that many of its greatest exponents had always chosen to live in Europe. To be told bluntly that his crusades about the Greeks and poetry missed the mark was alarming. The future set out on drawing boards in America had no place for him.

Then there was the total commitment in America to living with boredom. The citizens of a country with only shallow, spiritual values had no choice in the matter. Maurice described one professor at Stamford as 'a very fine bore indeed, notable even in a country which is pre-eminent in producing bores'.[138] In boredom, 'a 2nd XI from any village in Wisconsin could defeat an all-England team'.[139] President Nixon was dismissed as 'a terrible bore and rather too like a Rhodes Scholar from Arkansas. I think this is to overestimate him.'[140] The American male seemed, like some winged insect, to go through a predictable life cycle, in which tedium played a large part. 'I rather agree with you', he assured Julian Mitchell, 'about American undergraduates. It is extraordinary that those horrible, assertive, noisy, unkempt children become for a few years quite nice, polite and presentable young man [*sic*], and then relapse into those purple, bum-faced, bespectacled business men, tight at 6 pm, and all repeating the same formulaic phrases for the rest of their lives.'[141] Later in life, he sent 'condolences' to Evelyn Waugh,[142] who was about to visit America, and told a young friend that he had 'lost my taste for the New World'. New York and Washington still had a certain interest for him, 'but the rest of the country bores one to paralysis'.[143]

Most worrying of all was the American tendency to lapse, from time to time, into spasms of national paranoia, in which the joyful persecution of real and supposed enemies was undertaken with relish. In 1949, the hounding of Alger Hiss was a case in point. The guilt or innocence of 'poor Hiss' on charges of spying, had of course to be established, but 'the hysteria behind it all made a fair trial unlikely'. He told Felix Frankfurter that 'it seems quite insane to me and makes me rather dislike the Americans'.[144] Immediately after, America condoned the brutal persecution supervised by Senator McCarthy and his Committee on Unamerican Activities. While in theory commissioned to root out communist influence, McCarthy took the opportunity to attack all manifestations of liberal thinking. Writers and academics were inevitably caught up in his net. Contemplating these events, Bowra knew that most Americans were not bigots, and was therefore puzzled by the failure of his friends to restrain McCarthy. In January 1953, he told Alice James that

> We all watch American politics with eager and anxious eyes. I wish there was not so much witch-hunting in the air. I can't believe it does any good, and feel that it must do a lot of harm to innocent people. Why must we always adopt the ways of our enemies? I hope the General [Eisenhower] will stop it. He surely has enough prestige to do so and I imagine that he would have the bulk of the people behind him.[145]

Under McCarthyism, he himself would never be allowed into America, because 'a) I was born in China, b) I have been to Russia, c) I did not fight for Franco, d) I am an academic, notoriously the least American of all classes.'[146] All in all, 'this McCarthy stuff... ages one [sic]'.[147]

Ominously, his letters to American friends begin to contain comparisons to the German tragedy he had witnessed at first hand.

> I have a dark feeling that [the] US is suffering from something like what assailed Germany in 1870—a mixture of pride and envy, of a desire to boss and a feeling that somehow no one wants it to. Of course, there are millions of people who think otherwise, but the noisy ones get the press and the publicity.[148]

The rejection of Adlai Stevenson in the Presidential Election of 1952 was a terrible blow. Stevenson was hailed as 'a true liberal, a splendid speaker and a man of great courage', whereas Eisenhower was ignorant of politics and surrounded by 'ghastly, anti-liberty men'.[149] Even more to the point, one of Stevenson's ancestors had been a Wadham man.[150]

From a great distance, Maurice joined the battle. At his instigation, Stevenson was invited to give the Romanes Lecture in Oxford. On his insistence, Dean Acheson was given an honorary degree, and Bowra proudly reported that he had

> put him up, not so much for his policy as for his magnificent moral courage, both in speaking up for Hiss, and in defying all the jackals who attack him. He really is a brave man, and that stirs one's admiration. I hope he will not be prevented at the last minute from coming. I met him once with the Frankfurters, and was delighted by his gaiety and candour.[151]

In Oxford, Acheson met all Bowra's expectations. He had 'a complete indifference to all the nasty things which are said about him', and 'a lack of pomposity or any traces of a public face'.[152] Maurice had praised Gaitskell for the same qualities. In the same year, Oxford honoured Robert Oppenheimer 'for being a good socialist', but also for 'speaking his mind about freedom of thought and speech'. Maurice found him 'a highly-strung, jumpy, not very easy man', but 'extremely honest' and free of the vices that all too often affect 'the head of an academic institution ... to develop a public face and a public manner, and to say the right thing, no matter how wrong it may be'.[153] The depth of Bowra's interest in America may be measured by these politically inspired acts in a man who normally abstained from politics.

Hope in America was briefly reborn with the election of J. F. Kennedy in 1960, even though Maurice was 'not madly keen'[154] on the new President's

Catholicism. Suddenly, no doubt through the good offices of McGeorge Bundy and Dean Acheson, Bowra became high fashion on the East Coast. Leading politicians seem to have identified him as a political pundit. The most bizarre example of this occurred in February 1963. Bundy wrote to Wadham, requesting Maurice to compose 'a report on the character and quality of Mr Harold Wilson'. The letter was sure that 'Bowra on Wilson' would be 'an extraordinary promising subject',[155] and that his views would be passed on to President Kennedy. The project was quixotic, even absurd. Bowra had never met Wilson,[156] and, as a friend of Gaitskell, could only be expected to hold highly coloured views. For the Kennedy Administration to give Maurice this task is instructive of his standing in their eyes, but may also suggest limitations in the American method of gathering intelligence.

In June 1963, Bowra returned to Harvard to receive an honorary degree. The other honorands included George Kennan, 'melancholy', and U. Thant, 'jolly, serious, and friendly'.[157] After the ceremony, he travelled to Washington, where he was introduced to the Kennedys and the McNamaras. Predictably Kennedy's assassination was deeply felt. Lyndon Johnson brought a more coarse-grained style to Washington, which could not accommodate Bowra. When he returned to America in January 1964, he knew that there would be 'alas, no more White House'.[158] Even so, he was still welcome 'in the Kennedy set'. One evening, in particular, was memorable, because 'Mrs Kennedy came to a small dinner—her first night out and made a splendid effort, but kept on thinking of her husband and bursting into tears. She has got it into her head that she might have saved his life, and, though she couldn't have, it must be pretty gruelling to have him shot at your side.'[159] All in all, Maurice found the Kennedy world reasonably congenial: 'It is like 18th century England, rich and powerful, but not uncultivated and with a few nice people.'[160]

But even Democrats could go badly wrong. The brief promise of the Kennedy presidency was soon overshadowed by the conflict in Vietnam. Bowra described the war as one which had the capacity 'to haunt my conscience. I don't like the thought of all those very pretty and happy little people being mucked up.'[161] He was alarmed to hear rumours that even Bundy might think the war justified. Once again, the Americans, even his kind of American, talked theory instead of practicalities: 'They think they are fighting Communists, but you can only fight people: that is what they are doing, they are fighting the Vietnamese.'[162] Even so, when Graham Greene suggested that all the British members of the American Academy of Arts and Literature should resign by way of protest, Bowra declined the idea. Instead, 'we could do more good by writing to the members, and telling them what we think'.[163] To do more would be to injure American friends who also deplored the Vietnam adventure.

Maurice, half-jokingly, always maintained that nothing of importance or interest had happened after 1939. His autobiography deliberately ended with the outbreak of war. This argument rested on many supports, but two of them were represented by Germany and America. In the first, he had witnessed one of the greatest European cultures undermined by a popularly based barbarism. In the second, a great culture, in Bowra's sense of the word, had never taken root. After 1945, the superpower of the democratic west was a country in which Maurice could never have settled permanently and which held little that excited his intellect. In one country, his friends had been expelled and murdered. In the other, they huddled together in coastal cities looking for sustenance from overseas. Democracy had not protected the cultural traditions of Germany; in America, it had not generated much of value. The United States was 'a place where no bird sings, no flowers smell, no food tastes'.[164] Neither offered a welcoming environment for the poet and writer. It remained to be seen whether they had a future in England. Observing developments in Germany and America, Bowra could only have been powerfully reminded of the process by which the aristocratic world of sixth-century Greece gave way to the demagogues and unstable democracies of the fifth century. Bowra was no uncritical admirer of aristocracy or its physical representatives. Nor was he unhappy with democracy in principle. The overriding aim was to find a political system that offered security for someone with his values. With this priority in mind, the German and American models suggested little that was hopeful.

10

Warden of Wadham, 1938–1970

For all his cosmopolitanism, Maurice always regarded Oxford in general, and Wadham College in particular, as his preferred stage. It was here that he held court, and where he gave his most accomplished performances. Here, he could influence affairs, and steer them in directions he thought good. Only occasionally did Oxford fail him, producing spasms of doubt. A remarkable letter, written to Roy Harrod in 1924, reads oddly, coming from the pen of a man whose whole personality was committed to life in academia. In it, he confessed that he could not persuade himself to like '90% of dons, I find them boring in the worst, conventional way ... I like people, who surprise or amuse or sympathise, but I like them to do it with some show of life. I find very few who do this.' Undergraduates, for the most part, were equally unsatisfactory: 'They don't know enough about life or learning to make intimacy possible.' As for teaching, too much of it simply 'kills' all interest in the subject taught.[1] In fact, dons would be his companions for nearly half a century, and undergraduates an enduring challenge. Maurice went on teaching them till he died. This strange letter was really an anguished realization of how few people, even in Oxford, could really respond to the possibilities of life as Bowra defined them. But he also knew very well that there were even fewer outside the University's walls.

A few months away from Oxford quickly readjusted his perspectives. Returning from Harvard in 1937, Maurice found Oxford 'very agreeable'.

I can't think why anyone lives anywhere else. In my absence, my College has changed from being a study for lower-middle-class seekers after truth into a gay country club, bursting with sherry parties, Swedish girls, and undergraduates in hunting clothes or in yellow pull-overs ... The old characters have all moved forward a step on their fatal path of decay.[2]

By Oxford, of course, Bowra usually meant Wadham. He was right to do so, because throughout his career, the Oxford colleges were self-contained republics enjoying the independence offered by their own endowments and eccentricities. The head of such an establishment was someone of consequence. A man or woman of character could create a community in their own image. For this reason, Wadham and Bowra became indistinguishable.

Bowra's arrival in Wadham, in 1922, was less than triumphal. Warden Wells and five Fellows of the College met to fill a vacancy open to all subjects. Seven candidates only applied for the position. Two candidates, Bowra and a chemist called Pilley, attracted three votes each.[3] 'After much discussion', Warden Wells gave his casting vote for Bowra, not in recognition of superior promise as a scholar, but on the rather more unflattering grounds that he was 'the more all round man'.[4] The College was in need of a Dean of extrovert character who would live permanently in Wadham and exercise disciplinary and pastoral functions. Bowra would hold the office until 1932. For his pains, he was offered a substantial salary. In 1927, he earned £711.9.2d. Bowra's academic credentials were impeccable, but it was his other qualities which eventually carried the day.

Three men had voted against him, and they were people of consequence. Reggie Lennard was a distinguished economic historian, who, with a taste for long walks and spartan diets, would never thaw in his icey relations with his new colleague. Frederick Lindemann, later Lord Cherwell, would go on to become Churchill's principal scientific adviser. He regarded Bowra's exuberance as suspicious at the very least. In return, Maurice regarded him as an incorrigible snob. But the two men recognized the power in the other, and, according to David Astor, they 'made a deal', which required each of them to be wary of the other's sensibilities.[5] There would be little teasing of Cherwell and no high moral tone used against Bowra. The third objector, Theodore Wade-Gery, eventually changed his mind. As an ancient historian he had to work closely with Maurice in teaching classics in Wadham. Over the years, he came to recognize Bowra's deep seriousness of purpose, to collaborate with him on academic projects, and to welcome him into his family circle.[6] Even so Bowra's entry into Wadham was contested and controversial.

In the 1920s, the Dean of Wadham became a figure of fame or notoriety within the University, and a power within his college. When Warden

Wells retired, Wade-Gery and Bowra were instrumental in establishing his successor.[7] In fact, manoeuvring through the shoals of College politics gave Maurice great pleasure. Defeating the cautious and those he labelled philistine would always have an appeal. He told Ottoline Morrell that 'as I get older, I find I don't mind crushing offensive people, and am more confident of pushing my own plans through, and that gives a zest to life'.[8] Inevitably, Bowra had an agenda, and Wadham would be the testing ground for his ideas.

The College was to become more academic in atmosphere and more colourful. English schoolboys were to be saved from the baleful effects of their education to date, and offered alternatives. In 1923, one of his first pupils, Norman Brook, who would go on to become Cabinet Secretary and Head of the Civil Service, took a First in classical Moderations. Bowra was delighted, but only wished there were many more: 'My heartiest congratulations. I am entirely glad you got your first. You certainly deserved it. My only regret is that you had no Wadham man to keep you company. You are now in the distinguished position of being the only man with a first in the College.'[9] When Brook passed the examination to enter the Civil Service with equal distinction, Maurice again wrote with real warmth: 'It must be an enormous relief to you to get a job which you want, and to know you are financially secure for life. I think anxiety about a career is the worst thing in one's undergraduate life, and I am most awfully glad that you are now free of it.'[10] Such praise begat gratitude. Years later, Brook, now Lord Normanbrook, helped his old tutor to put the British Academy on to a sound, financial footing.

As Wadham's academic reputation rose, Maurice found a new vein of humour in ridiculing the poor performances of other Colleges. A raw nerve in Evelyn Waugh could always be touched by reporting that only 1.7% of Hertford College men achieved a First. Only 'the unmentionable St Peter's did worse'.[11] To effect this change in Wadham's character, a new energy was needed at all levels. First and foremost, there had to be a Senior Common Room of dons who took matters academic seriously. In too many Colleges, conversation revolved around the minutiae of parish politics or the likelihood of crews and sports teams doing well. At Wadham's High Table, by contrast, Bowra kept up a keener pace, with real 'enthusiasm, like an old schoolmaster, happy to be back in the classroom with the boys, happier here than anywhere'.[12] Stuart Hampshire wrote these words after discussing Thucydides over four courses in 1953. In addition, dons must be conscientious tutors or lecturers for twenty years or so. To do less was frivolous and sold the young short; to do more ran the risk of boring themselves and their audiences. Even so, Bowra himself went on teaching in nearly every Oxford term. As he put it, 'if you don't have to do it—then one chips in gladly'.[13] For many reasons, the election of a new Fellow was, for Maurice, a matter of extreme importance.

On 5 October 1938, Maurice was formally elected Warden of Wadham. The College Convention Book blandly records that he 'was unanimously elected Warden, no other name being proposed'. He would still be required to teach for a few hours a week and to live in College.[14] According to the *Oxford Magazine*, the election was generally welcomed in the University as imaginative. It was given 'an enthusiastic press'. The new Warden was a conversationalist 'with few equals'. He was also 'remarkable for the great number and wide variety of his friends'.[15] In July 1939, he was elected to Hebdomadal Council, the University's governing body. He was still only forty-one years old. According to the official report, his new career had begun smoothly enough.

Under the surface, however, the waters had been much disturbed. Two candidates had been on offer; Bowra and a lawyer named Bill Hart, 'a dull stick'[16] who had given the College years of effective service as Bursar. Lennard led Hart's campaign. No choice could have been starker. With Hart, Wadham would be in safe, if undistinguished, hands; with Bowra in charge there was the risk of something wonderful or something calamitous. In the event, Bowra won because Lindemann decided to support him. Although Maurice always regarded his ally as combining 'the worst points of the Philistine, the Pharisee, and the Snob',[17] the two men had a common interest in German politics, and admired each other's robust refusal to consider policies of appeasement. Maurice was genuinely pleased when Lindemann was given a government post in 1943.[18] In return, Lindemann took a chance on Bowra. He knew that many people in Oxford could not regard him as 'respectable'.[19] He resolutely refused to give him war-work of any consequence. Undergraduates speculated about Bowra's sexuality.[20] Yet, despite all this, Bowra offered the College the possibility of distinction, whereas his rival only suggested a future of worthy mediocrity.

On the day of Bowra's election, the omens were not propitious. During a thunderstorm, one of the Fellows' wives retired to a gardener's shed, and committed suicide with the assistance of 'a large saw'.[21] Someone as knowledgeable about the Greek world as Bowra might have found the episode daunting. Instead, he thought the coincidence of all these events mildly comic and dined out on retailing them. In fact, his insouciance in the face of sinister events was fully justified. Bowra would be Warden for thirty-two years. It would be one of the most talked about reigns in Oxford's history. Under his direction, Wadham would acquire more consequence than it had enjoyed for much of its existence.

Success, however, came at a cost. As a Head of House, Maurice had no choice but to tone down the more extravagant aspects of his public and private life. The Warden would have to nod to convention and public expectation just a little more. In some matters, the poacher would have to turn gamekeeper. It was not possible to be always anti-establishment if you were the establishment. Just before his election, Bowra had lunched with Stuart Hampshire and John Betjeman in Merton College. After a very good meal, they repaired to the chapel, where Maurice first gave an impromptu sermon, and then 'turned a somersault on the steps of the altar', before being removed by an angry porter.[22] Such escapades were now out of the question. A contemporary undergraduate noted the change and regretted it: 'His great success subdued him a little I feel—which is a pity. But the Warden must appear severely respectable I suppose: even to those who remember his past.'[23] In private and on paper, the Bowra style was unchanged, but the public face, of necessity, had to be given a certain gravity. Perhaps it was in the spirit of irony that Evelyn Waugh congratulated his friend by sending him a monkey-puzzle tree for the Warden's garden.[24]

Maurice's new home would be the Warden's Lodgings, a substantial building in Wadham's front quadrangle. From the beginning, he found it 'really charming', despite 'a shortage of bath-rooms and wcs'. Furnishing it would be an absorbing hobby, and a first-rate antidote to the fear of 'war and national humiliation'.[25] Housekeepers and cooks had also to be hurriedly found.[26] After the War, the Lodgings was given a new library. With this 'and four other reasonably large sitting-rooms', he found he could 'just jog along', being 'against the idea that scholars can work in cells'.[27] His surroundings and furnishings robustly suggested his own tastes and preferences, which were criticized at one's peril. When Lord David Cecil described the Lodgings as furnished in 'the Edwardian English Middle Middle Class Bowra Trust House style',[28] Bowra described Lord David as 'china in a bull shop'.[29]

Space, however, could not guarantee comfort. Staying in the Lodgings was something of an ordeal. The food and drink came in copious quantities, but, apart from suspect plumbing, there was the problem of cold. Apparently, the public schoolboy and old soldier in Bowra regarded too much heating as effete. Ann Fleming discovered that she was at 'grave risk after enduring the temperature of the water at Wadham in November. I was expected to appear in an unheated dining-room for breakfast at 8.30, and Maurice's only comment on the bath situation was, "I could wash without positive pain this morning." '[30] Lady Annan solved the problem by bringing electric heating pads for her bed. Every evening before retiring, she removed the light bulb, connected the pads, and slept soundly, remembering only to return the room to its usual state before morning tea appeared.[31] In Wadham, a guest could die of laughter or hypothermia.

Elected in 1938, Maurice had one year of Wardenship before the War came. The atmosphere was hardly normal. Oxford was too full of refugees, and Bowra's knowledge of Germany too extensive for him or his friends to indulge in self-delusion. A time of sackcloth and ashes was approaching. As a result, it was important to play the old games with a new intensity. At Christ Church, there was an undergraduate whose father had been a friend of the Warden's, as a result of which he was co-opted into Wadham circles. He kept a diary for the academic year 1938–9, which chronicles the last months of an *ancien régime*. After the War, there would be only increasingly pale imitations of what had once existed.

Under Maurice's tutelage, Clive experienced a series of 'enormous days that epitomize everything I worship in an Oxford term; something that cannot happen anywhere but in a university with university people; the change of tempo, the contrasting types, the small world seriousness about everyone and everything, the unwarranted belief that Oxford is the lynch-pin of England, the quintessence of civilized remains.' Conversations at a Bowra party started with the topic of lampshades and ended with arguments about Géricault and Delacroix. Reputations were 'carved up' or 'rammed home'. Maurice was so 'very good on everyone's sex life before and after marriage' that the boy 'choked with laughter'. On these occasions, 'all of us sank fathoms' before the Warden's 'brilliance'. He particularly enjoyed Bowra insisting that the postal address of Brasenose College was S.W.19. A year of this treatment left the undergraduate convinced that 'vice had more compensations than virtue'. Only politics could not be discussed. There would soon be time enough for those topics. When someone tried to raise the question of events in Spain, Bowra switched the focus sharply to the reputations of Ibsen and Eugene O'Neill.[32]

For the moment, reporting the peccadilloes of others was not only a customary amusement but also a necessary distraction. When the wife of A. J. Ayer left her husband for Stuart Hampshire, she provided just that opportunity for acerbic comment that the times required. Having suffered philosophy at New College, Bowra inevitably relished this, perhaps illogical, behaviour among philosophers. As he reported to Felix Frankfurter,

> The Hampshire–Ayer entanglement goes on. I went to a party given by Mrs Ayer. It was no fun, as they only ask guests who do not give them Persecution Mania ... But my evening was enlivened by Miss Bonham-Carter fainting on top of me. I carried her home in heroic style to a bed, where she soon recovered and said she had enjoyed it.[33]

A verse or two of poetry was obviously called for;

> One goes out, in comes another;
> Husbands play at Box and Cox.
> Perfect wife and perfect mother,
> Making love and making socks—
> Still they whisper in Japan:
> She's the girl for everyman.[34]

Thirty years later, Maurice enjoyed the irony of Stuart and Renée Hampshire taking up residence in Wadham's Lodgings as his successors.

Superficially, therefore, Bowra's Oxford was intact. Becoming Warden of Wadham had merely enlarged the stage on which he could perform. When Nigel Clive left the University, his comments echoed those which had often been written previously: 'When one leaves Oxford or Cambridge, one goes out into the wilds—presumably to stay there for ever and ever. I should like to go on living here for always, if only because the rest is barbaric. Oxford only fits you for Oxford.'[35] Maurice would understand and sympathize with these remarks, but he was also acutely aware that a line was about to be drawn through Oxford's history. At the age of forty-two, one phase of his life was firmly being brought to an end. What he had known and valued was about to be tested. It is no coincidence that his *Memories* stop in 1939. He had no interest or motivation to write about the post-War world.

In talking about the Second World War, Bowra found his American friends to be the most suitable audience. Alice James and the Frankfurters were the recipients of his thoughts on the conflict and on how it impacted on his world. At the same time that he was reducing the Christ Church undergraduate to helpless laughter and teasing Ayers and Hampshires, he was writing to Alice James very differently. She was told that War was inevitable, and that everyone would be brutalized by it.

> Here I find that one gets used to the endless air of crisis and feels ready for almost anything. I quite agree with you that war was the worst thing possible; we should then only defeat Hitler by becoming like him. The real problem is how far one can defeat him by pretending to play his own game. I confess I don't like it, because I can't see that there is anything else to be done. One's chief duty is to be sane, and not indulge in hate, which only creates lies and trouble for the future. (How very moral all this sounds, but it is so extremely real now).[36]

When 'the blow fell', he knew that his undergraduates would be marched away, 'helpless and innocent before what lies ahead of them'.[37] Three weeks after war was declared, Bowra was assailed by 'frightful thoughts that come all the time'. He admitted that there were 'worse things than death, and civilisation can't exist if there are no rules and no sense of honour. But I fear it is wrong to think that war will give us half of what we want.' It was much more likely to 'make us just like what we wish to destroy'.[38] Nazism had to be fought, but, won or lost, the conflict would not guarantee Bowrista values.

The first year of war was quite as terrible as he had predicted. Young men returned to Wadham with stories about Narvik and Dunkirk. In Europe, the German armies seemed to be unstoppable. Ten days after the invasion of France, Maurice reported to the Frankfurters that he had joined John Sparrow and Sylvester Gates for one last dinner at Boulestin's before he and all his friends faced the apocalypse. The letter then became more sombre.

> It is no use pretending that I am not fearfully depressed and anxious. This German rush to the Channel, through places which I knew so well in 1918 is an absolute nightmare. Every wireless news or paper brings something worse, and it is very hard to put much trust in one's few little hopes—that there will be a counter-ttack [sic], the tanks may break down, the RAF blow up communications. The devil moves with great speed and cunning, and I can't help feeling that we are all too nice to be able to resist him... At the

moment there is a real chance that England will be invaded from the air. It will certainly mean fearful destruction, disorganization and hysteria; it may even mean defeat. And then ... One's job is to stay here and stick it out.

To suggestions that he should take refuge in America, he answered that 'guilt forbids me, until I can come as a hero. I don't see myself as a success without the blood of some Huns on my hands, or at least a wooden leg.'[39]

Humour was still possible, but it was of the gallows variety. In June 1940, he spent an evening with Pauline and Sylvester Gates in London, where 'we had a very enjoyable blitz together ... Quite a show—fireworks, whistles, etc., and a nice mess in the West End. It was a good excuse for cracking a bottle, and the Gates are never averse to that.'[40] Everyone, including Bowra, was convinced that an invasion was imminent. Waiting for it was 'very wearying and wearing'. The only consolation was to be found in the idea that now he could look young men in the face, because it was no longer they alone who faced dangers and uncertainties: 'One comfort is that now we are all in it together, old and young, men and women. The sacrifice is equally shared, and I have less guilt about sending out the young to fight now that I know that I shall have a chance to take a risk myself.' With terrible irony that summer was one of warmth and blue skies. Bowra reflected that 'I doubt if I shall ever enjoy a fine summer again, as it will always remind me of 1940.'[41]

Worst of all was his inability to find suitable war-work. All his friends had been recruited into one organization or another, but there was no invitation for Bowra. Isaiah Berlin, 'pillowed on pink, satin sheets',[42] was working in the British Embassy in Washington. Roy Harrod and John Sparrow were also given posts in America. Every other Oxonian of prominence was breaking codes at Bletchley. Even John Betjeman was allegedly collecting intelligence in Dublin. But Maurice was only offered a lecture tour in India, which he found 'an odd, absurd idea'.[43] It was hurtful to remain on the sidelines. He confessed to Lindemann that 'he was deeply anxious to do some war job', even, as 'an old soldier', in the regular forces: 'I find it almost unendurable sitting here when the whole country is in deadly peril, and I want to do something of real use. What is the good of looking after the College if, after the war, there is no College left?'[44] Lindemann, however, could not, or would not, help.

Of necessity, Maurice had to settle for something more mundane. He joined the Home Guard, serving from 5 July 1940 until 31 December 1944.[45]

Initially, he was second-in-command of South Company, Oxford Home Guard, whose commanding officer was his old friend Frank Pakenham.[46] In registering for service, he was immediately confronted with the mindless bureaucracy which he remembered so well in the Great War: 'I had some difficulty in explaining my position, and the man decided I was a schoolmaster. He asked me if it was a whole time job. I unhesitatingly answered "Yes".'[47] Once established, he was put in charge of one hundred and fifty postal workers, who were drilled in Wadham's quadrangles. He found them 'perfectly charming and extremely keen. Many of them are old soldiers, and know much more about the business than I do.'[48] When Isaiah Berlin heard of Maurice's situation, he sarcastically observed that, whatever else might happen, 'our mails are safe at any rate'.[49] It was indeed hardly glorious, but Bowra decided to make the best of it.

> As for me, I imitate Flaubert when he joined the Garde Nationale in 1870. I now command a company—a rank usually held by retired Lieutenant-Generals. It is very agreeable and costs a great deal, as it means beer all round whenever we have a field day. The boys are almost entirely proletarian which I like a great deal. The few dons in it are kept down at the lowest rank, and not trusted with dangerous weapons. We are now armed with some fearful American guns, and would certainly do a lot of damage (not necessarily to the enemy) on Der Tag.[50]

But it was obvious to everyone that Bowra's talents were being underemployed, and he and others wondered why. His failure to find employment inevitably provoked speculation.[51] In fact, all his applications were blocked, not only by Lindemann but also by old acquaintances like Harold Nicolson. As Maurice put it, 'Harold Nickleby is being very unhelpful.'[52] When Isaiah Berlin tried to find him a post in New York, the file was returned stamped 'unreliable'.[53] Cyril Radcliffe, his New College contemporary was yet another who thought that he should not be employed, seeing him as 'someone who never grew up'. Establishment figures, so long mocked and teased in dinner party stories and scurrilous verse, took a terrible revenge. Leaving Bowra isolated in Oxford was a public affirmation that he was not wanted. When such doubtful characters as Guy Burgess and Donald Maclean were acceptable, Maurice was not. He was more 'unsuitable' than they apparently.[54]

Such a 'rebuff' hurt Bowra and he 'suffered' greatly as a result of its being so open to view.[55] For someone who had never felt completely English, his disappointment proved just how much of an outsider he really was.

Outside Oxford, he was tolerated as amusing and interesting. In a crisis he was not wanted or trusted. Rumours about his private life no doubt contributed to this mistrust. Against this background, Wadham's gamble in electing him its Warden is the more remarkable. Not surprisingly, Maurice reported his predicament to Felix Frankfurter with some bitterness.

> War is a) very dull and b) brings all the crooks to the top. No one has got a job except Sir Kenneth Clark, John Maud, Bob Boothby and Dr Lindemann. Everyone else is a hack or worse. The successful are intolerable, a lot of 'You must join us, old boy', or 'You must get a place under K' ... but of course they do nothing about it. All my friends have left Oxford ... I fuss about the Home Guards and enjoy it, but it is an up-hill struggle to get anything done for them. I have even developed a pathetic keenness for drill. At intervals I am told in the strictest confidence that I am being seriously considered for an important job. Interviews follow, hush-hush talks, and then nothing. I am afraid that I am one of those, who, for every six friends, has seven enemies. This is incidentally not at all good for my persecution mania ... it is hell doing nothing. In the last war, one was a hero, rich, busy, healthy, and the contrast is disgusting.[56]

When, much later in life, he was offered honours by monarchs and governments, he accepted them with an almost childish gratitude for being recognized at last.

Sitting in Oxford alone, with so many friends away, was a bleak experience. Shortages of cigarettes, razor blades, and soap were bad enough, but the disappearance of lavatory paper was particularly galling. Maurice told Penelope Betjeman that he had tried using the *Daily Mirror*, but found that it blocked the drains.[57] Chickens were kept in the Warden's garden. All in all, Oxford was no longer the city of the young or the interesting. For Maurice, 'lady typists in Keble fill no long-felt want'.[58] Frank Pakenham was inexplicably enthusiastic about working for Lord Beveridge, 'who is a cold-hearted, boastful tyrant'.[59] As usual, war drew away talent, leaving only bureaucracy and desiccation. For the first time in his life, he found Oxford to be a city, in which lived 'hardly anyone ... that one knows and likes',[60] and other places were just as bad. Spending Christmas 1940 with the Kenneth Clarks meant living without heating, and sharing a bathroom with Edward Sackville-West, whose 'unconscious resented it, and whenever I entered, even for [the] humblest and most necessary functions of our mortal clay, his nose would bleed and I had to give place, willy-nilly, to him'.[61] Making a joke about privation, however, barely masked his isolation. His natural audience was otherwise engaged, and no new role had been found. Maurice could only flourish in a highly specialized environment, and that was temporarily unavailable.

In a sense, Bowra had no war. He lived in a kind of suspended animation, with his patriotism rejected and his friends dispersed. His Wardenship therefore began in 1945, and on new rules. No one was more acutely aware that, in victory or defeat, the world of 1939 had been fatally undermined. New ways of doing things had to be established. Goronwy Rees thought that the War had mellowed Bowra, turning him into 'an old peach with only a tart flavour',[62] but, in this assessment, he was certainly wrong. In the clean air of the post-war world, Maurice saw opportunity to promote the causes which he had always loved. Context had changed out of all recognition but not the mission. As he cheerfully explained to Edith Sitwell, 'We are settling down again with grave, war-scarred undergraduates, who are very modest and charming and terribly eager to learn. It is rather wonderful to be at it all again.'[63]

In 1945, the powers invested in the Head of an Oxford College were still substantial. He or she could admit undergraduates more or less at will, and it was unusual for Fellows to be elected who were positively antipathetic to the Head of House. If these powers were linked to a strong personality, the opportunity to influence was always present. For these reasons, it was not unreasonable for Bowra to talk of Wadham as 'my College', to describe its Fellows in completely proprietorial terms.[64] In return, his loyalty to the College and all its inhabitants was absolute. In Isaiah Berlin's view, Wadham's debt to him was incalculable: 'he doubled their size, put them on the map, and they were, rightly, intensely proud of him, and his loyalty to, and defence of, anybody at Wadham, bad, good, indifferent was passionate, uncompromising and magnificent... nobody would criticize *anybody* in Wadham with impunity.'[65] Under Bowra, Wadham changed character, and the transformation was almost an act of artistic creation. In 1938, the College had been not very rich, not very clever, not very anything. That had to change. In 1945, Stuart Hampshire reported that 'Maurice is absorbed in Wadham, which he dreams of making into a Czechoslovakia among Oxford colleges—small but enlightened and respected.'[66]

This remark probably underestimated Bowra's ambitions. A College was to be moulded in one's own image. Maurice was of the opinion that 'all Colleges taken in the lump are dire—look at mine, look at All Souls run by Monteith and Edwards, look at New College. It does not matter. It is up to oneself to make it enjoyable and reasonably distinguished.'[67] The formula for success was simple. In order to get 'a despised, dim college into fighting trim … stir envy ("it is better to be envied than pitied") and hatred (Trevor-Roper in the *Sunday Times*),[68] but at least there is something to be done, and the something in [*sic*] 70% social—knowing people, talking, making yourself agreeable and/or formidable.'[69] A Head of House had to be everywhere, to know everyone, and to have the kind of powerful personality that provoked reactions. If all these factors were in place, the only remaining requirement was to fill the college with the cleverest people on offer. As Sally Chilver put it, 'he took that small college, extremely poor, and built it up by getting the very best scholars he could find. His criterion was entirely their brains.'[70]

Routine also played a part. Maurice's day was governed by the clock, and he had a life-long distaste for unpunctuality or time wasted. From 8.30 to 12.30 every morning, he worked in the Lodgings, seeing no one except in emergencies. For these hours, a walk around the Front Quadrangle from 11 to 11.15 was the only distraction. At 12.30, there would be a drink before lunch, often vodka. Afternoons would pass in chairing college or university committees for the most part, although he could be found, from time to time, incongruously and inexpertly cheering on Wadham teams. During Eights Week, from a vantage point on the College Barge, he could be heard bellowing encouragement to the wrong crews. At 6.30, he and guests would assemble in the breakfast room of the Lodgings 'to tank up' before dinner. Such meals were elaborate, but always ended promptly at 10.30 for undergraduates and 11.30 for adults, in order to make possible and likely the prompt resumption of work the next morning.[71]

In order to raise Wadham's profile, he had to influence admissions. The Warden's prerogative of admitting undergraduates at will was one that Maurice much enjoyed exercising. According to him the College should be looking for, in hierarchical order, 'clever boys, interesting boys, pretty boys,—no shits'.[72] To gather in the first category, the grammar schools were to be courted; for the others, hunches were to be followed and risks taken. Bowra would always be drawn to the eccentric and the maverick, as someone who had himself miraculously survived the greying experience of the English educational system. Sometimes his methods were totally unorthodox. Apocryphal stories abounded. One asserted that he had offered a place to a young man whom he encountered on a train journey between Reading and Oxford; another that his housekeeper, Frau von Gräfe, would take the final decision. Her choices would be known as 'W.H.s', or 'Warden's Housekeeper's'. [73]

More authenticated stories were just as colourful. Soldiers returning from the War were invariably well treated. Peter Fleming had put himself down as a candidate for Keble College, but wandered into Wadham by mistake. To his surprise, he found himself being interviewed by the Warden, who admitted him on the spot as a tribute to the Gurkha uniform he was wearing.[74] Another ex-soldier's interview went as follows:

> We spoke of the differences between the poetry of Shakespeare and that of the French dramatists Corneille and Racine... When I say 'we', I should perhaps qualify the statement by saying he spoke practically the whole time; my contribution being a humble 'Yes sir; no sir' every now and then. At the end of twenty minutes, he said, 'I'm glad we hold the same views.'[75]

Yet another undergraduate was taken after Maurice had interviewed not him, but his father. Only after arriving in Wadham was there a discussion about which subject should actually be read.

> Bowra suggested we start, like the alphabet, with the letter A. Agriculture. 'Yes', I said, 'that would be a good thing.' 'No', said Maurice, 'you can't learn about manure off a blackboard.' Classics. 'No, I didn't do them at school.' English—'Do you want to be a schoolmaster?' 'No', I said. And so we came to L. Law. 'Excellent all round subject.' So I did law.[76]

Perhaps understandably, Wadham's Fellows grew restive. To be told, at the beginning of an academic year, that they were to teach pupils whom they themselves had not interviewed and accepted was increasingly irksome. Maurice was in the habit of admitting 'too many odd bods'.[77] Accordingly during the Warden's extended stay in Harvard in 1947–8, the Fellows changed the rules. Henceforth, the Warden would continue to admit all graduates, but would only be allowed to sit in on undergraduate interviews. To sugar the pill, the Warden would be allowed a very few bisques, to be cashed in as he thought fit. Allegedly, these reforms were accepted without fuss. Bowra 'took it like a lamb'.[78] After all, control of graduate admissions allowed him to exercise considerable influence, not least in exploiting his Harvard connections to bring clever Americans to Wadham. For the rest, he used his remaining powers judiciously, not least in personally giving a place to the playwright Julian Mitchell.[79] Just occasionally, as if to remind his Fellows of their relative importance, he would break the rules, reassume 'tyrannical powers',[80] and admit someone whom they were very likely to find difficult. There were few recriminations for these occasional flights of fancy, for Bowra was allowed the licence that overwhelming personalities always command.

Elections to fellowships were even more critical. Tutors were in a sense Bowra's shock troops. If they shared the Warden's views, generations of pupils would be challenged in the ways he demanded. He knew too well that 'unless the right people are appointed to posts, the whole of the intellectual liveliness and calibre of an institution will decline'.[81] Accordingly, Maurice bent rules, cajoled voters, and manipulated procedures to secure the success of his candidates. Careerists, who only saw a college fellowship as a stepping stone to further self-promotion, were not encouraged to apply. Such men were dismissed with the damning description of being 'able' or of 'winning golden opinions'. Nor was there room for the second rate. When the head of another college wondered whether a long-serving lecturer should be promoted to a fellowship, even though she was 'not top class', Bowra simply replied, 'Get rid of her.'[82] Too much was at stake to allow sentiment any role in an election. Inevitably, the Warden was sometimes thwarted. Once, he had to watch helplessly as his colleagues elected a rowing man from Cambridge.[83] But he won often enough to give his College as professional a set of tutors as possible. Overwhelmingly, they shared his view of what sort of College Wadham should become.

Once elected, a Fellow should put his talents to good use. Just as he berated his friends for wasting time and not fulfilling themselves, so he criticized dons in general. When J. I. M. Stewart of Christ Church found success in writing detective stories, Bowra found the situation demeaning. Stewart was 'far too able to waste his talent like that. Entirely wrong.'[84] The teaching and exposition of English literature had a higher purpose. By contrast, if academics played the game by his rules, he became 'a kind of father figure, patriarchal... He was admirable if you were in trouble. He was the least punitive. He had no desire to judge people, none whatsoever.'[85] The Warden understood only too well that clever people often led irregular lives, about which it was pointless to be too censorious. Heavy teaching loads and the increasing emphasis on research and publication recommended them to his protection.

Bowra's impact on undergraduates was even more profound. Eighteen year olds arriving at Wadham from restricted social or geographical backgrounds had few defences at their disposal against exposure to the Warden's personality. Relations between him and the junior members of the College were governed by the doctrines of 'our age'. When asked how old someone was, Maurice often replied 'our age'. This meant that the person in question, whether eighteen or eighty, shared, or aspired to share, Bowrista values. Age was a matter of cultural temperament, not chronology. People who were 'our age' were those he found 'agreeable'. Barriers between generations were non-existent, because 'the agreeable' could be found in every generation.[86] The phrase 'our age' was an invitation to a common culture. As one undergraduate put it, 'I was amazed and awe-struck as the talk flowed on, but always with the acknowledgement that if we had not read anything, it was purely an oversight and would be quickly remedied... In one way he seemed incredibly old and yet also one's own age.'[87]

Entertaining undergraduates was central to his idea of a well-run College. 'The boys', as he once put it, 'were to be entertained like no how.'[88] Every Sunday evening in term, supper parties would be held in the Lodgings, to which students would be invited in groups of six or eight. While being talked at, the Warden's guests would be wined and dined at a level that they had never before encountered. After such performances, they were just a little less constrained about life than they had been. Sometimes it was too much. One undergraduate fell off a chair with laughter.[89] Occasionally, a student would prove incontrovertibly that he was not 'our age' by being sick. But these rituals served Bowra's purpose. At the end of the year, he knew, or claimed to know, everyone in Wadham. Even undergraduates with identical surnames would have been sorted out into 'Beer Jones' and 'Sex Jones'.[90] More important still, these dinners were a winnowing process. Those who had been identified as of 'our age' would be invited back repeatedly for further edification, as Bowristas in the making.

In such encounters, Wadham men quickly understood that the Warden was only judgemental in matters of academic delinquency. No other fall from grace was to be considered venal. In fact, the high moral tone had never been part of Bowra's repertoire. In 1929, as Dean, he had defended an undergraduate who had, on his own admission, 'committed fornication'. Lindemann and others thought that all financial assistance to the man in question should be withdrawn immediately, giving Bowra the opportunity to argue that their stance represented an absurd overreaction to an enduring fact of life.[91] Two years later, he led the opposition to a proposal sponsored by Gilbert Murray and H. A. L. Fisher which would have denied undergraduates the right to own motor cars. The two men feared that such vehicles would be used to facilitate illicit lovemaking. In reply, Bowra and his allies pointed out that if Oxford men were intent on fornication, they could just as easily travel by train.[92] In all these battles, he cheerfully offered the libertarianism which had governed his own private life to younger generations.

In his view, sexual mismanagement was of minor importance. It was much worse to damage historic buildings. Maurice once told Edith Sitwell that he was in a

> furious temper with two boys who climbed in here, and tore down for pleasure some of our stone-work—1611. Fortunately, they were caught and did not enjoy their interview with me ... I can understand crimes due to temper or the flesh, but not this sort of nonsense ... How I hate violence, and how little I understand it.[93]

In this vein, he deeply deplored infantile rivalries between colleges, which all too often ended in drunken destruction. Sexual activity, by contrast, could not fail to have some educational component.

As Warden, no aspect of Wadham life was closed to Bowra. Even sportsmen were to be given their chance. Although he had played rugby at school and tennis in Kent, Maurice generally took the view that sporting events represented that wasting of talent which he had detected in so many other aspects of English life. In 1941, when an undergraduate improbably invited the Warden to play squash, Bowra answered, 'No, not fair. Can't see the ball; have to play entirely by ear.'[94] Yet, despite all this, Wadham's sportsmen were to be supported. He detested rowing, for example, plaintively asking how, after two World Wars, such a practice could be allowed to continue, but he regularly attended Eights Week. About football he knew nothing, but he once explained to a dignitary at the Foreign Office that it would be quite impossible for him to host a group of visiting European diplomats, because 'it seems that the College will either win a football cup that day, or lose it in the final, and in either case there will be a dinner which I *must* attend'.[95] On every occasion, the College, even when represented by perspiring sportsmen, came first.

Knowing everyone and being everywhere allowed Bowra to be helpful. When undergraduates recalled his name, it was memories of assistance that came to mind. Accommodation was found for new lecturers[96] and references were written on request. In composing the latter, Bowra proudly announced that he was not 'hampered by any pedantic adherence to the truth'. References 'belong not to scholarship but to politics, and should be composed as such'.[97] Undergraduates with money troubles were sometimes surprised to receive a cheque from the Warden himself.[98] Those with problems of the mind were even more certain to receive attention, for Maurice had seen the consequences of stress and apprehension in the Great War. Above all, he defended students against the absurdities of their elders. In 1951, he 'got the troops out' to ensure that a man with advanced tuberculosis should be allowed to take a shortened course in defiance of the university statutes.[99] In Bowra's view, all communities needed rules, but there was no rule that could not be bent just a little in order to meet an individual's circumstances. After all, he had broken so many in his own lifetime that he could hardly accord them undue regard.

Entertaining also had another function. If Wadham was to have a higher profile in the world, then the world must be brought to Wadham. Distinguished guests passed through the College's gates for occasions that left Michael Foot, a Wadham man himself, 'with my spirit renewed. What a place Wadham is, thanks to you. That's how thousands of us feel.'[100] Certainly Wadham had never been so socially distinctive since the seventeenth century. All the Bowristas of the 1920s and 1930s appeared from time to time, and they were supplemented by new Oxford acquaintances like Iris Murdoch and Kerensky. Agatha Christie, 'a nice old party',[101] sometimes joined the Wadham court with her husband, the archaeologist Max Mallowan. Hugh Gaitskell brought Ann Fleming to meet 'darling Maurice', and they consoled each other when the Labour leader died.[102] Around Oxford, such proceedings gave Wadham a polish which it had never enjoyed before. After dining in the College, Jean Cocteau assured its Warden that 'in ... the bric-a-brac of this age, the memory of Oxford and your dinner ... represents an oasis of nobility and peace'.[103]

Undergraduates were, of course, largely observers of such proceedings, but they can hardly have been unaware that visitors with famous names gave their Warden and their College a certain renown. Just occasionally, though, the Warden's two styles of entertaining collided. Once an undergraduate was requested to report to the Lodgings to answer on a point of discipline. To his surprise, the door was opened by Evelyn Waugh, who demanded his company while the Warden dealt with an emergency. The student in question did his best to keep Waugh amused. As a reward for undertaking such a difficult task, all disciplinary considerations were forgotten. Instead he was invited to lunch: 'I never did get the telling off the Warden intended to give me. I did get a three and a half hour lunch in the company of one of the greatest wits in the university and one of our most brilliant authors. Now that is what I call luck.'[104]

Social adventures in Wadham became so intimately entwined with his personality that vacations represented a real and painful problem for Bowra. If his audience was dispersed, life moved into slow motion. The Christmas vacation was particularly feared in that escape through travelling would prove difficult. For many years, he was rescued by Kenneth Clark and his family, who lived in 'that castle in Kent, whence the knights set out to kill that poop T Becket'.[105] Often he went in the company of John Sparrow, as the two men were both godfathers to a Clark daughter. Apart from 'inadequate supplies of hot water' and the real possibility of being defeated by the schoolboy Alan Clark in games of L'Attaque, everything was in order. It was always a question of 'high thinking and high living'.[106] In the Clark circle, he met new friends, like the actress Irene Worth, who flattered him by hailing him as 'an everlasting influence'.[107] Then there was the amusement of going to Canterbury Cathedral on Christmas Day in order to hear a communist Dean exhorting his 'audience' to live better lives.[108] His gratitude to the Clarks for providing a new venue for the party, when Oxford was closed, was totally genuine and heartfelt.

Should Clark hospitality not be available for any reason, the difficulty of dealing with the problem of Christmas could induce panic. To remain in Oxford in solitude was simply not an option. In 1961, Nancy Mitford, a friend of thirty years standing, came to the rescue by inviting him to join her in Paris. Maurice was relieved of a burden and deeply grateful. Although he was forced into the company of English expatriates, men 'with pin heads and crumpled wives',[109] his letter expressing thanks was fulsome:

> How agreeable that, in the evening of our days, we should be sitting together singing carols—not indeed with strict accuracy, but at least with bold invention, conscientious party spirit, and some degree of brio, if not bravura. I cherish the memory as of something deliciously unexpected. It was wonderful to see you, and I greatly enjoyed your Xmas tuck-in.[110]

Somewhere, there had to be the opportunity for the performance to be given.

The Easter and summer vacations were less of a problem. Oxford was not so dark or so empty. Better weather made the possibility of travelling more congenial. For a part of most summers, Bowra joined the house party at Porto Fino in Italy, for which the Berlins acted as hosts. In his sixtieth year, reflecting sometimes that 'it was after all better not to be born', he was cheered to find a house full of 'Gaitskells, Lady Rothschild and Emma, "Hampshire et Cie", Ben-Gurion's secretary, an American professor boldly with a boy in the French army of the Rhine, two Chilvers, Mrs Fleming'.[111] Light-hearted accounts of these gatherings should not mislead. Maurice had a positive need of them. With the Berlins in Italy, or Ann Fleming on Sardinia, or the Leigh Fermors in Greece, he found that highly specialized environment which, for the rest of the year, Wadham society guaranteed.

Only one aspect of Wadham life bored him, and that was administration. He had always been clear that those who enjoyed the endless cycles of committees, minutes, and agendas were half-dead. Such duties were to be undertaken conscientiously, but no one should give them status or undue importance. Mercifully, for most of his Wardenship, college business was light and of a parish pump variety. When John Bamborough left Wadham to became the head of Linacre College, Bowra assured him that he 'could run the College with his left hand'.[112] In chairing meetings, Bowra was always on top of his brief, but only so that his mastery of the topic in hand would allow him to conduct the debate at a speed that left others gasping. In this way, he often 'got away with murder'.[113] It seemed that he always wanted decisions rather than debate. If he unusually found himself in a hopeless minority, he was quite capable of changing his opinion in mid-sentence, in order to expedite matters. Inevitably, this combination of strong views being pushed through at speed sometimes reduced college meetings to 'blood-letting exercises'.[114] On these occasions, the Warden, who thoroughly enjoyed battle, would trust a good meal and a lot of wine to restore harmony. Conciliatory gestures came easily to a man whose real passions were only engaged by items on an agenda that referred to fellowships or the fate of an individual.[115]

On money matters he had very few views at all. What he understood of such things bored him. Prudently therefore, he allowed Wadham's long-serving Bursar, Jack Thompson, to govern his empire without interference. For Bowra, a governing body meeting spent in going through the College's accounts was tantamount to being 'on the wheel'.[116] In such discussions he had to be unusually silent. For some, this reticence represented a real weakness in his Wardenship. Wadham had never been a rich college, and its fabric had suffered badly from decades of neglect. Appeals for assistance became unavoidable, but such things simply embarrassed Bowra. Edwardian gentlemen were temperamentally unsuited to begging for money. Whenever Wadham launched an appeal, the Warden wriggled and complained. As he once lamented to an American friend,

> Here we are having great storms. The government has cut our grant, and we shall have to sack a lot of scientists. Not that I mind, but they do. Kind old Uncle the State is not so jolly when he decides to cut off the dough. Meanwhile we are appealing to our alumni to prevent us from falling down. Large pieces of stone flop through the air and damage the tourists. The alumni won't produce nearly enough. They are not broken into it as yours are, and we will have to resort to the Big Money of the Foundations. My house is already draped with scaffolding as evidence of our intentions, but God knows who will pay for it.[117]

When the process was repeated, five years later, Bowra began to think that 'this is a skilful move a) to bankrupt me and b) to kill me off or at least to reduce me to such a state that I shall be incapable of keeping my job'.[118] Questions involving the handling or raising of money coldly exhibited the limitations of Maurice's intellectual range, and he wisely left such matters to those who claimed the relevant interest and expertise.

For most of Bowra's Wardenship, college business was light, because changes, whether generated internally or provoked by external interference, were only contemplated at a moderate pace. The groaning agendas for meetings in modern universities, sclerotic in effect and hard on the nerves, lay in the future. But some change there was, and Bowra was quick to seize upon any new opportunities to promote his causes. Easily the most important measure to have an impact on Maurice's Oxford was the Butler Education Act of 1944. It created, through the 11+ examination, the grammar school, and state studentships, a new clientele for the university, drawn often from social groups which had never before considered higher education to be a possibility. Here was an innovation that suited Wadham and suited its Warden.

Bowra welcomed the Act without reservations.

> What saved and transformed Oxford was the Butler Act of 1944. But for it Oxford could hardly have continued to exist; for fees were too high for

the old clientele. By securing that the state financed all who were able to profit by a university education, the Act entirely altered the character of Oxford, and demolished the all too justifiable charges that it admitted only the rich. The enormous social changes which followed coincided with vast other social changes after the second world war, and largely for this reason took place without any noticeable tension. Oxford...was this time on the winning side, but made no fuss about it.[119]

All his life, he had promoted the idea that an aristocracy of intellect, open of access, was required to guarantee a culture. Politicians now seemed to agree. In his view, and remarkably, 'the erections of an aristocratic society...have been placed at the service of all who belong to the democratic society of Oxford'.[120] This was language that the Greeks would have understood.

Butler provided a ladder by which a whole new tranche of English society could climb into Oxford. These newcomers offered Wadham hope. The best public schoolboys would always beat a path to Balliol, Magdalen, and New College. Therefore, Wadham should look for cleverness elsewhere. The College's enhanced academic profile would be built on an enlarged social base. In addition, the new government money that grammar schoolboys brought with them looked like a solution to financial problems. In 1947, a college meeting recorded its view that it could not 'operate on the domestic side without an increase of at least 50% on the pre-war number of undergraduates'.[121] The solution to this problem lay in a simple formula; a significant increase in undergraduate numbers and a less dramatic rise in the number of Fellows. Each of these would simply have to teach longer and harder. Butler's scholars were therefore welcomed enthusiastically in Wadham. The Warden was clear that they alone were responsible for making standards in Oxford 'much higher' than they were 'thirty years ago'.[122] His Bursar could, at the same time, be a little more relaxed about the financial future.[123]

Other changes, however, were less welcome. Bowra viewed with suspicion the founding of new, underfunded colleges. In his opinion, there might be a case for new undergraduate colleges. He was, for example, hugely helpful to Alan Bullock in launching St Catherine's.[124] But there were now to be colleges reserved for graduates, whose Fellows, Bowra suspected, would be hopelessly specialized, uninterested in teaching, and weighed down with chips on their shoulders. He tended to accuse graduates of self-importance, as people who gave themselves airs, and yet knew far too much about far too little. In 1965, he was honestly appalled that Isaiah Berlin should have contemplated becoming the head of such an institution.

> Isaiah, as a result of living next to the Hampshires at Princeton, has gone off his head. He has been offered and accepted the headship of one of these new Colleges—Iffley, St Iffley, Stiffley, Stiffkey ... His reason is that nobody in this country is interested in this kind of work, which is true, but no excuse for taking on an apostolic slumming job, which should occupy all his time if he is to be any good at all.[125]

It would be 'a slum life among the scrubs'.[126] No senior Bowristas should 'waste his talents in this fashion'. By Maurice's standards, a graduate institution could only be 'bogus', a 'platform college', full of 'dud dons'.[127] Such a place offended on two counts. It diverted attention and resources away from Oxford's principal function, which was the teaching of undergraduates, and it encouraged a narrowing of intellectual range. No one trained within the confines of graduate life would have the breadth of academic experience to be a useful ally in the campaigns he espoused.

Another new creature in the Oxford undergrowth with whom Maurice never really came to terms was the scientist. Pre-war Oxford, his Oxford, had been dominated by the classicist and the historian. Scientists of distinction like Lindemann were an oddity. After 1945, however, they grew in numbers and pretensions. Watching this process, Maurice was clear that these people had very different priorities.[128] They spoke a language which the linguist in Bowra could never hope to understand; they worked in laboratories, not colleges, leaving them struggling with divided loyalties; they seemed to think that lectures served the same academic purpose as tutorials; and scientific professors increasingly acted like medieval barons, challenging Maurice and his kind for the loyalty of college fellows and demanding ever greater and more expensive empires. For all these reasons, if a college was 'in a hopeless state', it was likely that its scientists were to blame.[129] In the long term, he half-jokingly, half-seriously, prophesied that science would destroy Oxford as he defined it.[130]

Within Wadham, the battle of the two cultures was fairly joined. Scientists complained that the Warden could never bring himself to believe that their work was actually 'about thinking and adding to the culture', but rather concerned with 'playing about with test tubes'.[131] When governments cut Oxford's funding, Bowra found consolation in the idea that 'it will also mean, happily, that some of the vast building schemes for science will not be realised, and with luck some of the professors will commit suicide. They will not be missed.'[132] When scientific chairs were attached to Wadham, he refused to allow their holders a room in College, on the argument that they probably already had several in their laboratories. Teasing these men came naturally to him, and the Methodism of Charles Coulson or the attempted humour of Brebis Bleaney offered easy targets.[133] Only two scientists ever really commanded his respect, Frederick Lindemann and Cyril Hinshelwood, 'a cold remote' man who in turn described Maurice as 'a very interesting, sociological phenomenon'.[134] The reason for the Warden's approval was the same in both cases. Both men crossed cultural lines in a way that Bowra himself found impossible. Lindemann was both physicist and a man of deep culture; Hinshelwood was, at different times, President of the Royal Society and President of the Classical Association. Unfortunately, few of their colleagues had the same range. Instead, they were within Wadham politics 'rather a nuisance'.[135] The scientist, like the graduate, had no part to play in his crusades.

Often led by the scientists, all the Fellows of Wadham became increasingly difficult to handle. What he called 'the new scrub colleagues'[136] of the 1960s were less and less inclined to follow Bowrista values. Arts dons, as well as scientists, clamoured to teach less, to have the right to hold two positions at once, and to be paid greatly enhanced salaries. Everything they demanded was covered 'with self-pity'.[137] In letters to Dadie Rylands in Cambridge, Bowra bewailed these changes in language which two refugees from the 1920s could understand. Worst of all, the new Wadham dons were 'not interested in the place'.[138] Marrying earlier and earlier, they disappeared into a domesticity that undermined Wadham's social life, and gave them an excuse for refusing to contemplate taking on a college job. In fact, the Warden tried hard to ingratiate himself with his colleagues' wives, not least by smuggling nylons into England on returning from his American adventures,[139] but it was often uphill work. The new generation of academics had expectations and priorities with which he found it difficult to sympathize.

In an interview for a national newspaper given four years before his death, Maurice opined that 'the right time to visit Oxford' would have been around 1850. Then it was still possible to walk, perhaps in the company of a scholar gypsy, from a College Lodge straight into open countryside. After the reforms of 1872, dons were allowed to marry, and North Oxford was built to house their domesticity and 'meet their philoprogenitive needs'. What Gerard Manley Hopkins called 'the base and brackish skirt' of suburban life began to enfold the University.[140] Coming up as an undergraduate in 1919, Bowra was acutely aware of these changes, and was taught by a generation of dons who had lived through them. During his Wardenship, the pace of change quickened, with detrimental consequences for the well being of Wadham. In 1963, he wrote to Dadie Rylands, a man of his generation and temperament, after surviving 'a sticky term'. The letter sets out new ways of thinking and their inevitable results.

> Too much reform and counter-reform in the air. One can have one or the other, but both together are exacting…I see hours of committees ahead…My dear colleagues are hard to digest, and, although I take endless trouble with them and their wives, I feel that I have not yet got the hang of them. They seem to care for the College only as a place for promotion elsewhere. Hence we have had a flaming row about who is to be Dean. The bachelors all refuse, the married men say they can never leave their wives after 7 pm., and each side abuses the other for lack of public spirit with justice.[141]

In the last years of his Wardenship, those around him barely hid their opinion that he had become something of an anachronism.

By implication, the academic world was moving away from Bowra's preoccupations. The scientist, unless he were Cyril Hinshelwood, would have no reason to listen to the song of the Greeks. The research graduate would never have the breadth of reading or vision to proselytize on behalf of the poet. And the married man would never have the time or energy to take either message to the young. Changes of this magnitude had to be expected in a Wardenship lasting thirty-two years. The wonder is that Maurice survived for so long. By sheer force of personality, he met change head-on, sometimes moderating its impact, and always looking for ways in which his values could find a place in the new circumstances of university life. For someone who had struggled against the current all his life, these battles, when not actually tiring, could almost be enjoyed. Even when forced into a series of tactical retreats, there was consolation in the thought that, for three decades, Wadham and Bowra's name become synonymous.

11

Bowra at Large, 1945–1970

After 1945, the Warden was pulled more and more into public view, and academic and national honours were piled upon his name. These badges of success both amused and flattered him. On the one hand, he was dismissive of them, claiming that one accepted them in the same way that 'a schoolboy collects stamps'.[1] On the other hand, it was gratifying to an outsider, finally, to be recognized. He had become inescapable. Before the War, he had been the face of Oxford in certain selected literary circles. After its conclusion, he was seen as the University's representative on a larger stage. One American visitor, in 1969, thought him 'as dominant' in Oxford 'as a dreaming spire'.[2] A decade earlier, Stuart Hampshire described his friend as 'an academic Churchill, seeing everyone into their graves and surviving through the days of opposition into undisputed power larger, in a sense, than life'.[3] It was something of consequence to feel Maurice's displeasure or approval. Lobbying through telephone calls that went on forever, he was able to persuade strong men to compromise their independence of thought. After Bowra's death, Kenneth Wheare drew breath and reflected that it would be 'difficult to get round the idea that you can decide something without having a call on the telephone beginning: "Your old friend here wonders whether you have gone *completely*, but completely, out of your mind."'[4]

His prominence was, of course, partly to be explained as the consequence of a bullish personality, but it was also a function of his absolute conviction that Oxford had value. The University had no need to apologize or explain. What it stood for was self-explanatory. Any educated person would immediately understand this; no uneducated person ever would. Conviction produced authority, and his importance was recognized by the high and the low. On one occasion, Dick Cadman, the head scout at Trinity College, saw Bowra striding down Broad St. A gust of wind whipped his mortarboard from his head, but there was no looking back. As Cadman reflected, Maurice knew with some confidence 'that someone else would pick it up'.[5]

Not surprisingly, he was chosen to represent Oxford at many official functions. Shortly after the War, he was part of a delegation that took fraternal greetings to the Sorbonne. The journey allowed him to re-establish contact 'with several of the poets', preach the virtues of Dylan Thomas and Sydney Keyes, and wallow in an 'enchanting spasm of French anglophilia'.[6] It would only be the first of many such excursions. In addition, he was endlessly pestered to sit on panels judging literary prizes, as being an academic of distinction who was 'near business-like'.[7] His name lent weight to a letter to *The Times*, to John Betjeman's many campaigns to save historic buildings,[8] or to efforts to have a gasometer removed from the Oxford skyline. Inside and outside Oxford, he was a natural candidate to give prestigious lectures. In all these activities, he confidently preached, in a Pauline way, those values that animated his whole being. In any context, audiences were challenged by Oxford in physical form.

Bowra's standing in Oxford depended on personality, not on the holding of office, but, from 1951 to 1954, he was the University's Vice-Chancellor. Unofficially, he exercised these duties a little longer. His predecessor, Dean Lowe of Christ Church, had been so inactive, even inert, that his workload had fallen on Maurice. In December 1949, he complained that he

> had been moved into administration and dislike it extremely. I am not even paid for it. Our dear Vice Chancellor, who comes from Ontario and is a clergyman, works only on Sundays and expects me to do the other six days for him. I sit on endless committees, and, though I am developing a name for record-breaking in speed, it bores me to hell. No time to read, let alone to write. Heavy concentration on medical salaries and god knows what.[9]

Six months later, the wailing was still shrill: 'I am getting tired of sitting on committees, and I long to be a scholar again. We never know when we are well off. Now I am in for four more years of dull routine, and than [*sic*] I shall chuck all this rot about administration and learn something.'[10] When he voiced the same sort of lamentations to Edith Sitwell, she endeavoured to cheer him up by reporting that she had recently been kissed by a gorilla.[11]

Maurice protested against administrative duties before he took them up, while he exercised them, and after he had withdrawn from them. He never moved away from the proposition that a bureaucracy only existed to allow academics to function to best advantage. It had no other significance or importance. Since bureaucrats could not be expected to share this view, academics had to sacrifice themselves, from time to time, in order to oversee the government of the University. It was a waste of time and talent, but necessary if academics were to continue to enjoy the great privilege of running their own lives. But the prospect was bleak even so. Contemplating the Vice-Chancellorship, he confessed that 'the job has no appeal for me at all. It is three years out of my life, and most of the work is dull and difficult, statutes, science, finances etc.'[12] When he was finally 'churched' as Vice-Chancellor, he could only look forward to 'the hard times that lie ahead, as indeed they do if the Tories get in'.[13]

Although the scale of University business was still relatively light in the 1950s, the pressure on a Vice-Chancellor to coordinate policy and to act as troubleshooter in all disputes was considerable. The Vice-Chancellor's diary for the period records a committee nearly every morning and afternoon, with many evenings taken up by ceremonial of some kind. This diary was kept by Maurice himself. Only he could have entered 'Bob' for the evening of 1 March 1953, or 'Huns' for the afternoon of 20 December 1952.[14] Committees were grim experiences, and the necessity to represent Oxford at conferences grimmer. It was absurd that academics talked about education so much and did it so little. Meeting with Vice-Chancellors from all over the Commonwealth, for example, proved an 'appalling' waste of time: 'No one said anything of the slightest interest, and the discomforts, both mental and physical, were enormous.'[15] In such assemblies, Americans brazenly lectured Oxford on how to conduct itself, 'and of course we shall listen, because we are poor, and that proves that God no longer loves us'.[16] Weeks and months spent in 'damned administration' led him to regard 'these three years as a kind of War Service, and chalk them up to my great credit with the Recording Angel'.[17] He was in danger of becoming 'a machine'.[18]

So many aspects of the job should never have concerned a busy academic at all. Why should it be necessary to shore up Gilbert Murray's confidence in rejecting the offer of a Chair in Psychical Research?[19] He was surely rationalist enough to have taken the decision alone. Why was it necessary to join the Mayor of Oxford and other local worthies in signing a letter which began with the words, 'The siting of the gasworks affects the life of Oxford in all its aspects'?[20] If the Chief Constable complained about the loss of two policemens' helmets during confrontations with undergraduates on Guy Fawkes night, could it really be the Vice-Chancellor's responsibility to respond to such 'overcoloured' tales?[21] Too often, triviality seemed to vie with pettiness for his attention.

Retiring from office, in 1954, was an unalloyed pleasure.

> I am deeply releived [sic] at getting rid of my Vice-Cancellarial duties, and feel just as I did on getting out of the army, light in head and pocket, but free. I shall now have to get back to old habits without the awful feeling that if I read a book, I ought to be writing memoranda or squaring scientists. I am back to the Greek and think of nothing else.[22]

Not that he ever escaped administration completely. In June 1954, he was elected to the University's governing Council with the largest majority ever recorded. Also, when his successors as Vice-Chancellor collapsed from strain, he was invariably called upon to stand in. In the spring of 1960, he had to resume the situation when his old enemy, President Boase of Magdalen, 'collapsed with a dud eye (jokes about his "beaux yeux" are not thought funny)'. He found 'everything in a fearful muddle of sloth, chicanery, and ignorance', and 'the hard work' necessary to put matters right was 'not at all enjoyable'.[23] Even in less dramatic moments, his advice was sought on and off committees and in common rooms. All in all, being Vice-Chancellor held few attractions, but duty had to be done. When John Sparrow declined to take his turn in the office, he was reprimanded by his old mentor in terms that came near to contempt.[24]

If the academic suffered on becoming the administrator, so did the private man. In public, Maurice was all confidence and brisk efficiency. In private, concern about taking decisions and making mistakes often gave him sleepless nights. In 1952, he confessed that he had developed 'a habit of waking up at 4.15 am and thinking of my sins and failures in a highly New England way. The Puritan background always comes back on you in the end.'[25] Close friends knew of these anxieties, and associated them with Maurice's long-held fear of public humiliations. As Stuart Hampshire put it,

> he always thought the wrong thing would come out and he would somehow get into trouble. He was very sensitive. If somebody would say, 'But Vice-Chancellor, you've got the figures entirely wrong', the rest of us would think

this was just rather irritating, whereas Maurice would wake up in the middle of the night about it.[26]

In addition, there was the necessity to behave. Vice-Chancellors could not turn somersaults in Merton Chapel. Bowristas bemoaned the all-too-obvious softening of mood and tone. Isaiah Berlin was saddened to see 'the old Maurice' sowing symptoms 'of general subsidence, self-absorption, surrender, security before self-expression and pleasure and general anxiety'. Watching their leader become respectable was a terrible experience. As Oxford's Vice-Chancellor, Bowra adopted 'an Origen line' that took some getting used to.[27]

Amid all this lamentation, however, there was also the call to battle, and Bowra relished a fight. Leading the University gave him the opportunity to open up new fronts. Having assured Berta Ruck that there was 'no damned merit' in being Vice-Chancellor, he went on to admit that, in some ways, it was 'not bad fun'. There were 'too many meetings, too much civic life', but also some good parties. On balance it was better than 'the five years of war which we impose on the younger generation at intervals'.[28] For one who understood that 'in academic warfare, it is wise to take the offensive and keep the initiative',[29] the holding of office was all opportunity. Doing down long-term enemies and promoting favourite causes could be hugely satisfying. Among the former were self-important science professors 'who drew enormous salaries and refuse to teach anyone'.[30] Confronting the Vice-Chancellor was not for the squeamish. Even Cyril Hinshelwood, in walking from Trinity College to his laboratory, was careful to take a route that avoided Wadham.[31] On scoring a victory, Bowra would be 'in fine form: mellow and resonant, like an old cello. Success is good for him.'[32]

Of course, he could not always win. His 'Bakerloo' was met, when J. N. L. Baker and his allies defeated a proposal to reform the General Board of Faculties, which governed the academic life of the University.[33] But he won often enough. During his years in office, the retirement age for dons was raised from sixty-five to sixty-seven; generous grants for Oxford were secured from the University Grants Committee; the vexed question of medical salaries was settled for a time; and above all, European Studies, at least at the graduate level, became part of the Oxford syllabus. In all battles, he had had to face considerable opposition. Sometimes a tactical retreat had been unavoidable.[34] But the *Oxford Magazine*, in reviewing his years in office, had no doubt in recording energetic and successful management.[35]

One of the reasons why he often won an argument was that his method of conducting business was rather startling. Of course he went into meetings fully briefed, and very clear about the outcome he wanted. But, in addition, he then took meetings at such a speed that opposition had little time to organize or even appear. Any suggestion of long-windedness would be met with the brutal injunction, 'Get on with it.'[36] In theory, meetings of Council began at two and ended at four. Under Bowra, agendas were often dealt with by 2.30, and, on one memorable occasion, by 2.10. The University's great men were embarrassed to discover that they suddenly had a free afternoon on their hands.[37] Members of Council 'for the first time have known what it is to see St Mary's clock on a Monday afternoon stand at half past two'.[38] For Maurice himself, it became a kind of game; 'I play a game of seeing how quickly I can get through … and then try to beat my own record.'[39] Rumour had it that he encouraged the University's Registrar to write the minutes of all meetings before they had taken place.[40]

Inevitably, such methods divided opinion. Those who found time spent on committees unrewarding were delighted. The historian E. L. Woodward praised the Vice-Chancellor for having 'the remarkable—and rare—power of making every member of the committee over which you preside think that he is sharing in the decisions of the chair'.[41] Other people were not so pleased. Maurice himself had to admit that 'stuffed shirts' and 'bien pensants' were unhappy at business being taken 'too speedily'.[42] The matter was even raised in the Sunday press.[43] But, for Bowra, there could not be too much apology, when it was 'extraordinary how many people like to hear themselves talk without having anything to say'.[44] Chairing a committee was all about arriving at decisions, preferably decisions which were in accord with the Bowrista canon. Against this benchmark, indecision had been designated almost as great a sin as idleness.

When Bowra retired from office, his admirers significantly outnumbered critics. Alan Bullock, though seeing in Maurice 'a bit of a bully', had no doubt that he had been 'a very, very good V C'.[45] Lionel Curtis saw him as 'the first really *great* Vice-Chancellor that he had known'.[46] The *Oxford Magazine* certainly spoke for a majority in Oxford in reporting that

Everyone will regret that the Vice-Chancellor's term of office draws so near to an end. How stimulating it has been to sit on any of the numberless bodies and committees of the University, when the arrows of wit were flying abroad! In his conduct of business time invariably seemed short, and was. The wonder was how much sparkling entertainment and competently handled business was packed into such short periods.[47]

Bowra had the confidence of a man who had belief. He never doubted that what Oxford represented mattered. Within the University he had become 'a brilliant figure'.[48] On leaving office, he was re-elected to Council with a record number of votes.[49] Maurice had demonstrated so much administrative ability that some associates thought that Oxford was too small a stage for him. Perhaps he should be 'running a big international company'. Perhaps Oxford was 'in this sense' proving 'a trap for him'.[50] But these were questions that Bowra himself would have thought absurd.

To hold the office of Vice-Chancellor was to be offered the chance to influence the workings of the University significantly, in matters small and in matters great. Some men interested themselves in financial or administrative reform, but Bowra, characteristically, had other priorities. For him, the nomination to honorary degrees and elections to academic posts were of much more interest. To the outside world, these contests could be easily dismissed as the stuff of parochial politics, but to Maurice they were of the utmost importance. All his life, he had thought it vital to put people with Bowrista values into jobs. Whom the University chose to honour was a public statement about its own sense of purpose. Equally, the holders of prestigious chairs could set an example within their own faculties that might do incalculable good. These were encounters when the forces of light would often be confronted by philistinism and narrow-mindedness. They were exactly the kind of battle to which Maurice had always felt most committed.

Even before he became Vice-Chancellor, he was a veteran of campaigns to secure honorary degrees for the right people. As 'Big Stuff' Bowra brought up the names of great writers, he was able to link Oxford's reputation with what was best in literature, and to show off his acquaintance with its leading representatives. In these debates, he found levels of obscurantism that were barely believable. Shortly after the War, he secured an honorary degree for T. S. Eliot, but only after 'considerable time and patience', having to explain to some of his colleagues 'who he is and why he should be honoured'.[51] On the whole, it was easier to put up foreign writers, because no one in Oxford even pretended to know who they were. As Maurice explained to Julian Mitchell, 'I can put over foreigners without much trouble, but when it comes to English names, the poor ignorant academics think they know better than I do and vote me down.'[52] In 1965, for example, his championing of Ivy Compton Burnett came to nothing, while his promotion of Neruda proved successful, because 'they could not even pretend that they had heard of him'.[53]

As a former Vice-Chancellor, he enjoyed extra muscle in these debates, and he used it without compunction. Undoubtedly his greatest triumph was to persuade the University to honour Charlie Chaplin, a victim of McCarthyism, but also 'a genius, and geniuses should be honoured by universities'.[54] Hugh Trevor-Roper and others had threatened opposition, but Maurice had his 'battalions ready for him' and 'he lost his nerve'.[55] As a punishment, the Trevor-Ropers were threatened with not being invited to meet Chaplin when, in due course, he arrived in Oxford. Characteristically, Maurice chose biblical language of a manichaean kind to describe his success. It had been 'a great victory over the Midianites'.[56]

When Chaplin visited the University, he naturally stayed at Wadham. Bowra found him 'easy and delightful'.[57] He was 'not at all stagey or difficult, and I felt that we belonged to his world'.[58] There was an innocence and lack of pretension about him that appealed to Maurice enormously. His guest was apparently unable to tie his own shoelaces, but, on the other hand, was spontaneously tempted to break away from official programmes to talk to onlookers and to sign autographs. He described the Oxford crowds to Bowra as 'my people'.[59] True, Chaplin 'took some looking after'. He had no watch and kept disappearing up 'back streets' to satisfy curiosity.[60] But such an immediate approach to life could only win the Warden's approval. Chaplin's ebullience made him a soulmate. As a special treat, certified Bowristas were invited to meet the great man. Lady Quinton was promised an introduction, if she agreed 'to wear a nice hat'.[61]

Even when the honorands were politicians or musicians, their presence in the University brought it distinction. Vincent Auriol, the President of France, was 'rather an old pet', though his strong, Limousin accent tested Bowra's French to the limit.[62] Haile Selassie was summed up as 'a nice, quiet, polite, old murderer'.[63] Bowra had no expertise in music, but an encounter with Shostakovich was pure joy.

We got Shostakovich here for an honorary degree. He looks like a Canadian Rhodes Scholar doing a DPhil in economics. He talks nothing but Russian, and in that talks only about music. All other topics are strictly taboo. He was rather sweet, and played the piano like a tornado or Buster Keaton, tearing the notes out of it. Two spies followed him around, but were skilfully side-tracked to a College ball, which they left, plastered, at 4 am singing in English.[64]

Little wonder that, on Degree Days, Maurice was on top form. Even dull honorands would somehow be lost in a good dinner: 'Maurice is an awfully nice Vice-Chancellor, because, when he has to entertain some boring honorand, he asks all his friends too, and has lots of drink, and the bore passes unnoticed and even becomes quite amusing'.[65] To propose dud personalities for honorary degrees was at least 'a nuisance',[66] or, worse, a direct violation of the Bowrista creed. Such behaviour trivialized occasions which pronounced to the world what Oxford stood for. Having persuaded the University to recognize Picasso, Maurice was desperately keen that the offer should be accepted, for 'otherwise, we shall never get any more artists, and the pro-art party will be despised and done in'.[67] If degrees were offered to the right people, it was good for Oxford and good for the Warden of Wadham.

Of equal importance was the question of appointments. Every election was of significance, being a battle between the forces of darkness and the party of light. Bowristas would win or Bowristas would lose. In these engagements, Maurice behaved like a kind of 'tribal chief', because he 'always thought in terms of friends and enemies, and he liked to see black and white'.[68] Only one principle mattered. On every occasion, the best scholar should carry the day. When looking for a new Keeper of the Ashmolean Museum, Bowra insisted that the winning candidate '*must* be a scholar, not a mere administrator'. It was simply not good enough 'to deal very well with the old ladies'.[69] It was outrageous that Helen Gardner should be passed over for a Chair of English in favour of Nevill Coghill, who was 'not a scholar at all', but only 'a good college man'.[70] In looking for occupants of chairs, only established scholarship matter; in fellowship elections, only the promise of it. Even friendship should not be allowed to cloud the issue. In 1949, he refused to support Enid Starkie's translation to the leading Chair in French. Instead, he ran a campaign, 'like Robert E Lee at Bull Run, or wherever it was', to elect Jean Seznec.[71] He explained to Edith Sitwell that 'in such matters I *can't* go against my principles. It is just impossible, and I think Miss Starkie entirely second-rate.'[72] Since, 'France is one of the great things in our lives',[73] its culture in Oxford had to be as expertly represented as possible. Rumour suggested that Bowra was merely taking revenge on a woman who may have played some part in his failure to secure the Chair of Greek thirteen years earlier, but this is probably unfair. Bowra's elevated reading of Oxford's importance called for other motives.

If the claims of friendship had no part to play in elections, nor should other, more covert, loyalties. Some critics noted that Bowra had been the man, who had described the homosexual fraternity within England as 'the Homintern', and went on to accuse him of favouring his co-religionists in making appointments. Again rumour proved false. Someone like James Joll was to be supported, because he was 'a high minded Queen' who wrote good books. The fact that he was 'a nice brave boy' in addition was merely a kind of bonus.[74] Quite different was a clergyman who, having left Queen's College in rather murky circumstances, reappeared as a candidate for a leading Chair. Bowra was appalled that he might actually be appointed by electors 'towing the Trade Union line and voting on the straight International ticket'.[75] When academics betrayed their own calling by subordinating the claims of scholarship to any other consideration, Maurice even found it 'hard to walk with Queens and keep the common touch'.[76]

Just as sexual behaviour was no reason to promote the second rate, nor was it an argument justifying the persecution of a genuine scholar. This belief underpinned Bowra's rather oblique relationship with Hugh Trevor-Roper. In theory the two men should have been great friends. In many ways their expectations of Oxford were the same. But, initially, Bowra had doubts. In his view, Trevor-Roper, apart from being too fond of duchesses, 'shows off all the time, sucks up to me, boasts, is far from poor owing to his awful book, on every page of which there is a howler'.[77] He was always ready to write articles for the *Sunday Express* 'about matters on which he can know nothing at all'.[78] On one occasion, he even had the temerity to correct a mistake in one of Maurice's own books by sending a postcard. Bowra could not enjoy the thought that Oxford postmen could read of his flaws in scholarship. Taken together, all this led him to encourage Evelyn Waugh 'to persecute him as much as you can'.[79] The mood completely changed, however, when Christ Church chose to harass Trevor-Roper for the offence of living with a woman whose divorce had not been finalized but whom he would eventually marry. This persecution of a scholar was for Bowra clericalism gone mad. He went out of his way to have 'a great heart-to-heart with Trevor-Roper about his girl. He is cracky about her. I promised 100% support and the full alliance of the Immoral Front.'[80] Careers were not to be threatened by the moral codes of suburbia.

This campaign proved worthwhile. When Trevor-Roper was appointed Regius Professor of Modern History, Oxford escaped the threat posed by A. J. P. Taylor, 'who is a split personality and has probably finished with work for TV and other more profitable ends'. Trevor-Roper was at least 'a clever man, a good writer, on the right side in all academic matters, and a sturdy fighter'.[81] The two men would never be the close friends that similarities in views would have suggested. Bowra still thought that the younger man was 'quite inhuman', wanting to be admired rather than liked. In return, Trevor-Roper could never be a Bowrista. He was either above or beyond bending the knee to Maurice. But both men appreciated the strength of the other, notably a seriousness of academic purpose. Inevitably, they would find themselves allies in many university battles.

Measured against the exacting test of scholarship, every appointment was good, bad, or indifferent. The success of people he greatly respected always gave Bowra huge pleasure. To see the great art historian Edgar Wind established in Oxford was unalloyed triumph, not least because it gave pain to two of Bowra's long-term enemies, T. S. R. Boase, 'who is jealous', and Sir Anthony Blunt, 'who is a stuffed sausage'.[82] When a Bowrista took over a whole college, a real celebration was in order. Noel Annan's elevation to the Provostship of King's College, Cambridge, for example, was simply magnificent. Maurice told Dadie Rylands that 'It is a great comfort that the fight was in your hands, and the enemies of humanity were routed and routed handsomely.' The College would now continue to be run 'in the grand old way'.[83]

Unfortunately not all elections ended well. When Jack Westrup became Professor of Music, Maurice found him 'not at all clever, and not, apparently, interested in music'. It was only too clear that 'he would not advance the cause'.[84] On another occasion, after reporting a tea party given by Edith Sitwell at which Dylan Thomas had 'read a new poem about the Welsh seaside, very dotty and wonderful', he sadly had to reflect that a new Professor of English Literature at Oxford was, by contrast, 'an unknown editor of boring minor Elizabethans ... Why are electoral boards so idiotic?'[85] On this score, 1949 was a terrible year. Balliol elected 'a fearful bore' as its Master, with a wife 'who gives herself airs' while Jesus College went for 'a flogging headmaster'.[86] Then there was the Professor of Economics, who wanted 'to make the university a branch of the civil service, in which promotion will go by men's opinions, tone of voice and pompous hypocrisy'.[87] He of course had to be defeated. It was barely credible that such people should be appointed to positions of influence in Oxford. Their existence made Maurice 'vomit with rage and shame'.[88]

Of particular interest were elections to the Wardenship of All Souls. It was a College Bowra viewed with suspicion. Rich and aloof, it took no undergraduates and contributed little to the teaching strength of the University. As a result, 'the only justification for All Souls is that it should be a place of learning',[89] recruiting productive scholars of the highest repute. It was therefore maddening that the College repeatedly refused to elect Isaiah Berlin as Warden. Instead they thought of Lord Franks, 'a chilly fellow' and 'by no means on the right side'; Leslie Rowse, who was a lightweight; and Richard Pares, whose pretensions to scholarship had been ruined by a 'Dora Copperfield' of a wife, replete with 'silly, small-girl ideas'.[90] In the end, the Fellows of All Souls, 'that assembly of empty men',[91] elected first Humphrey Sumner and then John Sparrow. The latter, in Maurice's view, although a Bowrista in sympathy, could never be 'a proper head' of a college.[92] The personal inhibitions that checked his scholarly instincts would ensure that All Souls would remain moribund, directed by a policy of masterly inactivity. As Vice-Chancellor, Bowra attacked the College for wasting its resources, and denounced Sparrow for leading 'an anti-research campaign'.[93] Reprimanding a friend in this way, even in 'a bantering tone',[94] reaffirmed Bowra's priorities. Duty to Oxford came first.

In 1944, Isaiah Berlin incautiously suggested that Maurice had become tired of elections. He described him as 'a sated power: and not a very formidable one: rather like Italy [in] 1900'.[95] He could not have been more wrong. Bowra's campaigns to promote a particular culture depended on the right people being elected to the right jobs. Every election was of importance. In a University, there would always be a conflict between 'the Immoral Front and the Rest'.[96] When the battle was on, 'the Immoral Front cannot relax in the wards and the precincts'.[97] Not every engagement would end in victory. Bowra spectacularly lost in 1960 when his candidate failed to stop Harold Macmillan becoming Chancellor.[98] But he won often enough to make the game worth playing. It had, for him, the character of a mission. In discussing the career of Stuart Hampshire with Isaiah Berlin, Maurice reported that 're donning, he will only go where there is a missionary call. I suggested New College could only be considered a step in the right direction.'[99]

Bowra's experience and expertise gave him a voice in academic elections, but his reputation and standing within Oxford was such that his opinion was sought on all aspects of the city's life. During his Vice-Chancellorship, local politics began to throb with a debate about building a relief road through the city's centre. Congestion had become insupportable, and Maurice could see that something had to be done.

> There is much talk about replanning Oxford, but most of the cures are worse than the disease, and the whole thing will cost so much, that it will never be done. Nice though it would be to go back to 1820, that is an opium dream, and after all, people must have cars and shops and houses, and why not?[100]

Central to this scheme was the idea that the High Street must be preserved at all costs. This meant either diverting traffic to the south along a new road to be build across Christ Church Meadow, or to the north past New College and Wadham. Obviously, for Maurice, the second proposal was out of the question.[101] Equally, a road across the Meadow might have the advantage of seriously irritating the governors of Christ Church, but would otherwise be destructive and merely move congestion from one part of the city to another. Confronted with a straight choice, however, he voted for a road across the Meadow, in order to preserve Wadham's quiet, and his action led to a passage of arms with Professor Lindemann outside the Sheldonian, which descended into pure Billingsgate.[102] Facetiously, or unfacetiously, Bowra suggested that a tunnel might be the answer.[103]

In the end, no road of any kind was built. Instead, John Sparrow launched a campaign to limit access to the city's centre. First of all, Radcliffe Square would be completely closed to traffic. Rather in the manner of Don Quixote, he rode out against the arrogant claims of the motor car. As a non-driver, Bowra was only too happy to follow in his wake, like a rather bemused Sancho Panza. To their joint astonishment,[104] they carried the day, and thereby started a process which has more and more discouraged and disheartened the motorist. Optimistically, Bowra looked forward to a University through which passed 'about three cars a day'.[105]

In a similar vein, Maurice took much innocent and malicious pleasure in remodelling the Oxford landscape. Whenever anything aesthetic is in question, every academic regards himself as the arbiter of taste, and thereby exposes himself to raillery. Bowra took one look at the new chapel at St Antony's and decided that it would 'make a very nice gymnasium, and could be opened by Lady Clark in bloomers and black woollen stockings'.[106] As Vice-Chancellor, he protected himself by employing John Betjeman as an unpaid adviser.[107] Bowra admired the appearance of Oxford too much to take chances. On only one occasion did he slip from grace. Representing Oxford, he persuaded an American benefactress and the Duchess of Marlborough to establish a rose garden opposite Magdalen, knowing full well that the College's President, T. S. R. Boase, detested roses. Inevitably, the area became known as 'The Boase Garden'.[108] But, normally, his reactions to all proposals was severely pragmatic. A new building should not disfigure Oxford, and its construction should be well within the University's budget. When Neville Coghill led a campaign to build a new theatre, the Vice-Chancellor agreed that it was 'straight down our main road' and infinitely desirable, but bluntly pointed out that Coghill's grasp of finance was rudimentary. As an administrator, beneath all that wit and the malice, Maurice never took his eye off the main objective, namely Oxford's ability to provide an atmosphere in which the best scholarship flourished. It was 'Hell when our bloody universities do the wrong thing ... I can never take it quietly, and feel that such actions call to Heaven for vengeance.'[109]

Having proved himself in Oxford, it was almost inevitable that Bowra would be invited to lead the Humanities for a term, as President of the British Academy. In July 1959, he 'descended on Burlington Gardens in true Olympian character, thunderbolt and all'.[110] In his first Presidential Address, he set out his personal agenda. First, the government must be persuaded or coerced into providing the Academy with a regular income with which to support research. When Bowra took office, the Academy had no assured income, but rather lived from day to day on the generosity of benefactors. In 1960, Maurice had to ask All Souls for a subvention in order to continue publication of its journals.[111] In Bowra's view, no academic body could function on such terms. When compared to similar arrangements in Europe, the Academy's poverty was a national disgrace: 'in France or Germany or Holland ... the Humanities do not starve.' The new President told his audience that the Academy had been too passive, 'too ready to hide its light under a bushel'. It was time to come out fighting. Governments must be forcefully reminded that 'research is the living centre from which knowledge at all levels ultimately flows'.[112]

Fortunately, the times could not have been more propitious for a campaign of this kind. Bowra's predecessor, Sir George Clark, had secured a grant from the Rockefeller Foundation in order to produce a report on the state of funding for research in the Humanities. Using evidence provided by this enquiry, Maurice then 'drove through the project with characteristic energy'.[113] A committee, consisting of Bowra himself, Clark, E. Dodds, and Sir Mortimer Wheeler, met eighteen times between April 1958 and February 1961, in order to formalize an appeal to government. It fell to Maurice to draft the Committee's recommendations. Initially, the Academy's President could not convince himself that the battle would be won. He told Felix Frankfurter that he was 'faced with a hideous task. The British Academy is going to publish a report on the support or non-support of research in the humanities, and I can see that I will have to write it myself. What a bore, and really not in my line. It will at least be delightfully dull, and make no impact of any kind on anyone.'[114] In the event, the report was 'politely received'. Bowra announced privately that he would 'be happy with 1/100th of what is given by the Govt. to science. I wish I knew *why* we had to keep up with technological developments, and suspect that much of it is bogus.'[115]

The crucial meeting took place in the spring of 1961. The Academy's Committee was allowed an interview with Henry Brooke, the Financial Secretary to the Treasury, after 'ricocheting off Norman Brook, the head of the Civil Service and one of Bowra's first pupils in Wadham'.[116] The happy coincidence of having a former pupil in such a useful position undoubtedly helped the cause. The Financial Secretary listened to the Academy's case, seemed to be sympathetic, and then lapsed into silence. This lack of any response from official circles went on for over a year. Only in July 1962, in his valedictory address to the Academy, was Bowra able to announce triumphantly that a grant of £25,000 a year had been secured. This victory established an important principle. When writing up the story, Sir Mortimer Wheeler felt justified in describing Bowra's performance as 'vigorous'.[117] Thanks to him and his confederates, government had been brought to accept some measure of financial responsibility for the Academy's work.

Bowra himself took great personal pleasure at this result, not least because he was to be the first chairman of the committee, within the Academy, charged with the distribution of these new funds. From his point of view, arrangements were perfect. The state had acknowledged its financial obligations, but did not presume to direct academics on what or how they undertook research. In retrospect, Bowra thought that his report had 'not done so badly. The Treasury, despite our national bankruptcy, are giving us £25,000 a year at once, and doubling it in two or three years time ... It will be nice to help some worthy and discouraged scholars.'[118] Scholarship in unfashionable subjects could now be protected, and research across disciplines could now be promoted. England must not go in for 'inbreeding' but must rather be open to new ideas coming from abroad. Equally, the inter-reaction between different disciplines could be fruitful. The man who had been so keen to promote European studies in Oxford now took his campaign to the national level. Too much narrowness and introspection was not healthy. Taking his own discipline as an example, he told the Academy that close work on texts was no doubt valid, but it did little to advance the purpose of classical studies, which was 'to recapture, as far as we can, the living experience of the Greco-Roman world'.[119]

These views naturally led him to a second objective as President, namely the opening up of British scholarship to the claims of other cultures. British Schools already existed in Rome and Athens, but Bowra was anxious for more. He particularly wanted to see a similar institution in Teheran. Maurice had no personal expertise in Persian studies, but he knew that here was a civilization, which had predated the Greeks and defied the Romans. In terms of cultural variety and continuity, Persia had almost unparalleled claims to be taken seriously. Sadly, as far as the British were concerned, it was 'almost a virgin field', but, for that very reason, offered 'enormous returns', if new interest could be generated.[120] Accordingly, as President of the British Academy, he began to agitate for a British Institute in Teheran, which he always referred to, in private correspondence, as 'my Institute'.[121]

In December 1960, Bowra travelled to Iran to open negotiations. Teheran itself had 'nothing to be said for it, ugly and shapeless and sprawling', but the ruins at Isfahan and Persepolis had been breathtaking. In addition, there had been a 'heavenly climate, caviare and sturgeon from the Caspian, gazelles and birds from the mountains'.[122] Importantly, he and Sir Mortimer Wheeler were granted an audience with the Shah, who was thought an 'attractive, hard-boiled, knowledgeable fellow, who rattles off figures with much confidence, though I am told they are all wrong'. His wife was 'a good-looker and has artificial eye-lashes, a nice smile and a hard chin'.[123] A deal was struck. The Iranian authorities provided a building near Teheran University, and the British Treasury offered a grant of £8,000 a year to cover general running costs. In December 1961, Bowra returned to Iran to give the inaugural lecture at the new Institute.[124] Appropriately, he chose to speak about Edward Fitzgerald and his translations of the poetry of Omar

Khayyam. Max Mallowan noted how congenial Fitzgerald's 'deep-seated sense of poetry' was to Maurice's own character.[125] Within weeks, British archaeologists began the excavation of Cyrus's palace at Pasargadae. When Bowra visited the site, he was exultant: 'Our boys and girls ... have done wonders, marked out the boundary walls of the huge domain, unearthed great walls of masonry, found a cylinder seal of Cyrus and heaven knows what, all in two months. So, as I was largely responsible for starting the whole thing, I am more than delighted.'[126]

The whole experience gave Bowra a real taste for Iran and its people. He visited the country again in April 1968 and February 1971, bringing home funds with which to establish a fellowship in Persian Studies within Wadham. Cynical friends suggested that he liked Iran because, 'in roaring twenties form', he could sit 'underneath some Bough or other with some Thou or other'. Allegedly he told a New College friend that 'they are all buggers in Persia'.[127] No doubt such attributes might prove something of a bonus if they existed, but there were more powerful forces at work. Visiting Iran, 'with its wonderfully dotty people',[128] reminded him of his boyhood in Asia, of the fact that Asian peoples knew how to live. In many ways, their priorities were better grounded than any to be found in the West: 'The Persians are charming, entirely double-faced and irresponsible and unreliable, but full of honour and irony and fancy, and like talking about poetry. I drank a lot of arak with them, and became very voluble in many languages.'[129] Alone among the peoples of the Middle East, they 'seem to have no chips on their shoulders'.[130]

More personally, to visit Iran was to re-establish contact with the Asia of his youth. He delightedly told Felix Frankfurter that he still felt

the magic of Asia, the smell of camels, the chaos in the bustling streets, food being cooked out of doors, bright colours, and sense of timelessness with no clocks or schedules or programmes. Somehow, everything that matters works much more easily than with us. Better meals appear punctually; the stops on the desolate roads produce eggs and kebabs and tea at the shortest possible notice; everyone talks for the sake of talking and is infinitely polite. Echoes from my childhood gather round me, and make me feel that somewhere and somehow I have missed a bus, or perhaps several buses.[131]

Returning to Asia compelled Maurice to reflect on what he had lost in trying to turn himself into an Englishman. The establishment of a British Institute in Teheran dignified Bowra's term of office as President of the British Academy, but was also deeply therapeutic in a personal sense.

The success of the Persian venture led Maurice to try his luck elsewhere. In May 1954, he had become a member of a committee whose purpose was to establish a British School in East Africa. Initially, all proposals were checked by politics and a lack of funds. But in 1959, the new President of the British Academy persuaded the United Africa Company, the Nuffield Foundation, and the governments of the relevant colonial territories to create a fund that would meet his purpose. A British School in Dar-es-Salaam duly opened.[132] Unlike its counterpart in Teheran, this establishment faced an uncertain future, because African nationalists could only view its existence with suspicion. It was, therefore, fortunate that, in the first months of its existence, an archaeologist from the School discovered a prehistoric skull that substantiated the view that *Homo sapiens* had started life in Africa. That such a discovery should have been made under the aegis of the British Academy rather than the Royal Society was particularly pleasing. As Maurice put it to an American friend, 'The British School totters along. We had a coup presenting the pre-man skull and all from East Africa, long before the Royal Society had heard of it... One in the eye for Sir Cyril Hinshelwood.'[133]

Holding high office in major academic institutions inevitably made Bowra aware of just how dependent such bodies were becoming on funding provided by governments. Such largesse allowed for expansion and new initiatives, but there were obvious dangers. Immediately after the War, bureaucrats and politicians were prepared to subsidize universities without insisting on having a voice in the direction of those institutions, but Bowra suspected and feared that such self-restraint would not hold for long. Treasury men were 'purple-faced bastards',[134] who always wanted to meddle and control. He warned an incoming Vice-Chancellor that he 'must stand up to bureaucrats', even if 'the Minister of Education, is a 2nd in History, we can deal with him'.[135] As long as Whitehall was dominated by the products of Oxbridge, it appeared that his University might be safe. But there was always the chance that his University might not always be so, and, worse, there was always the possibility that Oxford's graduates might turn treasonous.

The dangers were all too obvious. The university expansion of the 1950s and 1960s brought into life new institutions which competed with Oxbridge for funds, and which often regarded those bodies with a mixture of envy and contempt. As Maurice bluntly explained to Felix Frankfurter:

Alas, we are to Redbrick what West Berlin is to East Germany—a centre of light and liberty, and therefore to be disliked and done down. Sir Charles Morris, Sir Philip Morris[136] etc., those ignorant fuddy-duddies, are the real niggers in this wood-pile. However, we are putting up quite a good resistance, displaying sweet reasonableness at every turn, and really showing some desire to help them. To Hell with them, but their students matter, and we really must evolve some better way of allotting them around the place. This does not mean that I do not want the best myself. Of course, I do, and I think I can do something with them.[137]

Any Minister of Education with foul intent could use this resentment among university leaders to divide and conquer.

Equally threatening, in the post-war world, was a tabloid press which seemed to have cast off all inhibitions about reporting delinquency or supposed failings in established institutions. Confronted by this kind of journalism, Oxford simply could not win. The University was condemned, at one and the same time, for being the setting for *Brideshead* fantasy, and the home of a new, ruthless meritocracy. As Maurice observed, in an article in *The Times*, the press could not agree about anything but the one fact that Oxford was always in the wrong.

Oxford, unlike Cambridge, is always news to the sensational Press, and the public is confused by accounts of undergraduates, who are at once miserably poor and flauntingly extravagant, who work twelve hours a day and have unlimited time for pleasure, who despise politics and are given to violent views whether of the right or of the left. Such contradictory views are to be expected of any university which is worthy of the name and fosters a variety of human types, but too much attention need not be paid to them.[138]

Bowra knew well that inquisitive bureaucrats, sceptical politicians, and journalists looking for a story at any cost were all expressions of the same phenomenon. As democratic values really took hold, no institution could expect privacy, particularly if it was in receipt of substantial public funds. Its values could no longer be taken for granted. Rather they had to be fought for.

In this warfare, the leaders of universities had to be clear about what was to be defended to the limit, and careful about choosing their ground. It would be absurd to be too provocative. In 1953, for example, Maurice had no sympathy with the proposal to restore Oxford's separate representation in Parliament. It would bring the university little real advantage, and merely mire it in unnecessary 'political controversy'.[139] Another tactic to be assiduously employed was to fix, as far as was possible, the chairmanship of all committees and enquiries whose decisions vitally affected Oxford.[140] Above all, no government money should be accepted if the strings attached to it were unduly constricting. A University that was seven hundred years old should not indulge in short-term compromises with governments if fundamental ideas about the independence of scholarship were thereby impaired. In his view, it was better by far to accept painful cuts in funding and wait for a fairer wind. Academics had to realise that 'they can no longer open their mouths wide knowing that they will be filled'.[141] They had to face the uncomfortable fact that relying on the generosity of governments and the sympathy of the public as a whole carried unquantifiable risks.

In these battles, Bowra was happy to be machiavellian, even brutal. A man of his generation could only be suspicious and fearful of outside opinion, which could be easily motivated by jealousy or ignorance. In confronting them, he never had any doubt that Oxford was probably in the right.[142] Confidence allowed him to be very clear about options. The University's independence of action had to be preserved at all costs. In the middle of his Vice-Chancellorship, he cheerfully noted that 'next year the university will have no money from the government. I don't think it matters if we have enough to carry on with. We can do without enormous new labs.'[143] Predictably, he had nothing but contempt for the quislings within the universities who were prepared to collaborate with the intrusive ambitions of governments. Even within Oxford there was the whiff of Vichy. He once told a friend that many Vice-Chancellors in Africa had shown more courage in the defence of academic freedom than their English counterparts.[144] For him, there could be no argument on this point. The independence of Oxford and institutions like it defined a culture and offered one guarantee of rationally-based freedoms.

By any standards, Bowra's presidency of the British Academy had not been unfruitful. His campaigns brought his name to the attention of many people outside Oxford who saw him as the personification of the University. In return, although Wadham would always be his favourite stage, Maurice began to enjoy performances in front of new kinds of audience, Some time in the middle 1950s, for example, he met a certain Kenneth Swan, who had ambitions to create a cruise ship that would pleasantly combine education with leisure. The Swan Hellenic line would take passengers to places of cultural and historical interest. Lectures would be provided on board by experts in the civilizations to be visited. Since many of the cruises would be undertaken around the Mediterranean, Bowra was an obvious candidate to lead the revels. Initially, he thought that Swan was too keen 'on rich smarties' who would be 'bored to death' by anything too intellectual, but he quickly changed his mind. Such cruises offered him so many advantages. Captive audiences could be told about the Greeks, while the ship took him to 'beautiful and un-get-at-able places' in the Aegean, 'which lures me back like a first love, and is the one place where I am blissfully happy'.[145] He had always thought that a taste of the Mediterranean was 'indispensable if one is to keep alive'.[146] Since he was given a free passage in return for lecturing, it was all 'too good to be true'.[147] As he chortled to Berta Ruck, 'I have got on to a good racket. A splendid man who runs cruises takes me to Greece on condition that I make a speech or two at suitable places. As I cannot help doing this anyhow, ça vaut bien le voyage.'[148] Most importantly, travelling with Swan Hellenic averted the threat of vacations spent in an empty Oxford.

For someone who was always in need of listeners, a cruise ship full of passengers with no means of escape was usually a congenial environment, even if the audience consisted of 'yearning spinsters and QCs and clergymen'.[149] Of course social danger lurked in every passageway. Sir Henry Willink proved to be a 'grinning sham hearty' who had the temerity 'to talk through my lectures and was hideously knowing'.[150] Equally, Sir John Wolfenden was found to have no sense of humour. He was the author of a famous report on homosexuality, and yet refused an offer to lecture on the island of Lesbos. Bowra thought this rather 'churlish'.[151] Reacting sharply to such encounters, Maurice took on the defensive strategy of encouraging known friends to join these excursions. On one cruise, the suggestions book carried the comment that Bowra had not circulated sufficiently among the passengers, preferring to be 'sitting with his cronies'.[152] As far as Maurice was concerned, a Swan Hellenic cruise should always include a quorum of Bowristas afloat.

His sparring partner on many of these voyages was Sir Mortimer Wheeler, the eminent archaeologist with whom he had worked closely at the British Academy. For Wheeler, Maurice proved 'the perfect travelling companion; and he and I have travelled a good many thousand miles together, talking and talking and occasionally listening. In our more idle moments, we used to cruise in the Aegean, often with a crowd of acolytes, with whom we would share our knowledge and our ignorance with equal zest.'[153]

In addresses to cruise audiences, fact and imagination could be blended. One passenger remembered visiting a Roman site where Bowra, 'planting himself like a tree on level ground, hands behind his burly back, simply roared at us: "In this *beautiful* theatre, Nero once had the temerity to give a performance. He sang, we don't know what ... but I have always thought of his voice as a rather high *tenor*." '[154] Among Kenneth Clark's papers, there is a drawing of Maurice with his back to the walls of Troy declaiming Homer to a reverent audience.[155] It was Oxford speaking. Bowra had no interest in appearing on television, and only rarely broadcast on the radio, because, in these media, audiences were too undifferentiated and too remote. He much preferred a Swan Hellenic assembly, full of people whose vague interests in the ancient world could be warmed into something more passionate, and who could be manipulated into laughter that he himself could hear.

Good performances on public stages attracted recognition and honours. In December 1950, he went to Paris to pick up an honorary doctorate from the Sorbonne for services to French literature. He already had the ribbon of the *Légion d'honneur*. Strangely, the citation awarding the degree placed him in the RAF in 1917, but also recalled 'a soldier on campaign in France ... We will therefore have the impression of honouring one of our own countrymen.' He represented 'a veritable synthesis of diverse cultures, ancient and modern, cultural interests sustained by an astonishing knowledge of many languages'. All his writings were marked by 'a jovial strain of humour' and by 'the finest wit'.[156] Such levels of flattery were entirely congenial, particularly if accompanied by 'a dinner more than memorable. I like the habit of covering the table with bottles of champagne. It saves waiting.'[157] At such moments, he could honestly say that 'France is Europe.'[158] This award was followed by many others. Germany gave him Pour le Mérite, America membership of its Academy, and Greece the Royal Order of the Phoenix. In addition, there were honorary degrees from Dublin, St Andrews, Hull, the University of Wales, Harvard, Columbia, and Aix-en-Provence.

Among his friends, Maurice always affected to talk of these decorations as matters of no consequence whatever. But for someone who had always seen himself as something of an outsider, they were important signs of acceptance. In this respect, English honours were particularly valued. The country, in which he had not been born and which had rejected his services in the Second World War, now offered him recognition. In 1951, he was given a knighthood, and, in 1970, was made a Companion of Honour. Some friends guessed that he hoped for even more. John Bamborough thought that Hugh Gaitskell promised him a peerage, a prospect that gave Maurice one of 'the happiest moments' of his life.[159] It was as though England had forgiven him, and had, to some extent, seen the point of his literary crusades. It was warming to be congratulated by national figures like Laurence Olivier, even if he did spell the word professor with two 'ffs'.[160]

News of Bowra's acceptance of a knighthood startled his friends. He appeared to be accepting favours from an Establishment he had spent a lifetime mocking. The poacher really had turned gamekeeper. In the circumstances, a certain amount of teasing was in order. Penelope Betjeman sent him a pair of spurs. Maurice thanked her with a straight face, and insisted that her gift would 'remind me of my old days in the Royal Regiment, though there we were not allowed rowels ... I feel the ascription of "Knight Bachelor" rules out any thought of marriage.'[161] Edith Sitwell wrote to say that the award would at least have the advantage of killing F. R. Leavis with envy.[162] Evelyn Waugh pretended to think that the award could only have been intended to honour Bowra's sexual adventures, 'something violent and unexpected' that 'happened in the Beef Steak cloakrooms between you and Lord Jowett'.[163] For long-standing members of the Immoral Front, the master had committed a kind of treason. John Sparrow thought of joining the raillery by innocently suggesting that 'they' had 'caught him—never gave him a chance to refuse'. He prophesied that Maurice 'will soon forfeit all respect. How *could* he?'[164] He blamed Kenneth Clark for leading Bowra into temptation.

Maurice himself was a little shame-faced. His attempts at self-justification could sound a little hollow: 'I am now indeed a sated power and want nothing else. This last thing came as a great surprise—and for the moment I debuted [*sic*], but one has to be as famous as Mr Gladstone or Mr Churchill to go without these aids, and that clearly I am not.'[165] More honestly, he explained to Noel Annan that he had accepted these handouts from the Establishment for two reasons; first they gave pain to academic enemies whose influence he had fought all his life; and, secondly, they recognized the campaigns on behalf of the Greeks and the poets.

It is all very gratifying, and I make no attempt to hide my pleasure. As you know I have my full share of persecution mania, and this has dealt it a blow. I am much enjoying the obvious discomfiture of enemies. Poor Page, who is a martyr to envy, tried to be nice in his letter but did not really succeed. Boase has not written. Nor has Fraenkel. All of which is as it should be ... So I don't complain. The great thing is to get it for learning and not for administration.[166]

As Bowristas regularly appeared in the Honours Lists of the 1960s, it seemed to Maurice that the slow-moving English might at last be coming to understand 'the system' which he had pioneered since the 1920s. When John Betjeman was knighted, Bowra wrote to 'the Dear Old Boy' to insist that 'it was nice, too, that Penelope should after all these years of upward struggle become a lady'.[167] Friends with radical views were alarmed by the spectacle of Maurice shuffling towards respectability. To them there was a measure of surrender in the movement. While not being entirely able to refute the charge, Maurice would have offered two points in his defence. National recognition was personally warming. He and the English had finally shaken hands. Secondly, if the acceptance of honours implied compromise on Maurice's part, there was an element of concession on the other side as well. In dignifying Bowra, 'they' also admitted that what he stood for had value.

PART IV

Reflection

12

The 1960s

On the surface, Maurice lived the last decade of his life with undiminished energy. The performance still had brio and attack. No junior member of Wadham in those years was aware of great change. Descriptions of the impact made by dining with the Warden echoed those of thirty years earlier. As one of them recalled,

> I still remember that dinner. A grammar schoolboy from a working-class family in the midlands. I had never experienced anything like it: the food, the room, above all that magic figure who seemed to have known everyone. We didn't of course have to talk much. To present a name or a book was enough to set him off.[1]

The Warden could still be tempted out to lunch with undergraduates in King Edward St., or in graduate flats at Sandford. As ever, a Wadham man who expressed a liking for a particular author might be startled to receive a first edition in the next post.[2] Apparently, Wadham and its Warden in the 1960s were unchanged and unchangeable.

But the reality of the situation was very different. For someone brought up in the Edwardian era, the 1960s were often baffling and upsetting. For one thing, the ghost of Joseph had still not been fully exorcised, and Bowra dreamt repeatedly that he had failed his Finals. In his cups, he would admit to colleagues that 'we're all no good'. These moods were not helped by a fellow-classicist reading his *Greek Experience*, and innocently remarking that 'it's alright if you want to write that sort of thing'.[3] Old scars still occasionally bled. But, now, there were new doubts to face. Above all, the restlessness of the 1960s, the determination to make all things new, seemed to threaten his world and the values it represented. On university campuses, tectonic plates were in motion. Bowra's long fought-for campaigns, to establish humane learning as he understood it, were being undermined from all sides. According to Noel Annan, this fear brought Maurice much 'unhappiness'. He 'suffered dark nights of the soul'. He and his Cambridge doppelganger, Dadie Rylands, would in conversation 'vie with each other for the position of greatest failure'.[4] There was too much in the university life of the 1960s that Maurice could not understand or care for. Evelyn Waugh knew that something had gone wrong, when he heard that the young had begun to call the Warden 'Old Tragic'.[5]

A sense of being out of step with the times is a common excuse for publishing memoirs. Maurice began writing his in May 1965, in order 'to have something to fill the day'.[6] The volume would only take the story of his life up to 1939, and he was very firm about not going any further. He told a New College contemporary that 'nothing seems to have happened since then'.[7] Memories would 'be largely about the dead, who are anyhow more interesting than many of the living'.[8] There was simply no point in producing a second volume dealing with the post-war world 'as I have nothing to say. Since 1939, nothing of interest seems to have happened to me, or I have repressed it. I might of course write not a sequel but a parallel to the Memories, giving the seamy side of things, but, however enjoyable, it would have to wait for my death to see the light. I am too old to go comfortably to gaol for slander.'[9]

Stopping in 1939 made a loud symbolic point. The world he had known before that date was infinitely more understanding of him and his circle than what came after. The year 1939, he frankly admitted, was 'the end of an era for the world as for me'.[10] Before the War, individualism could be flaunted; after 1945, the individual was submerged in one system or another, all defined by words ending in 'ism'. Friends could only speculate how far Maurice was able or willing to make the necessary adjustments. Noel Annan thought that Memories was 'a period piece'.

> The great view held by the Twenties about people comes across with bell-like clarity. Maurice's generation thought that people were the most important thing and all their literary criticism is coloured by this fact. Indeed what is literature for but to tell us how peculiar, idiosyncratic and dotty people are? The dottiness is the important aspect. Life is only tolerable—according to this view—when it is viewed as comedy … though it is thought now to be deeply shocking not merely by Leavis and his disciples but by the Marxists and the Existentialists.[11]

To talk of the Greeks and individual destiny was increasingly dismissed as hopelessly old-fashioned.

As a result, Bowra found himself living in a world that he considered more and more crude and malformed. Knowing nothing no longer seemed to be any impediment to expressing views. The evidence for this was everywhere. At a Foyle's lunch, sitting next to Henry Moore and talking 'about the human body, always a provocative and friendly subject', the Warden looked at 'the *publikum* below the salt', who 'were very odd indeed, and there seemed to be no reason why they should be there or indeed why they should exist'.[12] His remarks on Mallarmé were received with polite incomprehension. Similarly, in 1970, he was taken to a production of *The Tempest* at Stratford, which he thought 'mad'.

> Ariel stark naked except for a cache sexe, with his hair done in a bun at the back like Rachel Trickett.[13] The revels in pitch dark, also by naked actors. The whole in a wind tunnel. Caliban always crawling on the ground. Thought to be all very clever, as I expect it was. I now understand the play less than ever, and that is saying a lot.[14]

Here was a brave, new world indeed, but one in which due reverence for great writing had been thrown to the winds.

Much of this degradation could be blamed, in his view, on the new media. Television and radio inevitably trivialized, trying to make easy what was inherently difficult. According to Maurice, 'All television corrupts, and absolute television corrupts absolutely.'[15] He never appeared on it. As for radio, the temptation to embellish and sensationalize seemed to be rooted in every producer and director. Inevitably, he was frequently asked to make broadcasts but almost always declined the invitation. In 1967, he refused a request from Christopher Sykes to talk about Adam von Trott, informing his friend that 'this is a thing I never do, as I have a horror of it. I am sorry about it, but there it is.'[16] Shortly after, he turned down the idea of talking about Felix Frankfurter, claiming that he had nothing to say that was not already in the public domain.[17] For Bowra, instruction had to involve the written word. It was the only basis for his idea of culture. Attempts by radio or television to create short cuts merely offered debased imitation of the real thing.

Beyond England, the world in the 1960s set out bleak prospects. Having witnessed the rise and defeat of Nazism, Bowra now saw authoritarianism reappearing in new forms. He could no longer visit Greece, now governed by colonels who mangled their own language. In 1965, he refused an invitation to visit China, even though the temptation to recapture memories of his childhood must have been great. On such a journey, 'one could just see the Great Wall and the Ming Tombs, but only at the cost of first seeing infant schools, factories, crèches, girls doing bayonet drill and other neo-democratic activities'.[18] In other parts of the world, racial intolerance still defined political debate. When Ian Smith enshrined white supremacy in Rhodesia, Bowra felt helpless. There was no point in sending troops because 'the officers and the NCOs would join Smith at once' while the imposition of sanctions 'will do nothing except make it easier for the blacks to starve, and I gather that it is quite easy already'. Significantly, this diagnosis ends with the statement that, 'it is all very depressing and not at all like the world in which I was brought up'.[19] He had begun to feel out of time. A more worrying thought was that these events *exactly* mirrored the world he had known when young. Populist authoritarianism and claims to racial supremacy had filled the first decade of his life. The Marxism and apartheid of the 1960s were profoundly depressing less because they were new, than because they repeated old themes. After the huge costs of two World Wars, no lessons had been learnt, no quarter given.

Bowra was not, however, primarily a political animal. In commenting on the resurgence of barbarisms, he was always anxious to bring the argument back to literary ground. The fading away of the literary vein in Western culture was what concerned him most. He was happy to chronicle the stages of decline. The year 1922 had been 'the splendid year', seeing the publication of masterpieces by Proust and Joyce, but there followed in 'the thirties a steep decline with hardly any first class new names'.[20] As for the 1960s, good writing had all but disappeared. Edith Sitwell was still producing work of real quality and for that he could only be profoundly grateful: 'though I like to deplore the present and say, sometimes with reason, how awful it is, I sometimes think of the few, the very few achievements in poetry that it has seen, and then I know I have no right to be ungrateful.'[21] In parallel degradation, learning in universities had become the bogus science of education. Bowristas regarded education departments as 'a pain in the ass', since they were less interested in liberating the individual than in imposing systems. Noel Annan shared with Maurice his fear that 'the individual is clearly disappearing, no one cares any more about him ... something new and probably more abortive is likely to appear'.[22] Bowra wholeheartedly agreed. He confessed that he was 'lost in these educational discussions.

Nobody seems to be interested in *what* the boys learn ... I would not say no to popping quietly under the grass.'²³ An uncharacteristic defeatism entered his vocabulary.

Much was at stake. Throughout his life, Bowra had looked for a political system that would cheerfully embrace his crusades on behalf of the Greeks and poets, and had failed to find anything to the purpose. Bowristas wrote to him expressing only resignation and loss:

> Of course you're heroic to go on battling with those ungovernable seas: trying to stem the filthy tide. I doubt if you'll do it, though this is not at all the point, for the battle has to be fought, right down to the last ditch: it's a destiny, which is different from a fate. You say the universities are to blame ... The truth is we have lost our grip, have no direction, no future, none but the cheapest and most cynical values ... The best is backward looking—*Past Convictions*, youthful walks through the Balkans. We've become disengaged, outside history, and gyrate idly, vainly. Yeats and Joyce are the swan-song of what started when the turtle lost his mate.²⁴

In his last decade, at home and abroad, Bowra saw his values attacked on all sides. New barbarisms and newly dignified ignorance in governments, in universities and in the mass media left him disorientated. Not surprisingly, many of his last, public lectures took the form of warnings. They recorded the decline of humane learning as he understood it, and begged for a moment of reflection before so much of value was thrown away.

For Bowra the most cogent evidence of oncoming disaster was the steep decline of interest in classical studies throughout the educational system. All his life, he had fought for the influence of the Greeks. They asserted the power of the individual, and they gave access to that 'inner self' that was serene. Now, these studies were being superseded by subjects more narrowly related to surviving in the twentieth century. To study economics rather than Greek literature was to put living successfully before living well. Corporate, rather than individual, values were the fashion. Taken together, changes of emphasis in education threatened Bowra with a world of no colour or sound. As he put it to an American friend, 'Business men think that they [classicists] do not belong to "the real world". God, what a horrible place it must be—let me live among the shadows a shadow, and be but a spume that plays.'²⁵ To talk of himself as 'a shadow' dramatically expresses growing alienation from the England of the 1960s. The Edwardian looked at the modern and found it wanting.

In 1945, Maurice became President of the Classical Association. His presidential Address, entitled *A Classical Education*, was full of foreboding. He pointed out that since the Renaissance, Latin and Greek had ceased to be the languages of science and medicine. Their role in the study of ethics and politics diminished with the degradation of Plato and Aristotle. These changes left only humane literature as the preserve of the classicist, and that too was now under threat as aristocratic government gave way to democratic experiments: 'The classical education was created by men who believed in an aristocratic ideal, and was intended primarily for those who were free from pecuniary anxieties and could develop their interests and personalities freely ... in a democratic age, most education is expected to be in some degree useful and vocational'.[26] In response to this threat, it was a mistake, Bowra insisted, to try to play the game by contemporary rules. No doubt remembering the embarrassments he had suffered at the hands of Adorno and Fraenkel, he denounced the Germans for smothering the literature of the ancient world in 'Wissenschaft', so that its message could not come through.[27] Instead he invited his audience to fight back on traditional lines which set the Greeks up as models of living. Bowra agreed that, historically, classicists had 'erred in claiming a monopoly' in the curriculum, but what they offered still had unquantifiable value.[28] The lecture is partly prophecy in the style of Cassandra and partly a call to arms.

Seven years later, he was asked to give the Birkbeck Lecture at London University. On this occasion he felt obliged to defend the study of literature as a whole, which he saw as the victim of 'whispering campaigns, which are all the more effective because some of them have been directed from high places'. There was the argument that to read literature was merely escapism, a view which Bowra dismissed as 'the old enemy, Philistinism, brought up to date'. In fact, the study of literature was not escapism at all, since it invited the reader to engage with the human condition at its most sublime and at its most vile: 'we come back from it not merely refreshed but wiser and more intelligent, acquainted more fully with life than we can ever hope to be, if we confine ourselves to the narrow range of our immediate experience'.[29] In this way, the study of literature is redemptive. By showing struggle, and even failure, it ennobles life and gives it meaning. That such studies should be denigrated in the post-war world suggested to Maurice that the civilization he had known had been touched by gangrene.

Bowra was on the defensive in a steadily worsening situation. By 1966, when he was asked to give the Romanes Lecture in Oxford, it seemed to him that many of the battles to which he had committed himself had been lost. He asked Dadie Rylands, 'what can I talk about? I think some nasty remarks on the decay of humane learning, the silliness and/or dullness of scholars, their lack of belief in the subject etc. But not easy.'[30] This lecture was of importance, because it was the last time that he would have a public platform from which to address the University. In the event, some friends thought his language too hesitant and opaque, but the central point was clear enough. The lecture represented an appeal by a man of a certain generation that his intellectual preoccupations should be given a fair hearing in the brave, new world of the 1960s.

The lecture opened with the stark claim that 'humane learning, in the sense of man and his works, attracts less public honour in England than in any other civilized country'.[31] Scientists were 'looked on with awe', while the artists were disregarded. The discerning patron and an informed readership had all but disappeared. State funding had taken their place, with consequences that were likely to be baleful.

> we can easily imagine circumstances, when officialdom, backed by public opinion, turned nasty and claims that much scholarly work is a waste of time and money; when Philistinism, disguised as economy or public spirit or financial realism or common sense or scientific exclusiveness, attacks the present system of learning, denounces it as absurd or worse, and seeks to discredit or disendow it.[32]

In view of subsequent events, some of these remarks might be thought prescient. Against these real and pressing threats Bowra invited his audience to come out fighting, to meet the new democracy more than halfway. People as a whole felt a need for the spiritual and healing qualities in literature, and, in popularization, 'there is nothing for tears'.[33] Properly presented, the Greeks and the poets could be as acceptable to mass taste as they had been to aristocratic societies in the past.

Such optimism about the future was not reflected in Maurice's private correspondence, however. On public platforms, he seemed to be whistling cheerful tunes to keep his spirits up. In his study, the mood was altogether more sombre. Here, the warnings conveyed in these lectures are rehearsed without the necessity of lifting the morale of an audience with a happy ending. Too many of the things he believed important were at a discount. It seemed increasingly likely that the enemies of the Bowristas would inherit the earth. Bureaucrats, scientists, businessmen, and politicians carried upward on waves of populist fervour would take the place of the heroes of the ancient world.

The evidence of this mutation of values was everywhere, even within Oxford itself. For someone who was 'terrifically Oxford',[34] this was hard to bear. When challenged to explain its purpose, the University should have had the confidence to give bureaucrats and politicians robust answers. Instead, Oxford, apparently riddled with self-doubt, made equivocal and apologetic concessions. To Bowra, the trend was apparent as early as 1944. In that year, he complained to Felix Frankfurter that

> the Master of Balliol is busy in the anti-brains trust, which is enjoying much fame just now. After the war, we are to do away with the intellect and go in entirely for leadership. The brains-busters include Lord Elton and the Headmaster of Winchester. So they are very popular. Our sin, it seems, is 'over-balanced intellectualism'. I have not noticed it, but I am notoriously slow. We can have nice tests in All-in wrestling etc., instead of scholarship exams, and the curriculum, such as it is, will be decided by a Soviet of Soviets. That is the world for which we are fighting.[35]

As for Cambridge, there was even less hope. There, every kind of philistinism had been embraced with enthusiasm. The University had 'sold themselves to Big Business … and now they have gone Conservative, Christian, scientist, games-playing, dog-loving, public school'.[36] All this represented a treason of the clerks on a grand scale.

In a parallel development, the internal politics of Oxford were becoming more and more grim. Issues of all kinds were increasingly to be decided by a centralized administration rather than by the Colleges and their Fellows. In one of his last speeches in Congregation, the University's parliament, Bowra complained that the bureaucrats were starting 'to bully the Colleges', and urged his audience to maintain 'our individuality as best we can'.[37] Officialdom, in Maurice's eyes, was always tempted to play the tyrant, particularly if collaborators could be found among the academics. Some of them, unfortunately, exhibited all the qualities of 'long-winded Fascist beasts'.[38] In 1965, he was forced to fight the suggestion that the Vice Chancellor should be allowed to expel an MA from the University 'for disrespect'. 'That way', as Maurice put it, 'lies South Africa.'[39] In the last five years of his life, the Warden of Wadham dropped out of university politics. Its prescriptions had become unfamiliar. Bowra jokingly described the process as tantamount to being 'flung on to the streets in the prime of life'. In fact, he felt relieved. There were, after all, 'advantages in belonging to an outmoded civilisation ... All this new spirit is very boring and exacting. I dislike the vocabulary of the reformers.'[40] He now had time to read and to see friends. But he also had time to reflect that the Oxford he had cherished lacked the courage to defend itself.

The University certainly needed courage. As more and more of Oxford's funding came from government, politicians demanded that there should be accountability. Oxford was to explain itself to the democracy that paid for its activities. When Bowra entered New College as an undergraduate, no money came from government; by the 1960s, at least a third of all income was dispensed by bureaucrats. Such a change inevitably exposed the University to questionings and prying enquiries. A man of Bowra's generation could only view such governmental interference with deep suspicion. For him, the independence of thought and action in universities was a vital component of a free society. Further, in his view, scientists were entirely responsible for dragging government into Oxford's affairs. The cost of maintaining laboratories could only be met by outside bodies. Scientists, conscious of this dependence, were also a potential fifth column therefore, and the Warden's suspicion of the scientific world was accordingly both cultural and political. As he explained to a goddaughter in 1963, 'Reform is in the air and blows coldly about my feet. Perhaps we need not actually do anything but we shall have to pretend to. Otherwise, the poor scientists won't get the millions which they regard as their right, and will be much too sorry for themselves, with tears before the evening's out.'[41] As the shadow of government regulation fell across the University, the clear light over Oxford that Maurice had known in his youth grew blurred.

In theory, relations between Oxford and government should have been merely conversations within a family. So many of the University's former pupils held high positions in politics and the civil service that Westminster and Whitehall should, by instinct, have had the University's interests at heart. Bowra's dealings with Lord Normanbrook over the funding of the British Academy offered a useful precedent. A general election brought the prospect of new faces, but not new threats. In 1964, for example, a change of political mood could be accommodated.

> Our election, seen on television, was very enjoyable. I don't at all like Mr Wilson, who is sharp and Philistine, but he is vastly cleverer than poor Sir Alec who survives from the Stone Age. The new government is packed with Oxford men; so with luck we may survive and not have to do what the Ministry of Education tells us at every point.[42]

The generation of politicians represented by Harold Wilson and Edward Heath revered their old university, but Bowra was prescient enough to know that, sooner or later, Oxford's luck would run out. Sooner or later, governments would attack because their desire to control was one of the dynamics of their existence. In this respect, the wind was thick with straws.

In the 1960s, two major enquires signalled the end of Oxford's security. The first, under the chairmanship of Lord Robbins, argued the case for a major expansion in tertiary education. Quite simply, successful economies would in the future need the skills of more and more graduates. New universities offering new kinds of curriculums had to be founded. Henceforth, Oxford would have to compete for public funds and meet sharp competition. In public, Bowra saw the point of these arguments. In an interview given to *The Times*, he boldly asserted that the sort of expansion that Robbins envisaged was 'an essential prerequisite of almost all other important plans for the next two decades'. He merely added riders to the effect that standards should not be allowed to fall, and that it might be an idea to establish distinct institutions for the sciences and the arts, in which the two disciplines might be separately honoured. Otherwise, the new universities were to be unequivocally welcomed.[43]

In private, Bowra's mood was more sombre. He knew only too well that what Lord Robbins proposed was a threat to Oxford's peace. He saw a two-tier system emerging that would all too often pitch Oxford and Cambridge against the rest. By dividing the universities against each other, the bureaucrat and the politician would have their chance to meddle. As he explained to an American protégé, 'it looks as if we're soon to be nationalized or at least reduced in status, so that the poor boys at Hull and Nottingham may not feel humiliated. I view it all with alarm, and hope with luck to be dead before anything is done.'[44] When negotiating for funding with the University Grants Committee, he had already had battle experience of 'the hatred of the other universities', which was 'pathological'.[45] Enemies, in the persons of Vice-Chancellors of other universities like Sir Philip Morris and Sir Douglas Logan, seemed to delight in denigrating Oxford and, by implication, the standards it represented. The creations of Lord Robbins promised undeclared warfare without end.

More immediately worrying was the appearance of another beast from the bureaucratic jungle with powers to investigate and report on all aspects of Oxford life. Lord Franks was upright and teetotal, and had been Bowra's candidate for the Chancellorship in 1960. In principle, 'on anti-snob lines', the Warden could see a case for having all his 'linen, clean and dirty, ready to wash in public'. An enquiry might give the University the chance to prove to a sceptical public that 'what we want is clever boys',[46] coming from all social backgrounds. Watching 'some raspberries' being handed out to All Souls for misusing substantial resources might even be 'amusing'.[47] But, of course, there would also be danger. Discussing the mysteries of Oxford in public was bound to be costly in terms of time wasted, and was bound to lead to misunderstandings. Bowra found himself unable to do anything 'but write endless answers to Franks's impeccable questionnaires. He thinks of everything and then I have to find answers.'[48] Worse still, the opening up of every conceivable issue allowed hobby horses to be ridden all around Oxford. As Maurice put it,

> The University is busy washing its linen (not all clean) in public and whitewashing its sepulchre under pressure of events. Our Science professors fill the press with lunatic suggestions—abolition of colleges, science for all, admissions to be made only by themselves, accusation of graft (alas, very rare indeed in practice) and so on. Lord Franks turns his ham-slicing mind to all our troubles and has accumulated a vast amount of tendentious material. I have myself sent him two documents, both misrepresented in the press.[49]

In his view, good might have emerged from the Franks Commission, but, in all probability, sound and fury would be followed by less than nothing.

Bowra himself gave evidence to the Commission, or, as he himself described it, 'I have to spend several days interviewing Lord Franks. He is a wonderful performer, and I much enjoy it.'[50] In his testimony he was anxious to make two points. The first, and most important, was that Oxford tutors must retain the right to choose their own pupils. The effectiveness of the tutorial system depended on it, and so did the possibility of accepting 'artists and so on' who did not necessarily shine in examinations. He quoted the examples of his friends William Walton and John Betjeman. Neither man enjoyed academic success, but both enriched the University with their presence. Of course 'a great many human beings you can educate in an ordinary, straight-forward way'. These people may be assessed in examinations. But there was an 'odd class' who had to be assessed by other criteria. As he put it to Franks, 'I often think about choosing human beings as a human activity; you cannot do it by any yardstick.'[51] If tutors retained control of admissions, cleverness would not be narrowly defined, but would rather be accommodated in all its expressions. In making these

remarks he was defending the colour of the world he had known against
the threat of turning all things grey.

Such an opinion might have been expected. His second point, however,
was less predictable. It was a plea for more emphasis on research. It had
always been his view that, after twenty years of teaching, a tutor ceased to
be of use to either himself or his pupils. The expansion in undergraduate
numbers after 1945 had created an intolerable new burden. If Oxford was
not to choke with 'mere hack tutors', some research element had to become
a regular feature of their lives. Time spent in research would refresh them
and their teaching. In a paper submitted to the Commission, Bowra and
Helen Gardner argued for the right to regular sabbaticals, and for the establishment of more readerships that would allow long-serving tutors to spend
their last years in research.[52] If necessary, Colleges should be bullied into
making these concessions. Otherwise, he feared an exodus of the talented.[53]
Wadham itself had lost able men, and, on this point, Bowra showed himself to be entirely in touch with contemporary concerns. Change only
threatened Oxford when it was motivated by envy or ignorance.

In the event, Oxford's walls did not fall at a blast from Lord Franks's
penny trumpet, but Bowra could easily see that the scrutiny of the
University and its ways would henceforth be a permanent feature of life.
In his last two decades, accumulating evidence proved that Whitehall and
Westminster wished to meddle and control. In turn, this pressure produced
a new breed of academic quisling who joyfully cooperated in bringing
down the walls of the temple. One such 'villain' was Keith Murray, 'who
is at the best a male impersonator and at the worst a mass of jelly'. Such
men sold principle for 'kudos', wanting to be 'governor of Gambia or
something of the kind'.[54] When Maurice bowed out of university politics
in 1967, he did so without regret. Increasing deafness made it difficult for
him to hear the arguments, and no one seemed prepared to defend the
University with confidence. Everything was apology and confession. As he
candidly explained to Dadie Rylands,

> I am rapidly clearing out of university affairs. They are too dull, too compli-
> cated, and take too much time ... How I miss the days of Smith and Poole. The
> present lot are very cowardly and touchy, and are always afraid of something,
> like offending the city, alienating the UGC, getting into the newspapers. As
> we do these things anyhow, we might as well get our money's worth.[55]

It seemed all too likely that the politician and bureaucrat had already won.

In the last decade of his life, Maurice regularly admitted in correspondence to an incomprehension of a world that increasingly marginalized him
and what he thought important. Such disrespect might have been expected
from the enemies, who more and more dominated university life, but there
was real sadness in the realization that students, too, were now inclined to
join in the work of demolition. Bowra had always encouraged the young
to be critical and satirical. His Oxford had always laughed at the expense of
establishment figures. In the 1950s, he found undergraduates 'much nicer
to each other than my generation ever was, more careful and provident,
and much more occupied with the future ... the boys are very kind to me
and have no respect at all, which is as it should be'.[56] Until the 1960s, it
never occurred to him that students would attack the University itself, the
very forum in which they were encouraged to speak freely. Now, in his
last years, he had to account for the spectacle of undergraduates burning
books. To discover treason among the young was almost insupportable.

Every instinct in Bowra led him to try to understand, and even excuse.
The notorious anti-establishment figure of the 1920s remained true to his
libertarian values to the end, but he was sorely tested. Over and over again,
he reminded himself that rules were only systems of last resort: 'Of course
some rules are necessary for any community of young people living in close
proximity to one another, but it is too easy to be too ingenious in devising
rules for almost every emergency, and this the colleges did, only to find that
most of them were broken.'[57] For most of his Oxford career, he had sided
with the young when they protested about the impositions of their elders.
When undergraduates had wished to march in support of the Campaign
for Nuclear Disarmament, it had been absurd for the University to try to
stop them.[58] All too often, unrest among students was provoked by idiotic
decisions taken by older people who should have known better.[59] To give
junior members a measure of representation on university committees was
only common sense, and could only be opposed by John Sparrow and
some backwoodsmen from Merton, 'who convey the impression that their
college is like Paraguay under the Jesuits'.[60] Maurice had always held that
to attempt to interfere with the public or private lives of undergraduates
unduly, except to offer help when they stumbled, was always unseemly and
often made the old look ridiculous.

These liberal formulas were severely tested in the 1960s. Berta Ruck's
hope that, in his last years, Maurice would not be 'too worried by protesting
students and their noise',[61] was unlikely to be realized. In Bowra's view,

too many young people now had no sense of humour, no appreciation of basic hygiene, washing themselves instead in self-pity. He explained that they were

> very touchy and can't bear any criticism of themselves, from their lack of prose style to their lack of hair cuts ... Also they don't wash behind their ears, which I was taught to do by my nanny at the age of three. However, when asked out, they clean themselves up and look quite presentable. The classical scholars are still the best, but they are being rapidly exterminated like the Fuegans or the Great Auk.[62]

John Sparrow's obsessive denunciation of young men who wore their hair long made 'an odd impression on those who do not know him well',[63] but Maurice himself was alarmed to find himself in the company of students who 'give the impression of having lice in their hair'.[64] Assuring one Wadham man that he had no wish 'to butt into your private affairs, and this is plainly one of them', he went on delicately to suggest that the temporary removal of a beard might improve his pupil's chances in an interview.[65] Unkempt hair and clothes must have recalled memories of the trenches. It was simply bewildering that the young should, of their own volition, recreate such conditions.

In addition, undergraduates now complained about everything. They denounced all 'interference with their private lives. As they have no private lives, this is paradoxical of them. Nor does it prevent them howling for help when they are in trouble'.[66] They were 'a neurotic lot', who saw no incongruity in abusing their parents while recruiting them in campaigns against the College: 'They now bring their parents up to complain that the rooms of their offspring are too damp, too dark, too small, too big, and not sufficiently equipped with creative works of art. No wonder the boys rush off to the loony bin.'[67] Oddest of all, 'some of the young do not like being at the university. I find this hard to imagine, but there it is, and of course they are right to think that they have been sold a pup by having to live in our present world.'[68] Too many had a positive contempt for learning, as Bowra understood it. Argument gave way to threats of violence. Maurice worried that 'the riot-habit' might spread to Oxford. If it did, he had decided 'to fall down dead if they try it here, and that would scare them off'.[69] All in all, 'the whole business of student power is so boring'[70] that it made him 'pine for my retirement'.[71] Sadly, having championed the young all his life, he now confessed to friends that 'I just can't understand them.'[72]

At nineteen, Bowra had found himself mired in the stinking mud of the Great War's battlefields. Against this experience, the behaviour of young men and women of the same age in the 1960s could only look ungrateful. They complained of neglect and of too much supervision at the same time. Never having known want or danger, they cheerfully attacked the very institutions that guaranteed their freedoms and comforts. As Maurice explained to a friend,

> As yet we have not had any awful outbursts here. The 'students', as undergraduates are now called, rumble and fizz and sizzle, but have not yet become murderous. I have no doubt they will. We give them everything they want, and then they ask for more. It all comes from not suffering enough in youth. No boarding schools for them and no army. They don't know how lucky they are, and that makes them sorry for themselves. I also suspect that they are undersexed (a well known English fault); hence their inability to live without girls. How can I live without you? How can I let you go?, as Tosti used to sing to Queen Victoria. Most of them are perfectly polite and agreeable, but think it wrong to stop the lunatics from doing what they like.[73]

It was little consolation to be told that, elsewhere, the situation was worse.[74] He found it more warming to hail Evelyn Waugh's recreations of the 1920s, and to hope that some colour might return to Oxford's skies. As 'the cycle' came round, perhaps 'the old Adam' might once again be visible.[75]

It was merely a matter of time before his Edwardian values would be required to confront the new world head-on. In November 1968, a Wadham man wrote an article for an undergraduate newspaper, abusing All Souls in language which many of that College's inmates thought libellous. Among the more temperate remarks about 'Arse Ole College' was the description of Max Beloff as 'a grizzled oaf' and of Warden Sparrow 'as a prince of a sweetie'. No one in All Souls saw the joke. Both Sparrow and Beloff bombarded Bowra with demands that he should be 'firm' in the defence of 'decent standards of civilized life', and that he should expel the author of the article from Wadham forthwith.[76] These letters put Bowra into a quandary. On the one hand, he loathed the vulgarity and tastelessness of the attack on senior members of the University, but, on the other hand, he could 'not bear to persecute' an undergraduate for expressing opinions.[77] Every libertarian instinct was against the idea. The student's behaviour had nothing to recommend it, but Warden Sparrow was overreacting. Tactfully, he reminded him that his own youth had not been without blemishes, and positively refused to agree to the Wadham man being 'castrated' to relieve elderly irritation.[78] At the same time, the undergraduate in question was left in no doubt about the Warden's opinion of his behaviour, and was lectured on the virtues of the apology.[79]

This episode is instructive. When undergraduates attacked Oxford's institutions in the language of the gutter, they came to personify everything that he feared. Cleverness, wit, and sensitivity were overwhelmed by the violence of mobs literally hammering on college doors. Yet, even under such severe provocation, Bowra's liberalism held. The anti-establishment figure of the 1920s and 1930s was 'not going to betray them and their rights to the bien pensants'. He would ask, 'Have the undergraduates a right to do this? And if they have, why should they be stopped from doing so?'[80] Of course, taking a liberal line was made easier by the fact that the target for so much abuse was All Souls. For years, Maurice himself had criticized that College for indulging in high living and low productivity. In May 1966, he had gone public with his views in, of all places, the *Daily Mail*.[81] It was 'no place for a young man of intelligence and humanity. All the younger fellows seem to have married mid-European psycho-analysts ten years older than themselves, and this suggests that there is something wrong.'[82] In these circumstances, defending his man against Warden Sparrow was hardly painful. Even so, undergraduates had become students, debate had degenerated into threats of violence, and wit had been debased into vulgarity. Just before he retired, a storm brought down an ancient tree in the Warden's garden. For Bowra, this event was portentous. It was awful, not only because 'it makes Mansfield visible', but also because it seemed to be an omen of darker things to come.[83] When Wadham offered him a party to celebrate his seventieth birthday, he insisted that the dress code should be black tie, in order to 'annoy the milk-in-first boys and their wives'.[84]

As his university system was increasingly attacked by forces whose provenance he did not understand and whose values he suspected, it was peculiarly hard for Maurice to bear the loss of friends and allies. To watch death obliterating long-term associations was an inevitable consequence of growing older, but it was an uncomfortable experience none the less. Expressing apologies for not attending Cyril Connolly's sixtieth birthday celebrations, Bowra hoped that his friend had 'enjoyed it' and had seen

> some old friends—alas, they shrink in number every year. I rather hate large gatherings and develop suicidal tendencies towards midnight... It was no fun

being sixty—I find that my memory is not what it was and my brain addles even more easily than before. Don't give up sex whatever you do. Once you knock off, you are done.[85]

First to go was the generation of his tutors, people like Warden Smith of New College, who, back in the 1920s, had rescued the young Bowra from Joseph's clutches, and given him some clue about Oxford's purpose. Writing obituary notices became something of a speciality for Bowra, and his account of Smith's life was heartfelt. Smith had believed that

> undergraduates might indeed be tiresome, but still had, in his view, the right to live their own lives as long as they let others do the same. His belief in liberty and his refusal to allow victims to be sacrificed to conformity, self-righteousness, or hysteria arose from this central outlook...It is something beyond all reasonable price, and we shall be guilty of an unforgivable treachery if we ever neglect or forget it.[86]

Unfortunately, the generation that had held these views was passing away.

Then it was the turn of his own generation to step up to the plank. Shortly before her own death in 1964, Edith Sitwell received a letter from Maurice bewailing the passing of mutual friends, and claiming that he now 'drugged' himself 'with my own work'.[87] Even the death of a sparring partner, like Evelyn Waugh, was grim. Of course, there was still a joke to be made. He told Dadie Rylands that 'Evelyn's death was a blow...slipped off neatly after Mass on Easter Day, being anointed and all, and is now happily ensconced in Abraham's bosom, watching with much satisfaction the torments of the damned.'[88] But the sense of loss was real: 'I miss the old boy very much...I never thought him a *nice* man, but he was wonderfully generous and amusing and faithful.'[89] With these experiences in mind Bowra began to admire those who confronted death on their own terms, rather than waiting for the grim reaper to make all the running. When his old rival in the classical world, Eduard Fraenkel, committed suicide four hours after his wife's death, Bowra hailed his action as 'in the High Roman fashion', and thought that he had been 'lucky to have the pills and the right amount of them'.[90] No man had relied more on a support system of friends than Maurice, and now every year cut their number.

Evidence of his own mortality was become all too evident. He began to announce that 'the Bowars [*sic*] are dying out. I am the last male Bowra, and after that only girls. I am inclined to think this is a good thing.'[91] He half-seriously suggested that, if he had had a son, he would only have produced 'someone like Basil Murray'.⁹² In the late 1950s, he was despatched to a nursing home to be nursed through a bout of influenza. A bachelor, with no family to care for him, had no choice in the matter. But it was an unpleasant foretaste of what was to come: 'To parody a great man—Ah the sweat and the stink and the expense. All that washing of one's arse by elderly nurses and those bed pans ... Not again for me. Better a quiet ending and a good end to the long, cloudy day.'⁹³ When an elderly don collapsed in the street, Maurice rather envied his clean break with life: 'Dear Dawkins died very nicely in front of this college. He fell down in the street and was off to eternity ... A nice end, and may I have one like it.'⁹⁴

In his last years, letters to Evelyn Waugh take on the character of a medical inventory. In October 1965, he wrote that he was 'sorry about your failing health'.

> Mine, you will be relieved to hear, has taken a sharp turn for the worse in the last year. Kidneys and lungs cause trouble; deafness increases at an alarming rate. I find a multitone aid no use except in tête-à-tête conversation. My teeth are not my own, but the front barrier of them is genuine, though full of holes and fillings. I can still bite a bit now and then. Like you, I find old age horrible, and wish that I had died six years ago.⁹⁵

Three months later, he reported 'a hideous pain in the knee, the resurgence of an ancient woe ... Mrs Betjeman has had a serious car-accident, with a broken rib. She was, it seems, very near death. Too awful to think of it. But I wouldn't mind it happening to me.'⁹⁶ In 1967, mumps was added to the list.⁹⁷ These disabilities made his company less attractive to the hostesses who had traditionally filled his vacations with company and pleasure. Ann Fleming was not the only one to find 'You Know Who' becoming a heavier responsibility.⁹⁸ Giving up smoking improved his general sense of well being, but not his capacity for work.⁹⁹

Worst of all, he was becoming deaf. The problem started to be noticed in the autumn of 1965, and was initially dismissed as catarrh.¹⁰⁰ This diagnosis could not be held for long. Possibly a legacy from hearing the bombardments of the Great War, he was increasingly threatened with a world of silence. As he expressed the situation to Noel Annan, 'The term has lasted a thousand years. I am going deaf and blind, and losing my memory. It is time I became a bishop.'¹⁰¹ Joking apart, hardly any affliction could have been more terrible for someone whose whole life had been passed in the manipulation of words. Maurice's response to the

situation was to talk even more than usual, and to talk louder. John Sparrow
had to complain that, by force of circumstances, his friend had given up
listening.[102] As the Warden talked in self-defence, the consequences for his
academic and social life were severe. He gave up attendance at meetings
of the British Academy, because 'I can't hear what they say, and it drives
me frenzied.'[103] Invitations to speak and lecture had to be declined because
his 'increasing deafness makes it impossible for me to take part in any
discussion, and this is embarrassing to everybody, including myself'.[104] It
was no longer comfortable for a great conversationalist to face an audience.

Sadder still, friends were finding it harder to cope. Guiltily, they admitted
the fact. In August 1969, Isaiah Berlin confessed to Sylvester Gates:

> Our summer has, I regret to tell you, been positively *made* by the absence
> of the Old Boy: I mean our old friend, you know who (I daren't say his
> name: but you won't leave this letter about? He may call to visit, gaga as
> he is, and he sees and hears what one does not wish him to): every day this
> freedom, this marvellous freedom from the pathetic, oppressive, demanding,
> guilt-inducing, conversation-killing, embarrassing, gross, maddening, at once
> touching and violently repellent, paranoid, deaf, blind, thick-skinned, easily
> offended, presence is a source of relief and almost joy: how disloyal: how
> awful.[105]

Increasing illness exposed the limitations of how Maurice had constructed
his friendships. Many of those, to whom he had accorded the title of friend,
found it hard to undertake the duty of care. It was wearing to hear Maurice
talk more and more as he feared not hearing the words of others.

The onset of illness and the death of friends came at a difficult moment.
Retirement loomed. In theory, Maurice would be required to leave the
Warden's Lodgings in 1968, on his seventieth birthday. In fact, as an act
of kindness, the College allowed him to stay for two more years, but
he could only regard this extension as a stay of execution. The thought
of leaving the Lodgings filled him with a kind of panic. Since 1922,
he had lived in Wadham. Every meal had been provided, and college
servants had always been on hand. On becoming Warden in 1938, he had
employed his own staff, often a married couple, and freely admitted that
he could not 'live without them'.[106] Accounts of problems with servants
punctuate his correspondence. A Hungarian couple were delightful, but
'he is handsome and melancholy and will never learn English, so we
unterhalten auf Deutsch'.[107] They were followed by Transylvanians whose

honesty he doubted, but their appearance was welcome as he could not 'live without servants, as my old-fashioned engine is geared to them'.[108] In the 1960s, domestic help was becoming harder to find. He complained to Cyril Connolly that 'at our age we are tied to servants, and they get harder and harder to get... Alas, for the happy days of Peking in my youth.'[109] On leaving the Lodgings, he discovered that every cup and glass had been smashed.[110] Coping with the practicalities of day-to-day life was wearing. He told Dadie Rylands that the only good thing about retirement was that he would no longer have 'to run a household, and... I shall think anything bliss by comparison'.[111]

Difficulties with servants simply exposed the vulnerability of an Edwardian bachelor in the 1960s. Never having mastered the art of driving a car, he had to rely on one of his helpers to supply the deficiency. Otherwise, the world looked a little threatening. Late in the decade, he arrived at Paddington on New Year's Eve to discover that 'the British Railways ceased to function, and I travelled for hours in a freezing train, to find no taxis at the station, when, out of the darkness, my man appeared, suspecting that I might need help. I nearly burst into tears on seeing him.'[112] By contrast, on another occasion, he returned to Oxford from Cambridge on 'a non-stop train at 8.50, and spent a happy hour on Paddington platform reading, and then was met here by my cook in her car. Such is a well-ordered life.'[113] Unfortunately, such Edwardian moments were becoming increasingly difficult to rediscover.

Such incidents explain the sympathy which Bowra always felt for people who had been brutally required by circumstance to adapt from one way of living to something more constrained. Among such people might be counted the great classicist Wilamowitz, whom Maurice believed to have been 'gestört' by the loss of property in the Great War, and the fading Irish gentry that he had known in the 1920s.[114] The predicament was made worse by the understandable inability of most people in the 1960s to see his point. When he expressed nervousness about whether his new quarters had ceilings that would take the weight of chandeliers, or whether there would be bookshelves enough to accommodate a large personal library, it was easy to dismiss these concerns as old-fashioned. But they were very real fears to him. Retirement would bring on 'the evil hour of moving house and living in poverty', but 'with luck my rest in the Lord may come before'.[115] He began to give his address as 'Reduced Circumstances, Oxford'.[116] Altogether, the change in living 'was a great bore'.[117]

Maurice had begun to worry about retirement as early as 1961, so great was the menace that it presented. In that year, he asked the College to build him a house in its grounds, in return for a substantial benefaction. The Bursar had to report that such a project was not possible, but that 'we should look into the possibility of finding other accommodation which would meet your requirements'.[118] This formula proved to be too vague for the Warden's purposes, and he determined to buy a house in North Oxford's Belbroughton Road. But he never really believed that this property could be the solution. It would be 'Hell'. There would be 'no privacy or comfort, and no room for my books'.[119] Discussing the house with John Walsh, Maurice exclaimed, 'Hate it! Hate it! Of course, I'll never live there. If I did, I'd die like a rat in a trap'.[120] Realistically, he had no choice but to accept whatever Wadham could allow him. In October 1968, a deal was struck. The North Oxford house would pass to the College in return for a set of rooms in one of its quadrangles.[121] These were likely to be rather 'modernismo',[122] but Bowra's sense of gratitude for Wadham's generosity was deep. As he reported to an American friend, 'My College has nobly offered to give me rooms and service when I retire in 1970. It is a great relief. I hate looking for servants and can't live without them. Also, I like a little life around me. It is noble of them, as nobody wants a ghost, however substantial, hanging round the place after his demise.'[123]

Retirement, when it came, was eased by the fact that Stuart Hampshire was elected as his successor. He and his wife might be 'Babes in the Wood' but at least they were old friends. The new Warden was a Bowrista by upbringing and inclination. His wife, Renée, was delightfully innocent and well meaning. It was a clear victory 'for the Immoral Front, whose members have greeted it with cheers'. Of course, co-education would now be introduced into Wadham; there would probably be a crèche for the Fellows' children; quite likely, the Lodgings would see 'pill clinics' in its 'disused kitchen' and evenings for 'Black Moslems' in its drawing room. But Maurice affected not to be too troubled about any of these possibilities. The crucial point was that, like him, the Hampshires 'will be very good with the boys', and were 'academically sound as well as distinguished'. Nothing else really mattered. Bowra made 'a stern resolve not to interfere', and, surprisingly, did just that. Looking at the new order in Wadham, he admitted that he always felt that his 'life would have been happier if I had known any girls in my youth'.[124]

He moved into his new quarters in the summer of 1970. There were four rooms in a modern, but quiet, courtyard. To friends, he put a brave face on things:

> I hope you have survived the winter so far and will also survive what the poet Blok calls 'the cold and the darkness of the coming days'. I view the prospect without love. However, my Reduced Circumstances are a great success. Quiet. Quite big enough, especially as I have a cellar next door for spare books etc. Good young man brings me breakfast, and my old char comes three times a week, keeps the place clean and washes my clothes.[125]

He looked forward 'to a quiet old age'.[126] Anything was 'better than starving in North Oxford'.[127] But, at other times, the upper lip was not quite so stiff. The new quarters were described as 'the little white bungalow over the way',[128] or as a 'mixture of a dog-kennel and an aquarium. I look forward to floating around behind a large window.'[129] There would be an honest attempt to accommodate the necessary changes, but no one could underestimate the effort required.

Living behind glass in a modern building, however, was not the greatest of his difficulties. Much worse was a growing feeling of isolation. Deafness had began the process, and the move to new accommodation seemed to have completed the business of cutting him off from human contact. Visitors seemed unable or unwilling to seek him out. This idea was almost certainly too melodramatic, but it genuinely alarmed the old man. Missing a visitor hurt badly.[130] Conversation had become a shouting match. One month before he died, Maurice was visited by Julian Mitchell, who recorded the occasion:

> I went to see Bowra, in a new lead quad, deaf, sits one down and talks *at* one: a) his finances b) his health and work—his opening words, in reply to 'How are you?'—'Dying, of course—dying,' c) how his food was arranged, staff etc. Then gossip about Connolly and Waugh and the Eastbourne set and Robert Lowell's new girl and so on, and fortissimo indiscretions about Stuart Hampshire and college politics. 'Jews are very fond of him,' he boomed. We ended yelling about the fellows. He really ought to be fitted with a silencer. Seems very bored: I expect he is. Up to date with everything, though. I felt rather exhausted by him … Bowra said, when I said Daddy was ill, 'It takes up a tremendous lot of time, someone dying.'[131]

Mitchell then came away, carrying, as a gift, eleven first editions of novels by Henry James. Maurice lived in his new flat for just under a year. By the standards of the day, he had been most generously treated by Wadham, but, for a man of his generation and experience, it was all the most terrible anti-climax.

Maurice died suddenly on 2 July 1971. He had suffered a massive heart attack, and this was exactly what he had hoped for. Of course, death was a fearsome thing, and 'most men shrank from asking what death really means, and to think of it too precisely is to feel the reason unseated... the very essence of its terror... is precisely that it cannot be understood or imagined, and therefore cannot be faced'.[132] But, in Maurice's view, 'death is all right but not to be bed-ridden and gaga for years'.[133] What terrified him was the idea that he might witness the slow disintegration of his mental and physical powers, even becoming helpless. For six months before his death, he seemed to be aware that this process was under way.

> I have been enjoying some rare and interesting complaints. First hideous pains in the legs, which meant rather a jolly week in a Nursing Homer [sic], doing nothing at all but recover from being woken at dawn and kept waiting for hours for breakfast... Now I have a strange mixture of heart and breath—a bad day or so, and I have to stay in and do nothing.[134]

To prescribe inactivity was, however, an impossibility. On the day before he died, he had attended a wedding and then gone out for dinner. At the latter function, he was 'in cracking form', loudly proclaiming that he hated weddings and much preferred funerals. He went so far as to suggest that he would like black horses with plumes to draw him away on his last journey.[135]

The funeral, a few days later, of course took place in Wadham Chapel. All the Bowristas came, and so too did surviving members of the Bowra family. At the last, the two worlds of Maurice's youth were brought together. John Betjeman described the scene for the benefit of Kenneth Clark:

> We walked in burning heat to Wadham Chapel, and there was the coffin in the full chapel, and on it pink sprays of flowers. Except for some Bowra ladies we never met, all was Wadham. The service was bleakly C of E as Maurice would wish... He had a lively hope of personal survival and of the next life. 'Much looking forward to it'... All this knowledge of him made his funeral not depressing but remote. Maurice is is [sic] quite all right... Faith Hope and Charity—for the saint, he said, such as yours truly, the greatest of these is Hope... He had a lot more of Christ in him than most.[136]

The eulogy was given by Isaiah Berlin, who gave a heavily bowdlerized version of his friend's life, taking refuge in conventional pieties. As he confessed to John Dancy, 'fortunately, you see, on these occasions, while it is necessary to speak the truth and nothing but the truth, it is not necessary to speak the whole truth'.[137] Hugh Trevor-Roper had reason to regret missing the funeral, 'partly for love of Maurice, partly to hear your éloge'.[138] After the service, Maurice was laid to rest among the Oxford worthies already asleep in St Cross churchyard.

What struck the mourners most sharply was how firm a line the death of Bowra had drawn through the Oxford experience. The phrase 'end of an era' came easily to the lips. For Julian Mitchell, Maurice had been 'a living refutation of time'.[139] Lord David Cecil was more explicit to Isaiah Berlin:

> As you know well, my relations with Maurice were not the closest nor, at one time, the easiest. But I found myself thinking about his death often and sadly. I realise it was he, more than anyone, who was the central figure of the Oxford of my youth—he gave the tone, he struck the note ... That phase of life—of Oxford's life—is really over now and its particular vein of stylish intellectual gaiety, its mixture of impishness and genuine classic standards is gone.[140]

Berlin himself agreed: 'the whole era is over ... the combination of genuine admiration for masterpieces of all times and places with equally genuine high spirits, appetite for life in all its manifestations—that doesn't seem to me particularly prevalent at present, either in England or anywhere else.'[141] At Bowra's death, his disciples were brought sharply to the realization of just how much their leader had been of his time, with values now displaced. A New College contemporary observed that 'the young men of today are interested in Marcuse, Lucacs and the detestable Sartre. How far on this stage will Maurice's influence go on being felt? Maybe. I wish it would. But I entertain a doubt.'[142]

Bowra died a comparatively wealthy man, leaving, after the payment of estate duty, in excess of one hundred and thirteen thousand pounds. His will, only two pages long, was witnessed not by friends, but by a Bursar's clerk and a student. Apart from tiny bequests in money and books, everything went to Wadham.[143] It is the last document of a man who had lived a whole life behind the walls of institutions. He had never had the support of a family, either in childhood or later, and the stress had been considerable. When congratulating Evelyn Waugh on the success of *The Ordeal of Gilbert Pinfold*, in which he had honestly chronicled a catastrophic breakdown, Maurice, only half-jokingly, admitted his own fears: 'I see all the symptoms in myself—addiction to sleeping tablets, indulgences in alcohol, failing memory, persecution mania, horror of the BBC...What will happen to me? I have no wife to look after me. I have no sensible doctor...My fear is that I shall give in to the Voices.'[144] Solitude had always been difficult to bear. In old age, it became insupportable. In such moments, he felt that, for all his success, his emotional life had been impoverished. Love was 'a hard business', and, though he had 'felt it eg with Joan and Annie', and though it made a person 'nicer and cleverer', he had never himself been given enough: 'life without it is a terrible, impoverished affair, and the older one gets, the worse it is. I find myself drying up, without lust or rage to sting me on.'[145] It was all too obvious that the Greeks and the poets were dead, and that he lived on in a modern world, which gloried in brutalism. Thanking John Betjeman for a postcard showing a great cemetery in Rome, Bowra added, 'How I would like to be buried in this cemetery...But no doubt by then cremation will be compulsory, and my ashes will be scattered over a housing estate.'[146] In the end, he did better than that.

13

Heaven or Hell

At the age of eight, Maurice Bowra made a pact with the Almighty. A pet cat had gone astray. If the Almighty condescended to return the animal, the boy promised to be a believer evermore. In the event, the cat duly reappeared, but it had been poisoned and died within a few days. As a result of this experience, Maurice began 'to form a distrustful picture of the universe'.[1] He learnt, at an early age, that the gods toyed with humankind, juggling their fates and destinies with unblinking callousness. When he later discovered that some Greeks held the same view, he could hardly have been surprised. The mystery could never be sorted out. Ambiguity was everywhere. Bowra's father had been a freethinker, proudly proclaiming himself a pupil of T. H. Huxley and his friends, who had given the late Victorian Church such a drubbing.[2] Yet the diary of Edward Bowra records a regular pattern of family churchgoing. Similarly, no issue divided Maurice's friends more. Some, like John Betjeman, always insisted that the Warden had had a lively belief in an afterlife; others were adamant that he had none whatever. It was a confusion that almost certainly reflected the true state of Bowra's mind.

In this, as in much else, he was a Greek. Athenians and Spartans had worshipped the gods, but Zeus and his compatriots had been very human in their behaviour. Driven by lust, jealousy, pride, and kindness, they had inflicted good and bad fortune on mere mortals, as whim and circumstance dictated. Equally, some men, like Achilles, were half-god, half-man, and could aspire to a spiritual consanguinity with the immortals. The ambiguity was puzzling and, confronted by it, the Greeks came up with the only possible answer. As Maurice put it, 'The unique splendour of the Greeks is that, with all their sense of the divine qualities in man and of his closeness to the gods, they knew that he was not and could not be a god, and they were content and proud that he should find his own magnificence, and be ready to live and to die for it.'³ The question of whether God existed would always be of interest. There was the hope that He would be decently Anglican. In the meantime, life had to be lived without reference to anything beyond man himself.

It would be easy to cast Bowra in an exclusively humanist light. Describing himself as 'one of those who live in darkness' to Evelyn Waugh, he went on to congratulate the novelist on his depiction, in *Helena*, of the ghastliness of much ancient religion:

> Your idea of the fourth century cannot be very far from the mark. They were all in a fearful muddle and fear, and the Gnostics were just as silly as you make them. The Mithraists were, I suspect, rather more awful than you suggest—very provincial and Masonic and low-class regimental. I have never been able to understand Constantine, but your picture of him is quite charming. He was, after all, mainly a general, and that makes anything possible.⁴

Arguably, the conventional piety taken on in Putney and Cheltenham evaporated in the stink of the trenches in the Great War. A friend at New College remembered that: 'Like a good many who have returned from the war, he is not much given to attendance at Chapel.'⁵ Alick Smith chose to turn a blind eye to Bowra's delinquency.⁶ As Dean of Wadham, Bowra himself abolished all compulsory attendance at religious services.⁷ No clergymen were to be found among the Bowristas, and clerical sensibilities were not accommodated in the Lodgings. His 'first step' as Vice-Chancellor was to ensure that visiting preachers would be found board and lodging in other colleges.⁸

Revealed religion was a matter for jesting. Some of his most scurrilous verse was reserved for the mocking of belief. Amusing excursions into blasphemy were a speciality. In the poem 'Marcus Niebuhr Tod', an Oxford classicist discovers the alternative Ten Commandments, sculpted onto a cliff in Sinai:

> Go, worship other gods than me,
> I feel the need of company.
>
> And copy bird or beast or fish
> In wood or stone, if that's your wish.
>
> Rightly or wrongly, take my name:
> To me it's very much the same.

If toil on weekdays you must shirk,
Then keep the Sabbath for your work.

If what you want's a good long life,
With parents keep continual strife.

Kill anyone who worries you:
It's easier and safer too.

And if your neighbour's wife is free,
Of course commit adultery.

If others have what you have not,
Why not take steps to steal the lot?

False evidence against a friend
Brings much advantage in the end.

If someone has what takes your eye
Ask, and you'll get it by and by.[9]

In 'Confirmation Songs', satire and sexual innuendo mix freely:

The Bishop, while the organ plays
Dispenses grace divine
On lips God made for other ways
Of taking bread and wine.[10]

In charades, Bowra excelled in the role of God expelling Adam and Eve from the Garden of Eden.[11] There was a story in Wadham which alleged that he once bit a colonial bishop in the calf for having bored the company too long. For Bowra, formal religion was always a target.

For some reason, priests and their religions kept trying to intrude themselves into private life. Too many Protestants objected to drink; too many Catholics objected to sex; too many Christians objected to both. Their influence clearly had to be resisted. Equally, he was dismissive of Anglican 'pfaffen' if they set out to be 'beastly'.[12] All priests seemed to have a touch of the theatrical self-righteousness that had made Thomas Becket such a nuisance; 'I never liked him very much … Rather too much like the late Archbishop Lang.'[13] In the company of religious friends, like the Pakenhams, he affected to fear the possibility that they would suddenly 'fall down in a religious ecstasy'.[14] Queen's University, Belfast, was deserving of the highest praise for maintaining a sane neutrality amid the 'brutality and barbarism' of Ireland's combative religions.[15]

In Maurice's view, there was simply no getting away from the fact that religions had always shown themselves to be intolerant and persecuting. To claim a monopoly of truth inevitably led to the suppression of rivals. As he put it to Colette Clark,

> I have been reading a very sad book about Cape Horn. There used to be nice savages there, who wore no clothes at all, and lived by catching fish as they bathed in the icy sea. Then Darwin came along and was deeply shocked. The result—missionaries, who made them wear clothes, and they all died of pneumonia, taking their fantastic language, with no abstract words, with them to the grave. Two nice ones came to England for a year, and were sent back to convert their brothers, but sensibly became as native as could be, and the son of one killed a missionary with a stone. How hard it is to do good to anyone.[16]

To exterminate in the name of morality would always be comforting to some. By contrast, while visiting the monastery at Qumran, Bowra, looking at 'all those sheep and goats muddled together',[17] expressed the wish that religion could be just a little more inclusive. He knew, however, that this could only be described as pious hope.

Inevitably, therefore, any of his friends who took to religion could expect a merciless teasing. The Betjeman family, in particular, provided a great deal of innocent, and not so innocent, amusement. John seemed able to run a commitment to High Church Anglicanism and serial adultery in tandem. At the same time, Penelope Betjeman's religious odyssey meandered very agreeably. When an Anglican, she battled with the harmonium in her village church, until the vicar begged her to stop. Apparently, 'the discord between the harmonium and the congregation' was 'becoming destructive to devotion'.[18] She, in turn, blamed her husband, 'who would stand at my side to pull out the stops as the fancy took him'.[19] After converting to Rome, she would be invited to parties in Wadham on the assumption that she was 'not taking a seminar on the Seven Last Things'.[20] When Rome itself could not totally satisfy, she went on tours of India, looking for spiritual nourishment. According to Maurice, 'having totally demoralised my Institute in Teheran ... she has moved on to her old stomping-grounds in India, where she has attended an oriental Conference, and is back to the Guptas and Mohejodoro (spelling not guaranteed). She has now got dysentery and piles, but says that it is worth it.'[21] When the Betjemans' son, Paul, became a Mormon, Bowra could only see it as divine intervention: 'Excellent, excellent, Paul a Mormon, a Mormon. It combines the religious fervour of the mother and the polygamous tendencies of the father.'[22] At its best, religion could make people look ridiculous.

The problem with organized religion went deeper than harmoniums with a mind of their own, however. Too much of it could unhinge the brain. A Wadham man who had been allotted C. S. Lewis as a tutor was assured by the Warden that he was about to be taught by someone who was 'insane'.[23] The evangelicalism associated with the Buchmanite movement of the late 1920s filled Bowra with gloom. Associating with it destroyed the Bowrista potential in young men like John Maud, who went off into worthy careers in public life:

> Maud failed to get the BBC, because he was said to be a Buchmanite. A great victory, but as Sir K has rightly said, you cannot keep a second-rate man down. We wonder if he will move with Woolton to a wider sphere of uselessness. He has resigned from Troutbeck [Birkbeck] College; so he has evidently heard voices calling him.[24]

Even after two World Wars, Oxford undergraduates still sometimes searched for a loving God. To Maurice, this piety was incomprehensible and a waste.

> The boys here seems [sic] to be sadly given to it, and I feel more and more like a Regency rip surviving into the pure days of the Prince Consort. It is all very odd. They know nothing at all about it, and put on a condescending look if one ventures any doubts. It comes from having no good avant-garde literature. When I was young, we had 'Blast' and the Vorticists and Dada to keep us clean. Much better than fussing about the validity of Anglican orders.[25]

Formal subscription to an established religion was no final bar on entry into Bowra's court, but it required explanation and a formal dispensation from Maurice himself.

Worst of all was to succumb to the temptation of conversion. In particular, travelling to Rome was almost unforgivable. Bowra could never understand how so many of his acquaintances were impelled to take this road. It was saddening that Rome should become 'a haven for those who feel a natural aversion to thought'.[26] Oxford seemed to be full of Jesuits trying to ensnare the unwary. At Urquhart's Chalet in the Alps, a priest was usually in attendance, offering spiritual direction, between long walks and meaningful suppers, to people like Richard Crossman.[27] Some potential Bowristas were lost forever. In the middle 1920s, Billy Clonmore became involved with a man who was 'the real snake in Billy's grass'.

They talked about copes, albs and birettas...But for him, Billy would not dream of becoming a priest. At present there are only two solutions 1) Get Billy in with the Dublin high-brows and get him to do his good works in Ireland...or 2) let Billy become a Papist and rely on his laziness and incompetence preventing him becoming a priest.[28]

When Frank Pakenham swapped the Church of England for Roman Catholicism, Maurice was sincerely puzzled. It seemed to be an action unfair to Anglicanism and unfair to Pakenham.[29]

Most worrying of all was the rumour that Gilbert Murray, Maurice's mentor in everything Greek, had converted to Rome on his deathbed. If the story was true, Bowra could only regard his decision as an apostasy: 'We are much disturbed by the story, spread assiduously by his daughter, that Gilbert Murray made a death-bed repentance, and was received back into the arms of Rome. Alas, it may be true. He was a bit gaga, and he always liked to let down his own side. May it not happen to us.'[30] His character had always been ambiguous as a 'prudish' man who hugely enjoyed Aristophanes. Then again, he had deliberately married a woman full of principles whose aim in life was 'to boss and control'. But, on the other hand, he had been 'a poet manqué', with 'irony, humour' and the capacity for 'delicious nonsense'.[31] It was terrible that such a man should have surrendered at the last. Murray had always enjoyed retailing the story that his house on Boar's Hill was flanked, on one side, by an asylum and, on the other, by a Catholic community. If any Murray 'develops either trouble, he only had to cross the hedge'.[32] Bowra feared that the man he had admired more than any other in Greek studies had taken advantage of this convenient geography.

So pronounced were Bowra's views on this point that a knowledge of his disapproval was enough to prevent some of his friends taking the step. Cyril Connolly assured Winston Churchill that 'his greatest safeguard against conversion is the fact that, if he joined the Church of Rome, he could never look Maurice Bowra in the face again'.[33] Even committing to a fashionable High Church Anglicanism was not acceptable. Billa Harrod's defence was that she went to a clergyman, 'who is well known for his lightness of penalties in dealing with Pansies', and who offered her similar terms.[34] Worst of all was Evelyn Waugh's conversion to Rome. In Maurice's view, the novelist had 'been done in by a happy marriage (she is a water-colour girl who farms and bears quantities of children) and by the Catholic Church which he takes with a Calvinist seriousness'.[35] *Brideshead Revisited*

was a masterpiece, but 'a masterpiece of Papist propaganda'.[36] There was
something absurd about Waugh's behaviour, for he was 'the least Christian
person' Maurice had ever met.[37] He wrote well when he wrote out of hate.
His attempts to write out of love were simply 'too much'.[38] For Waugh to
call *Helena* the best book he had ever written was 'going over the top'.[39]

Before Waugh took to religion, the two men had been close. According
to Roy Harrod, Waugh 'at one time ... was seeing a great deal of Maurice'.

> That was before he became a Catholic. When his first wife left him he came
> and stayed with Maurice, who took infinite trouble to piece together his
> shattered world for him. I remember thinking at the time what a marvellous
> friend for Evelyn to have. Evelyn was of course a far greater writer than
> Maurice and had his own highly original wit. But I shouldn't be surprised
> if you went through his first two books (novels, I mean) with a fine
> comb, ... you might find a Maurice turn of phrase here or there.[40]

But Waugh's conversion changed everything, and the two men became
'estranged'. It was 'a pretty long interval before the friendship was revivified
when ... EW asked MB for guidance about books ... on the Crusades, and
MB kept sending him volumes of the Oxford History of England—Stuart
and Whig periods—an expensive sort of joke.'[41] Yet this was exactly the
right way to tease a man whom Bowra saw wasting great talent on religion.

So many stories and comments running in the same vein might lead to the
conclusion that Bowra's mind did indeed run along exclusively humanist
lines. But, at other times and in other contexts, ambiguity crept in. He
warned the atheistical J. B. S. Haldane that, on their deathbeds, 'you and
I will be screaming for a priest'.[42] Even as a young man, he had disliked
jejune assaults on religion. When Isaiah Berlin edited a severely anti-clerical
magazine called *The Oxford Outlook*, Maurice threatened to set up a pro-
church journal in competition.[43] It was infuriating to him that Anglican
bishops were generally so dull and timid, that they refused to fight their
own corner. That was not Bowra's way.

> As a Victorian Agnostic, I am horrified by the bishops in this country. They
> spend all their time explaining that they really think the same as I do. This
> is a patent lie, and, if it were not, they should be unfrocked at once. They
> know no theology: so I can't discuss it with them, and catch them out on
> vital points of doctrine.[44]

Quite why churchmen refused to defend what was theirs in beauty
and spirituality baffled him. Bowra joined many others in writing to

Paul VI imploring him to preserve the Latin Mass: 'In the materialist and technocratic civilisation that is increasingly threatening the life of the mind and spirit in its original creative expression—the word—it seems particularly inhuman to deprive men of word-forms in one of their most grandiose manifestations.'[45]

Organized religion was 'marvellous rot',[46] but it deserved respect. Without it, 'the boys will believe, alas, in science, and think it will cure all their ills, poor poops. It is more likely to frizzle them to death.'[47] Religion, after all, was a struggling after something deeper and more meaningful than what the modern world offered. This endeavour, which Maurice would call artistic, was encapsulated in music, stone, and glass. No doubt his early training in Putney and Cheltenham conditioned some of his responses, but the great festivals were regularly observed, even if commitment ran ahead of musicality: 'I insisted on going to Church on Christmas Day, singing carols out of tune.'[48]

When in positions of authority, Maurice always ensured that the forms were observed. During the Second World War, his Home Guardsmen were marched to St Mary's, Grandpont, for Sunday service. Even though the overall tone of the church was on the 'low' side, Maurice enjoyed himself: 'Clergyman with moustache, no cross or flowers on the altar, no turning to the East in the creed, but choir in gay purple gowns with ruffs, and sidesmen chosen for very esoteric reasons…I read the lessons, Isaiah and Revelations, the latter a particularly obscure and succulent passage.'[49] As Warden of Wadham, he regularly attended evensong in the College Chapel, and took pains to find the right kind of chaplain. Such men should be 'nothing absurdly High, but nothing disgracefully Low'. To one, he described his own beliefs as '50-50'.[50] Predictably, exchanging the poetry of the Prayer Book and the King James Bible for some more modern translations was out of the question. One chaplain was even summoned to explain why 'Hark the Herald Angels Sing' had been dropped from its usual place in the carol service.[51] At dinner, he took great pleasure in correcting the officially pious on points of theology.

As he grew older, what had been an attachment to the poetry and stately forms of the Anglicanism of his youth deepened into something more mystical. He decided that he simply could 'not be beastly anymore', and began to wonder whether it was more important to be good than to be clever.[52] Of course, the Greeks had known this, regularly bringing down those who showed too much pride. To fly too near the sun invited destruction. As Noel Annan perceptively observed, Bowra's religion was in fact 'the old pietas—not the formal creed, but a knowledge that the gods must be given their due, and that they destroy mortals who fall prey to hubris and the reaching for too much glory'.[53] To the end of his life, the jokes about religion still came thick and fast. He once observed that he was 'looking forward to meeting God. Got six questions to ask Him. UNANSWERABLE.'[54] But now, it was not just increasing frailty that stopped him turning somersaults in college chapels. He had now a larger perspective on life, and 'became less interested in social success (his own or anyone's), and concluded that he had mismanaged things'. His 'Wildean temperament' now led him 'to turn towards De Profundis', which was 'a natural swing away from brilliance, the desire to impress, towards a craving for easiness and naturalness'.[55] Like the Greeks, Maurice suspected that the world, as he knew it, was not enough or the whole.

Most witnesses agree that Maurice was never a subscriber to any formal creed or set of commandments. He was not an Anglican or anything else. He had little respect for priests, and deeply resented any attempt by clerics to regulate the terms of private life. Above all, he hated to see religion being used to cover up personal weaknesses. In his view such defects should be faced squarely, and a formal challenge issued to the gods. The Greeks and the poets had given every individual the opportunity and the burden of living a life. It was a responsibility that could not be shuffled off or surrendered to churchmen. Bowra's personality was not a yielding one. The attack was everything. Indeed, some friends believed that he had been wasted in academic life, when 'his natural proclivity...should have made him a test pilot or a dare devil driver at Brooklands, risking his life for something more dangerous than Homer or the Symbolists'.[56] But, for Maurice, there was nothing more dangerous than Homer and the Symbolists. The poets, speaking through the mystical language of religion or using other words, demanded that man should find his own immanence and meaning.

Understandably therefore, some friends, like Noel Annan, were 'distressed' by the nature of Maurice's funeral. There was too much talk of sin, repentance, and redemption. It was

> cold, heartless, and overlaid with an Anglican desire to get their own back on Maurice—how on earth could Stuart have allowed himself to read that awful lesson, which tells us with infinite smugness, that after the faithful have

been a little punished and refined in the fires of God's wrath, they are led into the unimaginable place?[57]

Such theological language missed the point. Bowra did indeed have the hope of a heaven to come, but it would be one in which he would be reunited with friends rather than angels. He told John Betjeman that he was 'much looking forward to it. I'll see Brother Tom and old friends. Of course I won't see important people'.[58] As his Edwardian world was overtaken by new creeds, as, in his opinion, the poets were falling silent, it was comforting to think that his culture might endure elsewhere. Taking up this theme, John Sparrow wrote his friend's epitaph:

> Which of the two, when God and Maurice meet,
> Will occupy—you ask—the judgment seat?
> Sure, our old friend—each one of us replies—
> Will justly dominate the Grand Assize:
> He'll seize the sceptre and annex the throne,
> Claim the Almighty's thunder for his own,
> Trump the Last Trump, and the Last Post postpone.
> Then, if his strong prerogative extends
> To passing sentence on his sinful friends,
> Thus shall we supplicate at Heaven's high bar:
> 'Be merciful! You made us what we are;
> Our jokes, our joys, our hopes, our hatreds too,
> The outrageous things we do, or want to do—
> How much of all of them we owe to you!
> Send us to Hell or Heaven or where you will,
> Promise us only you'll be with us still:
> Without you, Heaven would be too dull to bear,
> And Hell will not be Hell if you are there.'[59]

Endnotes

CHAPTER I — FROM CHINA TO CHELTENHAM

1. C. A. V. Bowra, *Memorials of the Bowra Family*, Wadham Coll., Oxford; Bowra MSS.
2. Ibid.
3. C. M. Bowra to J. Sparrow, [1927]; Sparrow MSS, Box 57.
4. *Memories*, 8–9.
5. C. M. Bowra to P. Synnott, 25 July 1926; Synnott MSS.
6. Ibid. 22 Dec. 1929; ibid.
7. BL Add. MSS 72728, f. 24; C. M. Bowra to R. Harrod, 21 Jan. [1921].
8. C. A. V. Bowra to C. M. Bowra, 10 July 1922; Bowra MSS.
9. C. A. V. Bowra, *Memorials of the Bowra Family*, iii, 11 Nov 1903; SOAS, Bowra MSS, pp/ms/69/19.
10. Ibid.
11. *Memories*, 56.
12. C. A. V. Bowra to E. Blair, 5 Nov. 1945; Bod. Lib. Oxford; Ms. Eng. c4856, f. 18.
13. *Memories*, 56.
14. BL Add. MSS 72728, ff. 14–15; C. M. Bowra to R. Harrod, 17 Aug. [1920].
15. C. A. V. Bowra to E. Blair, 7 March 1946; Bod. Lib. Oxford; Ms. Eng. c4856, f. 25.
16. *Memories*, 55.
17. Ibid. 59.
18. Ibid. 56.
19. Ibid. 59.
20. E. V. Bowra to E. Bowra, 15 Feb. 1903; Bowra MSS, Maurice once observed that he suspected 'that most Victorian parents did not care very much for their children and thought it bad for them if they took notice of them'. C. M. Bowra to J. Salmon, 21 June 1971; Salmon MSS.
21. BL Add, MSS 72728, f. 18; C. M. Bowra to R. Harrod, 24 Dec [?].
22. Ibid. ff. 14–15; 17 Aug. [1920].
23. C. M. Bowra to R. Dundas, 10 Sept. [1922]; Christ Church, Oxford; Dundas MSS.
24. BL Add. MSS 72728, f. 23; C. M. Bowra to R. Harrod, 12 Jan [1921].

25. C. M. Bowra to E. Starkie, 31 Jan. [1960]; Bod. Lib., Oxford, Starkie MSS.

26. *Idem* to P. Synnott, 26 Dec. [1926]; Synnott MSS.

27. Caroline Scott; Wadham Coll. Archives.

28. Davie/Isaiah Berlin; ibid.

29. Mitchell/Noel Worswick and Mitchell/J. Bamborough.

30. C. M. Bowra to P. Balfour, 7 Oct. [1926]; Huntington Lib., Calif., Balfour/Kinross MSS.

31. C. M. Bowra to J. Sparrow, 2 Oct. [1926]; Sparrow MSS, Box 57.

32. C. M. Bowra to P. Leigh Fermor, 15 Nov. [?]; Bowra MSS.

33. Davie/Sally Chilver.

34. *Memories*, 5.

35. C. A. V. Bowra, *Memorials of the Bowra Family*, 8 Feb 1902; SOAS, Bowra MSS, pp/ms/69/19, 101.

36. Ibid. 94.

37. Ibid. 74.

38. Ibid. 80.

39. Ibid. 92.

40. H. W. Parke, *Wadham Gazette*, 1986.

41. Wadham Coll. Archives.

42. C. Connolly to N. Blakiston, 26 May 1925; N. Blakiston, *A Romantic Friendship* (London 1975), 85.

43. C. M. Bowra to P. Synnott, 20 Sept. [1926]; Synnott MSS.

44. H. W. Parke, *Wadham Gazette*, 1986.

45. C. M. Bowra to Alice James, 24 June [1950]; Harvard, Houghton Library, bms am 1938 (152).

46. *Idem* to C. Connolly, 28 Dec. [*c*.1961]; Connolly MSS. See also *idem* to C. Clark, 10 Sept. [1961]; C. Clark MSS.

47. *Memories*, 5.

48. C. A. V. Bowra, *Memorials of the Bowra Family*, Dec. 1903; SOAS, Bowra MSS, pp/ms/69/19, 115.

49. Ibid. 119–20.

50. Ibid. 124.

51. Ibid. 130.

52. *Memories*, 13.

53. Ibid. 6–7.

54. C. M. Bowra to G. Rylands, n.d.; King's Coll. Cam., Rylands MSS, GHWR/3/57.

55. Diary of Edward Bowra, 8 April 1905; Wadham Coll. Archives.

56. Ibid. 8 April 1908.

57. Ibid. 25 Dec. 1907.

58. C. M. Bowra to C. Connolly, 24 Aug. [1938?]; Connolly MSS.

59. *Idem* to P. Synnott, 14 Dec. [1925]; Synnott MSS.

60. *Memories*, 14.

61. Willington School reports, April 1905; Wadham Coll., Bowra MSS.

62. Ibid. Dec. 1908; ibid.

63. Miss Annie Hale to C. M. Bowra, 7 Oct. 1938; ibid.

64. Miss E. Dell to C. M. Bowra, 4 Nov. 1951; ibid. Miss Dell was invited to stay in Wadham when her former pupil was Vice-Chancellor; C. M. Bowra to N. Annan, 1 Jan. [1951?]; King's Coll., Cambridge, Annan MSS.

65. *Memories*, 19.

66. Ibid. 22.

67. C. A. V. Bowra, *Memorials of the Bowra Family*, March 1910; SOAS Bowra MSS, pp/ms/69/19, 203.

68. Ibid. 196.

69. Ibid. 206.

70. Cheltenham College Rulebook; Cheltenham Coll. Archives.

71. C. Thornton to C. A. V. Bowra, 5 June 1910; Bowra MSS.

72. C. M. Bowra to H. Hugo, 11 Nov. 1964; Sparrow MSS, Box 57.

73. A. J. Ayer, *Part of My Life* (Oxford 1977), 99.

74. Lady Longford, *The Pebbled Shore* (London 1986), 77.

75. C. A. V. Bowra, *Memorials of the Bowra Family*, 27 June 1912; SOAS, Bowra MSS, pp/ms/69/19, 239.

76. OTC, Southern and Northern Commands Camp, Burden Hampshire, 1912; Cheltenham Coll. Archives.

77. Cheltenham College Junior Department Report, 16 July 1910; Bowra MSS.

78. C. Thornton to C. A. V. Bowra, 1 Jan. 1911; ibid.

79. *Memories*, 41, and Mitchell/C. M. Bowra.

80. *Memories*, 37–8.

81. Ibid. 36.

82. Ibid. 37.

83. Ibid.

84. BL Add. MSS, 72728, ff. 10, 14, 23; C. M. Bowra to R. Harrod; 8 Aug. [1920], 17 Aug. [1920] and 12 Jan. [1921]. C. M. Bowra to D. Woodruff, 31 July [1920]; Georgetown Univ., Woodruff MSS, Box 1, f. 19.

85. *Memories*, 28.

86. BL Add. MSS 72728, f. 14; C. M. Bowra to R. Harrod, 17 Aug. [1920].

87. L. Haslett to C. M. Bowra, 1 June 1958; Bowra MSS.

88. BL Add. MSS 72728, f. 14; C. M. Bowra to R. Harrod, 17 Aug. [1920].

89. Maurice Bowra, *New Bats in Old Belfries* ed. H. Hardy and J. Holmes (Oxford 2005), 9.

90. BL Add. MSS 71182, f. 64; C. M. Bowra to B. Harrod, 17 July [c.1952].

91. C. M. Bowra to H. Hugo, 25 July [1957]; Sparrow MSS, Box 57.

92. *Idem* to C. Connolly, 27 March [?]; Connolly MSS.

93. Ibid.

94. C. M. Bowra to J. Dancy, 6 Dec. [1952]; Bowra MSS.

95. *Memories*, 35.

96. C. Hollis, *Oxford in the Twenties* (London, 1976), 18.

97. C. M. Bowra to J. Betjeman, 12 Jan. [1942?]; Betjeman MSS.

98. *Eidem*, 8 Jan. 1950; ibid.

99. C. M. Bowra to G. Rylands, 24 April 1965; Rylands MSS, GHWR/3/57.

100. Sir R. Prain to Sir K. Clark, 1978; Tate Britain, Clark MSS, TGA/8812/1/3/451.

101. Davie/Longford, Wadham Coll. Archives.

102. C. M. Bowra to D. Woodruff, 31 July [*c*.1920]; Georgetown Univ., Woodruff MSS, Box 1 folder 19.

103. *Idem*, 'Sunday'; ibid.

104. BL Add. MSS 72728, ff. 6–7; C. M. Bowra to R. Harrod, 30 July [1920], and C. M. Bowra to P. Synnott, 13 July [1926]; Synnott MSS.

105. Ibid.

106. C. A. V. Bowra, *Memorials of the Bowra Family*, 6 Aug. 1925; SOAS, Bowra MSS, pp/ms/69/19.

107. BL Add. MSS 72728, f. 7; C. M. Bowra to R. Harrod, 30 July [1920].

108. *Idem* to P. Synnott, 24 Dec. [1925]; Synnott MSS.

109. *Eidem* 20 Dec. [1924]; ibid.

110. C. M. Bowra to S. Gates, 'Saturday' [1921 ?]; Gates MSS.

111. *Idem* to P. Synnott, 14 Dec. [1925]; Synnott MSS.

112. *Idem* to S. Gates, 9 April [1921]; Gates MSS.

113. *Idem* to P. Synnott, 1 Oct. 1927; Synnott MSS.

114. *Idem* to S. Gates, 9 April [1921]; Gates MSS.

115. BL Add. MSS 72728, f. 10; C. M. Bowra to R. Harrod, 8 Aug. [1920].

116. C. M. Bowra to P. Synnott, 1 and 4 Oct. [1927]; Synnott MSS.

117. *Idem* to F. Frankfurter, 28 March [1937]; Frankfurter MSS Box 25.

118. *Idem* to Ottoline Morrell, 22 April [?]; HRC, Morrell MSS, 17.

119. *Idem* to R. Dundas, 10 Sept. [1922]; Christ Church, Oxford, Dundas MSS, Box 1.

120. Mitchell/Peter Fraser.

121. Mitchell/Lady Berlin.

122. Mitchell/R. J. P. Williams.

123. C. M. Bowra to G. Rylands, [*c*.April 1967]; GHWE/3/57.

124. S. K. Ghosh, *A Tribute*; Sparrow MSS, Box 57.

125. E. Kantorowicz to C. M. Bowra, 27 April 1949; Bowra MSS.

126. J. Spence to L. G. Mitchell, 28 Jan. 2006; Bowra MSS.

127. Mitchell/John Bamborough.

128. B. Ruck, *A Smile from the Past* (London 1959), 229–30.

129. *Memories*, 26.

130. Mitchell/Lady Quinton.

131. C. M. Bowra to P. Synnott, Aug. [1931]; Synnott MSS.

132. *Idem* to C. Connolly, 25 May [1945]; Tulsa Univ., McFarlin Lib., Connolly MSS.

CHAPTER 2 — WAR, 1914–1918

1. Mitchell/George Richardson.
2. *Memories*, 39.
3. C. A. V. Bowra, *Memorials of the Bowra Family*, 12 Jan. 1916; SOAS, Bowra MSS, 294.
4. Ibid. 302.
5. Passport; Bowra MSS.
6. H. Lloyd-Jones, *Maurice Bowra* (London 1974), 23.
7. C. A. V. Bowra, *Memorials of the Bowra Family*, 8–22 May 1916; SOAS, Bowra MSS, 303.
8. *Memories*, 60.
9. Ibid. 64.
10. Ibid.
11. Ibid. 65.
12. Ibid. 67.
13. Ibid. 68.
14. Ibid.
15. V. Joscelyne to J. Sparrow, 4 Nov. 1974; Sparrow MSS, Box 57. Maurice told John Salmon that the Russian was 'the only girl I ever loved'. At the time, Salmon did not detect an emphasis on the word 'girl'. J. Salmon to L. Mitchell, 23 Oct. 2006; Wadham Coll. Oxford, Bowra MSS He also confided to Noel Annan that 'Petrograd... changed my life'; C. M. Bowra to N. Annan, 27 Nov, 1966; King's Coll. Camb., Annan MSS.
16. 'Nocturne', Wadham Coll. Oxford, Bowra MSS.
17. 'The Dreamer', ibid.
18. 'Out of Touch', ibid.
19. *Memories*, 68.
20. Ibid. 40.
21. Ibid.
22. Ibid. 39.
23. Ibid.
24. Ibid. 42.
25. 'Mecanophilus', *c*.1913; Wadham Coll. Oxford; Bowra MSS.
26. 'Gold Dancing in the Air'; ibid.
27. C. M. Bowra, *Poetry and the First World War* (Oxford 1961), 4.
28. C. A. V. Bowra, *Memorials of the Bowra Family*, 23 Oct. 1917; SOAS, Bowra MSS, 322–3.
29. File of Lt. C. M. Bowra, 1917; National Archives, Kew; WO 374/8155.
30. Ibid.
31. C. M. Bowra to P. Synnott, 25 March [1928]; Synnott MSS.
32. *Memories*, 74.
33. Ibid. 87.

34. War Diary, 298th Army Brigade, RFA; National Archives, Kew; WO 95/456.

35. *Memories*, 80.

36. Ibid.

37. Ibid. 81.

38. Ibid. 86.

39. Ibid. 87.

40. C. Connolly to N. Blakiston, 23 April 1925; N. Blakiston, *A Romantic Friendship* (London 1975), 71.

41. C. M. Bowra to F. Frankfurter, n.d. Frankfurter MSS, Box 25.

42. Transcript of a BBC Broadcast, 7 April 1972; Wadham Coll., Oxford, Bowra MSS.

43. C. A. V. Bowra, *Memorials of the Bowra Family*, March 1918; SOAS, Bowra MSS, 336.

44. *Idem* to E. Starkie, 1 Jan. 1965; Bod. Lib., Oxford, Starkie MSS, Box 1966.

45. Bowra, *Poetry and the First World War*, 14–15.

46. *Early Greek Elegists* (Cambridge 1936), 70.

47. *Idem* to E. Waugh, 12 July [1955]; Bowra MSS.

48. *Memories*, 78.

49. A. Powell, *Infants of the Spring* (London 1976), 182.

50. I. Berlin to Sir G. Catlin, 21 Sept. 1971; Berlin MSS, 195 f. 102.

51. C. Connolly to C. M. Bowra, n.d., Bowra MSS.

52. N. Annan, *The Dons* (London 1999), 140.

53. Bowra, *Poetry and the First World War*, 20.

54. 'Gold Dancing in the Air'; Wadham Coll. Oxford; Bowra MSS.

55. 'Reminiscence', 1921; ibid.

56. 'Gold Dancing in the Air'; Wadham Coll. Oxford; Bowra MSS.

57. C. Hollis, *Oxford in the Twenties* (London 1976), 22–3.

58. *Memories*, 95.

59. W. T. Rodgers *Hugh Gaitskell* (London, 1964), 22–3.

60. Bowra, *Poetry and the First World War*, 23.

61. Mitchell/A. F. Thompson.

62. Davie/Lord Longford.

63. E. Waugh to C. M. Bowra, 14 July 1955; Bowra MSS.

64. Davie/Jean Jones.

65. Davie/Noel Annan.

66. *Memories*, 75.

67. C. M. Bowra to H. Hugo, n.d.; Sparrow MSS, Box 57.

68. *Memories*, 91.

69. Ibid. 90.

70. Bowra, *Poetry and the First World War*, 103.

71. E. Longford, *The Pebbled Shore* (London 1986), 163.

72. A. Fleming to H. Charteris, [Aug. 1954]; M. Amory, *The Letters of Ann Fleming* (London 1985), 139.
73. Idem. to Duchess of Devonshire, 26 Aug [1967]; ibid. 387.
74. C. M. Bowra, *Memorial Address*, 30 Oct. 1958 (Oxford).
75. Revd A. W. R. Lodge to H. Hardy, 27 Dec 2005; Bowra MSS. J. Spence, *Wadham Gazette*, Jan. 2006, New Series 4, no 9, 57.
76. *Memories*, 88.
77. Mitchell/Colette Clark.
78. Bowra, *Poetry and the First World War*, 24.
79. *Idem* to P. Synnott; Synnott MSS.
80. Bowra, *Poetry and the First World War*, 35.
81. J. Garcia Villa, *A Celebration for Edith Sitwell* (New Jersey 1948), 27, 29, 31.
82. C. M. Bowra to C. Connolly, n.d.; *Sunday Times*, 29 Aug. 1971.
83. *Memories*, 89; and Mitchell/Julian Mitchell.
84. C. M. Bowra, *The Lyrical Poetry of Thomas Hardy* (Nottingham, 1946), 16−18.
85. Davie/A. L. Rowse. Rowse added, 'That's the real Maurice, under the bluster and everything else.'
86. C. M. Bowra, *Poetry and Politics* (Cambridge, 1966), 17−18.

CHAPTER 3 — NEW COLLEGE, 1919−1922

1. *Memories*, 71.
2. C. M. Bowra to F. Frankfurter, n.d.; Frankfurter MSS, Box 25.
3. *Idem* to C. Connolly, [*c.*1965]; Connolly MSS.
4. Mitchell/C. M. Bowra.
5. *Memories*, 103.
6. C. M. Bowra to Sir C. Cox, 31 Jan. [1935]; New Coll., Oxford, PA/C1/3/354−5.
7. *Idem* to A. Smith, [1948]; New Coll., Oxford, PA/32/12/1.
8. *Idem* to Mrs Fisher, 18 April [1940]; Bod. Lib. Oxford, Fisher MSS, 213 f. 190. *Idem* to M. Fisher, ibid.; ibid. 218 f. 112.
9. C. M. Bowra, Obituary of A. S. Owen, 23 Jan. 1941; Bowra MSS.
10. *Memories*, 100.
11. Davie/Sir Stuart Hampshire.
12. C. M. Bowra to J. Sparrow, 27 Oct. [1932]; Sparrow MSS, Box 57.
13. J. Sparrow to Sir K. Clark, 30 Aug. 1932; Tate Britain, Clark MSS, TGA/8812/1/3/2942.
14. *Idem* to C. M. Bowra, 30 Jan. 1966; Bowra MSS.
15. *Memories*, 111.
16. Davie/Sir Stuart Hampshire.
17. Mitchell/George Huxley.
18. Ibid.

19. C. M. Bowra to D. Woodruff, 11 April [1920]; Georgetown Univ., Woodruff MSS, Box 1 folder 19.

20. BL Add. MSS 72728, f. 10; C. M. Bowra to R. Harrod, 8 Aug. [1920].

21. *Eidem*, 17 Aug. [1920]; ibid. f. 16.

22. *Eidem*, 24 Dec. [1920]; ibid. f. 18.

23. Ibid.

24. C. M. Bowra to I. Berlin, 6 June 1943; Bowra MSS.

25. *Eidem* 20 Nov. 1945; ibid.

26. A. S. Owen to C. M. Bowra, 11 Nov. 1930; ibid.

27. I. Berlin, *Memorial Address*, 17 July 1971; ibid.

28. Audrey Beecham to S. Hampshire, 28 Oct. 1971; ibid.

29. C. M. Bowra to P. Synnott, [March 1927]; Synnott MSS.

30. Mitchell/George Huxley.

31. BL Add. MSS 72728, f. 24; C. M. Bowra to R. Harrod, 12 Jan. [1921].

32. R. Harrod, *The Prof.* (London, 1959), 40.

33. C. M. Bowra to H. Hugo, 30 June [1958]; Sparrow MSS, Box 57.

34. BL Add. MSS 72762, f. 74; 'The Pale Student' to R. Harrod, 27 Dec. 1920.

35. E. Siepmann, *Confessions of a Nihilist* (London, 1955), 53.

36. BL Add. MSS 72728, f. 1; C. M. Bowra to R. Harrrod [1922?].

37. Ibid. ff. 44, 14; *eidem*, 25 and 17 Aug. [1922].

38. Ibid. 71610, f. 2; *eidem*, 14 Sept. [1922].

39. Ibid.

40. C. M. Bowra to D. Woodruff, 31 July [1920]; Georgetown Univ., Woodruff MSS, Box 1, folder 19.

41. J. Laver, *Museum Piece* (London 1963), 80−1.

42. C. Hollis, *Oxford in the Twenties* (London 1976), 42.

43. *Memories*, 120.

44. Mitchell/C. M. Bowra.

45. *Memories*, 120.

46. BL Add. MSS 72728, f. 1; C. M. Bowra to R. Harrod, [1922].

47. J. Laver, *Museum Piece* (London 1963), 60.

48. 'Milord'; Maurice Bowra, *New Bats in Old Belfries* ed. H. Hardy and J. Holmes (Oxford, 2005), 61−2.

49. BL Add. MSS 71182, f. 62; C. M. Bowra to R. Harrod, 18 July [?].

50. BL Add. MSS 72733, f. 77; D. Woodruff to R. Harrod, 21 Dec. [1920].

51. Ibid. 78112, f. 58; C. M. Bowra to R. Harrod, 21 Oct. 1963.

52. C. M. Bowra to S. Gates, 16 April [1922]; Gates MSS.

53. BL Add. MSS 72730, f. 117; B. Murray to R. Harrod, 21 April 1922.

54. BL Add. MSS 72728, ff. 26−7, 33−5; C. M. Bowra to R. Harrod, [1921] and 21 Jan. [1921].

55. Ibid. ff. 36−7; *eidem*, 30 July [1921].

56. 'Leavetaking'; Bowra MSS.

CHAPTER 4 — GREECE

1. I. Berlin, *Memorial Address*, 17 July 1971; Wadham Coll., Oxford, Bowra MSS.

2. C. M. Bowra, *Speech Given at the Cambridge Arts Theatre*, 21 March 1971.

3. Ibid.

4. Ibid.

5. *Idem, From the Greek* (Oxford, 1943), introduction.

6. C. Connolly, draft review; Connolly MSS.

7. C. M. Bowra, *The Greek Experience* (London, 1957), 46.

8. Ibid.

9. Ibid. 64.

10. Ibid. 46.

11. Ibid. 41.

12. Ibid. 23.

13. C. M. Bowra, *Ancient Greek Literature* (London, 1933), 250.

14. *The Criterion,* draft review; Bowra MSS.

15. Davie/A. L. Rowse.

16. *London Magazine*, I(10), Nov. 1954, 90.

17. Davie/Lady Longford.

18. Bowra, *The Greek Experience*, 127.

19. Ibid. 163.

20. C. M. Bowra to F. Frankfurter, 5 Jan. [1953]; Frankfurter MSS, Box 25.

21. *Idem, Landmarks in Greek Literature* (London, 1966), iv. 115.

22. *Oxford Magazine*, 4 May 1933, 612.

23. C. M. Bowra, *The Simplicity of Racine* (Oxford, 1956), 9.

24. Ibid. 32.

25. Bowra, *Landmarks in Greek Literature*, 76.

26. *Zeitschrift für Sozialforschung*, Jahrgang, 6 (1937), 391.

27. Ibid. 397.

28. C. M. Bowra, *Early Greek Elegists* (Cambridge, 1935), 170.

29. *Idem, Pindar* (Oxford 1964), 1–2.

30. *Idem, Problems in Greek Poetry* (Oxford, 1953), 91.

31. *Idem, The Greek Experience*, 73.

32. Ibid. 83.

33. C. M. Bowra to C. Connolly, 13 Feb. 1966; Connolly MSS.

34. BL Add. MSS 72728, f. 13; C. M. Bowra to R. Harrod, 17 Aug. [1920].

35. Mitchell/Lord and Lady Quinton.

36. C. M. Bowra, *On Greek Margins* (Oxford, 1970), and *Miscellaneous Papers* in Wadham Coll. Library.

37. A. L. Rowse, *Friends and Contemporaries* (London, 1990), 90.

38. C. M. Bowra to C. Connolly, 18 Oct. [1957]; Connolly MSS.

39. Ibid. H. Hugo, 30 Nov. [1958?]; Sparrow MSS, Box 57.

40. C. M. Bowra to F. Frankfurter, 4 June [?], Frankfurter MSS, Box 25.

41. *Idem* to Prof Craik, 5 Feb. [?]; Murray MSS, 55 f. 74.

42. Draft review of Denniston's book on Greek particles, 1934; Bowra MSS.

43. C. M. Bowra, 'The Scholarship of Housman'; Bowra MSS.

44. *Memories*, 260–1.

45. BL Add. MSS 72728, f. 13, C. M. Bowra to R. Harrod, 17 Aug. [1920].

46. *Idem* to H. R. Trevor-Roper, 13 Sept. 1963; Christ Church, Oxford, Trevor-Roper MSS, '1963' folder.

47. C. M. Bowra to W. M. Calder III, 17 Sept. 1966; *Greek, Roman and Byzantine Studies*, XL, (2005), 213–17.

48. N. Annan, *The Dons* (London, 1999), 163.

49. T. W. Adorno to M. Horkheimer, 26 Mai 1936; C. Gödde and H. Lonitz, *Briefe und Briefwechel von T. W. Adorno, 1927–37* (Frankfurt 2003), 150.

50. *Eidem*, 25 June 1936; 166.

51. *Eidem*, 28 Nov. 1936; 235–6.

52. *Zeitschrift für Socialforschung*, Jahrgang 6 (1937).

53. M. Horkheimer to T. W. Adorno, 12 März 1937; Gödde and Lonitz, *Briefe und Briefwechel von T. W. Adorno, 1927–37*, 319–20.

54. Mitchell/Peter Fraser.

55. Davie/Stuart Hampshire.

56. Davie/Noel Annan.

57. C. M. Bowra to A. James, 3 Dec. [1950]; Harvard, Houghton Lib., BMS AM 1938 (152).

58. *Idem* to C. Clark, 28 Dec. [1960], C. Clark MSS.

59. *Idem* to Sir G. Catlin, 27 July [?]; McMaster Univ., Hamilton, Ontario, Catlin MSS.

60. *Idem* to C. Clark, 26 Jan. 1964; C. Clark MSS.

61. *Eidem*, 8 Jan. 1965; ibid.

62. Mitchell/G. Huxley.

63. Ibid.

64. Morwood/P. Leigh Fermor.

65. C. M. Bowra to E. Sitwell; 16 Nov. [?]; Sitwell MSS HRC, Sitwell 15.

66. E. Fitzgibbon to C. M. Bowra, 29 Nov. 1964; Bowra MSS.

67. Davie/Hampshire.

68. C. M. Bowra to I. Berlin, 3 Dec. [1951]; Bowra MSS.

69. A. Powell, *Infants of the Spring* (London 1976), 193.

70. *Memories*, 228.

71. *Oxford Magazine*, 30 May 1957.

72. Sir G. Murray to C. M. Bowra, 17 Sept. 1933; Murray MSS, 65 f. 35. See also C. M. Bowra to Sir G. Murray, 10 Nov. 1930 and 28 Jan. [1935], Bowra MSS.

73. Sir G. Murray to C. M. Bowra, 14 May 1934; Murray MSS, 67 f. 186.

74. C. M. Bowra to Sir G. Murray, 13 May [1930]; ibid. 57 ff. 28–9.

75. T. W. Adorno to M. Horkheimer, 26 Mai 1936; Gödde and Lonitz, *Briefe und Briefwechel von T. W. Adorno, 1927–37*, 150.

76. I. Berlin to E. Bowen, [July 1935]; H. Hardy, *Flourishing* (London, 2004), 135.

77. *Idem* to M. Frankfurter, 3 June 1936; ibid. 169–70.

78. *Idem* to E. Bowen, [June 1936]; ibid. 177.

79. Ibid.

80. Sir G. Murray to S. Baldwin, 2 June 1936; National Archives, Kew, MP77/138.

81. Ernst Kantorowicz to C. M. Bowra, 8 July 1936; Bowra MSS.

82. *Eidem*, 8 Nov. 1949; ibid.

83. Ibid.

84. I. Berlin to C. M. Bowra, [Jan. 1937]; Sir Christopher Cox, T. S. R. Boase and John Redcliffe-Maud.

85. *Idem* to M. Frankfurter, 24 June 1936; Hardy, *Flourishing*, 178.

86. C. M. Bowra to G. Murray, 25 June [?], Murray MSS.

87. E. R. Dodds to C. M. Bowra, 2 Jan. 1968; Bowra MSS.

88. T. W. Adorno to M. Horkheimer, 28 Nov. 1936; Gödde and Lonitz, *Theodor W. Adorno, Briefe und Briefwechel 1927–37*, 235.

89. M. Fisher to I. Berlin, [1937]; Murray MSS, 243, f. 85.

90. G. Murray to C. M. Bowra, 24 June 1936; ibid. 77 f. 218.

91. C. M. Bowra to G. Murray, 26 June [1936]; ibid. f. 247.

92. *Idem* to F. Frankfurter, 28 March [1937]; Frankfurter MSS, Box 25.

93. 'Gilbert and Mary: An Eclogue'; Maurice Bowra, *New Bats in Old Belfries* ed. H. Hardy and J. Holmes (Oxford, 2005), 87–91.

94. I. Berlin to C. M. Bowra, 8 Dec. 1936; Bowra MSS.

95. R. Mynors to C. M. Bowra, I Jan. 1937; ibid.

96. C. M. Bowra to I. Berlin, 21 Jan. [1937]; ibid.

97. I. Berlin to M. Fisher, [*c*.17 Dec. 1936]; Hardy, *Flourishing*, 220.

98. E. Kantorowicz to C. M. Bowra, 8 July 1936; Bowra MSS.

99. Davie/Sir Stuart Hampshire.

100. *Memories*, 269.

101. Ibid.

102. Mitchell/Noel Worswick.

103. BL Add., MSS 71182, f. 53; C. M. Bowra to R. Harrod, 11 Sept. [1952]. *Idem* to H. Hugo, 11 Sept. [1952]; Sparrow MSS, Box 57.

104. *Idem* to E. Bowen, 7 Sept. [1935?]; HRC, Bowra MSS, 2.

105. *Idem* to I. Berlin, 12 Oct. [1932]; Berlin MSS, 246 f. 2.

106. Morwood/P. Leigh Fermor.

107. S. Tabachnik, *Fiercer than Tigers* (Michigan, 2002), 220.

108. C. M. Bowra to J. Mitchell, 22 April 1961; J. Mitchell MSS.

109. *Idem* to Lord Simon, 7 Oct. [1946]; Bod. Lib., Simon MSS, 96 f. 213.

110. Details of these tours may be found in the National Archives at Kew, BW 83/1 and BW 83/19.

111. BL Add., MSS 71182, f. 64; C. M. Bowra to B. Harrod, 17 July [?]. See also *idem* to J. Betjeman, 8 Jan. 1950; Betjeman MSS.

112. Ann Fleming to H. Charteris, [Aug. 1954]; M. Amory, *The Letters of Ann Fleming* (London, 1985), 138–9.

113. *Idem* to E. Waugh, 26 June [1964]; ibid. 346. See also P. Levi to C. M. Bowra, n.d.; Bowra MSS.

114. C. M. Bowra to Isaline Blew Horner, 8 June [?]; Fac. of Oriental Studies, Camb., Horner MSS.

115. *Idem* to I. Berlin, 6 Oct. 1962; Bowra MSS.

116. *Idem* to Alice James, 15 March [1955]; Harvard, Houghton Lib., bMS AM 1938 (152).

117. *Idem* to Berta Ruck, 28 Dec. [?]; Bowra MSS. See also *The Times*, 16 March 1956.

118. Morwood/P. Leigh Fermor.

119. C. M. Bowra to Berta Ruck, 12 Dec. 1968; Bowra MSS.

120. W. G. Forrest to C. M. Bowra, 'Sunday'; ibid.

121. Mitchell/Noel Worswick.

122. C. M. Bowra to C. Connolly, 14 July 1968; Connolly MSS.

123. *Eidem*, 18 Sept. 1967; ibid.

124. Lecture given at the Cambridge Arts Theatre, 21 March 1971; Bowra MSS.

125. J. Finley to C. M. Bowra, 3 Jan. 1965; Bowra MSS.

126. *The Cornhill Magazine*, winter 1971–2.

CHAPTER 5 — POETRY

1. H. Lloyd-Jones, *Maurice Bowra* (London 1974), 46.

2. Unpublished essay by Cyril Connolly; Bowra MSS.

3. Ibid.

4. Mitchell/Colette Clark.

5. S. Hampshire to I. Berlin, [*c*.1955]; Berlin MSS, c256 f. 180.

6. N. Annan, *The Dons* (London, 1999), 144.

7. C. M. Bowra to S. Gates, 3 Jan. [?]; Gates MSS.

8. C. Day-Lewis, *The Poet's Task* (Oxford, 1951), 3.

9. C. M. Bowra, *Guillaume Apollinaire, Choix de Poésies* (London 1945), xv.

10. *Idem, In General and Particular* (London 1964), 223.

11. *Idem, Pindar* (Oxford 1964), 5.

12. *Idem, Inspiration and Poetry* (London, 1955), 10.

13. *Idem* to E. Sitwell, 30 Aug. [?]; HRC, Sitwell MSS, 22.

14. *Idem* and T. Higham, *The Oxford Book of Greek Verse* (Oxford 1938), xi.

15. *Idem, The Heritage of Symbolism* (London 1943), 12.

16. C. M. Bowra, *Greek Lyric Poetry* (Oxford 1961), 136; *idem, Problems in Greek Poetry* (Oxford, 1953), 37; *idem, Pindar*, 394.

17. *Idem* to P. Synnott, 6 March [1928]; Synnott MSS.

18. *Horizon*, 8 (43), July 1943.

19. Davie/Stuart Hampshire.

20. Bowra, *The Heritage of Symbolism*, preface.

21. I. Berlin, *Personal Impressions* (London 1980), 126.

22. Tape of a BBC broadcast, Bowra MSS.

23. E. Sitwell to C. M. Bowra, 21 April 1949; ibid.

24. *Horizon*, 10 (55), 27 June 1944; ibid.

25. C. M. Bowra, *Primitive Song* (London 1962), 286.

26. *Idem* to J. Sparrow, 21 June 1952; Sparrow MSS, Box 57.

27. Bowra, *In General and Particular*, 225 and 231.

28. Ibid. 237.

29. *Idem, The Heritage of Symbolism*, 221.

30. Ibid.

31. *Idem, The Background of Modern Poetry* (Oxford, 1946), 9.

32. E. Sitwell to C. M. Bowra, 12 Jan. 1944; Bowra MSS.

33. E. Kantorowicz to C. M. Bowra, 19 Nov. 1943; ibid.

34. I. Worth to Sir K. Clark, n.d.; Tate Britain, Clark MSS, TGA 8812/1/3 3548.

35. *Memories*, 230.

36. Ibid. See also H. Acton, *Nancy Mitford, A. Memoir* (London 1975), 20.

37. W. B. Yeats to C. M. Bowra, 31 May 1934; Bowra MSS.

38. *Memories*, 238.

39. W. B. Yeats to C. M. Bowra, 24 April [1938]; Bowra MSS.

40. *Memories*, 236.

41. *The Times*, 8 June 1959.

42. E. Sitwell to C. M. Bowra, 12 and 24 Jan. 1944; Bowra MSS.

43. *Eidem*, 8 July 1955; ibid.

44. *The Cornhill Magazine*, no. 965, July 1945, 378–9, and C. M. Bowra, 'The War Poetry of Edith Sitwell', in J. Garcia Villa (ed.), *A Celebration for Edith Sitwell* (New Jersey, 1948), 21 and 26.

45. C. M. Bowra to E. Sitwell, 22 July [?]; HRC, Sitwell MSS, 14.

46. E. Sitwell to C. M. Bowra, 23 March 1958; Bowra MSS.

47. R. E. Norton, *Secret Germany: Stefan Georg and his Circle* (Cornell, 2002), 454.

48. Ibid. 450.

49. Bowra, *The Heritage of Symbolism*, 106.

50. K. Clark, *Another Part of the Wood* (London, 1974), 114.

51. Lloyd-Jones, *Maurice Bowra*, 26. See also C. M. Bowra to G. Rylands, 25 June 1964; King's Coll., Cambridge; GHWR/3/57.

52. C. M. Bowra, *Sappho: Dichtung* (Berlin, 1936). The book was reprinted in 1938.

53. *Memories*, 286–91. After his death, at Kantorowicz's request, all Bowra's letters to him were destroyed. For his association with Oxford in the 1930s, see Bod. Lib., Oxford, Society for the Protection of Science and Learning MSS, f508/2.

54. Ibid.

55. C. M. Bowra to J. Sparrow, 27 Oct. [1932]; Sparrow MSS, Box 57.

56. *New Oxford Magazine*, 1 (3), Feb. 1934, 317, 322.

57. Bowra, *The Heritage of Symbolism*, 142.

58. Ibid. 116.

59. Ibid.

60. Ibid. 134.

61. Ibid. 178.

62. *New Oxford Magazine*, 1 (3), Feb. 1934, 331.

63. G. Weidenfeld, *Remembering my Good Friends* (London 1994), 247–8.

64. S. Spender, *Journals 1939–1983* (London 1985), 258.

65. University of Tulsa, PEN Archive.

66. C. M. Bowra, *Poetry and Politics* (Cambridge, 1966), 2.

67. *Idem, The Heritage of Symbolism*, 7.

68. *Idem, Poetry and Politics*, 13.

69. *Idem* to J. Sparrow, 2 April [1933]; Sparrow MSS, Box 57.

70. Ibid. 5 Jan [1934]; ibid.

71. C. M. Bowra, *An Anthology of Mexican Verse* (London, 1958), 10.

72. *Idem, In General and Particular*, 24–5.

73. Mitchell/C. M. Bowra.

74. C. M. Bowra, *The Oxford Outlook*, 12 (57), Feb. 1932.

75. *Idem, The Cornhill Magazine*, no. 961, Jan. 1945.

76. Ibid.

77. Bowra, *Guillaume Apollinaire: Choix de Poésies*, introduction.

78. *Idem, An Anthology of Mexican Verse*, 11.

79. Natasha Spender to L. G. Mitchell, 3 Aug. 2005.

80. C. M. Bowra to Mr Blaser, 16 Oct. [?]; University of Tulsa, McFarlin Lib., Pound MSS.

81. *Idem* to Cyril Connolly, 28 Dec. [1960s]; ibid. Connolly MSS.

82. Ibid. 25 June [?]; ibid.

83. C. M. Bowra to E. Sitwell, 17 March [?]; HRC, Sitwell MSS, 7.

84. E. Sitwell to C. M. Bowra, 24 March 1947; Bowra MSS.

85. C. M. Bowra to E. Sitwell, 17 May [?]; Washington State University, Sitwell MSS.

86. *Idem* to G. Rylands, 24 May 1964; Bowra MSS.

87. *Idem* to C. Connolly, 24 May 1964; Connolly MSS.

88. *Idem* to E. Sitwell, 16 Nov. [1948?]; HRC, Sitwell MSS, 14.

89. *Eidem*, 2 July [?], ibid. 8/9.

90. Ibid.

91. C. M. Bowra to E. Sitwell, 25 July [?]; ibid. 10.

92. C. M. Bowra to E. Jennings, 28 Oct. 1967; Georgetown University, Washington; Jennings MSS, Box 1, folder 4.

93. *Idem* to ? Guillen, [1951]; Rare Books and Manuscripts, Pennsylvania State University Libraries.

94. E. Sitwell to L. Russell, 6 Oct. 1957; Eton College, Tower Store, Horner 02.

95. Typescript of BBC broadcast, 7 April 1972, Bowra MSS.

96. Mitchell/Jill Day-Lewis. Some friends thought he would remain neutral in the contest between Day-Lewis and C. S. Lewis; R. Lehmann to E. Starkie, 27 Feb. 1951; Bod. Lib., Starkie MSS, '1951'.

97. Mitchell/Lady Berlin.

98. C. M. Bowra, *A Book of Russian Verse* (London, 1943), xiv.

99. *Idem* to S. Colefax, 13 Sept. [?]; Bod. Lib., MS Eng. c.3160, f. 39.

100. M. Ignatieff, *Isaiah Berlin* (London, 1998), 233.

101. V. Ivanov to C. M. Bowra, 1 Oct. 1946; Bowra MSS. D. Ivanov, *Poems of Vyacheslav Ivanov* (Oxford, 1962), introduction. See also P. Davidson, *Vyacheslav Ivanov and C. M. Bowra* (Birmingham, 2006).

102. V. Ivanov to C. M. Bowra, 20 Dec. 1947; Bowra MSS.

103. C. M. Bowra to I. Berlin, 5 Nov. [1945]; ibid.

104. B. Pasternak to C. M. Bowra, 5 Nov. 1956; ibid.

105. *Eidem*, 25 Dec. 1945; ibid.

106. C. M. Bowra to E. Sitwell, 1 May [1946]; ibid.

107. P. Levi, *Boris Pasternak* (London, 1990), 207, 237, 245.

108. B. Pasternak to C. M. Bowra, 1 Sept. 1956; Bowra MSS.

109. *Eidem*, 5 Nov. 1956; ibid.

110. C. M. Bowra to F. Frankfurter, 11 Oct. [1958]; Frankfurter MSS, Box 25.

111. *Idem* to the Pasternak Family, 23 May [?]; Stanford University, Hoover Institution, Pasternak MSS, Box 14, folder 19.

112. *Idem* to E. Starkie, 5 Jan. 1966; Bod. Lib., Starkie MSS, Box '1966'.

113. Ibid. [Oct. 1947]; ibid. Box '1947'.

114. C. M. Bowra, *Memorial Address for Enid Starkie* (Oxford, 1970), 8.

115. Mitchell/Walter Hooper.

116. Bowra, *Memorial Address for Enid Starkie*, 7.

117. *Oxford Magazine*, 14 and 28 Feb. 1946.

118. E. Sitwell to C. M. Bowra, 8 May 1946; Bowra MSS.

119. C. M. Bowra to E. Sitwell, 17 May and 18 Dec. [?]; ibid.

120. BL Add., MSS 71182, f. 56; C. M. Bowra to R. Harrod, 5 Dec. [1955].

121. C. M. Bowra to H. Hugo, 26 Jan. [1956]; Sparrow MSS, Box 57.

122. *Idem* to E. Starkie, 8 Feb. [1956], Bod. Lib., Starkie MSS, '1956'.

123. *Idem* to U. Niebuhr, 23 May 1958; Nat. Lib. of Congress, Niebuhr MSS. When Auden found himself supporting the same candidate as Bowra in a later election he found the experience uncomfortable. W. Auden to E. Starkie, 1 Feb. 1966; Bod. Lib., Starkie MSS, '1966'.

124. C. M. Bowra to G. Rylands, 9 Feb. 1966; Rylands MSS, GHWR/3/57.

125. *Idem* to G. Donaldson, 8 Feb. 1966; Bowra MSS.

126. V. Joscelyne to C. M. Bowra, 30 Nov. [?]; ibid.

127. Bowra, *Poetry and Politics*, 67.

128. Ibid. 69.

CHAPTER 6 — SEX AND SEXUALITY

1. Davie/Stuart Hampshire.

2. Davie/Isaiah Berlin.

3. Davie/Leslie Rowse.

4. W. Clonmure to P. Balfour, [1926]; Huntington Lib., Kinross MSS.

5. Ibid.

6. Mitchell/Walter Hooper.

7. Davie/Leslie Rowse.

8. Davie/Stuart Hampshire.

9. Ibid.

10. Mitchell/Lady Annan.

11. A. Fleming to E. Waugh, [June 1960]; M. Amory, *The Letters of Ann Fleming* (London, 1985), 262.

12. Noel Annan's Commonplace Book; King's Coll., Cambridge, Annan MSS.

13. Wadham Coll., Oxford, Bowra MSS.

14. J. Sparrow to P. Synnott, 6 April 1927; Synnott MSS.

15. Mitchell/Walter Hooper.

16. Davie/Noel Annan.

17. Mitchell/C. M. Bowra and C. M. Bowra to J. Sparrow, 19 May 1963; Sparrow MSS, Box 38.

18. C. M. Bowra to J. Betjeman, 8 June 1950; Betjeman MSS.

19. *Idem* to P. Synnott, 21 April [1928]; Synnott MSS.

20. F. Partridge, *Diaries* (London 2004), 27.

21. Davie/Noel Annan. Though some friends remembered a surprisingly weak handshake: J. Salmon to L. Mitchell, 23 Oct. 2006; Bowra MSS.

22. Davie/Leslie Rowse.

23. Davie/Stuart Hampshire. Hampshire did not believe that Bowra and Boothby were ever anything more than friends, but it was a friendship with strange consequences. In 1960, Bowra opposed the candidacy of Harold Macmillan for the Chancellorship of Oxford University, because Macmillan detested Boothby as the long-term lover of his wife.

24. C. M. Bowra to F. Frankfurter, 16 June 1963; Frankfurter MSS, Box 24.

25. C. Connolly to C. M. Bowra, n.d.; Connolly MSS.

26. A. Powell, *Infants of the Spring* (London, 1976), 182.

27. Ibid. 193.

28. C. M. Bowra to P. Synnott, 1 Oct. 1927; Synnott MSS.

29. A. J. Ayer, *Part of My Life* (Oxford, 1977), 230, and J. Rees, *Looking for Mr Nobody* (London, 1994), 54.

30. C. M. Bowra to G. Rylands, 17 March [1944]; Rylands MSS, GHWR/3/57.

31. 'E. D.' to C. M. Bowra, 1 Sept. 1942; Bowra MSS.

32. I. Berlin to F. Frankfurter, 23 June 1940; H. Hardy, *Flourishing* (London, 2004), 305.

33. Mitchell/Noel Worswick.

34. C. M. Bowra to J. Mitchell, 20 July 1970; Mitchell MSS.

35. Davie/Stuart Hampshire.

36. Ibid.

37. R. Glasser, *Gorbals Boy at Oxford* (London, 1988), 165–7.

38. Davie/Isaiah Berlin, and N. Annan, *The Dons* (London 1999), 156.

39. Davie/Isaiah Berlin.

40. Diary of Nigel Clive, 2 May 1939; Bowra MSS.

41. 'Captain Courageous' is a poem about an officer disgraced for immoral behaviour. Maurice Bowra, *New Bats in Old Belfries* ed. H. Hardy and J. Holmes (Oxford, 2005), 47–9. It includes the verse; 'The Captain's stuck upon the mat, | And guilt is in his eye. | He knows that all who sin like that | Disgrace the Old School Tie, | That he who tries to fuck a | Lance Corporal isn't pukka | And suffers by and by.' He had enjoyed the tale of such an incident at Sandhurst in 1926; C. M. Bowra to P. Kinross, 7 Oct. 1926; Huntington Lib., Calif.; Kinross MSS.

42. C. M. Bowra to J. Sparrow, 19 May 1963; Sparrow MSS, Box 38.

43. N. Annan to C. M. Bowra, 14 June [?]; Bowra MSS.

44. S. Tabachnik, *Fiercer Than Tigers* (Michigan, 2002), 261.

45. E. Starkie, 'André Gide's Visit to Oxford', 1947; Bod. Lib., Oxford; Starkie MSS.

46. Ibid.

47. J. Sparrow to H. Trevor-Roper, 14 Oct. 1971; Christ Church, Oxford, Trevor-Roper MSS, '1970–1973', unfol.

48. R. Lehmann to E. Starkie, [1947]; Bod. Lib., Oxford, Starkie MSS, '1947'.

49. Starkie, 'André Gide's Visit to Oxford'; ibid.

50. R. Lehmann to E. Starkie, 13 June 1947; ibid.

51. *Eaedem*, [May 1947]; ibid.

52. E. Starkie, 'André Gide's Visit to Oxford'; ibid.

53. G. Rylands to C. M. Bowra, 26 Dec. 1962; Bowra MSS.

54. *Eidem*, 4 Feb. 1969; ibid.

55. A. Bishop to G. Rylands, 28 June 1923; ibid. Michael Davie's notes, Wadham College.

56. *Memories*, 56.

57. E. Kantorowicz to C. M. Bowra, 22 March 1962; ibid.

58. Davie/Stuart Hampshire.

59. Ibid.

60. C. M. Bowra to J. Betjeman, 19 Sept. [1931?]; Bowra MSS.

61. Tape of BBC Broadcast, 7 April 1972; ibid.

62. 'Old Croaker'; Bowra, *New Bats in Old Belfries*, 50–60.

63. C. M. Bowra to J. Betjeman, 17 July [1940]; Betjeman MSS.

64. A. Bishop to C. M. Bowra, 16 June 1942; Bowra MSS.

65. BL Add. MSS 71182, f. 50; C. M. Bowra to Billa Harrod, n.d.

66. C. M. Bowra to A. S. Sproatt, 18 June [?]; King's Coll. Camb., WJHS/9.

67. *Memories*, 122.

68. D. Carrington to G. Brennan, 15 Oct. 1924; HRC, DC/9B.

69. BL Add. MSS 72728, f. 6, C. M. Bowra to R. Harrod, 30 July [1920].

70. C. M. Bowra to M. McCarthy, 20 Sept. [1927]; Lilly Library, Indiana University, Bloomington, Ind., McCarthy MSS.

71. J. Lewis, *Cyril Connolly* (London, 1997), 187.

72. *Memories*, 123.

73. P. Synnott to P. Balfour, [Jan. 1926]; Huntington Lib., Kinross MSS.

74. C. M. Bowra to P. Synnott, 9 Nov. [1925]; Synnott MSS.

75. *Eidem*, 14 Dec. [1925]; ibid.

76. *Eidem*, 20 Dec [1924]; ibid.

77. C. Connolly to P. Balfour, Jan. 1925; Huntington Lib., Kinross MSS.

78. *Eidem*, Jan. 1925; ibid.

79. P. Synnott to P. Balfour, 7 Jan. [1925]; ibid.

80. C. M. Bowra to P. Synnott, 11 Jan. [1925]; Synnott MSS.

81. *Idem* to C. Connolly, 3 Aug. [1925]; Connolly MSS.

82. C. Connolly to C. M. Bowra, n.d.; ibid.

83. *Idem* to P. Balfour, 12 Aug. [1926]; Huntington Lib., Kinross MSS.

84. C. M. Bowra to J. Sparrow, 20 July [1927]; Sparrow MSS, Box 57.

85. *Idem* to P. Balfour, 11 Jan. 1927; Huntington Lib., Kinross MSS.

86. *Eidem*, 18 Sept. [1926]; ibid.

87. C. M. Bowra to C. Connolly, 22 April [?], Connolly MSS.

88. *Idem* to P. Synnott, 19 Feb. [1928]; Synnott MSS.

89. 'Anxiety', April 1927; Wadham Coll., Bowra MSS. Another copy exists in the Synnott MSS.

90. 'Separation', [3 April 1928]; Synnott MSS.

91. Davie/Lady Harrod.

92. C. M. Bowra to J. Sparrow, 4 July 1928; Sparrow MSS.

93. *Eidem*, 6 Aug. [1928].

94. C. M. Bowra to P. Synnott, 19 Spet. [1929]; Synnott MSS.

95. *Idem* to J. Sparrow, 14 Sept. [1929]; Sparrow MSS, Box 57.

96. *Idem* to P. Balfour, 23 Aug. [1930]; Huntington Lib., Kinross MSS.

97. *Eidem*, 23 Aug. 1931; ibid., and C. M. Bowra to J. Betjeman, 19 Sept. [1931]; Betjeman MSS.

98. Ayer, *Part of My Life*, 99.

99. Davie/Lady Longford.

100. C. M. Bowra to J. Sparrow, 29 Dec. [1929]; Sparrow MSS, Box 57. Maurice described bisexual people as those who played 'strokes all around the wicket'; Morwood/P. Leigh Fermor.

101. C. M. Bowra to J. Sparrow, 13 Sept [1928]; ibid.

102. E. Dell to C. M. Bowra, 19 Jan. 1922; Bowra MSS.

103. Davie/Lady Longford.

104. Morwood/P. Leigh Fermor.

105. Davie/Sally Chilver.

106. C. M. Bowra to J. Sparrow, [1927]; Sparrow MSS, Box 57.

107. Mitchell/Jill Day-Lewis.

108. BL Add. MSS 72728, f. 49; C. M. Bowra to R. Harrod, 27 April [1935].

109. 'Prothalamium', 1927. Maurice Bowra, *New Bats in Old Belfries*, 13.

110. 'Heldengesang', June 1950; ibid. 102–3.

111. 'Uffington Downs', 1937; ibid. 21–3; and C. M. Bowra to N. Annan, 25 Oct. [1944]; King's Coll. Camb., Annan MSS.

112. C. M. Bowra to F. Frankfurter, 4 Dec. ?; Frankfurter MSS, Box 25.

113. Mitchell/Jill Day-Lewis.

114. C. M. Bowra to F. Frankfurter, 12 Sept. ?; Frankfurter MSS, Box 25.

115. *Eidem*, Sept. ?; ibid.

116. C. M. Bowra to I. Berlin, 18 June 1943 and 25 Oct. 1945; Bowra MSS.

117. Ibid.

118. C. M. Bowra to J. Betjeman, 21 Aug. 1930; Betjemann MSS. Penelope Betjeman was called 'propellor' as a commentary to her whirring energy.

119. *Idem* to E. Waugh, 2 March [?]; Bowra MSS.

120. Revd A. W. R. Lodge to H. Hardy, 27 Dec. 2005; ibid.

121. C. M. Bowra to P. Synnott, 21 April [1928]; Synnott MSS.

122. *Eidem*, [Oct. 1927]; ibid.

123. Mitchell/C. M. Bowra.

124. *Memories*, 333.

125. C. M. Bowra to G. Rylands, 22 Dec. 1922; Rylands MSS, GHWR/3/57.

126. C. Connolly essay, 17 July 1971; Bowra MSS.

127. C. M. Bowra to J. Sparrow, 10 July [1927]; Sparrow MSS, Box 57.

128. *Eidem*, 3 Oct. [1927], ibid.

129. *Eidem*, 18 Aug. [1927], ibid.

130. Lady Longford, *The Pebbled Shore* (London, 1986), 211.

131. Ibid. 62–3.

132. Davie/Lady Longford.

133. Ibid.

134. Ibid.

135. C. M. Bowra to J. Sparrow, 23 Dec. [1927]; Sparrow MSS, Box 57.

136. *Idem* to P. Synnott, 30 May [1928]; Synnott MSS.

137. *Eidem*, 7 June [1928]; ibid.

138. Davie/Lady Longford; and Lady Longford, *Pebbled Shore*, 90–1.

139. Ibid. 117. Curiously though, Lady Longford's daughter was never invited to Wadham, while an undergraduate at Lady Margaret Hall; Mitchell/Lady Antonia Fraser.

140. C. M. Bowra to F. Frankfurter, 24 Sept. [1936]; Frankfurter MSS, Box 25.

141. I. Berlin to F. Frankfurter, 23 Aug. 1937; H. Hardy, *Flourishing: Letters 1928–46* (London 2004), 250–1.

142. Davie/Isaiah Berlin.

143. Davie/Sally Chilver.

144. C. M. Bowra to C. and J. Connolly [1937]; Connolly MSS.

145. BL Add. MSS 72776, f. 103; B. Harrod to R. Harrod, 25 Aug 1937. See also BL Add. MSS 72777, f. 22; R. Harrod to B. Harrod, 9 Oct. 1937.

146. C. M. Bowra to C. Connolly, 11 Aug. [1937]; Connolly MSS.

147. Ibid. In fact, she became a successful academic.

148. *Eidem*, [1937]; ibid.

149. C. M. Bowra to I. Berlin, 11 Aug. [1937]; Bowra MSS.

150. 'The Late Lorn Lesbian', 1937; Maurice Bowra, *New Bats in Old Belfries*, 20.

151. I. Berlin to F. Frankfurter, 23 Aug. 1937; Hardy, *Flourishing*, 250–1.

152. M. Fisher to I. Berlin [1937]; Berlin MSS, 243, ff. 85, 89. See also M. Frankfurter to I. Berlin, 26 April [1938]; ibid. 106, f. 48.

153. Davie/Stuart Hampshire.

154. J. Mitchell, *A Disgraceful Anomaly* (London, 2003), 20. The story is also discounted by Ann Fleming's daughter; Mitchell/Fionn Morgan.

155. I. Berlin to N. Annan, 31 Aug. 1973; Berlin MSS, 241, f. 132; and C. M. Bowra to N. Annan; 29 Sept. [?]; King's Coll. Camb., Annan MSS.

156. Aline Berlin found Bowra to be 'all kindness' to women; Mitchell/Lady Berlin.

157. J. Leigh Fermor to C. Clark, 19 July [1971]; C. Clark MSS.

158. Maurice often talked of 'the incompatibility of love and sex'; Davie/Noel Annan.

159. N. Annan to I. Berlin, 8 Aug. 1973; Berlin MSS, 241, f. 127.

160. S. Hastings, *Rosamond Lehmann* (London, 2002), 269.

161. C. M. Bowra to E. Sitwell, 14 Feb. ?; HRC, Sitwell MSS, 11.

162. Mitchell/Colette Clark.

163. J. Mitchell, introduction to Maurice Bowra, *New Bats in Old Belfries*.

164. Draft Notes by Cyril Connolly in Bowra MSS.

CHAPTER 7 — OXFORD, 1922–1938

1. C. M. Bowra to R. Lennard, 14 Dec. 1925; Bowra MSS.

2. *The Times*, 17 March 1967.

3. Ibid.

4. A. J. Ayer, *Part of My Life* (Oxford, 1977), 99.

5. Lady Longford, *The Pebbled Shore* (London, 1986), 81–92.

6. Mary ? to C. M. Bowra, 16 Dec. 1936; Bowra MSS.

7. Mitchell/Mary Bennett.

8. R. Mynors to K. Clark, 6 July 1947; Tate Britain, Clark MSS, TGA 8812/1/3 2201.

9. Mitchell/Lady Quinton.

10. *Oxford Magazine*, 1933.

11. Ibid.

12. C. M. Bowra to I. Berlin, 12 and 29 Oct. 1932; Berlin MSS.

13. S. Day-Lewis, *Cecil Day-Lewis* (London 1980), 31.

14. K. Clark, *Another Part of the Wood* (London, 1974), 99–100.

15. Ibid.

16. Ibid.

17. Davie/David Astor.

18. C. Connolly, unpublished essay, 14 July 1971; Bowra MSS.

19. J. Betjeman, tape of BBC broadcast; ibid.

20. J. Lowe, *The Warden* (London, 1998), 51.

21. N. Annan, tape of BBC broadcast, Bowra MSS.

22. I. Berlin, tape recording; H. Hardy, *Flourishing* (London, 2004), 705–6.

23. I. Berlin to C. M. Bowra, 27 Aug. [1952]; Bowra MSS.

24. C. M. Bowra to J. Sparrow, [1927]; Sparrow MSS, Box 57.

25. *Eidem*, July [1927]; ibid.

26. *Eidem*, 20 Aug. [1927]; ibid.

27. Mitchell/George Richardson.

28. *The Sunday Times*, 19 Oct. 1974.

29. Mitchell/George Richardson. Undergraduates who had taken too much on board would be quite literally shown the door.

30. O. Lancaster, *With an Eye to the Future* (London, 1953), 71.

31. Mitchell/George Richardson.

32. D. Pryce Jones, *Cyril Connolly* (London, 1983), 83.

33. C. M. Bowra to P. Synnott, 19 Feb. [1928]; Synnott MSS.

34. *Idem* to J. Sparrow, n.d.; Sparrow MSS, Box 57.

35. *Idem*, *Proceedings of the British Academy*, 35 (1953), 223.

36. A. Powell, *Infants of the Spring* (London, 1976), 179–80.

37. Mitchell/John Bamborough. Maurice Platnauer was a Fellow of Brasenose.

38. Mitchell/C. M. Bowra.

39. J. Betjeman, *Summoned by Bells* (London 1960), 101.

40. Lady Longford, *The Pebbled Shore*, 81–92.

41. BL Add. MSS 71189, f. 50; E. Starkie to R. Harrod, [1943].

42. W. M. Calder III to L. Mitchell, 21 Dec 2005; Bowra MSS.

43. 'Friends of my Youth', [1921]; Maurice Bowra, *New Bats in Old Belfries* ed. H. Hardy and J. Holmes (Oxford, 2005), 17–18.

44. Ibid.

45. S. Spender, *Journals, 1939–1983* (London, 1985), 155.

46. C. M. Bowra to J. Betjeman, n.d.; Betjeman MSS.

47. 'The Architect to his Lady', 1927; Maurice Bowra, *New Bats in Old Belfries*, 15–16.

48. I. Berlin to Lady Diana Cooper, n.d., Eton Coll. Archives, Tower Store, DC 03.

49. 'Major Prophet'; Maurice Bowra, *New Bats in Old Belfries*, 32.

50. C. M. Bowra to J. Sparrow, 4 Jan. [1930]; Sparrow MSS, Box 57.

51. This included the practice of reading other people's letters; *eidem*, 20 Aug. [1927]; ibid.

52. N. Annan to I. Berlin, 8 Aug. 1973; Berlin MSS, 241, f. 27.

53. C. M. Bowra to G. Rylands, 24 Aug. 1965; Rylands MSS, GHWR/3/57.

54. M. Bennett to I. Berlin, 10 Aug. 1971; Berlin MSS, 243, f. 179.

55. Ibid.

56. *Eadem* to I. Berlin, 14 Nov. 1935; ibid. f. 46.

57. S. Day-Lewis, *Cecil Day-Lewis*, 31, 251.

58. C. Connolly to N. Blakiston, 24 Nov. 1924; N. Blakiston, *A Romantic Friendship* (London, 1975), 26.

59. N. Annan, in H. Lloyd-Jones, *Maurice Bowra* (London, 1974), 61.

60. Ibid, 62, 64.

61. I. Berlin to N. Annan, 31 Aug. 1971; Hardy, *Flourishing*, 706.

62. A. L. Rowse, *Friends and Contemporaries* (London 1990), 76.

63. Mitchell/C. M. Bowra and C. M. Bowra to E. Waugh, 27 Sept. 1964; Bowra MSS: E. Waugh to C. M. Bowra, 'Michaelmas', 1964; ibid.

64. Mitchell/John Bamborough. Martin Tupper was a famous Victorian moralist.

65. H. Carpenter, *W. H. Auden* (London, 1981), 65.

66. 'Momotombo'; Maurice Bowra, *New Bats in Old Belfries*, 133–5.

67. Ibid.

68. I. Berlin to S. Spender, 20 June [1936]; Hardy, *Flourishing*, 176.

69. Davie/Noel Annan.

70. Powell, *Infants of the Spring*, 128.

71. Mitchell/C. M. Bowra.

72. Ibid.

73. C. Connolly to N. Blakiston, 14 May 1925; Blakiston, *A Romantic Friendship*, 78–9.

74. C. Hollis, *Oxford in the Twenties* (London 1976), 22.

75. C. M. Bowra to C. Clark, 28 Dec. [1960]; C. Clark MSS.

76. *Idem* to P. Synnott, [27 April 1926]; Synnott MSS.

77. *Eidem*, 19 Feb. [1928]; ibid.

78. C. M. Bowra to C. Connolly, 3 Aug [1925?]; Connolly MSS.

79. *Wadham Gazette*, new series, 1 (1), 1975.

80. C. M. Bowra to P. Synnott, [Oct. 1927]; Synnott MSS, and *idem* to P. Balfour, 28 July [1925]; Huntington Lib., Calif., Kinross MSS.

81. *Idem* to P. Synnott, 14 July [1925]; Synnott MSS.

82. C. Radcliffe to J. Sparrow, 28 Nov. 1966; Sparrow MSS, Box 64.

83. J. Sparrow to Sir K. Clark, 29 Dec. 1964; Tate Britain, Clark MSS, TGA/8812/1/3 f. 2963.

84. C. M. Bowra to J. Sparrow, n.d.; Sparrow MSS, Box 57.

85. Mitchell/George Huxley.

86. Mitchell/Peter Fraser.

87. C. M. Bowra to C. Connolly, 22 April [?], Connolly MSS.

88. R. Blake to H. Trevor-Roper, 7 Sept. 1962; Christ Church, Oxford, Trevor-Roper MSS, Box '1962'.

89. C. M. Bowra to A. James, 27 April [1952]; Harvard, Houghton Library, bMS AM 1938 (152).

90. M. Ignatieff, *Isaiah Berlin* (London 1998), 51.

91. S. Hampshire to I. Berlin, 9 March 1945; Berlin MSS, 256 f. 46.

92. Ayer, *Part of My Life*, 99.

93. H. Lloyd-Jones, Tape of BBC broadcast, 7 April 1972; Bowra MSS.

94. Ignatieff, *Isaiah Berlin*, 51.

95. S. Hampshire, Tape of BBC broadcast, 7 April 1972; Bowra MSS.

96. Powell, *Infants of the Spring*, 183.

97. Lady Longford, *The Pebbled Shore* (London 1986), 86.

98. N. Annan to I. Berlin, 8 Aug. 1973; Berlin MSS, 241 f. 127.

99. Powell, *Infants of the Spring*, 181.

100. C. M. Bowra to P. Synnott, [Oct. 1927]; Synnott MSS.

101. *Idem* to A. James, 15 Jan. [1950]; Harvard, Houghton Library, bMS AM 1938 (152).

102. BL Add. MSS, 71610, f.13; *idem* to R. Harrod, 6 April [1924].

103. P. Vibert to L. Mitchell, 8 March 2006; Bowra MSS.

104. C. M. Bowra to J. Sparrow, 2 Aug 1928; Sparrow MSS, Box 57.

105. BL Add., MSS, 72728, f. 14; *idem* to R. Harrod, 17 Aug. [1920].

106. *Memories*, 128.

107. Ibid. 149.

108. C. M. Bowra to H. Trevor-Roper, 6 Feb. [1961]; Christ Church, Oxford, Trevor-Roper MSS, '1961'.

109. Claude [?] to B. Arber, 6 July 1971; Bowra MSS.

110. S. Tabachnik, *Fiercer than Tigers* (Michigan, 2002), 51–2.

111. Ibid.

112. C. M. Bowra to C. Clark, 4 Oct. [1961]; C. Clark MSS.

113. *Idem* to E. Sitwell, 17 March [?]; HRC, Sitwell MSS, 7.

114. N. Annan, in Lloyd-Jones, *Maurice Bowra*, 53.

115. C. M. Bowra to J. Sparrow, 1 April [1928]; Sparrow MSS, Box 57.

116. *Idem* to P. Synnott, 25 March [1928]; Synnott MSS.

117. When Betjeman retreated to a prep school in Buckinghamshire, Bowra visited him regularly. He was also helpful in securing his friend a post on *The Architectural Review*.

118. C. M. Bowra to F. Frankfurter, 18 Dec. [1949]; Frankfurter MSS, Box 25.

119. *Idem* to C. Connolly, n.d.; Connolly MSS.

120. Revd A. W. R. Lodge to H. Hardy, 27 Dec., 2005; Bowra MSS.

121. C. M. Bowra to J. Sparrow, 2 April [1929]; Sparrow MSS, Box 57.

122. *Eidem*, [Jan. 1934]; Lowe, *The Warden*, 75–6.

123. C. M. Bowra to J. Sparrow, 19 May 1963; Sparrow MSS, Box 38.

124. *Eidem*, 16 Jan [1962]; ibid., Box 37.

125. I. Berlin to N. Annan, 18 Jan. 1962; Berlin MSS, 241, f. 72.

126. C. M. Bowra to J. Sparrow, 12 June 1934; Lowe, *The Warden*, 80–1.

127. *Idem* to C. Clark, 8 Jan. 1965; C. Clark MSS.

128. *Eidem*, 6 Jan. 1971; ibid.

129. C. Radcliffe to J. Sparrow, 28 Nov. 1966; Sparrow MSS, Box 64.

130. Mitchell/Colette Clark.

131. Ibid.

132. Mitchell / J. Bamborough.

133. I. Berlin to N. Annan, 20 May 1949; Berlin MSS, 241 f. 1.

134. Powell, *Infants of the Spring*, 189.

135. C. M. Bowra to P. Synnott, 25 July [1925]; Synnott MSS.

136. C. Connolly to C. M. Bowra, n.d.; Connolly MSS.

137. E. Bowen to I. Berlin, [Sept. 1935]; Berlin MSS, 245 f. 37. See also C. Connolly to N. Blakiston, 25 Dec. 1926 and March 1927; Blakiston *A Romantic Friendship*, 200.

138. C. M. Bowra to M. McCarthy, 18 Jan. [1927?]; Lilly Library, Indiana University, Bloomington, Ind.; McCarthy MSS.

139. C. Connolly to C. M. Bowra, n.d.; Bowra MSS.

140. Ibid.

141. C. M. Bowra to M. Frankfurter, 28 March [1937]; Frankfurter MSS, Box 25.

142. I. Berlin to E. Bowen, [*c*.26 Aug. 1936]; Hardy, *Flourishing*, 182.

143. C. M. Bowra to F. Frankfurter, 16 Sept. 1962; Frankfurter MSS, Box 25.

144. N. Annan, *The Dons* (London, 1999), 151.

145. Mitchell/George Huxley and Mitchell/Mary Bennett.

146. S. Day-Lewis, *Cecil Day-Lewis*, 33.

147. Mitchell/George Huxley.

148. C. Day-Lewis to C. M. Bowra, [*c*.1927]; Bowra MSS.

149. Tabachnik, *Fiercer than Tigers*, 311; and C. Day-Lewis, *The Buried Day* (London, 1960), 177.

150. J. Betjeman, Tape of BBC broadcast, 7 April 1972, Bowra MSS.

151. C. M. Bowra to C. Connolly, n.d.; Connolly MSS. See also *eidem*, 3 Aug. [1925 or 6]; ibid.

152. Mitchell/Colette Clark.

153. K. Clark to J. Sparrow, 25 Aug. [1926]; Sparrow MSS, Box 58.

154. J. Lewis, *Cyril Connolly* (London, 1997), 145. After the Minehead incident, Connolly penned the following verse: 'How many geese has Maurice

cooked | The time I've been away? | Why only one, but that's been done | To last to judgement day' (ibid. 129).

155. *Sunday Times*, 17 July 1971.
156. Ibid.
157. J. Sparrow to I. Berlin, [1934]; Berlin MSS, 281, f. 23.
158. M. Hastings to P. Balfour, 9 Aug. 1961; Huntington Lib., Calif., Balfour MSS.
159. I. Berlin to J. Sparrow, 23 March 1954; Sparrow MSS, Box 56.
160. BL Add., MSS 72728, ff. 44–5; C. M. Bowra to R. Harrod, 25 Aug. [1922].
161. C. M. Bowra to E. Bowen, 7 Sept. [1935]; HRC, Bowen MSS, 2.
162. Mitchell/Lady Berlin. Berlin himself sometimes needed reassurance about Maurice's opinion of him; see M. Frankfurter to I. Berlin, [1953]; Berlin MSS, 136, f. 442.

CHAPTER 8 — BOWRA AND THE WIDER WORLD, 1922–1939

1. F. Wolsey to C. M. Bowra, n.d.; Bowra MSS. For a variation on the Parson's Pleasure story, see G. H. Paton to L. G. Mitchell, 7 Feb. 2006; ibid.
2. S. Hampshire to C. H. Moore, 26 Jan. 1973; Bowra MSS. If the remark was ever made by anyone, it might be more properly ascribed to the Principal of Hertford.
3. 'Maggie Bowra' to J. Sparrow, 10 Dec. 1967; Sparrow MSS, Box 81.
4. I. Berlin to F. Frankfurter, 23 Aug. 1937; H. Hardy, *Flourishing* (London, 2004), 250–1.
5. N. Blake, *The Shell of Death* (London, 1936).
6. M. Innes, *Operation Pax* (London, 1951).
7. M. Amory, *Lord Berners* (London, 1999), 180, 184.
8. Lord Berners, *Far From the Madding War* (London, 1941), chap. 4.
9. J. Lewis, *Cyril Connolly* (London, 1997), 160.
10. E. Bowen, *To the North* (London, 1932).
11. I. Berlin to E. Bowen, [15 and 27 Sept. 1938]; Hardy, *Flourishing*, 288.
12. S. Spender to L. Mitchell, 2 Aug. [19]90; Mitchell MSS.
13. E. Sitwell to C. M. Bowra, 21 Sept. 1953; Bowra MSS.
14. Noel Annan's Commonplace Book; King's Coll., Cambridge, Annan MSS.
15. Ibid.
16. Stuart Hampshire; BBC broadcast tape; Bowra MSS.
17. Ibid.
18. E. Kantorowicz to C. M. Bowra, 3 Sept. 1963; ibid.
19. A. Fleming to Lady Diana Cooper, 'Wednesday', Morgan MSS.
20. *The Eton College Chronicle*, 30 Nov. 1950.
21. BL Add. MSS 71610, f. 4; C. M. Bowra to R. Harrod, 6 Sept. [1923].
22. M. Frankfurter to I. Berlin, 29 March [1949]; Berlin MSS, 118 f. 209.
23. N. Annan in H. Lloyd-Jones, *Maurice Bowra* (London, 1974), 56–7.

24. Mitchell/Lord Quinton.

25. Annan in Lloyd-Jones, *Maurice Bowra*, 56–7.

26. C. M. Bowra to I. Berlin, 7 Nov. 1945; Bowra MSS.

27. I. Berlin to N. Annan, 3 Aug. 1973; Berlin MSS, 241 f. 129.

28. Davie/Stuart Hampshire.

29. Ibid.

30. Davie/Noel Annan.

31. C. M. Bowra to J. Sparrow, 10 July [1927]; Sparrow MSS, Box 57.

32. Mitchell/C. M. Bowra.

33. C. M. Bowra to J. Sparrow, n.d.; J. Lowe, *The Warden* (London, 1998), 75–6. C. M. Bowra to Ottoline Morrell, he described Bloomsbury as full of 'dead sensualists'; *idem* to Lady Ottoline Morrell, 22 April [?]; HRC, Morrell MSS, 17.

34. K. Clarke, *Another Part of the Wood* (London, 1974), 99.

35. C. M. Bowra to F. Frankfurter n.d.; Frankfurter MSS, Box 25.

36. The Wharf's Guest Books; Bod. Lib., Oxford; Bonham Carter MSS, 698. Philip Ritchie, Sylvester Gates, and Eddie Sackville-West were also regular visitors.

37. C. M. Bowra to P. Synnott, 5 July [1925]; Synnott MSS.

38. *Idem* to Lady Ottoline Morrell, 22 April [?]; HRC, Morrell MSS.

39. *Eidem*, 27 April [1928].

40. C. M. Bowra to J. Sparrow, 19 Sept. [1928]; Sparrow MSS, Box 57.

41. *Idem* to P. Synnott, 19 Feb. [1928]; Synnott MSS.

42. *Eidem*, [7 June 1929]; ibid.

43. C. M. Bowra to Lady Ottoline Morrell, 'Sunday'; HRC, Morrell MSS, 16.

44. *Idem* to P. Synnott, 5 April [1925]; Synnott MSS.

45. *Idem* to Lady Ottoline Morrell, 3 April [1928]; HRC, Morrell MSS, 16.

46. *Eidem*, 22 April [?]; ibid.

47. C. M. Bowra to J. Sparrow, 1 April [1928]; Sparrow MSS, Box 57.

48. Ibid.

49. C. Day-Lewis, *The Buried Day* (London 1960), 173.

50. C. M. Bowra to P. Synnott, 25 March 1928; Synnott MSS.

51. *Idem* to Lady Ottoline Morrell, 26 May [?]; HRC, Morrell MSS, 17.

52. Ibid.

53. Mitchell/C. M. Bowra. See also C. M. Bowra to G. Rylands, 5 April 1968; Rylands MSS, GHWR/3/57.

54. C. Beaton to Lady Diana Cooper, n.d., Eton Coll. Tower Store, DC 07.

55. C. M. Bowra to M. Frankfurter, 18 Dec. [1949]; Frankfurter MSS, Box 25.

56. Lady Hartwell to I. Berlin, 27 March [?]; Berlin MSS, 244 ff. 27–8.

57. Mitchell/Colette Clark.

58. Lord Boothby, *Recollections of a Rebel* (London, 1978), 13–14.

59. Noel Annan's Commonplace Book; King's Coll., Cambridge, Annan MSS.

60. C. M. Bowra to G. Rylands, 24 May 1964; Bowra MSS. See also *idem* to C. Connolly, 24 May 1964; Connolly MSS.

61. C. Hollis, *Oxford in the Twenties* (London 1976), 30. 'Maurice was beyond question Samgrass.' C. Sykes, *Evelyn Waugh* (London, 1975), 254.

62. C. M. Bowra to C. Connolly, 6 June 1971; Connolly MSS.

63. Sykes, *Evelyn Waugh*, 254.

64. Ibid.

65. C. M. Bowra to N. Mitford, 29 Dec. 1966; Chatsworth, Mitford MSS, with permission from 'The Estate of Nancy Mitford'.

66. A. Pryce-Jones, *The Bonus of Laughter* (London, 1987), 230. For a variation on the story, see the obituary of James Lees-Milne, *Daily Telegraph*, 29 Dec. 1997. Bowra of course shared the patois of his time and class in using, for example, LMC for Lower Middle Class, or, when travelling abroad, ENT for English at Next Table. Mitchell/Lady Annan.

67. C. M. Bowra to Lady Ottoline Morrell, 26 May [?] and 14 Sept. [?]; HRC, Morrell MSS, 17.

68. A. Fleming to P. Leigh Fermor, 28 [Oct. 1954], M. Amory, *The Letters of Ann Fleming* (London, 1985), 129.

69. C. M. Bowra to P. Synnott, 23 Dec. [1925]; Synnott MSS. The company for the weekend consisted only of Bowra himself, Sackville-West, and one of his uncles.

70. *Eidem*, 29 Dec. 1927; ibid.

71. C. M. Bowra to J. Sparrow, 4 Jan. [1928]; Sparrow MSS, Box 57.

72. *Eidem*, 11 Jan. [1926]; ibid. According to the Naas guest book, Bowra was also there in July 1926, Sept. 1927, and Aug. 1931; Synnott MSS.

73. C. M. Bowra to M. McCarthy, 27 Sept. [1927]; Lilly Lib., Univ. of Indiana, McCarthy MSS; and *idem* to J. Sparrow, 11 Jan. [1926]; Sparrow MSS, Box 57.

74. *Eidem*, 12 Aug. 1926; J. Lowe, *The Warden* (London, 1998), 52.

75. C. M. Bowra to P. Synnott, 25 March [1928]; Synnott MSS.

76. Noel Annan Commonplace Book; King's Coll., Cambridge, Annan MSS.

77. C. M. Bowra to A. James, 5 June [1953]; Harvard, Houghton Lib., bMS AM 1938 (152).

78. P. Vibert to L. Mitchell, 8 March 2006; Bowra MSS.

79. C. M. Bowra to A. James, 29 May [1952]; Harvard, Houghton Lib., bMS AM 1938 (152).

80. *Idem* to H. Hugo, [1951]; Sparrow MSS, Box 57.

81. *Eidem*, 30 July 1963; ibid.

82. C. M. Bowra to G. Rylands, 28 March 1971; Bowra MSS.

83. *Idem* to H. Hugo, 30 July 1963; Sparrow MSS, Box 57.

84. Memoir by P. Leigh Fermor; Morgan MSS.

85. C. M. Bowra to C. Clark, 22 Sept. 1967; C. Clark MSS.

86. *Idem* to H. Hugo, 14 Oct. ?; Sparrow MSS, Box 57.

87. *Idem* to C. Clark, 22 Sept, 1967; C. Clark MSS.

88. *Idem* to G. Rylands, 15 Oct. 1967; Rylands MSS, GHWR/3/57.

89. Mitchell/Colette Clark.

90. A. Fleming to the Duchess of Devonshire, 26 Aug. [1964]; Morgan MSS.

91. Mitchell/Walter Hooper.

92. A. Fleming to Clarissa Eden, 7 Oct. [?]; Morgan MSS.

93. *Eadem* to Lady Berlin, 14 Aug. 1964; ibid.

94. C. M. Bowra to H. Hugo, 14 Oct. 1964; Sparrow MSS, Box 57; and *idem* to N. Annan, 14 Oct. 1967; King's Coll., Cambridge, Annan MSS.

95. 'Prize Song' in Maurice Bowra, *New Bats in Old Belfries* ed. H. Hardy and J. Holmes (Oxford, 2005), 140–1.

96. C. M. Bowra to F. Frankfurter, 28 March [1937]; Frankfurter MSS, Box 25.

97. *Idem* to P. Balfour, 7 Oct [1926]; Huntington Lib., Calif., Kinross MSS. To go into politics, 'one has to be inconceivably stupid'.

98. *Idem* to C. Clark, 10 Jan. 1970; C. Clark MSS. Maurice once abruptly told Winston Churchill that he could no longer have the services of Bill Deakin as a special adviser, because it was much more important that he should become the first head of St Antony's College: *Idem* to W. Churchill, 9 March [?]; Churchill Coll., Cambridge, Churchill MSS, CHUR/2/168 B.

99. *Idem* to J. Salmon 21 June 1971; Salmon MSS.

100. N. Annan to C. M. Bowra, 8 May 1967; King's Coll., Cambridge, NGA/5/1/892.

101. Untitled fragment; Bowra MSS. See also 'Workers' (1922) in the same collection.

102. *The Times*, 17 March 1967.

103. G. Burgess to I. Berlin, [Sept. 1934]; Berlin MSS, 103, f. 244.

104. Davie/Lady Longford.

105. C. M. Bowra, 'Hugh Gaitskell', in W. T. Rodgers, *Oxford in the Nineteen Twenties* (London, 1964), 20.

106. H. Gaitskell to C. M. Bowra, 3 Jan. 1955; UCL., Gaitskell MSS, f19.2; and P. Williams, *Hugh Gaitskell* (London, 1979), 754.

107. Bowra, 'Hugh Gaitskell', 29.

108. Ibid.

109. C. M. Bowra to J. Betjeman, 29 Oct. [1950?]; Betjeman MSS.

110. *Idem* to F. Frankfurter, 18 Dec. [?]; Frankfurter MSS, Box 25.

111. P. Williams, *Hugh Gaitskell* (London, 1979), 367–8.

112. C. M. Bowra to F. Frankfurter, 1 Feb. 1963; Frankfurter MSS, Box 25. See also *idem* to G. Rylands, 19 Jan, 1963; Rylands MSS, GHWR/3/57.

113. Hollis, *Oxford in the Twenties*, 27. For Gaitskell's influence, see Williams, *Hugh Gaitskell*, 17–18.

114. *The Times*, 17 May 1967: the Strike had been 'a sad and pathetic affair'.

115. Hollis, *Oxford in the Twenties*, 24.

116. *Oxford Magazine*, 3 June 1926.

117. *The Times*, 23 June 1937.

118. Mitchell/C. M. Bowra. See also Hollis, *Oxford in the Twenties*, 28.

119. See Chap. 9.

120. Hollis, *Oxford in the Twenties*, 28. Bowra later remarked that 'I did not fight in Spain, but kept most of my hate for the Germans'; C. M. Bowra to N. Annan, 27 Nov. 1966; King's Coll., Cambridge, Annan MSS.

121. E. Waugh to C. M. Bowra, 2 July 1960; Bowra MSS.

122. Hollis, *Oxford in the Twenties*, 29.

123. C. M. Bowra to R. Colby, 78 Feb [1936]; Scheetz MSS.

124. Mitchell/C. M. Bowra.

125. *The Times*, 7 May 1958, 23 Jan. 1959, 2 Jan 1962.

126. Ibid. 23 Oct. 1957, 10 April 1959, 11 May 1965, 8 May 1967.

127. C. M. Bowra to E. Waugh, 14 Jan. [1960]; Bowra MSS.

128. *Idem* to Lady Ottoline Morrell, 24 July [1928]; HRC, Morrell MSS, 19.

129. *Idem* to F. Frankfurter, 25 Feb. [1955/6]; Frankfurter MSS, Box 25.

130. *Oxford Mail*, 5 Nov. 1956.

131. *The Times*, 3 Nov. 1956.

132. C. M. Bowra to H. Trevor-Roper, 26 Nov. and 10 Dec. [1956]; Christ Church, Oxford, Trevor-Roper MSS, '1956'.

133. *Idem* to H. Hugo, 31 Jan. 1957; Sparrow MSS, Box 57.

134. *Eidem*, 30 July 1963; ibid.

135. C. M. Bowra to J. Sparrow, 18 Aug. [1927]; ibid.

136. *Eidem*, 3 Oct. 1927; ibid.

CHAPTER 9 — GERMANY AND AMERICA

1. C. M. Bowra to M. Frankfurter, 28 Aug. [1939]; Frankfurter MSS, Box 25.

2. Ibid.

3. Mitchell/George Huxley.

4. *Memories*, 271. See also J. Lowe, *The Warden* (London, 1998), 57–8.

5. Mitchell/Lord and Lady Quinton, and Mitchell/Lady Annan.

6. C. M. Bowra, *Poetry and the First World War* (Oxford, 1961), 23.

7. *Memories*, 94–5.

8. Mitchell/C. M. Bowra.

9. Ibid.

10. Ibid.

11. C. M. Bowra, in W. T. Rodgers, *Hugh Gaitskell* (London, 1964), 22.

12. *Idem* to Lady Ottoline Morrell, 14 Sept. [?]; HRC, Morrell MSS, 19.

13. *Idem* to P. Synnott, 14 Sept. [1927]; Synnott MSS.

14. *Eidem*, [Oct. 1927]; ibid.

15. *Eidem*, 24 Dec. [1925]; ibid. See also C. M. Bowra to C. Connolly, 27 Aug. [1925]; Connolly MSS.

16. C. M. Bowra to P. Synnott, 24 March [1927]; Synnott MSS.

17. *Idem* to J. Sparrow, 26 March [1927]; Sparrow MSS, Box 57.

18. *Idem* to 'Ug', 13 July [1934]; Bowra MSS.

19. *Memories*, 281.

20. M. Cooper to I. Berlin, 26 June 1932; Berlin MSS, 250, f. 4.

21. *Memories*, 275.

22. Ibid. 279–80.

23. Ibid. 284.

24. Ibid.

25. Ibid.

26. Lord Boothby, *Recollections of a Rebel* (London, 1978), 110.

27. *Memories*, 284.

28. C. M. Bowra to Ottoline Morrell, 23 Sept. [1933]; HRC, Morrell MSS, 20.

29. *Idem* to Jean Connolly, 24 Aug. [1938]; Connolly MSS.

30. *Idem* to Ottoline Morrell, 7 Sept. [1935]; HRC, Bowen MSS.

31. *Idem* to M. and F. Frankfurter, 8 Jan. [1935?]; Frankfurter MSS, Box 25.

32. *Idem* to M. Frankfurter, 28 Aug. [1938]; ibid. Frau Grafe was the housekeeper in the Lodgings in Wadham for twenty years; E. Hamilton to R. Dugdale, 13 Nov. 2006; Bowra MSS.

33. C. M. Bowra to M. Frankfurter, 28 Aug. [1938]; Frankfurter MSS, Box 25.

34. *Idem* to Sir G. Murray, 3 Sept. [1936]; Murray MSS, 79, f. 13.

35. *Idem* to A. von Trott, 14 March 1936; C. Sykes, *Troubled Loyalty* (London, 1968), 168–9.

36. E. Kantorowicz to C. M. Bowra, Oct. 1938; Bowra MSS.

37. P. Marnham, *Wild Mary* (London, 2006), 75. Mary Wesley also remembered that the friendship between Bowra and the Baroness had been so close that some friends thought that there might have been an *affaire*: Davie/Mary Welsey; Bowra MSS.

38. Diary of Nigel Clive, 24 Oct. 1938; ibid.

39. She would later die in a concentration camp.

40. E. Kantorowicz to C. M. Bowra, 30 Sept. 1938; ibid.

41. *Eidem*, 11 Oct. 1938; ibid.

42. *Eidem*, 29 Oct. 1938; ibid. and *Memories*, 297.

43. *Memories*, 304.

44. E. Kantorowicz to C. M. Bowra, 29 Oct. 1938; Bowra MSS.

45. *Eidem*, 6 June 1939; ibid.

46. *Memories*, 306.

47. C. M. Bowra to F. Frankfurter, 1 Nov. 1963; Frankfurter MSS, Box 25.

48. R. Giesey to C. M. Bowra, 29 Sept. 1963; Bowra MSS.

49. M. Frankfurter to I. Berlin, 8 June 1937; Berlin MSS, 105, f. 227.

50. Davie/David Astor.

51. A. von Trott to I. Berlin, 26 Aug. [1935]; Berlin MSS, 104, f. 52.

52. *Eidem*, 11 May [1936], 18 March 1937, 25 Nov. 1938; ibid. 105, ff. 51, 53 and 106, f. 108.

53. A. von Trott to I. Berlin, 18 March 1937; ibid. 105, f. 53.
54. Memoir by Diana Hubback, 17 Dec. 1934; Balliol Coll., Oxford, von Trott MSS, IV iii. See also D. Hopkinson, *The Incense Tree* (London, 1968), 131.
55. David/David Astor.
56. Mitchell/A. F. Thompson. See also Davie/Stuart Hampshire.
57. C. M. Bowra to F. Frankfurter, 4 Dec. [1937]; Frankfurter MSS, Box 25.
58. *Memories* puts the meeting in May. Christopher Sykes in *Troubled Loyalty* gives June, and David Astor July; Davie/David Astor.
59. Davie/David Astor.
60. H. von Moltke to L. Curtis, 15 Feb. 1939; Bod. Lib., Oxford, Curtis MSS, 99, f. 7.
61. C. M. Bowra to F. Frankfurter, 1 March [1952]; Frankfurter MSS, Box 25.
62. M. Ignatieff, *Isaiah Berlin* (London, 1998), 76.
63. Ibid. Marian Frankfurter believed Trott 'to be not Pro Nazi', while her husband was more suspicious; M. Frankfurter to I. Berlin, 8 June 1937; Berlin MSS, 105, ff. 22–3.
64. C. M. Bowra to Lord Lindemann, 13 July [1939]; Nuffield Coll., Oxford, Cherwell MSS, B122/36.
65. Davie/David Astor.
66. *Memories*, 305–6.
67. D. Astor, *Encounter*, June 1969. This article in fact delivered an uncompromising attack on Bowra. Sheila Grant-Duff condemned Astor's comments as 'monstrous'. Others heard the remark about Trott being one of the few Nazis to be hanged; Mitchell/A. F. Thompson.
68. S. Grant-Duff to I. Berlin, 2 July 1962; Berlin MSS, 254, f. 176.
69. Davie/David Astor.
70. C. Sykes to C. M. Bowra, 7 Dec. 1968; Bowra MSS.
71. C. M. Bowra to H. Hugo, 13 Dec. 1968; Sparrow MSS, Box 57.
72. C. M. Bowra to A. von Trott, 14 March 1936; Sykes, *Troubled Loyalty*, 168–9.
73. *Memories*, 346.
74. BL Add. MSS 71186, f. 117; D. Mitford to N. Mitford, 17 May 1943.
75. J. Sparrow to K. Clark, n.d.; Tate Britain, Clark MSS, TGA/8812/1/3 2975. Also Mitchell/Colette Clark.
76. K. Clark, *Another Part of the Wood* (London, 1974), 274.
77. *Memories*, 349 and M. Gilbert to C. M. Bowra, 28 June 1964; Bowra MSS.
78. Mitchell/C. M. Bowra.
79. Davie/Alan Bullock. Bullock was 'surprised' and delighted by Bowra's declaration, having hitherto seen him as too much of an 'aesthete' to be concerned with politics. For a similar view, see A. L. Rowse, *Friends and Contemporaries* (London, 1990), 78–80.
80. Mitchell/C. M. Bowra.
81. F. Frankfurter to C. M. Bowra, 11 May 1937; Frankfurter MSS.

82. C. M. Bowra to G. Murray, 11 June [1934]; Murray MSS, 68, ff. 25–9.

83. *Idem* to C. Cox, 13 July [1934]; New Coll., Oxford; Cox MSS, PA.C1/3/350.

84. *Idem* to ? Herlitochka, 31 July 1938; Reading Univ. Lib., 1409/62/19.

85. C. M. Bowra, *The Study of Literature* (London, 1952).

86. E. Kantorowicz to C. M. Bowra, 21 Sept. 1944; Bowra MSS. In April 1938, Hugh Trevor-Roper recorded the following remarks in his diary: 'Maurice said that the trouble was that they would beat us in war, as we have no wish to fight and they are all so anxious to die. "I must say" he added, "that I don't blame them. If I were a German, I should want to die too!" '; Diary of H. R. Trevor-Roper, Christ Church Archives.

87. C. M. Bowra, Speech, 11 April 1951; Bod. Lib., Oxford, Curtis MSS, 165.

88. *Idem* to I. Berlin, 5 Nov. [1945]; Bowra MSS.

89. *Eidem*, 29 Sept. and 3 Dec. [1951]; ibid; and C. M. Bowra to A. James, 10 Dec. [1951]; Harvard, Houghton Lib., bMS AM 1938 (152).

90. *Idem* to C. Clark, 12 Dec. 1969; C. Clark MSS.

91. *Eidem*, 13 Oct. 1970; ibid. See also M. L. Mouck to S. Hampshire, 20 Sept. 1971; Bowra MSS.

92. C. M. Bowra to I. Berlin, [1936]; Bowra MSS.

93. *Idem* to E. Bowen, 20 Oct. [1948]; HRC, Bowra MSS.

94. *Idem* to J. Betjeman, 4 Jan. 1937; Betjeman MSS.

95. A. Pryce-Jones, *The Bonus of Laughter* (London, 1987), 212.

96. *Memories*, 329.

97. C. M. Bowra to I. Berlin, [28 Sept. 1936]; Berlin MSS, 246, f. 8.

98. Ibid.

99. *Idem* to F. Frankfurter, 25 June [1940]; Frankfurter MSS, Box 25.

100. *Memories*, 316.

101. M. Frankfurter to I. Berlin, 24 Nov. 1936; Berlin MSS, 105, f. 116.

102. C. M. Bowra to J. Mitchell, 13 Oct. 1960; Mitchell MSS.

103. *Memories*, 319.

104. M. Frankfurter to I. Berlin, 30 Nov. 1936; Berlin MSS 105, f. 112.

105. Ibid.

106. Ibid.

107. *Eidem*, 8 June 1937; ibid. ff. 222–3.

108. T. Higham to C. M. Bowra, 31 Dec. 1936; Bowra MSS.

109. R. Harrod to C. M. Bowra, 17 Jan. 1939; ibid.

110. C. M. Bowra to F. Frankfurter, 25 June [?]; Frankfurter MSS, Box 25.

111. The book would be dedicated to the Master and Fellows of Eliot House in Harvard.

112. I. Berlin to C. M. Bowra, [1949]; Bowra MSS.

113. C. M. Bowra to P. Hadley, 30 Jan. [1949]; ibid.

114. *Idem* to U. Niebuhr, 31 Dec. [1948]; National Library of Congress, Washington, DC, Niebuhr MSS.

115. C. M. Bowra to E. Bowen, 20 Oct. [1948]; HRC, Bowen MSS, 4.
116. Ibid.
117. C. M. Bowra to F. Frankfurter, 30 Sept, 1948; Frankfurter MSS, Box 25; *idem* to G. Rylands, 14 Dec. [1948]; Bowra MSS; *idem* to E. Sitwell, 11 Nov. [1948], HRC, Sitwell MSS, 7.
118. *Idem* to F. Frankfurter, 13 April [1949]; Frankfurter MSS, Box 25.
119. *Idem* to I. Berlin, 12 April [1949]; Bowra MSS.
120. *Eidem*, 1 Aug. [1949]; ibid.
121. *Eidem*, 4 Jan. [1949]; ibid.
122. C. M. Bowra to P. Hadley, 30 Jan. [1949]; ibid.
123. 'Howard and Adèle'; Sparrow MSS, Box 57. Hugo was told that 'If you ever want a job, or a dirty turn done to an enemy, remember that I am your man.' C. M. Bowra to H. Hugo, 12 April [1949]; ibid.
124. *Idem* to A. James, 24 June [1950]; Harvard, Houghton Lib., bMS AM 1938 (152).
125. *Idem* to H. Hugo, 12 April [1949]; Sparrow MSS, Box 57.
126. Ibid.
127. Ibid.
128. C. M. Bowra to A. James, 26 April [1949]; Harvard, Houghton Lib., bMS AM 1938 (152).
129. *Idem* to U. Niebuhr, [27 April 1949]; Nat. Lib. of Congress, Washington DC, Niebuhr MSS.
130. *Idem* to A. James, 26 April [1949]; Harvard, Houghton Lib., bMS AM 1938 (152).
131. Ibid.
132. *Eidem*, 2 July [1949]; ibid.
133. *Wadham Gazette*, New Series, 3(7); 1992.
134. E. Kantorowicz to C. M. Bowra, 19 Nov. 1943; Bowra MSS.
135. C. M. Bowra to P. Synnott, 29 March [1927]; Synnott MSS.
136. *Idem* to E. Waugh, 28 Nov. [1951]; Bowra MSS.
137. *Idem* to H. Hugo, 27 April [1952]; Sparrow MSS, Box 57.
138. *Idem* to E. Waugh, 1 Oct. 1964; Bowra MSS.
139. *Idem* to P. Balfour, 13 March 1956; Huntington Lib., Calif., Kinross MSS.
140. *Idem* to F. Frankfurter, 9 Dec. [?]; Frankfurter MSS, Box 25.
141. *Idem* to J. Mitchell, 13 March 1965; J. Mitchell MSS.
142. *Idem* to E. Waugh [*c.*1960]; Bowra MSS.
143. *Idem* to J. Mitchell, 21 Feb. 1961; J. Mitchell MSS.
144. *Idem* to F. Frankfurter, 25 Aug. and 18 Dec. 1949; Frankfurter MSS, Box 25.
145. *Idem* to A. James, 4 Jan. [1953]; Harvard, Houghton Lib., bMS AM 1938 (152).
146. *Idem* to F. Frankfurter, 5 Jan. [1953]; Frankfurter MSS, Box 25.
147. *Eidem*, 1 March [1952?]; ibid. Bowra also confided in Frankfurter that he was praying that McCarthy might be shot; *eidem*, 5 July [1953].

148. C. M. Bowra to A. James, 18 March [1953]; Harvard, Houghton Lib., bMS AM 1938 (152).

149. BL Add. MSS 71182, f. 53; C. M. Bowra to R. Harrod, 11 Sept. [1952].

150. Ibid.

151. *Idem* to A. James, 27 April [1952]; Harvard, Houghton Lib., bMS AM 1938 (152).

152. *Idem* to F. Frankfurter, 26 June [1953]; Frankfurter MSS, Box 25.

153. *Idem* to A. James, 15 Dec. [1953?]; Harvard, Houghton Lib., bMS AM 1938 (152).

154. *Idem* to J. Mitchell, 13 Oct. 1960; J. Mitchell MSS.

155. M. Bundy to C. M. Bowra, 23 Feb 1963; Bowra MSS.

156. Mitchell/Lady Wilson.

157. C. M. Bowra to F. Frankfurter, 16 June 1963; Frankfurter MSS, Box 25.

158. *Idem* to G. Rylands, 8 Dec. 1963; Rylands MSS, GHWR/3/57.

159. *Idem* to H. Hugo, 26 Jan. 1964; Sparrow MSS, Box 57.

160. *Idem* to C. Clark, 26 Jan. 1964; C. Clark MSS.

161. *Idem* to I. Berlin, 20 Dec. 1965; Berlin MSS, 246, f. 108.

162. Interview for *Pi*, 19 Jan. 1967; Bowra MSS.

163. C. M. Bowra to G. Greene, 4 Sept. 1967; Georgetown Univ., Washington, DC, Greene MSS, part 2.

164. N. Mitford to D. Mitford, 28 Dec. 1961; C. Mosley, *The Mitfords* (London, 2007), 361.

CHAPTER 10 — WARDEN OF WADHAM, 1938–1970

1. BL Add. MSS 71610, f. 8; C. M. Bowra to R. Harrod, 1 July [1924].

2. *Idem* to F. Frankfurter, 28 March [1937]; Frankfurter MSS, Box 25.

3. Wells, Dixey, and Stenning voted for Bowra; Lindemann, Lennard, and Wade-Gery voted for Pilley.

4. Warden's Memoranda Book, 1922; Wadham Coll., Oxford. One of the other defeated candidates was T. S. R. Boase, the future President of Magdalen.

5. Davie/David Astor.

6. Mitchell/Sir Robert Wade-Gery.

7. T. Wade-Gery to F. Lindemann, n.d.; Nuffield Coll., Oxford, Cherwell MSS, B122/5.

8. C. M. Bowra to Ottoline Morrell, 22 April [?]; HRC, Morrell MSS, 17.

9. *Idem* to N. Brook, 6 April [1923]; Bod. Lib., Oxford, MS. Eng. Lett. C273, f. 10.

10. *Eidem*, 1 Oct. [1925]; ibid. f. 28. Hart went on to become the chief administrator of the London County Council.

11. C. M. Bowra to E. Waugh, 1 Oct. 1964; Bowra MSS.

12. S. Hampshire to I. Berlin, 8 Nov. 1953; Berlin MSS, 256, ff. 134–5.

13. C. M. Bowra to I. Berlin, 11 Nov. [1953]; Bowra MSS. For a more caustic view, see S. Gates to I. Berlin, 15 Feb. 1956; Berlin MSS, 146, f. 221.

14. Convention Book, 5 Oct. 1938; 517; Wadham Coll. Archives.

15. *Oxford Magazine*, 13 Oct. 1938; 10.

16. Mitchell/A. F. Thompson.

17. C. M. Bowra to F. Frankfurter, 1 Nov. 1959; Frankfurter MSS, Box 25. Maurice adapted a nursery rhyme to read 'Tinker, Tailor, Soldier, Sailor, Rich Man, Poor Man, Lindemann, Thief'; C. Hollis, *Oxford in the Twenties* (London, 1976), 35. See also *Memories*, 135–6; A. Fort, *The Prof* (London, 2004), 92.

18. C. M. Bowra to Lord Cherwell, 1 Jan. 1943; Nuffield Coll., Oxford, Cherwell MSS, A47, f. 3.

19. Davie/Mary Wesley.

20. Mitchell/J Bamborough.

21. Noel Annan's Commonplace Book; King's Coll., Cambridge, Annan MSS.

22. Davie/Stuart Hampshire. For a full account of this incident, see diary of H. R. Trevor-Roper, April 1938; Christ Church, Oxford, Trevor-Roper MSS.

23. Diary of N. Clive, 12 Oct. 1938; Wadham Coll. Archives.

24. C. M. Bowra to E. Waugh, 9 Jan. [?]; Bowra MSS.

25. *Idem* to E. Bowen, 23 Sept. [1938]; HRC, Bowen MSS.

26. *Idem* to J. Connolly, 29 Aug. 1938; Connolly MSS.

27. *Idem* to H. Hugo, 13 April [1950]; Sparrow MSS, Box 57.

28. Lord D. Cecil to I. Berlin, [*c*.1951]; Oxford, Berlin MSS, 162, f. 49.

29. J. Dancy to H. Hardy, 17 Nov. 2005; Bowra MSS.

30. A. Fleming to D. Cooper, 22 April [1955]; Morgan MSS.

31. Mitchell/Lady Annan.

32. Diary of N. Clive, 16 Oct., 20 Oct., 6 Nov. 1938 and 22 Jan., 15 Feb., 7 May 1939; Wadham Coll. Archives.

33. C. M. Bowra to F. Frankfurter, 28 Aug. [1938]; Frankfurter MSS, Box 25.

34. 'Air Populaire', in Maurice Bowra, *New Bats in Old Belfries* ed. H. Hardy and J. Holmes (Oxford, 2005), 34–5.

35. Diary of N. Clive, 16 June; Wadham Coll. Archives.

36. C. M. Bowra to A. James, 4 April [1939]; Harvard, Houghton Lib., bMS AM 1938 (152).

37. *Eidem*, 24 Sept. 1939; ibid.

38. Ibid. See also C. M. Bowra to M. Frankfurter, 9 Sept. [1939]; Frankfurter MSS, Box 25.

39. *Idem* to F. Frankfurter, 25 July [1940]; ibid.

40. Ibid.

41. C. M. Bowra to A. James, 18 July [1940]; Harvard, Houghton Lib., bMS AM 1938 (152).

42. *Idem* to A. S. Sproatt, 18 June [1940?]; King's Coll., Cambridge, WJHS/9.

43. *Idem* to I. Berlin, 18 June 1943; Bowra MSS.

44. *Idem* to Lord Cherwell, 3 June [1940]; Nuffield Coll., Oxford, Cherwell MSS, B123/1.

45. Certificate of Service, Bowra MSS.

46. Lady Longford, *The Pebbled Shore* (London, 1986).

47. C. M. Bowra to P. Betjeman, 7 April [1941?]; Betjeman MSS.

48. *Idem* to A. James, 18 July [1940]; Harvard, Houghton Lib., bMS AM 1938 (152).

49. I. Berlin to M. Frankfurter, 23 June 1940; H. Hardy, *Flourishing* (London, 2004), 304.

50. C. M. Bowra to A. James, 25 June [1940]; Harvard, Houghton Lib., bMS AM 1938 (152).

51. *Idem* to P. Betjeman, 17 July [1940]; Betjeman MSS.

52. Davie/Isaiah Berlin.

53. Davie/Noel Annan.

54. Davie/Stuart Hampshire.

55. Ibid.

56. C. M. Bowra to F. Frankfurter, 13 Sept. [1940]; Frankfurter MSS, Box 25.

57. *Idem* to P. Betjeman, 7 April [1941?]; Betjeman MSS.

58. *Idem* to E. Waugh, 15 March [1942]; Bowra MSS.

59. *Eidem*, [1942?]; ibid.

60. BL Add. MSS 71182, f. 50; C. M. Bowra to B. Harrod, [1942].

61. *Idem* to J. Sparrow, 2 Jan. 1941; Sparrow MSS, Box 57.

62. G. Rees to I. Berlin, [1946]; Berlin MSS, 274, f. 39.

63. C. M. Bowra to E. Sitwell, 5 Nov. [1945]; HRC, Sitwell MSS, 12.

64. Mitchell/J. Bamborough. See also C. M. Bowra to R. Chapman, 14 Oct. [?]; Bod. Lib., Oxford, Ms. Eng. Lett. c462, f. 208.

65. I. Berlin to N. Annan, 31 Aug. 1973; Berlin MSS, 241, f. 131.

66. S. Hampshire to I. Berlin, 9 March 1945; ibid. 256, f. 47.

67. C. M. Bowra to I. Berlin, 11 Nov. [1953]; Bowra MSS.

68. Trevor-Roper had recently published an essay in this newspaper denouncing 'the corrosive ingenuities' taught in Wadham.

69. C. M. Bowra to I. Berlin, 25 Nov. 1964; Berlin MSS, 246, f. 102.

70. Davie/Sally Chilver.

71. Mitchell/A. F. Thompson.

72. John Potter Interview; Wadham Coll., Oxford, Bowra MSS.

73. Mitchell/J. Bamborough.

74. P. Fleming to L. Mitchell, 27 June 2006; Bowra MSS.

75. *Wadham Gazette*, New Series, 3 (3), 1988, 53.

76. Ibid. New Series, 3 (12), 1997, 64.

77. Mitchell/J. Bamborough.

78. Ibid. and Mitchell/A. F. Thompson.

79. J. Mitchell, *A Disgraceful Anomaly* (London, 2003), 9.

80. C. M. Bowra to F. King, 30 Sept. [?]; HRC, King MSS.

81. N. Annan; typescript of BBC broadcast, 7 April 1972; Bowra MSS.

82. Mitchell/Mary Bennett.

83. C. M. Bowra to I. Berlin, 16 March 1965; Berlin MSS, 246, f. 103.

84. Memoir by D. Dean; Wadham Coll., Oxford, Bowra MSS.

85. Davie/Stuart Hampshire.

86. Mitchell, *A Disgraceful Anomaly*, 20.

87. P. Kilty to L. Mitchell, 17 May 2006; Wadham Coll., Oxford, Bowra MSS.

88. Mitchell/C. M. Bowra.

89. Memoir by D. Dean; Wadham Coll., Oxford, Bowra MSS.

90. P. Rhodes to L. Mitchell, 16 Aug. 2006; ibid.

91. Convention Book, 18 Oct. 1929; Wadham College Archives.

92. *Memories*, 153.

93. C. M. Bowra to E. Sitwell, 18 June [?]; HRC, Sitwell MSS, 10.

94. Memoir by D. Dean; Wadham Coll., Oxford, Bowra MSS.

95. C. M. Bowra to Sir J. Nicholls, 7 March 1964; ibid.

96. J. Dancy to H. Hardy, 17 Nov. 1996; ibid.

97. C. M. Bowra to H. Hugo, 5 Oct. [1953]; Sparrow MSS, Box 57.

98. P. R. L. I. Morgan to L. Mitchell, 9 Feb. 2006; Bowra MSS.

99. C. M. Bowra to I. Berlin, 3 Dec. [1951]; ibid.

100. M. Foot to C. M. Bowra, n.d.; ibid.

101. C. M. Bowra to G. Rylands, 29 Oct. [?]; ibid. See also Agatha Christie to
C. M. Bowra, 24 June [?]; ibid.

102. A. Fleming to C. M. Bowra, 18 Jan. [?] and 24 Jan. [?]; ibid.

103. J. Cocteau to C. M. Bowra, 8 July 1956; ibid.

104. *Wadham Gazette,* New Series, 4 (9), 2006; 57.

105. C. M. Bowra to F. Frankfurter, 18 Dec. [1958]; Frankfurter MSS, Box 25.

106. *Idem* to P. Betjeman, 17 Dec. [1956?]; Betjeman MSS. See also *idem* to
G. Rylands, 24 Jan. 1965; Rylands MSS, GHWR/3/57.

107. I. Worth to I. Berlin, 28 Sept, 1971; Berlin MSS, 195, f. 151.

108. C. M. Bowra to P. Betjeman, 17 Dec. [1956?]; Betjeman MSS. See also *idem*
to J. Betjeman, 12 Jan [1942?]; ibid.

109. N. Mitford to D. Cooper, 26 Dec. 1961; Eton Coll., Tower Store, DCOS.

110. C. M. Bowra to N. Mitford, 31 Dec. [1961]; Chatsworth Archives, Mitford
MSS, by permission of 'the estate of Nancy Mitford'.

111. *Idem* to G. Rylands, 16 Sept. [1961]; Rylands MSS, GHWR/3/57.

112. Mitchell/J. Bamborough.

113. Ibid.

114. Mitchell/R. J. P. Williams.

115. Mitchell/A. F. Thompson.

116. C. M. Bowra to I. Blew Horner, 5 March [?]; Faculty of Oriental Studies,
Cambridge, Blew Horner MSS.

117. *Idem* to H. Hugo, 25 July [1957]; Sparrow MSS, Box 57.

118. *Idem* to G. Rylands, 22 Dec. 1962; Rylands MSS, GHWR/3/57.

119. *Idem*, Introduction to F. Markham, *Oxford* (London, 1967), 11.

120. *Daily Telegraph*, 26 May 1967. See also Davie/Sally Chilver. He told Noel Annan that 'the trouble with the public schools is that a) they are full of spivs and hardly any gentlemen ... and b) the teaching is going steadily downhill', C. M. Bowra to N. Annan, 4 June [?]; King's Coll., Cambridge, Annan MSS.

121. Convention Book 1945–66, 12 Dec. 1947; Wadham Coll. Archives.

122. *The Times*, 13 Dec. 1949.

123. Mitchell/R. J. P. Williams.

124. Davie/Alan Bullock. Bullock admired Bowra as a man 'who didn't care a damn what anyone said', but could not cope with his homosexuality, which seemed to involve too much 'malice and doing down'.

125. C. M. Bowra to G. Rylands, 13 Dec. 1965; Rylands MSS, GHWR/3/57.

126. *Eidem*, 9 Feb. 1966; ibid.

127. A. Fleming to E. Waugh, 21 Jan. [1966]; M. Amory, *The Letters of Ann Fleming* (London, 1985), 374.

128. C. M. Bowra to G. Rylands, 5 July and 13 Dec. 1967; Rylands MSS, GHWR/3/57.

129. *Idem* to C. Clark, 10 Jan. 1970; C. Clark MSS.

130. Mitchell/C. M. Bowra.

131. Mitchell/R. J. P. Williams.

132. C. M. Bowra to G. Rylands, 22 March [1962]; Rylands MSS, GHWR/3/57.

133. Mitchell/R. J. P. Williams. See also C. M. Bowra to C. Coulson, 2 Aug. 1951; Bod. Lib., Oxford, Coulson MSS, A 1 2 2.

134. Mitchell/R. J. P. Williams.

135. C. M. Bowra to G. Rylands, 13 Dec. 1965; Rylands MSS, GHWR/3/57.

136. *Eidem*, 5 Oct 1965; ibid.

137. *Eidem*, 13 May 1970; ibid.

138. Ibid.

139. Mitchell/Mrs J. Bamborough.

140. *Daily Telegraph*, 26 May 1967.

141. C. M. Bowra to G. Rylands, 8 Dec. 1963; Rylands MSS, GHWR/3/57.

CHAPTER 11 — BOWRA AT LARGE, 1945–1970

1. Mitchell/C. M. Bowra.

2. H. Martin to P. Balfour, 8 Sept. 1969; Huntington Lib., Calif., Kinross MSS.

3. S. Hampshire to I. Berlin, 17 Feb. [1952]; Berlin MSS, 256, f. 113.

4. K. Wheare to I. Berlin, 20 Aug. 1971; ibid. 194, f. 195.

5. Mitchell/David Bell.

6. C. M. Bowra to E. Sitwell, 6 May [?]; HRC, Sitwell MSS, 12; and BL Add. MSS 71182, f. 52; *idem* to B. Harrod, 28 May [?]. See also H. Gaitskell to C. M. Bowra, 29 May 1954; UCL London, Gaitskell MSS, c 296, 1.

7. R. Hart-Davis to Lady D. Cooper, 1 Feb. 1956; Eton College, Tower Store, DC 05.

8. B. Hillier, *John Betjeman: The Bonus of Laughter* (London, 2004), 264.

9. C. M. Bowra to H. Hugo, 17 Dec. [1949]; Sparrow MSS, Box 57.

10. *Idem* to A. James, 24 June [1950]; Harvard, Houghton Lib., bMS AM 1938 (152).

11. E. Sitwell to C. M. Bowra, 5 March 1951; Bowra MSS.

12. C. M. Bowra to I. Berlin, 10 Nov. [1948]; ibid.

13. *Eidem*, 9 Oct. [1951]; ibid.

14. Vice-Chancellor's Diary, 1951–4; Oxford Univ. Archives, CV2/4/2/3.

15. C. M. Bowra to E. Sitwell, 10 July [1953]; HRC, Sitwell MSS, 11.

16. *Idem* to F. Frankfurter, 5 July [1953]; Frankfurter MSS, Box 25.

17. *Idem* to C. Connolly, 20 Dec [1953]; Connolly MSS.

18. *Eidem*, [1953]; ibid.

19. *Idem* to G. Murray, 19 Oct. 1953; Murray MSS, 487, f. 252.

20. *The Times*, 20 Dec. 1951.

21. C. M. Bowra to the Chief Constable, 14 Nov. 1952; Oxford Univ. Archives, VC Correspondence VC1/101/114.

22. *Idem* to C. Connolly, 17 Oct. [1954]; Connolly MSS.

23. *Idem* to J. Mitchell, 13 March [1960]; J. Mitchell MSS.

24. J. Lowe, *The Warden* (London, 1998), 186–7.

25. C. M. Bowra to H. Hugo, 20 Dec. [1952]; Sparrow MSS, Box 57.

26. Davie/Stuart Hampshire.

27. I. Berlin to J. Sparrow, 23 March 1954; ibid. Box 56.

28. C. M. Bowra to B. Ruck, 2 Jan. [1953]; Bowra MSS.

29. *Idem*, in *Proceedings of the British Academy*, vol. 35 (1953), 232.

30. *Idem* to H. Hugo, 27 April [1952]; Sparrow MSS, Box 57.

31. Mitchell/David Bell.

32. BL Add. MSS 71612, f. 181; J. Sparrow to B. Harrod, 11 Nov. 1952.

33. J. Bamborough, *Times Literary Supplement*, 1 Nov. 1974.

34. C. M. Bowra to Franks Committee, 17 Nov. 1964; Oxford Univ. Archives, HCH/50/23–24.

35. *Oxford Magazine*, 5 Nov. 1953.

36. Davie/Alan Bullock.

37. Sir K. Wheare, in H. Lloyd-Jones, *Maurice Bowra* (London, 1974), 123.

38. *Oxford Magazine*, 16 Oct. 1952.

39. C. M. Bowra to A. James, 29 May 1952; Harvard, Houghton Lib., bMS AM 1938 (152).

40. Davie/Stuart Hampshire.

41. E. L. Woodward to C. M. Bowra, 1 June 1951; Bowra MSS.

42. C. M. Bowra to H. Hugo, 10 Dec. [1951]; Sparrow MSS, Box 57, and *idem* to F. Frankfurter, 10 Dec. [1952]; Frankfurter MSS, Box 25.

43. *Sunday Times*, 27 April 1952.

44. C. M. Bowra to A. James, 29 May [1952]; Harvard, Houghton Lib., bMS AM 1938 (152).

45. Davie/Alan Bullock.

46. J. Sparrow to I. Berlin, 15 Dec. 1951; Berlin MSS, 281. f. 135.

47. *Oxford Magazine*, 17 June 1954.

48. Ibid.

49. Ibid. 9 June 1954.

50. Davie/Alan Bullock.

51. C. M. Bowra to E. Sitwell, 1 May [1946?]; HRC, Sitwell MSS, 13.

52. *Idem* to J. Mitchell, 4 Dec. 1964; J. Mitchell MSS.

53. *Eidem*, 13 March 1965; ibid.

54. *Idem* to F. Frankfurter, 16 Sept. 1962; Frankfurter MSS, Box 25.

55. *Idem* to B. Ruck, 30 Dec. 1962; Bowra MSS.

56. Ibid.

57. Ibid.

58. C. M. Bowra to C. Clark, 6 July [1962]; C. Clark MSS.

59. *Idem* to G. Rylands, 30 June [1962]; Rylands MSS, GHWR/3/57.

60. Ibid.

61. Mitchell/Lady Quinton.

62. BL Add. MSS 71182, f. 64; C. M. Bowra to B. Harrod, 17 July [?].

63. *Idem* to H. Hugo, 27 April [1952]; Sparrow MSS, Box 57.

64. *Eidem*, 30 June [1958]; ibid.

65. B. Harrod to I. Berlin, 30 Jan. 1952; Berlin MSS, 129, ff. 162–3.

66. C. M. Bowra to I. Berlin, 7 May [1949]; Bowra MSS.

67. *Idem* to D. Cooper, 19 Feb. [?], Getty Research Centre, Los Angeles, Cooper MSS, 860161.

68. Stuart Hampshire, Tape of BBC Broadcast, 7 April 972; Wadham Coll., Oxford, Bowra MSS.

69. C. M. Bowra to H. Trevor-Roper, 3 Jan. [1962]; Christ Church, Trevor-Roper MSS, '1962'.

70. *Idem* to F. Frankfurter, 25 Feb. [1955?]; Frankfurter MSS, Box 25.

71. *Idem* to H. Hugo, 17 Dec. [1949]; Sparrow MSS, Box 57.

72. *Idem* to E. Sitwell, 16 Nov. [?]; HRC, Sitwell MSS, 14.

73. *Idem* to E. Starkie, 23 Oct. [1949]; Bod. Lib., Oxford, Starkie MSS, '1949'. See also E. Starkie to I. Berlin, 23 Oct. 1949; Berlin MSS, 120, f. 120.

74. C. M. Bowra to I. Berlin, 12 April [1949?]; Bowra MSS.

75. *Eidem*, 20 Nov. 1945; ibid.

76. *Eidem*, 21 Sept. [1951]; ibid.

77. C. M. Bowra to E. Waugh, 1 July [1947]; ibid. The book in question was *The Last Days of Hitler*.

78. *Eidem*, [1947]; ibid.

79. *Eidem*, 1 July [1947]; ibid.

80. BL Add. MSS 71182, f. 64; C. M. Bowra to B. Harrod, 17 July [?].

81. C. M. Bowra to F. Frankfurter, 22 July [1957]; Frankfurter MSS, Box 25.

82. *Idem* to I. Berlin, 3 Dec. [1951?]; Bowra MSS.

83. *Idem* to G. Rylands, 22 June 1953, Rylands MSS, GHWR/3/57.

84. *Idem* to P. Hadley, 25 Jan. [1947]; Bowra MSS.

85. *Idem* to S. Colefax, 13 Sept. [?]; Bod. Lib., Oxford, MS. Eng. c3160, f. 39.

86. *Idem* to M. Frankfurter, 18 Dec. [1949]; Frankfurter MSS, Box 25.

87. BL Add. MSS 72728, f. 51; *idem* to R. Harrod, n.d.

88. *Idem* to H. Trevor-Roper, 10 Dec. [1956]; Christ Church, Oxford, Trevor-Roper MSS, '1956'.

89. *Idem* to I. Berlin, 20 Dec. [1951?]; Bowra MSS.

90. *Eidem*, 26 Oct. [1953]; ibid.

91. C. M. Bowra to F. Frankfurter, 20 Dec. [1952]; Frankfurter MSS, Box 25.

92. *Idem* to I. Berlin, 4 Jan. [1952]; Bowra MSS.

93. J. Sparrow to I. Berlin, 2 Dec. 1952; Berlin MSS, 281, f. 153.

94. Ibid.

95. I. Berlin to H. Hart, [Oct. 1944]; H. Hardy, *Flourishing* (London, 2004), 498.

96. *Idem* to Stuart Hampshire, 15 Oct. 1953; Berlin MSS, 256, f. 122.

97. S. Hampshire to I. Berlin, [1955]; ibid. f. 185.

98. For details of this very enjoyable contest, see H. Trevor-Roper to W. Notestein, 23 March 1960; Christ Church, Trevor-Roper MSS, and C. M. Bowra to J. Mitchell, 13 March [1960]; J. Mitchell MSS, and I. Berlin to F. Frankfurter, 29 Feb. 1960; Berlin MSS, 253, f. 142.

99. C. M. Bowra to I. Berlin, 22 Sept. [1946]; Bowra MSS.

100. *Idem* to A. James, 9 Nov. [1953]; Harvard, Houghton Lib., bS 1938 (152).

101. *Eidem*, 16 Nov. [1955]; ibid.

102. R. Blake to H. Trevor-Roper, 29 Dec. 1955; Christ Church, Trevor-Roper MSS.

103. C. M. Bowra to F. Frankfurter, 23 Oct. [1956]; Frankfurter MSS, Box 25.

104. *Idem* to J. Betjeman, 26 Jan. and 13 June 1966; Betjeman MSS.

105. *Idem* to H. Trevor-Roper, 26 Nov. [1956]; Christ Church, Oxford, Trevor-Roper MSS.

106. *Idem* to J. Betjeman, 29 Oct. [1950?]; Betjeman MSS.

107. *Eidem*, 6 Jan. [?]; ibid.

108. B. Hillier, 'The Boase Garden'; *The Betjemanian*, vol. 9. I am grateful to Jonathan Brewer for this reference.

109. C. M. Bowra to N. Coghill, 20 April 1954; Bod. Lib., Oxford, MS Eng. Lett. c803, f. 103; and *idem* to N. Annan, 13 Sept. [1961]; King's Coll., Cambridge, Annan MSS.

110. *Proceedings of the British Academy*, 45 (1959), 151.

111. J. Sparrow to C. M. Bowra, 22 March 1960; Sir M. Wheeler, *The British Academy 1949–1968* (London, 1970), 26–7.

112. Presidential Address, 11 July 1962; *Proceedings of the British Academy*, 48, 32–4.

113. A. L. Rowse, *Friends and Contemporaries* (London, 1990), 89.

114. C. M. Bowra to F. Frankfurter, 5 Dec. [1960]; Frankfurter MSS, Box 25.

115. *Eidem*, 9 Dec. [1960]; ibid.

116. Sir M. Wheeler, *The British Academy 1949–1968*, 47.

117. Ibid. 48.

118. C. M. Bowra to F. Frankfurter, 16 Sept. 1962; Frankfurter MSS, Box 25.

119. Presidential Address, 11 July 1962; *Proceedings of the British Academy*, 46, 32.

120. C. M. Bowra to F. Frankfurter, 15 Jan. [1961]; Frankfurter MSS, Box 25.

121. *Idem* to C. Clark, 14 March [?]; C. Clark MSS.

122. *Idem* to E. Waugh, 13 Feb. [1961]; Bowra MSS.

123. *Idem* to F. Frankfurter, 15 Jan. [1961]; Frankfurter MSS, Box 25, and *idem* to S. Hampshire, 21 Dec. [1960]; Bowra MSS.

124. *Proceedings of the British Academy*, 47 (July 1961), 27.

125. M. Mallowen to J. Sparrow, 1971; Sparrow MSS, Box 57.

126. C. M. Bowra to F. Frankfurter, 29 Dec. [1961]; Frankfurter MSS, Box 25.

127. M. Hastings to P. Balfour, 18 Dec. 1961; Huntington Lib., Calf., Kinross MSS.

128. C. M. Bowra to G. Rylands, 26 April 1968; Rylands MSS, GHWR/3/57.

129. *Idem* to C. Clark, 20 Dec. [?]; C. Clark MSS.

130. *Idem* to G. Rylands, 25 March 1971; Rylands MSS, GHWR/3/57.

131. *Idem* to Frankfurter, 29 Dec. [1961]; Frankfurter MSS, Box 25.

132. Sir M. Wheeler, *The British Academy 1949–1968*, 72.

133. C. M. Bowra to F. Frankfurter, 1 Nov. [1959]; Frankfurter MSS, Box 25.

134. Davie/Isaiah Berlin.

135. Mitchell/Mary Bennett.

136. Vice-Chancellors of provincial universities.

137. C. M. Bowra to F. Frankfurter, 9 Dec. [1954?]; Frankfurter MSS, Box 25.

138. *The Times*, 25 June 1956.

139. C. M. Bowra to Lord Monkton, 6 Feb. 1953; Bod. Lib., Oxford, Monkton MSS 3, f. 144.

140. *Idem* to Lord Cherwell, 26 June 1953; Nuffield Coll., Oxford, Cherwell MSS B 137, f. 2. See also N. Annan, BBC Broadcast Tape, 7 April 1972; Bowra MSS.

141. *Idem* to H. Hugo, 10 Dec. [1951]; Sparrow MSS, Box 57.

142. Sir K. Wheare, in Lloyd-Jones, *Maurice Bowra*, 128.

143. C. M. Bowra to I. Berlin, 3 Dec. [1951]; Bowra MSS.

144. *Idem* to C. Clark, 7 Oct. 1957; C. Clark MSS.

145. *Idem* to F. Frankfurter, 21 April [195?]; Frankfurter MSS, Box 25.

146. *Idem* to C. Connolly, 12 Oct. 1963; Connolly MSS.

147. *Idem* to H. Hugo, 23 July [1957]; Sparrow MSS, Box 57.

148. *Idem* to B. Ruck, 3 Jan. [?]; Bowra MSS.

149. *Eidem*, 7 Dec. [?]; ibid.

150. C. M. Bowra to G. Rylands, 19 April 1964; Rylands MSS, GHWR/3/57.

151. *Idem* to F. Frankfurter, 21 April [195?]; Frankfurter MSS, Box 25.

152. E. Longford, *The Pebbled Shore* (London, 1986), 364.

153. Sir M. Wheeler, *The British Academy, 1944–1968*, 151–2.

154. E. Pernyi, 'A Thoroughly Highbrow Cruise'; Wadham Coll., Oxford, Bowra MSS.

155. J. Dancy to H. Hardy, 17 Nov. 2005; ibid.

156. Citation for the Doctorate from the Faculté des Lettres, Sorbonne; ibid.

157. C. M. Bowra to H. Hugo, 9 Dec. [1950]; Sparrow MSS, Box 57.

158. *Idem* to E. Starkie, 7 March [1960]; Bod. Lib., Oxford, Starkie MSS, '1960'.

159. Mitchell/John Bamborough.

160. Sir L. Olivier to C. M. Bowra, 3 Jan. [1951]; Bowra MSS.

161. C. M. Bowra to P. Betjeman, 9 Jan. [1955]; Betjeman MSS.

162. E. Sitwell to C. M. Bowra, 17 Feb. 1951; Bowra MSS.

163. E. Waugh to C. M. Bowra, 3 Dec. [1951]; ibid.

164. J. Sparrow to I. Berlin, 1 Jan 1951; Berlin MSS, 281, ff. 99–100.

165. C. M. Bowra to E. Starkie, 2 Jan. [1951]; Bod. Lib., Oxford, Starkie MSS, '1951'.

166. *Idem* to N. Annan, 5 and 9 Jan [1951]; King's Coll., Cambridge, Annan MSS.

167. *Idem* to J. Betjeman, 15 June 1969; Betjeman MSS.

CHAPTER 12 — THE 1960S

1. P. Kilty to L. Mitchell, 17 May 2006; Wadham Coll., Oxford, Bowra MSS.

2. Ibid.

3. Mitchell/R. J. P. Williams.

4. N. Annan to I. Berlin, 11 Sept. 1973; Berlin MSS, 241, f. 135.

5. E. Waugh to Lady Longford, 4 Jan. 1969; Lady Longford, *The Pebbled Shore* (London, 1986), 384; also Mitchell/Dowager Duchess of Devonshire.

6. C. M. Bowra to G. Rylands, 25 May 1965; Rylands MSS, GHWR/3/57.

7. *Idem* to Sir G. Catlin, 5 June [1965]; McMaster Univ., Hamilton, Ontario, Catlin MSS.

8. *Idem* to C. Clark, 17 Sept. 1966; C. Clark MSS.

9. *Idem* to J. Mitchell; 13 March 1965; J. Mitchell MSS.

10. *Idem* to G. Rylands, 5 Oct. 1965; Bowra MSS.

11. N. Annan to I. Berlin, 16 Dec. 1966; Berlin MSS, 241, ff. 98–9.

12. C. M. Bowra to C. Clark, 12 Dec. 1969; C. Clark MSS.

13. The Principal of St Hugh's College, Oxford.

14. C. M. Bowra to G. Rylands, 13 Dec. [1970]; Bowra MSS.

15. A. Briggs, *History of Broadcasting* (Oxford, 1961), iv. 14.

16. C. M. Bowra to C. Sykes, 6 May 1967; Georgetown Univ., Sykes MSS, Box 3, Folder 16.

17. *Idem* to U. Niebuhr, 25 Aug. 1968; Nat. Lib. of Congress, Washington, DC, Niebuhr MSS.

18. *Idem* to E. Waugh, 30 Nov. 1965; Bowra MSS.

19. *Idem* to I. Berlin, 22 Sept. 1965; ibid.

20. *Idem* to C. Connolly, 28 Nov. 1965; Connolly MSS.

21. *Idem* to E. Sitwell, 18 Dec. 1964; Washington State Univ., Sitwell MSS.

22. N. Annan to C. M. Bowra, 14 June [?]; Bowra MSS.

23. C. M. Bowra to G. Rylands, 26 Oct. 1967; Rylands MSS, GHWR/3/57.

24. P [?] to C. M. Bowra, 5 Jan. 1964; Bowra MSS.

25. C. M. Bowra to H. Hugo, 26 Nov. 1966; Sparrow MSS, Box 57.

26. *Idem*, *A Classical Education* (Oxford, 1945), 7.

27. Ibid. 23.

28. Ibid. 24–30.

29. *Idem*, *The Study of Literature* (London, 1952), 4.

30. *Idem* to G. Rylands, 7 May 1966; Rylands MSS, GHWR/3/57.

31. *Idem*, *A Case for Humane Learning* (Oxford, 1966), 3.

32. Ibid. 8.

33. Ibid. 22.

34. Davie/Stuart Hampshire.

35. C. M. Bowra to F. Frankfurter, 19 April [1944]; Frankfurter MSS, Box 25.

36. *Eidem*, 18 Dec. [1958]; ibid.

37. *Oxford Gazette*, 17 July 1968.

38. C. M. Bowra to I. Berlin, 22 Sept. 1965; Bowra MSS.

39. Ibid.

40. *Idem* to H. Hugo, 2 June [1967]; Sparrow MSS, Box 57.

41. *Idem* to C. Clark, 14 Dec. 1963; C. Clark MSS.

42. *Idem* to H. Hugo, 11 Nov. 1964; Sparrow MSS, Box 57.

43. *The Times*, 22 Feb. 1964.

44. C. M. Bowra to H. Hugo, 26 Jan. 1964; Sparrow MSS, Box 57.

45. *Idem* to I. Berlin, 6 March [1960]; Bowra MSS.

46. *Idem* to F. Frankfurter, 11 Oct. [1958]; Frankfurter MSS, Box 25.

47. *Idem* to G. Rylands, 9 Feb. 1965; Rylands MSS, GHWR/3/57.

48. *Eidem*, 24 Jan. 1964; ibid.

49. C. M. Bowra to H. Hugo, 11 Nov. 1964; Sparrow MSS, Box 57.

50. *Idem* to G. Rylands, 24 April 1965, Bowra MSS.

51. Bowra's evidence to the Franks Commission, 17 Nov. 1964; Oxford Univ. Archives, HC/4/50/24.

52. Ibid. HC/4/50/23.

53. *Oxford Gazette*, 15 March 1967.

54. C. M. Bowra to F. Frankfurter, 26 July [195?]; Frankfurter MSS, Box 25.

55. *Idem* to G. Rylands, 3 Feb. 1967; Rylands MSS, GHWR/3/57.

56. *Idem* to B. Ruck, 2 Jan. [1953?]; Bowra MSS.

57. *Idem*, introduction to F. Markham, *Oxford* (London, 1967), 11.

58. *Idem* to F. Frankfurter, 5 Dec. [1954?]; Frankfurter MSS, Box 25.

59. *Idem* to N. Annan, 18 July 1970; King's Coll., Cambridge, Annan MSS, and *idem* to J. Mitchell, 21 Feb. 1961; J. Mitchell MSS.

60. C. M. Bowra to N. Annan, 18 July 1970; King's Coll., Cambridge, Annan MSS.

61. B. Ruck to C. M. Bowra, 11 June 1970; Bowra MSS.

62. C. M. Bowra to H. Hugo, 26 Nov. 1966; Sparrow MSS, Box 57.

63. *Idem* to G. Rylands, 27 Oct. 1968; Rylands MSS, GHWR/3/57.

64. *Idem* to H. Hugo, 7 Aug. 1965; Sparrow MSS, Box 57.

65. *Idem* to J. Salmon, 30 April 1965; Salmon MSS.

66. *Idem* to J. Mitchell, 13 March 1965; J. Mitchell MSS.

67. *Idem* to G. Rylands, 26 Oct. 1967; Rylands MSS, GHWR/3/57.

68. *Idem* to U. Niebuhr, 15 April 1970; Niebuhr MSS.

69. *Idem* to G. Rylands, [April 1967]; Rylands MSS, GHWR/3/57.

70. *Eidem*, 27 Oct. 1968; ibid.

71. *Eidem*, 16 April [1969]; ibid.

72. Mitchell/Lord Quinton.

73. C. M. Bowra to B. Ruck, 12 Dec. 1968; Bowra MSS.

74. W. G. Forrest to C. M. Bowra, n.d.; ibid. Classics students at Yale had declared it intolerable that they should be required to know Latin and Greek.

75. C. M. Bowra to E. Waugh, 15 Oct. 1963; ibid. *Idem* to J. Mitchell, 21 Feb. 1961; J. Mitchell MSS.

76. J. Sparrow to C. M. Bowra, 2, 8, 9 Nov. 1968; Bowra MSS; and M. Beloff to C. M. Bowra, 7 Nov. 1968; ibid.

77. C. M. Bowra to I. Berlin, 2 April 1969; ibid.

78. *Idem* to C. Clark, 12 Dec. 1969; ibid.

79. Mitchell/A. F. Thompson. See also M. Rosen, *In the Colonie* (London, 2005), 85.

80. N. Annan, BBC Broadcast Tape, 7 April 1972; Bowra MSS.

81. J. Sparrow to C. M. Bowra, 15 May 1966; Berlin MSS, 281, f. 269.

82. C. M. Bowra to J. Mitchell, 13 March [1960]; J. Mitchell MSS.

83. *Idem* to G. Rylands, 24 Sept. [?]; Rylands MSS, GHWR/3/57.

84. *Eidem*, 5 April 1968; ibid.

85. C. M. Bowra to C. Connolly, 12 Oct. 1963; Connolly MSS.

86. *Idem*, *Memorial Address for A Smith* (Oxford, 1958).

87. *Idem* to E. Sitwell, 18 Dec. 1963; Washington State Univ., Sitwell MSS.

88. *Idem* to G. Rylands, 7 Aug. 1966; Rylands MSS, GHWR/3/57.

89. *Idem* to N. Mitford, 29 Dec. 1966; Chatsworth MSS, Mitford MSS: by permission of 'the Estate of Nancy Mitford'.

90. *Idem* to G. Rylands, 27 Oct. 1970; Bowra MSS.

91. *Idem* to C. Connolly, 6 July 1970; Connolly MSS.

92. *Eidem*, 17 May 1970; ibid.

93. C. M. Bowra to P. Hadley, 10 Dec. [1958/9]; Bowra MSS.

94. *Idem* to N. Annan, 12 June [1955]; King's Coll., Cambridge, Annan MSS.

95. *Idem* to E. Waugh, 27 Oct. 1965; Bowra MSS.

96. *Eidem*, 28 Jan. 1966; ibid.

97. *Idem* to J. Betjeman, 29 Sept. 1967; Betjeman MSS.

98. A. Fleming to Lady Berlin, 5 Aug. 1969; Morgan MSS; and Mitchell/ F. Morgan; Mitchell/Lord and Lady Quinton.

99. C. M. Bowra to G. Rylands, 5 July 1966; Rylands MSS, GHWR/3/57.

100. *Eidem*, 5 Oct. 1965; Bowra MSS.

101. C. M. Bowra to N. Annan, 8 March [196?]; King's Coll., Cambridge, Annan MSS.

102. J. Sparrow to K. Clark, 29 Dec. 1964; Tate Britain, Clark MSS, TGA/8812/ 1/3 2963.

103. C. M. Bowra to H. Trevor-Roper, 6 Jan. 1971; Christ Church, Oxford, Trevor-Roper MSS, o 1970–3.

104. *Idem* to P. Mansel, 13 July 1968; Eton Coll., Archives.

105. I. Berlin to S. Gates, 30 Aug. 1969; Gates MSS.

106. C. M. Bowra to H. Hugo, 13 Dec. 1968; Sparrow MSS, Box 57.

107. *Idem* to B. Ruck, 3 Jan. [?]; Bowra MSS.

108. *Idem* to C. Clark, 30 June [?]; C. Clark MSS.

109. *Idem* to C. Connolly, 8 Nov. 1968; Connolly MSS.

110. *Idem* to G. Rylands, 27 Oct. 1970; Rylands MSS, GHWR/3/57.

111. *Eidem*, 20 July 1970; ibid.

112. *Idem* to N. Mitford, 31 Dec. [196?]; Chatsworth, Mitford MSS.

113. *Idem* to N. Annan, 1 May [1949?]; King's Coll., Cambridge, Annan MSS.

114. Mitchell/George Huxley.

115. C. M. Bowra to G. Rylands, 15 June 1966; Bowra MSS.

116. *Eidem*, 27 Oct. 1970; Rylands MSS, GHWR/3/57.

117. C. M. Bowra to N. Annan, 18 July 1970; King's Coll., Cambridge, Annan MSS.

118. J. Thompson to C. M. Bowra, 27 Jan. 1961; Convention Book 1945–66; Wadham Coll. Archives.

119. C. M. Bowra to G. Rylands, 26 April 1968; Bowra MSS.

120. Mitchell/John Walsh.

121. C. M. Bowra to G. Rylands, 27 Oct. 1968; Rylands MSS, GHWR/3/57.

122. *Eidem*, 20 July 1970; ibid.

123. C. M. Bowra to H. Hugo, 13 Dec. 1968; Sparrow MSS, Box 57.

124. *Idem* to C. Connolly, 17 May 1970; Connolly MSS; *idem* to G. Rylands, 9 Feb. 1970; Rylands MSS, GHWR/3/57; *idem* to C. Clark, 6 Jan. 1971; C. Clark MSS.

125. *Idem* to G. Rylands, 13 Dec. [1970]; Bowra MSS.

126. *Idem* to G. Huxley, 21 Aug. 1970; ibid.

127. *Idem* to C. Connolly, 15 April 1970; Connolly MSS.

128. *Idem* to C. Clark, 1 April 1970; C. Clark MSS.

129. Ibid.

130. C. M. Bowra to H. Trevor-Roper, 12 Nov. 1970; Christ Church, Trevor-Roper MSS, o 1970–3.

131. Diary of J. Mitchell, 26 June 1971; J. Mitchell MSS.

132. C. M. Bowra, *Inspiration and Poetry* (London, 1955), 257.

133. *Idem* to C. Connolly, 17 May 1970; Connolly MSS.

134. *Idem* to C. Clark, 30 May 1971; C. Clark MSS, and *idem* to N. Annan, 29 May 1971; King's Coll., Cambridge, Annan MSS.

135. Mitchell/Mrs J. Bamborough.

136. J. Betjeman to K. Clark, 11 July 1971; Tate Britain, Clark MSS, TGA 8812/1/3 337.

137. J. Dancy to H. Hardy, 17 Nov. 2005; Hardy MSS.

138. H. Trevor-Roper to I. Berlin, 13 Aug. 1971; Berlin MSS, 274, f. 171.

139. Diary of J. Mitchell, 5 July 1971; J. Mitchell MSS.

140. Lord David Cecil to I. Berlin, [1971]; Berlin MSS, 196, f. 283.

141. I. Berlin to G. Catlin, 21 Sept. 1971; ibid. 195, f. 102.

142. G. Catlin to I. Berlin, 15 Aug. 1971; ibid. 196, f. 269.

143. Maurice Bowra's Will, 13 Jan. 1951; Bowra MSS.

144. C. M. Bowra to E. Waugh, 25 July [1955]; ibid. See also *idem* to R. Boothby, 30 July [1957]; ibid.

145. *Idem* to C. Connolly, 7 Feb. [196?]; Connolly MSS.

146. *Idem* to J. Betjeman, 5 Sept. [194?]; Betjeman MSS.

CHAPTER 13 — HEAVEN OR HELL

1. *Memories*, 15.

2. C. Hollis, *Oxford in the Twenties* (London, 1976), 37.

3. C. M. Bowra, *The Greek Experience* (London, 1957), 202.

4. *Idem* to E. Waugh, 6 Oct. [1950]; Bowra MSS.

5. *Wadham Gazette*, New Series, 1 (11) (1984), 28.

6. Hollis, *Oxford in the Twenties*, 37.

7. *Wadham Gazette*, New Series, 1 (11) (1975), 31.

8. C. M. Bowra to I. Berlin, 20 Nov. 1945; Bowra MSS.

9. 'Marcus Niebuhr Tod', in Maurice Bowra, *New Bats in Old Belfries* ed. H. Hardy and J. Holmes (Oxford, 2005), 3–5.

10. 'Confirmation Songs, II'; Sparrow MSS, Box 57.

11. Mitchell/Colette Clark.

12. E. Kantorowicz to C. M. Bowra, 11 Nov. 1955; Bowra MSS.

13. C. M. Bowra to B. Ruck, 30 Dec. 1962; ibid.

14. *Idem* to P. Synnott, June 1931; B. Hillier, *The Young Betjeman* (London, 1988), 316.

15. C. M. Bowra to G. Huxley, 21 Aug. 1970; Bowra MSS.

16. *Idem* to C. Clark, 21 Jan. [1957]; C. Clark MSS. Maurice once claimed to disapprove of a tax on luxuries, 'Necessities we agreed might well be taxed, as we could dispense with them—we never use them; but luxuries

no!' Diary of Hugh Trevor-Roper, 22 April 1938; Christ Church, Oxford, Trevor-Roper MSS.

17. C. M. Bowra to G. Rylands, 16 April [1969]; Bowra MSS.

18. Revd F. P. Horton to P. Betjeman, 7 May [?]; ibid.

19. P. Betjeman to C. M. Bowra, n.d.; ibid.

20. C. M. Bowra to J. Betjeman, 20 May [?]; Betjeman MSS.

21. *Idem* to C. Clark, 26 Jan. 1964; C. Clark MSS.

22. A. N. Wilson, *John Betjeman* (London, 2006), 4. My thanks to Jonathan Brewer for this reference.

23. David Dean Memorandum; Wadham Coll., Oxford, Bowra MSS.

24. C. M. Bowra to I. Berlin, 20 Nov. 1945; ibid.

25. *Idem* to H. Hugo, 26 Jan. [1956]; Sparrow MSS, Box 57.

26. *Idem* to J. Betjeman, 29 Oct. [?]; Betjeman MSS.

27. *Idem* to P. Synnott, 14 Sept. [1927]; Synnott MSS. It was embarrassing for Bowra that, as he followed the twists and turns of 'the barbarian rows between Prots and Caths. in Ulster', he had to sympathize with persecuted Catholics. *Idem* to J. Salmon, 12 Jan. 1967; J. Salmon MSS.

28. *Idem* to P. Balfour, 11 Jan. [1927]; Huntington Lib., Calif., Kinross MSS.

29. *Idem* to E. Waugh, 26 May [1953]; Bowra MSS.

30. *Idem* to H. Hugo, 23 July [1957]; Sparrow MSS, Box 57.

31. BL Add. MSS 72728, f. 52; C. M. Bowra to R. Harrod, 29 July [1957].

32. Ibid.

33. W. Churchill to E. Waugh, n.d.; J. Lewis, *Cyril Connolly* (London, 1957), 413 n.

34. C. M. Bowra to E. Waugh, 12 July [1955]; Bowra MSS.

35. *Idem* to H. Hugo, 11 Sept. [1952]; Sparrow MSS, Box 57.

36. BL Add. MSS 71182, f. 51; C. M. Bowra to B. Harrod, 20 Dec. [1944].

37. Mitchell/C. M. Bowra.

38. C. M. Bowra to H. Hugo, 9 Dec. [1950]; Sparrow MSS, Box 57.

39. Ibid.

40. BL Add. MSS 71613, f. 218; R. Harrod to D. Woodruff, 13 July 1971.

41. Ibid. f. 220; D. Woodruff to R. Harrod, 15 July 1971.

42. Hollis, *Oxford in the Twenties*, 37.

43. Ibid.

44. C. M. Bowra to H. Hugo, 31 Dec. 1967; Sparrow MSS, Box 57.

45. *Idem* and others to Paul VI, 1971; Bowra MSS.

46. Mitchell/C. M. Bowra.

47. C. M. Bowra to H. Hugo, 31 Dec. 1967; Sparrow MSS, Box 57.

48. K. Clark, *The Other Half* (London, 1986), 199.

49. C. M. Bowra to P. Betjeman, 7 April [1941]; Betjeman MSS.

50. Mitchell/Walter Hooper.

51. P. Rhodes to L. Mitchell, 16 Aug. 2006; Bowra MSS.

52. Mitchell/Colette Clark.

53. N. Annan, *The Dons* (London, 1999), 168.

54. Ibid.

55. S. Hampshire to I. Berlin, 21 July [1971]; Berlin MSS, 256, f. 314.

56. 'N' to N. Annan, Oct. 1974; King's Coll., Cambridge, Annan MSS.

57. N. Annan to I. Berlin, 28 Sept. 1971; Berlin MSS, 241, f. 122.

58. J. Betjeman to K. Clark, 11 July 1971; C. Lycett-Green, *John Betjeman. Letters* (London, 1994–5), ii. 417–18. See also *idem* to J. Sparrow, 11 July 1971; Sparrow MSS, Box 56, and B. Hillier, *The Bonus of Laughter* (London, 2004), 289.

59. J. Sparrow, in H. Lloyd-Jones, *Maurice Bowra* (London, 1974), 155.

Select Bibliography

I. MANUSCRIPT SOURCES

British Library
Harrod MSS. Papers and Correspondence of Sir Roy and Lady Harrod

Cambridge University
Churchill College. Papers and Correspondence of Sir Winston Churchill
Faculty of Oriental Studies. Papers and Correspondence of I. B. Horner
King's College. Papers and Correspondence of Lord Annan
     Papers and Correspondence of G. W. Rylands

Chatsworth House
Mitford MSS. Papers and Correspondence of Nancy Mitford

Eton College
Connolly MSS. Papers and Correspondence of Cyril Connolly
Literary Society. Minutes Book

Getty Research Centre, Los Angeles
Cooper MSS. Papers and Correspondence of Douglas Cooper

Hoover Institution, Stanford
Pasternak MSS. Papers and Correspondence of the Pasternak family

Houghton Library, Harvard
James MSS. Papers and Correspondence of Alice and William James

Harry Ransom Humanities Research Center, Austin
Bowen MSS. Papers and Correspondence of Elizabeth Bowen
Morrell MSS. Papers and Correspondence of Lady Ottoline Morrell
Sitwell MSS. Papers and Correspondence of Edith Sitwell

Huntington Library, Los Angeles
Kinross MSS. Papers and Correspondence of Patrick Balfour

Indiana University, Bloomington
McCarthy MSS. Papers and Correspondence of Desmond and Mollie McCarthy

McMaster University, Hamilton
Catlin MSS. Papers and Correspondence of Sir George Catlin

National Archives, Kew

War Office Records. War Service File of C. M. Bowra

National Library of Congress, Washington, DC

Frankfurter MSS. Papers and Correspondence of Felix and Marian Frankfurter
Niebuhr MSS. Papers and Correspondence of Reinhold and Ursula Niebuhr

Oxford University

All Souls
  Papers and Correspondence of John Sparrow
Balliol College
  Papers and Correspondence of Adam von Trott
Bodleian Library
  Papers and Correspondence of Sir Isaiah Berlin
  Papers and Correspondence of the Bonham Carter Family
  Papers and Correspondence of Sybil Colefax
  Papers and Correspondence of Neville Coghill
  Papers and Correspondence of Sir Lionel Curtis
  Papers and Correspondence of Charles Coulson
  Papers and Correspondence of H. A. L. Fisher
  Papers and Correspondence of Lord Monkton
  Papers and Correspondence of Sir Gilbert Murray
  Papers and Correspondence of Sir J. L. Myers
  Papers and Correspondence of Lord Simon
  Papers and Correspondence of Enid Starkie
  Papers of the Society for the Protection of Science and Learning
Christ Church
  Papers and Correspondence of Tom Driberg
  Papers and Correspondence of Robin Dundas
  Papers and Correspondence of Hugh Trevor-Roper
New College
  Papers and Correspondence of Sir Christopher Cox
Nuffield College
  Papers and Correspondence of Lord Cherwell
University Archives
  Evidence given to the Franks Committee
  Vice-Chancellor's Correspondence, 1951–4
Wadham College
  Papers and Correspondence of Sir C. M. Bowra
  Convention Books, 1922–70
  Warden's Memoranda Book

Reading University

Chatto and Windus MSS. Papers and Correspondence relating to Chatto and
Windus

School of Oriental and African Studies
Bowra MSS. Papers and Correspondence of C. A. V. Bowra and his family

Tate Britain
Clark MSS. Papers and Correspondence of Sir Kenneth Clark

University of Tulsa, Oklahoma
Connolly MSS. Papers and Correspondence of Cyril Connolly
P.E.N. Archive. Papers of the P.E.N. Society

University College, London
Gaitskell MSS. Papers and Correspondence of Hugh Gaitskell

University of Victoria, British Columbia
Betjeman MSS. Papers and Correspondence of Sir John Betjeman

Washington State University
Sitwell MSS. Papers and Correspondence of Edith Sitwell

2. PRINTED SOURCES

H. Acton, *Nancy Mitford: A Memoir* (London, 1975)
M. Amory, *The Letters of Ann Fleming* (London, 1985)
——— *Lord Berners* (London, 1999)
N. Annan, *The Dons* (London, 1999)
A. J. Ayer, *Part of My Life* (Oxford, 1957)
——— *More of My Life* (Oxford, 1985)
E. Barker, *Golden Ages of the Great Cities* (London, 1952)
I. Berlin, *Personal Impressions* (London, 1980)
G. Berners, *Far From the Madding War* (London, 1941)
J. Betjeman, *Summoned by Bells* (London, 1960)
N. Blake, *Thou Shell of Death* (London, 1936)
N. Blakiston, *A Romantic Friendship* (London, 1975)
R. Boothby, *Recollections of a Rebel* (London, 1978)
E. Bowen, *To the North* (London, 1932)
C. M. Bowra, *Tradition and Design in the Iliad* (Oxford, 1930)
——— *Ancient Greek Literature* (London, 1933)
——— *Sappho: Dichtung* (Berlin, 1936)
——— [with T. Higham], *Oxford Book of Greek Verse* (Oxford, 1938)
——— [with T. Higham], *From the Greek* (Oxford, 1943)
——— *The Heritage of Symbolism* (London, 1943)
——— *Oxford Book of Russian Verse* (Oxford, 1943)
——— *Sophoclean Tragedy* (Oxford, 1944)
——— *A Classical Education* (Oxford, 1945)
——— *Guillaume Apollinaire, Choix de Poésies* (London, 1945)
——— *From Virgil to Milton* (London, 1945)

C. M. Bowra, *The Background to Modern Poetry* (Oxford, 1946)

_____ *The Lyrical Poetry of Thomas Hardy* (Nottingham, 1946)

_____ *The Creative Experiment* (London, 1949)

_____ *The Romantic Imagination* (London, 1950)

_____ *Heroic Poetry* (London, 1952)

_____ *The Study of Literature* (London, 1952)

_____ *Problems in Greek Poetry* (Oxford, 1953)

_____ *Homer and his Forerunners* (Edinburgh, 1953)

_____ *Inspiration and Poetry* (London, 1955)

_____ *The Simplicity of Racine* (Oxford, 1956)

_____ *The Greek Experience* (London, 1957)

_____ *Memorial Address for Alick Smith* (Oxford, 1958)

_____ *Greek Lyric Poetry* (Oxford, 1961)

_____ *Mediaeval Love Song* (Oxford, 1961)

_____ *Poetry and the First World War* (Oxford, 1961)

_____ *Primitive Song* (London, 1962)

_____ *In General and Particular* (London, 1964)

_____ *Pindar* (Oxford, 1964)

_____ *A Case for Humane Learning* (Oxford, 1966)

_____ *Landmarks in Greek Literature* (London, 1966)

_____ *Memories* (London, 1966)

_____ *Poetry and Politics* (Cambridge, 1966)

_____ *Memorial Address for Enid Starkie* (Oxford, 1970)

_____ *On Greek Margins* (Oxford, 1970)

_____ *Periclean Athens* (London, 1971)

_____ *Homer* (London, 1972)

_____ *New Bats in Old Belfries*, ed. H. Hardy and J. Holmes (London, 2005)

H. Carpenter, *W. H. Auden* (London, 1981)

K. Clark, *Another Part of the Wood* (London, 1974)

_____ *The Other Half* (London, 1986)

P. Davidson, *Vyacheslav Ivanov and C. M. Bowra* (Birmingham, 2006)

C. Day-Lewis, *The Poet's Task* (Oxford, 1951)

_____ *The Buried Day* (London, 1960)

S. Day-Lewis, *Cecil Day-Lewis* (London, 1980)

A. Doria, *Da Poesia Medieval Portuguesa* (Lisboa, 1947)

A. Fort, *The Prof.* (London, 2004)

J. Garcia Villa, *A Celebration for Edith Sitwell,* (New Jersey, 1948)

R. Glasser, *Gorbals Boy at Oxford* (London, 1988)

C. Gödde and H. Lonitz, Theodor W. Adorno, *Briefe und Briefwechsel, 1927–1937* (Frankfurt, 2003)

H. Hardy, *Flourishing. Letters 1928–1946. Isaiah Berlin* (London, 2004)

R. Harrod, *The Prof* (London, 1959)

S. Hastings, *Rosamond Lehmann* (London, 2002)

B. Hillier, *Young Betjeman* (London, 1988)

_____ *New Fame, New Love* (London, 2002)

_____ *The Bonus of Laughter* (London, 2004)

C. Hollis, *Oxford in the Twenties* (London, 1976)

D. Hopkinson, *The Incense Tree* (London, 1968)

M. Ignatieff, *Isaiah Berlin* (Lndon, 1998)

M. Innes, *Operation Pax* (London, 1951)

D. Ivanov, *Poems of Vyacheslav Ivanov* (Oxford, 1962)

O. Lancaster, *With an Eye to the Future* (London, 1953)

J. Laver, *Museum Piece* (London, 1963)

P. Levi, *Boris Pasternak* (London 1990)

J. Lewis, *Cyril Connolly* (London 1997)

H. Lloyd-Jones, *Maurice Bowra* (London, 1974)

E. Longford, *The Pebbled Shore* (London, 1986)

J. Lowe, *The Warden* (London, 1998)

C. Lycett-Green, *John Betjeman. Letters* (London, 1994–5)

F. Markham, *Oxford* (London, 1967)

P. Marnham, *Wild Mary* (London, 2006)

J. Mitchell, *A Disgraceful Anomaly* (London, 2003)

R. Norton, *Stefan Georg and His Circle* (Cornell, 2002)

O. Pax, *An Anthology of Mexican Poetry* (London, 1958)

A. Powell, *Infants of the Spring* (London, 1976)

A. Pryce-Jones, *The Bonus of Laughter* (London, 1987)

D. Pryce-Jones, *Cyril Connolly* (London, 1983)

J. Rees, *Looking for Mr Nobody* (London, 1994)

W. Rodgers, *Hugh Gaitskell* (London, 1964)

M. Rosen, *In the Colonie* (London, 2005)

A. Rowse, *Friends and Contemporaries* (London, 1990)

B. Ruck, *A Smile for the Past* (London, 1959)

E. Siepmann, *Confessions of a Nihilist* (London, 1955)

S. Spender, *Journals 1939–1983* (London, 1985)

C. Sykes, *Troubled Loyalty* (London, 1968)

_____ *Evelyn Waugh* (London, 1975)

S. Tabachnik, *Fiercer than Tigers* (Michigan, 2002)

G. Weidenfeld, *Remembering My Good Friends* (London, 1994)

M. Wheeler, *The British Academy, 1939–1953* (London, 1970)

P. Williams, *Hugh Gaitskell* (London, 1979)

A. Wilson, *John Betjeman* (London, 2006)

3. JOURNALS AND MAGAZINES

Cornhill Magazine

Encounter

London Magazine
New Oxford Magazine
Oxford Gazette
Oxford Magazine
Oxford Outlook
Proceedings of the British Academy
Wadham Gazette

Index